MAGILL'S SURVEY OF CINEMA

Silent Films

VOLUME 3
PRI-Z
INDEXES

Edited by

FRANK N. MAGILL

Associate Editors

PATRICIA KING HANSON

STEPHEN L. HANSON

SALEM PRESS
Englewood Cliffs, N.J.

LIBRARY OF CONGRESS CATALOG CARD NUMBER: 82-60577

Complete Set: ISBN 0-89356-239-4
Volume 3:   ISBN 0-89356-242-4

PRINTED IN THE UNITED STATES OF AMERICA

LIST OF TITLES IN VOLUME THREE

LIST OF TITLES IN VOLUME THREE

MAGILL'S
SURVEY
OF
CINEMA

THE PRIVATE LIFE OF HELEN OF TROY

Released: 1927
Production: Associated First National
Direction: Alexander Korda
Screenplay: Carey Wilson; based on the novel of the same name by John Erskine
Titles: Ralph Spence, Gerald Duffy, and Casey Robinson
Cinematography: Lee Garmes and Sid Hickox
Editing: Harold Young
Costume design: Max Ree
Music: Carl Edouarde
Length: 8 reels/7,694 feet

Principal characters:
Helen	Maria Corda
Menelaus	Lewis Stone
Paris	Ricardo Cortez
Eteoneus	George Fawcett
Adraste	Alice White
Telemachus	Gordon Elliott
Ulysses	Tom O'Brien
Achilles	Bert Sprotte
Ajax	Mario Carillo
Aphrodite	Alice Adair
Athena	Helen Fairweather
Hera	Virginia Thomas

What novelist John Erskine wrote about in his much-admired novel *The Private Life of Helen of Troy* is not what the film is about. He told a slight comedy of manners, all of which took place after King Menelaus brought home his errant wife, Helen. She was still beautiful, but middle-aged, and the novel was about how a woman settles down and makes a home for a cranky old man, who, in his prime, attempted to bring her home when she was kidnaped, an event which was the catalyst for the Trojan War.

The film, however, relates the more interesting story of the rape of Helen, Queen of Sparta (Maria Corda), by Paris (Ricardo Cortez), one of the princes of Troy, and how her husband dared the elements and the wrath of the gods to bring her home. Ethel Barrymore had admired the novel when it was first published and was asked if she would appear on the stage as Helen if a dramatization were written, but she said quite rightly, "No, it would become a very talky play."

The film could have been the stupendous humorless bore that it was when remade as a talkie and released by Warner Bros. late in 1955. That version was full of battles and obvious production value. This early version, however, has none of that; it is a masterpiece of good taste, since it was directed by Alexander Korda. The sets are all simple, stark, classic, and quite wonderful. The people are real and speak English via subtitles written by three of the wittiest writers of the time, Ralph Spence, Gerald Duffy, and Casey Robinson. It also has musical arrangements that are delightfully tongue-in-cheek. Carl Edouarde arranged the score, based on modern tunes, and one example of the film's musical wit occurs when the siege of Troy nears its end and the great Trojan Horse is rolled in: the accompaniment on the score is to the tune of "Horses, Horses, Horses."

The best performance in the film is naturally rendered by Lewis Stone as Menelaus, who catches the audience's sympathy at once. They realize that traveling all that way from Sparta to Troy is a headache, especially when it is done to fetch home a wife who had no business running away, regardless of any legends. The truth, Menelaus seems to be saying, is that he lost interest in Helen long ago; she was beautiful but vain and rather silly, and it serves Paris right for being stuck with her. If Menelaus could have given her enough rope, she would have crawled home on her own, once she got bored with life behind those Trojan walls. Now for all these years of siege, he has been stuck in Asia Minor, and it is he who is bored. At least he does not have her dressmaking bills to pay, and he is glad that the first thing he did when he found that his wife was gone, was to hunt out the shop of his wife's couturier and sack it. Stone as Menelaus epitomizes all the long-suffering husbands ever tormented by vain and frivolous wives.

Maria Corda, the wife of Alexander Korda (who spelled her husband's surname with a "C" rather than the proper Hungarian "K"), is photographed stunningly by Lee Garmes and Sid Hickox. She has one expression—self-admiration—and so is probably right for the role. Much more piquant is Alice White as Adraste, the maidservant. As for Paris, played by Ricardo Cortez, he seems a little too old to have been a young princely shepherd tending his flocks.

Menelaus, when he bursts into the throne room and finds his wife waiting to be rescued, does not run her through with his sword, not even when she drops her robe and stands naked before him, waiting. It is the time-honored tradition of a husband's privilege. Menelaus, however, simply takes a good look at what he has been missing all these years, wraps her up in her robe, and takes her home. The audience knows, however, that when he gets her safely home, he is going to get his fishing gear ready and resume his favorite pastime, leaving Helen to look around his court for another likely prince. Next time, however, viewers get the impression that she can get home on her own.

The film had its premiere in New York at the Globe Theater simply because Associated First National had three weeks left on its rental agreement, and thus they got two shows a day for three weeks at top prices. The picture did well, however, even outside of the big cities, where talking equipment was not yet installed. On opening night, Erskine, the author of the novel, came onstage as master of ceremonies. The weekly *Variety* reported that he offered "what was probably the best verbal introduction any New York film ever had. It was funny and short. It also served to introduce Maria Corda in person."

Corda never succeeded as a star in the United States. Associated First National presented her in another silent film, but even by that time she still did not speak English, and with the advent of sound, a strong Hungarian accent would have presented great difficulties. She and Alexander Korda divorced soon after *The Private Life of Helen of Troy*, and eventually, Korda married Merle Oberon and was knighted by the Queen. Corda went into obscurity except for occasional lawsuits against Korda and his estate.

The Private Life of Helen of Troy received a nomination at Academy Awards time—the first Awards of 1927-1928—for Best Title Writing, an award that was discontinued immediately because of the advent of sound. It also received another nomination for Best Engineering Effects, another award that was discontinued after its first year. It was, however, an extraordinarily beautiful picture to look at; it was written by Carey Wilson and directed by Korda with impeccable taste.

DeWitt Bodeen

PRUNELLA

Released: 1918
Production: Famous Players-Lasky for Paramount
Direction: Maurice Tourneur
Screenplay: Charles Maigne; based on the play of the same name by H. Granville Barker and Laurence Housman
Cinematography: John van den Broek
Art direction: Ben Carré
Length: 5 reels

Principal characters:
Prunella .... Marguerite Clark
Pierrot .... Jules Raucourt
Scaramel .... Harry Leoni
Prim .... Isabel Berwin
Prude .... Marcia Harris
Privacy .... Nora Cecil
The Gardeners .... William J. Gross
                                   A. Voorhees Wood
                                   Charles Hartley
The Gardener's boy .... Arthur Kennedy

Any discussion of fantasy in films would warrant much attention devoted to the contributions of director Maurice Tourneur. Even early films like *The Wishing Ring* (1914) bear the whimsical lightness of his touch, as did other later achievements such as *Poor Little Rich Girl* (1917) with Mary Pickford. The following year, he directed both *The Blue Bird* and *Prunella*, which were essentially fairy tales and had to be treated with a feather-light touch. *Prunella* especially was like a screen pantomime. Much of it was done in the spirit of ballet with graceful movement and mimic action and reaction. Tourneur permitted nothing extraneous or "natural"; it was all lightly impressionistic.

Marguerite Clark seemed to be a star who was born to be directed by Tourneur, and it is regrettable that *Prunella* is the only film on which they collaborated. A very proficient director, J. Searle Dawley, directed sixteen of Clark's films. He was good, but not of the caliber of Tourneur. Clark specialized in fairy tales at Paramount—*The Goose Girl* (1915), *Snow White* (1916), *The Seven Swans* (1917)—and those features were usually programmed to be released at Christmas. She had done *Prunella* on Broadway for Winthrop Ames, and audiences, falling in love with it and her as Prunella, demanded that Paramount immortalize her performance on the screen, and they did. Unfortunately, the only complete print of any of Clark's films is in the British Institute, a charming romantic comedy called *Silks and Satins* (1916), in which she plays a dual role.

Adolph Zukor brought her to the screen in 1914 in *Wildflower*, a romance directed by Allan Dwan, with Harold Lockwood and Jack Pickford. Clark was an immediate favorite with American audiences, who felt as if they had discovered her for themselves, which is exactly how Zukor had hoped they would feel. Before she came to pictures, she had enjoyed a long and busy career on the legitimate stage, appearing first as the soubrettish heroines opposite DeWolf Hopper in a series of musicals and playing the lead role in the national tour of James M. Barrie's *Peter Pan*. She was starred by the Shuberts in 1909 in *The Wishing Ring*, and New Yorkers took her to their hearts in *Snow White, Prunella, Anatol,* and *Merely Mary Ann*.

When Clark accepted Zukor's 1914 invitation to become one of his Famous Players, she did so only on the advice of her older sister Cora, because the money (a three-year contract at one thousand dollars a week) was fantastic and much more than the meager stage salaries of the time. Cora told her "that pictures were a fad and in three years would be dead, and that therefore she might as well sign."

Marguerite Clark almost immediately loved filmmaking; she understood the medium as if she had been born to it and never returned to the theater. She was dainty, very petite, and very brunette, with large, hazel-colored eyes that were always laughing. She was wistful, playful, even mischievous, and playing a Pierette/Columbine character came to her naturally. Fans took sides, some championing Clark, others vowing that Pickford was their screen sweetheart. There was no rivalry between the actresses themselves, however, for they knew that while they might rightly play the same roles, each would play them differently to conform to her established screen image. Any tension that existed was between Cora Clark and Mrs. Smith, Pickford's mother, who fostered a rivalry that was otherwise simply nonexistent. Fans worshiped "Our Mary," and those same fans adored Clark. Clark came to pictures considerably older than most of the girls who became film stars in their teens, for she was reputedly born in 1883, thus making Pickford almost exactly ten years younger.

In the story, Prunella (Marguerite Clark), a demure orphan girl, lives in a pretty little house at the side of a road, protected by her three spinster aunts, Prim (Isabel Berwin), Prude (Marcia Harris), and Privacy (Nora Cecil). The three maiden ladies guard Prunella with extreme care, because her mother, Priscilla, had run away years earlier with a French landscape gardener, who had carved the statue of Love gracing the garden. A year after her departure, the baby named Prunella was left on the aunts' doorstep, and Priscilla was known to have died.

Now the three aunts sit with their niece in the garden hearing Prunella recite her lessons. In the distance, they hear music and quickly urge Prunella into the house. Privacy, however, has forgotten the key to the gate, and she sends Prunella for it, warning her to return at once.

The music grows louder, and Prunella, her curiosity aroused, stands up on a little stool and looks over the garden hedge. A troupe of mummers are coming down the road; and a very dashing young man, Pierrot (Jules Raucourt), steals into the garden. Prunella is bewildered but overjoyed when he makes passionate love to her. He swears that he will come back later that same night, fetch her, and she will be Queen of the Mummers. When the moon is high and full, he steals back into the garden, and Prunella is ready and waiting for him.

For three years Prunella travels with the Mummers as their leading light, and Pierrot carefully tends her with love. There is no real fidelity in the fickle heart of Pierrot, however, although he and Prunella are married and should be living happily ever after. He is in love with love, and when Prunella becomes the leading actress in Paris, he steals off with a new flame. Her heart broken, Prunella abandons her career and leaves Paris.

Meanwhile, two of the aunts have died, and Privacy, the remaining aunt, decides to sell the little house at the side of the road. A gentleman buys it, sight unseen, and when he comes to take possession, Privacy is surprised to find that her anonymous buyer is a sadder and very lonely Pierrot. He does not know where Prunella is. When he had wearied of the world, he had returned to his and Prunella's home, but he found it deserted. She had left with none of the gifts he had lavished upon her; everything was intact. In the garden, inscribed on a rock were the words, "Here lies—Pierette," which was the pet name he had given her. He prays that she is not dead and will come back to the home of her girlhood.

Later that night, when the moon rises, Prunella enters the garden and walks to the statue of Love. Mummers passing by on their way to the party inside the house do not recognize her. In despair, she crumples in a heap at the foot of the statue of Love.

Pierrot deserts the party given for him in his new home and comes out unhappily. Prunella rises, recognizing him at once. She goes to him, but he withdraws, thinking her a ghost. On his knees he swears it is only she whom he loves, and she asks that if she were a ghost, would he give up his life to come to her? With a cry of avowal that he would, he seizes her in his arms and finds that she is very much alive and breathing. He sobs for joy, and Prunella caresses his hair and looks up with a smile to the moon.

Clark stayed young in features and heart throughout her life, dying at the age of fifty-seven. In 1918, she married an aviator, Lieutenant Harry Palmerson Williams; and in 1936, when he was killed in a plane crash, she and Cora moved to New York. When Clark retired in 1921, after her "comeback" film, *Scrambled Wives*, she told a *New York Times* reporter who had queried her about any future films she might do, "I know enough to go home when the party's over, and the guests are gone."

DeWitt Bodeen

QUEEN ELIZABETH
(LA REINE ELISABETH)

Released: 1912
Production: Film d'Art; released by Famous Players Company
Direction: Louis Mercanton and Desfontaines
Screenplay: Emile Moreau
Cinematography: no listing
Length: 4 reels/1,059 feet

> *Principal characters:*
> Queen Elizabeth .... Sarah Bernhardt
> James Devereaux
> (The Earl of Essex) .... Lou Tellegen
> Countess of Nottingham .... Romaine
> Earl of Nottingham .... M. Maxudian

Queen Elizabeth frequently has been designated the film that initiated the multireel feature, a distinction also attributed to *Quo Vadis?* (1912), the eight-reel Italian spectacle produced by Cines in Italy. Adolph Zukor brought the French-made film to the United States where it became the first feature-length film viewed in America and the first in which the famous stage actress Sarah Bernhardt was seen on screen by an American audience.

In 1907, a company known as Film d'Art was formed in France for the purpose of introducing, on film to a mass audience, the great artists and plays of the French national theater. While only a few of these offerings made an impression on the French audiences, they created a great sensation and many imitators in other countries, particularly the United States. The Film d'Art produced standard repertory pieces such as *Tosca* and *Phedre*, many ballets, and a few films of real quality such as *Les Miserables* (1912) and *Les Mysteres de Paris* (1913), both directed by Albert Capellani for Pathé. The great French actress Réjane appeared in a stage version of *Madame Sans-Gêne* for Film d'Art, and the outstanding *La Reine Elisabeth* (*Queen Elizabeth*) which was made in a London studio by Desfontaines and Louis Mercanton directing the great Bernhardt, who had also appeared in *La Dame aux Camélias* (*Camille*) for that company in 1910.

From the first Film d'Art production, *The Assasination of the Duc de Guise* (1908), the directors, most of whom were from the theater, such as Charles Le Bargy and André Calmettes, made no attempt to achieve a sense of realism in their films. Preferring not to see scenery exposed for what it was, the masses did not attend the Film d'Art productions, but prestige was conferred on them by the "elite" audiences who flocked to see the more "aesthetic" and intelligent fare. Filmmakers in Italy, Germany, England, and America were impressed not only with the documentation of great art but also with the three-, four-, and even five-reel length of these elaborately produced classics. Until that time, American productions were geared to the fifteen-minute, fast-paced nickelodeon pieces. When Zukor secured a license to import *Queen Elizabeth* to the United States, the American Motion Picture Patents-Trust group regarded the move as an invasion and a threat. The trade papers were in favor of ousting the foreigners, but Zukor, a Hungarian immigrant with a short career in the fur business and then in Arcades and nickelodeons behind him, was undaunted, and went against the Motion Picture Patents Company rule of one reel. He persuaded David Frohman, a leading impressario of the New York theater, to let him present Bernhardt on film in a legitimate showcase.

On July 12, 1912, America saw the feature-length film at the Lyceum Theater for the unprecedented amount of one dollar a ticket. The evening was a great success even though the "divine Sarah" could only be seen flailing about the screen to subtitles. Zukor decided to form the company Famous Players in Famous Plays in order to produce similar films in America, all of which would run the "ridiculous" length of four reels. Little did a horrified industry realize that in the near future, Zukor would merge with Jesse L. Lasky's Feature Picture Company (which Lasky fashioned after Zukor's success) to become the ancestor of today's Paramount Pictures Corporation. Unable to enlist D. W. Griffith, Zukor persuaded Edwin S. Porter to direct and Frohman to continue to lend his name and various affiliations to the Famous Players' enterprise. The successes of this company proved that quality and quantity were acceptable to the American public and, at the same time, demolished the Trust's one- or two-reel myth, paving the way for the D. W. Griffith epics a few years later.

Bernhardt played no small part in helping to establish this new policy. Her consent to act in motion pictures made considerable headway in liberating film from the prejudices of the intelligencia. Certain films could now be considered in the same league as the legitimate theater. Bernhardt's reasons for undertaking this adventure, of which many of her fellow artists looked askance, was, perhaps, more personal than altruistic. When she, at age sixty-five, was asked to film *Camille* and *Queen Elizabeth*, her comment upon accepting was, "This is my last chance at immortality." Fortunately, Bernhardt was correct in that a permanent record of several of her later performances does exist.

Unfortunately, the quality and charisma that Bernhardt projected from the legitimate theater was not captured on the screen. Her emphasized, representational style of theatrical acting was too stylized for palatability on film, which inherently renders everything larger than life. Apparently, she was as shocked as a spectator today might be if he or she did not understand the conventions of turn-of-the-century theater. Her extraordinary voice was absent and the stage gestures for which she was revered became ludicrous when blown out of theatrical proportion. It is said that Bernhardt fainted when she saw herself on screen in the role of *Camille*. The stilted camerawork was not cinematic; the film employed theatrical staging, acting, and set painting as well as unedited scenes, the results being very similar to Georges Méliès' films without the imaginativeness. Characters enter from right and left as if the edges of the screen were the stage. Some of the most famous and skillful actors in the world grimace for the camera like a Samurai in an Akira Kurosawa film while indulging in up to four double takes. The charasmatic vitality of Bernhardt's living presence is absent and the result is expressionistic gesticulating with arms swinging wildly, fists clenching, chest beating, and eyes rolling as her wrist is pressed to her forehead, and her fingers tear at her breasts and clothing.

Prior to Griffith's work, the camera had not yet been tuned to the actors. For the majority of viewers, however, who never had the opportunity to see one of the greatest actresses of the nineteenth century in person, it is a pleasure to be able to accept the dramatic conventions of turn-of-the-century drama and watch England's Queen Elizabeth I be portrayed by one of the most magnificent actresses the theater has ever known.

Queen Elizabeth is a gripping drama which was filmed in Bernhardt's own theater during a special performance given for the Film d'Art. Bernhardt's portrayal of Elizabeth was one of her most highly praised roles and considered one of the best interpretations in the history of the theater. The film runs approximately one hour and was originally narrated by a reader in the theater who explained the action to musical accompaniment.

Although *Queen Elizabeth*, like most examples of "filmed theater," is not as interesting or entertaining to watch as other historical dramas, even from the same period, such as *Quo Vadis?*, it was an important landmark. It brought a kind of legitimacy to films by its relationship to the stage. The narrative of the film, and even Bernhardt's acting, is unimportant in relationship to the film's place in the advancement of the cultural merits of motion pictures in the minds of many critics.

Tanita C. Kelly

THE QUEEN OF SHEBA

Released: 1921
Production: Fox Film Corporation
Direction: J. Gordon Edwards
Screenplay: Virginia Tracy and J. Gordon Edwards
Cinematography: John W. Boyle
Editing: Hettie Grey Baker
Length: 9 reels/8,279 feet

Principal characters:
Queen of Sheba .... Betty Blythe
King Solomon .... Fritz Leiber
King Armud of Sheba .... George Siegmann
Adonijah .... George Raymond Nye
Princess Vashti .... Nell Craig
Sheba's son .... Pat Moore
Queen Amrath .... Claire De Lorez

The search for an actress to play the title role in *The Queen of Sheba* was quite extensive, with several major stars vying for the part. When director J. Gordon Edwards awarded the role to newcomer Betty Blythe, she was instantly vaulted to star status. Filming took six months, and after the picture was previewed, producer William Fox knew that he not only had a hit but also a new box-office star for his company. Blythe's career was aided by the fact that she was taller than the average actress, and, in her exotic costumes, she looked very desirable. In fact, she told an interviewer that "I wear twenty-eight costumes in *The Queen of Sheba*, and if I put them all on at once, I could not keep warm."

According to some sources, Fox called her into his office, after the film was released, determined to make her his mistress as well as his brightest star. When Blythe finally realized what he wanted, however, she announced to her employer that she loved her husband, director Paul Scardon, and would never be unfaithful to him. Although Fox made her offers of money and fame, she refused to compromise herself. The producer next threatened to blacklist her, at which point she walked out of his office. He kept his word, though, and used his considerable influence to make work difficult for her to find in Hollywood. Finally, she and her husband went East for a while and then sailed for England, where she was able to get some good roles. Five years after her "blacklisting" she came back to Hollywood to play in independent productions and second leads.

The Queen of Sheba was the brainchild of J. Gordon Edwards, Fox's most prominent director who had directed Theda Bara in twenty-three of her best pictures: spectacles such as *Cleopatra* (1917), *Madame DuBarry* (1918),

Salome (1918), *Romeo and Juliet* (1916), and *Camille* (1917). A film about the Queen of Sheba and her visit to King Solomon had been growing in his mind for some years before he was finally able to work out the whole plot to his satisfaction. Bara's star had set by then, however, and she had stopped making films entirely to become the devoted wife of Fox director Charles Brabin.

Edwards had no trouble getting Fox to agree to spend the vast sums that the production of *The Queen of Sheba* would require, for Edwards' earlier great expenditure on *Cleopatra* had brought millions of dollars back to Fox. King Solomon's palace and temple set, for example, expanded across the Fox Western Avenue lot until the camera practically had to be placed on the street to capture the entire panorama.

The film takes place one thousand years before the birth of Christ. The action begins as the Queen of Sheba (Betty Blythe) makes a grand entrance with a train of slaves bearing gifts for the ruler of Judea, King Solomon (Fritz Leiber). She has heard accounts of his great wisdom, and she hopes to make him an ally to her kingdom located on the southwest tip of Saudi Arabia. Among her gifts to the King are four white Arab steeds, which she claims are the fastest in the world. One of Solomon's one thousand wives, Vashti (Nell Craig), however, steps forward and calls Sheba a liar, claiming that there are no faster horses than those of King Solomon. To settle the issue, it is decided that a chariot race will determine which are the better horses, and thus the Queen of Sheba finds herself pitted against Vashti.

A huge, lavish stadium track was built just outside Los Angeles, and Fox cowboy star and champion rider Tom Mix was placed in charge of staging the race itself. Excellently filmed and edited, the chariot race became the most talked-about scene in the film. One reviewer thought that Fox was quite clever to include a chariot race in *The Queen of Sheba*, thus upstaging the best scene of *Ben-Hur*, a novel whose screen rights were being offered at that time for one million dollars. After the Queen of Sheba wins the race, the picture was interrupted by an intermission before the second half began.

Sheba spends her last night in Judea in Solomon's bedchamber, then she goes back to her kingdom, where she gives birth to a son. When the child is four, she sends him back to the court of King Solomon. Adonijah (George Raymond Nye), Solomon's brother, however, fears that the King will make the boy his heir and kidnaps the child. Then an attempt is made to overthrow Solomon, but when Sheba learns of the revolt, she leads her army to the King's aid. The revolution is crushed, and Solomon and Sheba find their son hidden and drugged in a tomb. At the end, Sheba and her son bid farewell to Solomon and begin their journey home.

Fritz Leiber, who portrayed King Solomon, was actually a distinguished Shakespearean actor who appeared in only a few Fox pictures: *Cleopatra* and *If I Were King* (1920). His son is today a famous writer of science-fiction novels. Edwards went to Europe shortly after *The Queen of Sheba* and directed a few epics for the Fox Company, the most famous and beautiful of which was *The Shepherd King* (1923), before his death on Christmas Day, 1925. His grandson is the present-day director Blake Edwards.

Blythe's later career in England produced a number of interesting films. Two of them were exotic epics in the sumptuous style of *The Queen of Sheba*. The first, *Chu Chin Chow* (1925), was a lavish Arabian fantasy, which was remade as a talkie in 1934 with Anna May Wong. The second, *She* (1925), was a very popular film. It is a fairly faithful adaptation of H. Rider Haggard's incredibly popular novel, in which Blythe played Ayesha (She-Who-Must-Be-Obeyed), a two thousand-year-old queen who keeps her beauty by bathing in fire. Blythe played the ruler of the lost African kingdom, clad in bead costumes which were similar to those of *The Queen of Sheba* and just as revealing. *She* was remade in 1935 with Helen Gahagan in the title role and again in 1965 starring Ursula Andress.

Blythe was married for thirty-four years to Paul Scardon who had been responsible for her career before *The Queen of Sheba*. He had first seen her in a two-reel version of an O. Henry short story in late 1917 and hired her to play opposite Harry T. Morey in a number of features he directed for Vitagraph. Theirs was one of the longer marriages in Hollywood. After his death, she retired to the Motion Picture Country House in Woodland Hills, California, where she died in 1972.

Larry Lee Holland

QUO VADIS?

Released: 1912
Production: Enrico Guazzoni for Cines Studios
Direction: Enrico Guazzoni
Screenplay: Enrico Guazzoni; based on the novel of the same name by Henryk Sienkiewicz
Cinematography: no listing
Length: 9 reels/7,800 feet

> *Principal characters:*
> Vinicius .... Amletto Novelli
> Petronius .... Gustavo Serena
> Lygia .... Lea Gunghi
> Poppaea, Nero's wife .... Amelia Cattaneo
> Ursus .... Bruto Castellani
> Nero .... Giovanni Gizzi
> St. Peter .... Leo Orlandini

Enrico Guazzoni's first version of *Quo Vadis?* in 1912 was one of a select number of motion pictures which, on their appearance, forever altered the course of filmmaking. As the greatest spectacular of its day, it was an enormous worldwide success from both a financial and an artistic point of view and briefly shifted international attention to Italy as the leading producer of feature films. In a very real sense, *Quo Vadis?* actually defined the feature film as it has come to be known today. At a length of nine reels, corresponding to a playing time of two hours on the normal projection speed for silent films, it was the longest film made up to that time, and its immense success amply demonstrated the viability of the longer running time. Today, however, a running time of two hours is about the norm for feature films.

The success of the film also paved the way for the elevation of cinema as an art form. It was shown in premier theaters that had been leased for the entire season, which enabled ambitious directors, particularly in the United States (D. W. Griffith, for example), to raise their own aspirations for their productions. In New York, it sustained itself through two performances a day over a number of months at full theatrical ticket prices with orchestral accompaniment. This sounded the death knell for the old style of nickelodeon shows which featured any number of miscellaneous reels. A significant number of the American filmgoing public was so stirred by the Italian spectacle that a frenzied interest in feature films swept the country and challenged head-on the Patents Company's conservative production policies and indeed the very existence of short one- and two-reel films. After *Quo Vadis?*, film programs were built entirely around a feature film and the shorter productions were used only on a supplemental basis. Such programming encouraged the construction of theaters designed specifically for the showing of the new "first-class" films rather than the previous practice of converting existing buildings or of leasing legitimate theaters. The first of these "movie theaters," the Strand, which seated 2,900 people, opened in New York City on April 11, 1914.

The demand for prints of the film was so unprecedented on a worldwide basis that for the first time in cinema history, a production studio, the Rome-based Cines Company, was required to keep its staff on a twenty-four-hour work shift daily for weeks, merely to keep up with the demand for prints from all parts of the world.

Adapted from the immensely popular novel by Nobel Prize-winning author Henryk Sienkiewicz, *Quo Vadis?* was an even greater success than the novel. It brought to life the enormous crowd scenes with thousands of extras, the monumental sets, the burning of Rome, the chariot races, and an arena populated with real lions to devour the Christians. Lavish staging on such a large scale was completely new, and the rich images engendered by the spectacle of real lions or a burning city enthralled audiences all over the world.

The sculptor Auguste Rodin pronounced it a masterpiece, and in France, it was featured at the Gaumont Palace in Paris, the largest film theater in the world at that time. The theater even commissioned composer Jean Nogues to write a special musical score, and it was performed by a live orchestra and a choir of 150 voices. In London, the film sold out the Albert Hall, which could seat an audience of twenty thousand at each showing. It was also the first major film to be presented to King George V and Queen Mary, showing how far the form had come in only two decades. It established the film as a legitimate art and became the first undisputed "hit" in cinema history, earning more than $150,000 (a monumental sum given the price of tickets in 1912) in the United States alone.

The title, *Quo Vadis?*, means literally "Where are you going?" in Latin. As employed by Sienkiewicz in his novel and by Enrico Guazzoni in the film, it alludes to a legend in which St. Peter (Leo Orlandini), confronted with a vision of Christ said "Quo Vadis?" and was told "I go to Rome to be crucified again." The film begins at this point and concerns the patrician soldier Vinicius (Amletto Novelli). As the film opens, Vinicius and his legion are returning to Rome over the Appian Way following the conquest of Britain. Reaching Rome, Vinicius is greeted by the emperor Nero (Giovanni Gizzi), who honors him with a pagan orgy of dining and celebration.

After the feast, Vinicius' uncle Petronius (Gustavo Serena), a member of the emperor's entourage, arranges for the hero to lodge with a retired Roman general. During Vinicius' stay, he meets a former slave girl who has become the general's adopted daughter, Lygia (Lea Gunghi). She is a recent convert to Christianity, a fact that Vinicius only comes to realize after he has fallen in love with her. Then he, too, gradually converts to Christianity.

Vinicius' conversion establishes a major point of conflict among himself, his patron Nero, and ironically, Poppaea (Amelia Cattaneo), the emperor's wife. Poppaea is a wanton who tries to make Vinicius one of her conquests, but he rebuffs her. At this same time, with his own power starting to erode, Nero devises the idea of blaming the empire's problems on the new religious sect of Christians. He has the city of Rome set on fire and then charges the Christians with the willful destruction of the city. He then throws the sect to ferocious lions in the Circus Maximus for the entertainment of the masses.

Lygia and Vinicius are arrested with the other Christians. In the arena, the soldier is forced to watch as his love is tied to the back of a ferocious bull. As the bull rushes into the arena, however, Ursus (Bruto Castellani), a very strong man whom Lygia had nursed when he was wounded and who is now sworn to protect her, runs forward and locks his arms around the animal. The spectators are astonished as he kills the bull, prompting the chant to go up that the pair should go free. Reluctantly, the emperor lets all three of the prisoners go. Subsequently, Nero is confronted with his crimes by the dying Christians, and the angry mob rises up in a revolution that ends with the Emperor's death. Vinicius and Lygia are then free to marry, and the film ends on an optimistic note.

Scholars attributed the unprecedented success of *Quo Vadis?* primarily to its monumental scale and the energy of its frenzied crowd scenes. Yet, most overlooked certain new qualities that Guazzoni infused into the form itself. His primary contribution to the film was a unique feeling for space—a quest for a third dimension. Space and a largeness of scale, he reasoned, would result in a degree of verisimilitude heretofore unknown in the cinema or, in fact, upon the stage. Guazzoni, thus, introduced and codified the conventions that would set the standard for the genre of the historical spectacular. His massive sets fully expressed the flavor of first century Rome, and he said later, during the production of *Marcantonio e Cleopatra* (1913), "I was offered the chance to show spectators the most characteristic places in ancient Rome and Egypt, places we may all have dreamt of as children." According to Pierre Leprohon, a historian of Italian cinema, Guazzoni intended to direct his film "in such a way that the smallest detail will be in conformity with the strictest historical truth." In fact, he insisted upon complete historical authenticity, even to the point of employing real lions in the Colosseum scenes.

The film expressed to the viewer a strong impression of depth and space through the use of huge sets and large crowds. Guazzoni was able to manipulate his hordes of actors and extras in and around his enormous structures better perhaps than any director before or since. His staging of the crowd scenes were very smooth and revealed an almost complete mastery of the physical aspects of his production. There was a conscientious and meticulously detailed effort to achieve a third dimension of depth through the establishment of immense vacuums of luminous space between the large outdoor sets and the director's cameras. Neopolitan film historian Roberto Paeolla viewed the spectacular architectural masses on different visual planes and the compilation of a large amount of visual detail as expressing the "supreme majesty of space." Yet, the production lacked one fundamental element—camera movement. The lone perspective was one consisting of a long, stationary, wide-angle shot with the frame pretty much duplicating the proscenium of a theater and confining all of the action within its perimeters. Thus, there was no intimacy except that of the stage. Guazzoni's contemporary, Giovanni Pastrone would put the camera on a dolly and employ the first tracking shots in his 1914 production of *Cabiria*, thus fulfilling the technical promise of *Quo Vadis?*, which Guazzoni attempted with the relatively limited concepts at his disposal in 1912.

Quo Vadis? was the first feature film, and it not only established the conventions for the historical costume spectacles but also, to some degree, for every feature film from *The Birth of a Nation* (1915) to *Apocalypse Now* (1979) and *Heaven's Gate* (1981). D. W. Griffith, in fact, saw both *Quo Vadis?* and *Cabiria* while he was devising *The Birth of a Nation*, and there is no doubt that both influenced him heavily at a point in his life when he was at a loss as to the perfect form in which to express his epic vision of a pivotal period in American history. *Quo Vadis?*, undoubtedly gave him some suggestions.

The film sustains itself today and has been remade twice. An Italian-German production directed by Gabriellino d'Annunzio and Georg Jacoby in 1925 featured a cast of twenty thousand, including Emil Jannings, Lilian Hall-Davies, and Bruto Castellani who repeated his role as Ursus from the 1912 version. M-G-M made a lavish $8,250,000 version in 1925 that occupied Rome's Cinecittà Studios for two years. Like Guazzoni's epic, it featured chariot races, the burning of Rome, and the barbaric bloodletting of the Circus Maximus, but today it is best remembered for Peter Ustinov's beautifully effete interpretation of Nero in the 1951 production. Guazzoni's epic, after seventy years, is still the definitive treatment and a landmark in the development of the motion picture as well.

Stephen L. Hanson

THE RAT

Released: 1926
Production: Michael Balcon for W & F; released by Artlee
Direction: Graham Cutts
Screenplay: Graham Cutts; based on the script by David L'Estrange (Ivor Novello and Constance Collier)
Cinematography: Hal Young
Art direction: Charles W. Arnold
Length: 8 reels/7,323 feet

Principal characters:
Pierre Boucheron .... Ivor Novello
Odile Etrange .... Mae Marsh
Zelie de Chaumet .... Isabel Jeans
Herman Stetz .... Robert Scholtz
Madeleine Sornay .... Esme Fitzgibbons
Paul ....Hugh Brook
Detective Caillard .... James Lindsay
Mere Colline .... Marie Ault
Rose .... Iris Grey
Mou Mou .... Julie Suedo

"A British picture that will do much to encourage the future of native effort," is how the principal British film trade paper greeted the release of *The Rat* in the winter of 1925. It was, in fact, highly regarded in its native country as one of the most sophisticated productions of the decade, although receiving only a limited release in the United States—in 1926—by the minor distributor, Artlee.

Ivor Novello wrote *The Rat* as a film script while starring as Joseph Beaugarde in D. W. Griffith's production of *The White Rose* (1923), a film which effectively introduced the British matinee idol to American filmgoers. Novello showed his script to stage actress Constance Collier, and she persuaded him to rewrite it in play form. It was to be the first play written by Novello and also his first production as actor-manager. British drama critic James Agate once noted that Novello "played in the tradition of Sir John Martin Harvey," and there is, indeed, an extraordinary similarity of style between Novello and Harvey, one of Britain's better-known actor-managers. The stage production of *The Rat* opened in Brighton, Sussex, on the southern coast of England, on January 15, 1924, and was transferred to London's Prince of Wales Theatre in June of the same year. It proved to be a tremendous success and established Isabel Jeans, in the role that she also played in the film version, as a star.

Michael Balcon approached Novello regarding the possibility of a film version of *The Rat* and production began early in 1925 at London's Islington studios. Novello, of course, played the title role, but that of his sweetheart, Odile, was assigned to the American actress Mae Marsh, with whom Novello had appeared in *The White Rose*, and who had already been seen in two previous British features, *Paddy-the-Next-Best-Thing* (1922) and *Flames of Passion* (1922). Novello's biographers claim that Marsh was ill during most of the production, but if this is so, she certainly shows no signs of it onscreen and gives a quiet, yet emotionally charged performance.

The Rat is pure romantic melodrama and, as such, appears dated today. What has not been dated, however, is the sophisticated direction and the fluid camerawork of cinematographer Hal Young. There is little cutting within a given scene, but, instead, the camera follows the action around the set. When a character moves from one side of the room to the other, there is not a cut from the subject's first position to the next, but rather the camera moves along with that person. Strangely enough, such camerawork does not distract the observer. In fact, during the final scenes when the Marsh character is charged with murder and the Novello character is wandering hysterically through the streets of Paris, it adds to the frenzy of the situation.

Novello portrays Pierre Boucheron, commonly known as the Rat, a Parisian apache who magnetically attracts women and who earns his living by stealing from the rich. The Rat lives, platonically, as the story makes clear, with a timid waif named Odile Etrange (Mae Marsh). Zelie de Chaumet (Isabel Jeans), a demimondaine who has become bored with her sophisticated world, visits a low dive, where the Rat hangs out, and is physically attracted to him. In turn, Zelie's protector, Herman Stetz (played in an overblown, melodramatic fashion by Robert Scholtz) is attracted to Odile. Stetz has Zelie decoy the Rat to her apartment while he goes off to visit Odile. Odile tries to halt Stetz's advances, pleading with a statue of the Virgin Mary, as the villain corners her and attempts what is a fairly realistic depiction of vicious rape. The Rat returns to his apartment just in time to save Odile and to stab Stetz to death. When the police arrive, Odile insists on assuming guilt for the Rat's crime. Desperately, the Rat pleads with her not to go through with her admission of guilt, but she remains steadfast and is eventually acquitted after a verdict of self-defense. When Odile is released from prison, the Rat realizes and admits his love for the little waif.

The Rat boasts some remarkably realistic sets by art director Charles W. Arnold and has a fairly realistic French atmosphere. The film, in fact, opens with shots of Parisian nightclubs, and, later in the production, there is a long sequence shot live at Follies Bergere.

As a leading man, Novello has his problems. His looks are effeminate, and with the addition of the heavy white makeup that he insists on using here and also in Alfred Hitchcock's *The Lodger* (1926), he appears emasculated. He was a popular playwright and composer, with a large following among middle-aged spinsters, and his film career lasted through the 1930's.

The Rat is the most accessible of the films directed by Graham Cutts (1887-1958), one of the most important British directors of the 1920's, and one for whom Hitchcock once worked as an assistant. To many of his contemporaries, Cutts was regarded as "the British D. W. Griffith." He had entered the film industry as a cinema proprietor and made his first film, *The Wonderful Story*, in 1922 in collaboration with Herbert Wilcox. Among his other important films are *Woman to Woman* (1923), *The Passionate Adventure* (1924), and *The Sea Urchin* (1926). With the coming of sound, Cutts's career declined, and he retired in 1946. Film critic Iris Barry, who was later to found the film department of the Museum of Modern Art, was one of the first to appreciate Cutts's talent. She wrote in her 1926 volume, *Let's Go to the Movies*,

> Mr. Graham Cutts is another British picture-maker, very definitely not of the sheep and water school. He knows, and very rightly, what American jazz films are like, and though he does not make American pictures . . . he makes smart, English pictures which prosper. . . . He understands the art of timing his incidents much better than anyone else in England. . . . His horizon needs broadening, and then his ability and surefire punch could carry him far.

There can be no question that *The Rat* was one of the most popular British films of the decade. Its success led to two sequels, both directed by Cutts and both starring Novello and Jeans: *The Triumph of the Rat* (1926, with Nina Vanna as the heroine) and *The Return of the Rat* (1929, with Mabel Poulton as Novello's leading lady). In addition, there was a somewhat ludicrous 1937 remake of the original story, under the direction of Jack Raymond and featuring Anton Walbrook, Rene Ray, and Ruth Chatterton.

Anthony Slide

REBECCA OF SUNNYBROOK FARM

Released: 1917
Production: Artcraft Pictures Corporation/Paramount
Direction: Marshall Neilan
Screenplay: Frances Marion; based on the novel of the same name by Kate Douglas Wiggin
Cinematography: Walter Stradling
Length: 6 reels

Principal characters:
Rebecca Randall	Mary Pickford
Adam Ladd	Eugene O'Brien
Mrs. Randall	Jane Wolff
Miranda Sawyer	Josephine Crowell
Mr. Cobb	Charles Ogle
Jane Sawyer	Mayme Kelso
Mrs. Simpson	Kate Toncray
Mr. Simpson	Frank Turner
Minnie Smellie	Violet Wilkey

In 1917, Mary Pickford had several successful films. *Poor Little Rich Girl*, *A Romance of the Redwoods*, and *The Little Princess* were all, in their way, representative of the "Little Mary" who became known as "America's Sweetheart." Of all her films that year, perhaps none represents the epitome of Pickford's appeal quite as much as *Rebecca of Sunnybrook Farm*. This appeal has held through the decades. For many fans, the image of the actress is quite vivid, while the titles of her films tend to fade. Most fans, and buffs, remember only two or three of her films, usually *Rebecca of Sunnybrook Farm*, *Poor Little Rich Girl*, and perhaps *Little Lord Fauntleroy* (1921). Other films which were perhaps more indicative of Pickford's versatility as an actress, such as *Stella Maris* (1918) or *Suds* (1920), are usually remembered only by a relative handful of film scholars.

Pickford, who was born in Toronto, Canada, in 1893 as Gladys Smith was the first "superstar" of motion pictures. She had an appeal which would be difficult to measure in terms of today's stars. Although she did not begin working in films until the age of seventeen, her child-woman beauty and golden sausage curls made her a natural choice for parts which would normally be only for children. She became the top box-office star in motion pictures throughout the teens and held a high position through the mid-1920's. When other women were sirens, vamps, or flappers, Pickford still retained her childish looks, and the public wanted it that way. The childlike innocence, enthusiasm, and vitality would probably not be appreciated in a modern actress. In fact, Pickford's own films are not particularly popular with revival houses perhaps for this same reason.

Yet, Pickford's screen *persona* was not sickeningly sweet. Film historian Kevin Brownlow has noted in his book *The Parade's Gone By* that Pickford represented "the ideal American girl." She was "extremely attractive, warm-hearted, generous, funny—but independent and fiery-tempered when the occasion demands." Whatever the subsequent evaluations of her character have been, they are incorrect and demeaning if they see her in the same light as some of her more saccharine imitators. Two decades after Pickford was at her peak, another sausage-curled actress—this time an actual child, Shirley Temple—would appear in films which fit the description which some critics have applied to Pickford. Pickford, however, was not "too sweet," either in her films or in her life. She was an extremely astute businesswoman whose salary rose to $350,000 per film by the time she made *Rebecca of Sunnybrook Farm*, and who had the foresight to preserve her films. She made numerous attempts to go away from her child roles, but the public never accepted her as anything but "Little Mary."

In *Rebecca of Sunnybrook Farm*, Rebecca Randall (Mary Pickford) is one of many children who live on a farm with their mother (Jane Wolff). Because the family is poor, Rebecca is sent to live with her spinster aunts, Jane Sawyer (Mayme Kelso) and Miranda Sawyer (Josephine Crowell). The two sisters are staid New England women who are somewhat shocked by Rebecca's free spirit. Among other things of which they disapprove is Rebecca's friendship and help to Mrs. Simpson (Kate Toncray), a local woman scorned by the townspeople because she has no wedding ring and apparently is the common-law wife of Mr. Simpson (Frank Turner).

Rebecca's help for Mrs. Simpson is not only kind but is also an indication of the girl's strength of character, for she stands up against not only her aunts but virtually the entire town as well. Rebecca is assisted by Adam Ladd (Eugene O'Brien), a young man in the town who gives Rebecca his deceased mother's wedding ring to give to Mrs. Simpson. They are immediately taken with each other, although Rebecca is still a child.

One of the best scenes in the film, and one which is indicative of Pickford's spunkiness in her "girl" films, concerns blackberry pie. Because Rebecca's aunts will not allow her to eat some blackberry pie, she sneaks into the kitchen and takes some. Just as she snatches the pie, however, she sees one of her aunt's hand-stitched samplers which reads "Thou Shalt Not Steal," so she starts to put the pie back. Just as she does, however, she sees another sampler which reads "The Lord Helps Those Who Help Themselves," so she reconsiders and finally eats the pie.

Another enjoyable sequence in the film involves a backyard circus. Rebecca and some of her friends decide to hold a circus in the barn with the assistance of one of Rebecca's many newfound friends, Mr. Cobb (Charles Ogle). Everything is going well until Aunt Miranda stops the show just as a bare-back rider is about to perform some of her more daring stunts.

Because Rebecca is getting older and the aunts feel that she needs a more disciplined atmosphere, she is sent off to boarding school. When she returns several years later, she is a lovely young woman, and she renews her friendship with Adam. They eventually marry, but only after Rebecca has seen to it that her brothers and sisters are taken care of when the Sunnybrook Farm is sold to the railroad.

The plot, in the retelling, does *sound* saccharine, but Pickford's performance, as well as some of the acting in minor roles raises the film above that level. One of the minor characters, Minnie Smellie (Violet Wilkey) is particularly good as the Preacher's daughter who is Rebecca's rival at the school in her aunts' village. Minnie is delightfully two-faced and a good foil for Rebecca, who matches her snarl for snarl. Another actress who has a very minor part which is not even billed is ZaSu Pitts. Pickford had hired Pitts as an extra when the film was on location in Pitts's hometown. This small beginning eventually led to a career which lasted almost fifty years.

Rebecca of Sunnybrook Farm was the first film which Pickford made after a rather unhappy professional association with Cecil B. De Mille. Two other films from 1917, *A Romance of the Redwoods* and *A Little American*, had been directed and cowritten by De Mille with Pickford as their star. It had been a tenuous relationship at best, and both seemed happy to end what was supposed to have been a long and profitable association.

Rebecca of Sunnybrook Farm was more of a labor of love for Pickford than her previous two efforts. Her friend Frances Marion wrote the screenplay based on Kate Douglas Wiggin's best-selling novel of the same name, and Marshall Neilan, who directed the film, had been an actor and leading man opposite Pickford at the Selig Company in the early teens. Later, he turned to directing and supervised or directed a number of Pickford's films. He continued directing and occasionally acting and writing on her films through the mid-1920's.

Although Pickford was almost twenty-five when *Rebecca of Sunnybrook Farm* was made, she would go on playing little-girl and ingenue parts for several more years. In 1929, she made her first talkie, *Coquette*, and won an Academy Award for Best Actress of the year in a role which was not a "little girl" part. She made only two more films, *Kiki* (1931) and *Secrets* (1933), neither of which was successful, before her retirement. Over the next two decades there was talk that she would come out of retirement, but she never did, preferring to live a relatively quiet life with her third husband, Charles "Buddy" Rogers at her estate Pickfair. She received an Oscar for her lifetime contribution to the film industry in 1975 and died in 1979.

Janet Curry

THE RED KIMONO

Released: 1925
Production: Mrs. Wallace Reid for Vital Exchanges
Direction: Walter Lang
Screenplay: Dorothy Arzner; based on an original story by Adela Rogers St. Johns
Cinematography: James Diamond
Length: 7 reels

> *Principal characters:*
> Gabrielle Darley .... Priscilla Bonner
> Mrs. Wallace Reid .... Herself
> Frederick .... Theodore von Eltz

Until her husband's death, from drug addiction, in 1923, Mrs. Wallace Reid (1895-1977) had been little more than a minor screen actress, working under her real name of Dorothy Davenport. With her husband's death, however, Mrs. Reid embarked on a new career as a producer-director, with her first effort being *Human Wreckage* (1923), an exposé of the dangers of narcotics. Mrs. Reid continued to produce films of a somewhat sensational nature, such as *Broken Laws* (1924), which criticized neglectful parents, but none of her films were as exploitative as *The Red Kimono*, a drama of prostitution, which she produced with her own company. The film was very much a woman's picture, for in addition to its subject matter and its producer, the script for *The Red Kimono* was written by director-to-be Dorothy Arzner from an original story by magazine writer Adela Rogers St. Johns. It starred an attractive young actress named Priscilla Bonner, who specialized in portraying innocent young girls, and is best remembered as the blind girl in Harry Langdon's *The Strong Man* (1926).

The film opens with Mrs. Reid in the "morgue" of a newspaper office, where she opens a 1917 newspaper to the story of Gabrielle Darley (Priscilla Bonner). The heroine is first seen in the "crib" district of New Orleans, when she learns from a neighboring girl that her boyfriend has left her and is on his way to Los Angeles to marry another woman. Gabrielle follows her lover to Los Angeles, and when she sees him in a jewelry store purchasing a wedding ring, she shoots and kills him.

At her trial, Gabrielle tearfully recounts the story of her life which is a melodramatic tale of an innocent young village girl lured into prostitution by the "village sport" and forced to support both him and herself. A sympathetic jury acquits the girl, and later, in an unintentionally amusing scene, Gabrielle Darley encounters a Red Cross poster as she leaves the prison cell, which bears the slogan, "At the service of all mankind." Penniless, Gabrielle is taken up by a wealthy socialite, who finds Gabrielle's salvation an easy way to gain publicity. At first, Gabrielle is an amusing novelty who can be shown off to the woman's friends, but in time, the society woman tires of Gabrielle and asks her to leave.

The poor girl tries to obtain work, but, of course, she is too well known thanks to the socialite's publicity-seeking efforts. In desperation, Gabrielle wires back to her neighbor in the "crib" for money to return to New Orleans and her old life-style. In the meantime, the socialite's chauffeur has fallen in love with Gabrielle and searches in vain for her. Then America enters World War I, Gabrielle goes to work in a hospital, and the chauffeur enlists. In the hospital, just as the chauffeur is about to go overseas, he finds Gabrielle, now a scrub woman. He asks her to marry him immediately, but she insists on waiting until he returns from the front; thus, she will be completely regenerated. At the film's end, Mrs. Reid reappears with a suitable Biblical quotation.

The plot of *The Red Kimono* is a silly one, but, unfortunately for Mrs. Reid, it was based on fact. There really was a Gabrielle Darley, who had married well and was living happily in St. Louis. When she viewed the film, Miss Darley was more than a little upset, and she won a sizeable lawsuit against the producer. Aside from the lawsuit, Mrs. Reid had to contend with far from favorable reviews. *Variety* (February 3, 1926) recalled that it was films such as this that set back the German film industry ten years, and noted, "Mrs. Reid or someone else may believe she is doing something for the fallen woman in turning out a picture of this sort, but the chances are that she will do tremendous harm to the picture industry as a whole and to herself." *Photoplay* (March, 1926) was even more outspoken: "Something terrible. It started out with a good story by Adela Rogers St. Johns and was directed by Mrs. Wallace Reid. But somewhere the great qualities of those ladies' talents got completely lost." Mordaunt Hall in *The New York Times* (February 3, 1926) outdid both *Variety* and *Photoplay*, writing "There have been a number of wretched pictures on Broadway during the last year, but none seem to have quite reached the low level of *The Red Kimono*."

In truth, *The Red Kimono* has much to recommend it. It moves along at a fast pace and the plot line is not entirely without surprises. The direction by Walter Lang, making his debut, is faultless, although quite obviously much of the credit should go to Mrs. Reid, who remained continuously on the set. In their refusal to condemn Gabrielle, the producer and scriptwriter show remarkable courage. Not once is there any suggestion that Miss Darley might have chosen a life-style other than prostitution, and the chauffeur-hero never condemns her for returning to that life.

Particular praise should go to Bonner, who never overacts and never gives way to the melodramatics that perhaps some of the scenes might suggest. In *Variety* (December 26, 1925), Arthur James presented an opposing viewpoint from his fellow critics:

Put *The Red Kimono* right up in the front row as a box office production and weave a wreath of fame for Priscilla Bonner who, for consistent acting, appealing personality and a developed talent takes her place among the foremost actresses of the screen. Priscilla Bonner has a Gish quality with a greater vitality and in a role requiring the utmost delicacy to conserve its sympathy she demonstrates unusual power. Cast in the right roles and well directed, this young woman has no handicap to place her at the top rung of the ladder.

Aside from Louis Malle's *Pretty Baby* (1978), starring Brooke Shields, *The Red Kimono* appears to have been the only film documenting the Storyville district of New Orleans, named after Mayor Story, who attempted to confine all crime—drugs, gambling, prostitution, and the like—to one area of the city. The expensive prostitutes were listed in the "Blue Book," while the poorer ones, such as Gabrielle Darley, maintained one-room shacks, called cribs. (The slang term, to crib, meaning to cheat, derives from the cribs of New Orleans, where men might cheat, or crib, on their wives.)

Mrs. Reid followed *The Red Kimono* with *The Earth Woman* (1926), also directed by Lang and starring Bonner. It received reviews as critical as those for *The Red Kimono*, and for a while, Mrs. Reid returned to acting. She became a producer again in the late 1920's; and as late as the mid-1950's, Mrs. Reid was still active, working as an associate to Arthur Lubin on the "Francis, the Talking Mule," series.

Anthony Slide

THE RED LANTERN

Released: 1919
Production: Richard A. Rowland and Maxwell Karger for Metro
Direction: Albert Capellani
Screenplay: June Mathis and Albert Capellani; bàsed on the novel of the
same name by Edith Wherry
Cinematography: Tony Gaudio
Length: 7 reels

Principal characters:
Mahlee, an Eurasian/Blanche Sackville .... Nazimova
Sir Philip Sackville .... Frank Currier
Dr. Sam Wang .... Noah Beery
Dowager Empress of China .... Yukio Ao Yama
General Jung-Lu .... Edward J. Connelly
Andrew Handel .... Darrell Foss

Alla Nazimova was much attracted to dual roles in films. She assayed double
roles in four of the starring films she made for Metro: three times as mother
and daughter in *Toys of Fate* (1918), *Out of the Fog* (1919), and *Madame
Peacock* (1920). Her most dramatic dual role, however, was in *The Red
Lantern* (1919), in which she played half-sisters: the Eurasian named Mahlee
and the Englishwoman, Blanche Sackville, who share the same father. There
are double exposure scenes in *The Red Lantern* where Mahlee confronts
Blanche, and the viewer is amazed by the faint resemblance the two girls
share and overwhelmed by the difference in their physical and psychological
makeups.

Nazimova had made her screen debut in *War Brides* (1916), a powerful
five-reel indictment of war in which she starred for Lewis J. Selznick. The
film was adapted from a one-act play in which Nazimova had been highly
successful on the Orpheum circuit. Two years later, Metro signed the actress
to a starring contract, and beginning with *Revelation*, she made eleven feature
films, becoming known as the most intelligent and exotic of all stars. Her
name was high on popularity lists during the late teens, but she became too
difficult to relate to after her stylized version of *Camille* (1921), in which
Rudolph Valentino played Armand. By the time she made *Salome* (1923),
she had completely alienated her audience, and those few who sat through
a screening of it were convulsed with laughter by her outrageous fright wig
designed by Natacha Rambova. Metro would not release the film, nor would
United Artists, and it was finally introduced to the public by Allied Producers
and Distributors.

After Metro, only three character roles came to Nazimova for Associated
First National and Vitagraph, after which her name disappeared from the

screen. She enjoyed a remarkable renaissance of her fame as an actress on the stage, especially with her appearances on Broadway in *The Cherry Orchard*, *A Month in the Country*, and *Mourning Becomes Electra*, but she did not return to the cameras until 1940, when she played with Norma Shearer and Robert Taylor in M-G-M's *Escape*, the first of four talking features she did before she died on July 13, 1945.

For a few brief years, from 1918 to 1921, she had flourished as Metro's top box-office attraction, but nothing she did for the cinema equaled the great performances she had played on Broadway in the beginning years of her career, when she not only learned to speak English, but also became the most important interpreter of Henrik Ibsen in *Hedda Gabler*, *A Doll's House*, *The Master Builder*, *Little Eyolf*, and *Ghosts*.

Her most vivid performance at Metro was in *The Red Lantern*, a dramatic story of the Boxer Rebellion in China at Peking, of which *The Moving Picture World* critic wrote that it stands "not only as the most satisfactory production which Nazimova has yet given us, but it ranks with the really big stories of the screen catalogue."

In the film, Mahlee (Nazimova) is first introduced as a teenaged girl of the native quarter, whose father is Sir Philip Sackville (Frank Currier), known as "an English mandarin," who had bought the favors of the daughter of Madame Ling. Eventually, when he tired of her and the daughter she bore him, he left them money with the instructions that Mahlee was to be reared with her feet unbound. At the beginning of the action, young Madame Ling is dead and Mahlee's old grandmother is dying. Mahlee is a constant reproach to her grandmother because of her unbound feet. Mahlee prepares a poisoned drink for her grandmother, and when the old woman drinks and falls senseless, Mahlee, torn by remorse, seizes a knife and starts to cut into the flesh of her feet, crying, "Watch, grandame, I shall do as you wish." The old lady, however, roused from her death pangs, seizes the knife and throws it away before she dies. Mahlee then collapses, but is discovered and brought to the Ark of the Covenant Mission, where she is adopted by the missionaries.

Time changes her from a shy outcast to a young mission convert who tries to dress her hair in the style of the picture of the Virgin Mary that hangs in her room. As a young woman, she falls in love for the first time with a young American missionary, Andrew Handel (Darrell Foss), who has taught her to sing, play, and read his language. She thinks of herself as a white girl, but then Sir Philip Sackville comes to the mission with his daughter Blanche, and Mahlee sees in her legitimate half-sister proof of her own oriental ancestry forever mocking her. Every day Mahlee's oriental features bear witness to the purity of Blanche's features, and Mahlee turns from her Christian beliefs to favor the philosophy first taught her, Buddhism. It is a torment fanned persistently by the evil Dr. Sam Wang (Noah Beery), a Chinese who cunningly turns Mahlee into a young girl who at first resents and then later loathes

Blanche because Andrew Handel has fallen in love with her instead of Mahlee. It is not difficult, subsequently, for Dr. Wang to awaken a devotion in Mahlee's heart for the dreaded Boxers, championing their cause of killing the white foreigners who are taking power in China.

Mahlee, arrayed in a golden robe, rides in the jeweled palanquin of the Goddess of the Red Lantern and is presented to the Dowager Empress of China (Yukio Ao Yama) as the Boxer Goddess reincarnated. Even General Jung-Lu (Edward J. Connelly), Chief of the Manchu Army, is fascinated by her. Yet, though she is enjoying her new power, when she sees her father with his legitimate daughter, she humbles herself to him. She explains that he is a European Mandarin and if he will only say that she is his daughter, she can belong to him and his people, and she will forget the terrible Boxer cause. "My poor girl," says Sackville, pityingly, "I cannot help you." Crushed by her failure, Mahlee vanishes. The Boxers, meanwhile, have clashed, been defeated, and have scattered, thus causing the Dowager Empress to abandon her throne.

Andrew Handel, whom Mahlee has loved so hopelessly, comes into the deserted throne room. It is, however, not quite deserted. Huddled in the depths of the peacock throne is the small childlike figure of Mahlee who looks at Handel sadly, murmuring "East is East, and West is West. . . ." At her feet is an overturned cup of poison called "The Wine that brings sweet sleep."

The Red Lantern was Nazimova's finest film at Metro. Playing roles that were brilliantly contrasted, she gained great sympathy for both Mahlee and the helpless English girl, Blanche. Noah Beery, as the infamous Dr. Wang, was more Oriental looking than Warner Oland ever was in his films; in fact, some of the stills of *The Red Lantern* are labeled as being "Oland," who made a career of playing Orientals including many films as Charlie Chan. The entire cast was very impressive, and the production, with scenes of the Temple of Buddha were so exquisitely re-created as to be breathtaking. The Feast of the Red Lantern was magnificently staged, adding dramatic color and power to the picture. Albert Capellani's direction got every ounce of drama from the exotic situations, and Tony Gaudio's cinematography was always dramatically beautiful; his double exposure scenes involving the two sisters were immaculately done.

It is unfortunate that *The Red Lantern*, like most of Nazimova's Metro releases, is a "lost film," but those who did see it remember it fondly. Perhaps someday it will resurface to be enjoyed again.

DeWitt Bodeen

REDSKIN

Released: 1929
Production: Victor Schertzinger for Famous Players-Lasky/Paramount
Direction: Victor Schertzinger
Screenplay: Elizabeth Pickett
Titles: Julian Johnson
Cinematography: Edward Cronjager
Color cinematography: Ray Rennahan and Edward Estabrook
Editing: Otto Lovering
Music: J. S. Zamecnik
Length: 9 reels/7,453 feet

Principal characters:
Wingfoot	Richard Dix
Cornblossom	Gladys Belmont
Judy	Jane Novak
John Walton	Larry Steers
Navajo Jim	Tully Marshall
Chief Notani	George Rigas
Chahi	Bernard Siegel
Yina	Augustine Lopez
Pueblo Jim	Noble Johnson
Commissioner	Joseph W. Girard
Wingfoot (age nine)	Philip Anderson
Cornblossom (age six)	Loraine Rivero
Pueblo Jim (age fifteen)	George Walker

More than anything else, *Redskin* is a classic example of both the potentiality and the limitations of the two-strip Technicolor process. The rich, lustrous reds, browns, and greens that were popular with silent-film audiences in the late 1920's are showcased to exceptional effect, enhancing the grandeur of the Arizona location and the earthy colors and designs of Indian clothes. The color enables the audience to appreciate realistically the Indian fabrics and the majestic flat-top mountains that create the atmosphere of Enchanted Mesa, where the story takes place. The palette of the two-strip process was limited, however, because it gave the denim shirts, streams, and turquoise ornamentations an odd green hue.

In addition to the seductive color cinematography, *Redskin* is an unusual film for its time in that it portrays Indians sympathetically, taking their side—to an extent—against the white government which forces Indian children to leave the reservation and learn the ways of white society. The redskin of the title is Wingfoot (Philip Anderson), a Navajo boy who is taken away from his culture at age nine by John Walton (Larry Steers), a handsome but stern man who believes in harsh discipline instead of compassion and understanding.

When Wingfoot is enrolled by Walton at the government-run Indian school, he is forced to mingle with Pueblo children, the sworn enemy of his people. He is also shorn of his long hair, his traditions, and his native pride. Completing the degradation, Walton severely whips Wingfoot for refusing to salute the American flag. Hereafter, he is known to his Indian peers as Do-Atin, the Whipped One, branding him for life as an outsider. Walton, however, suffers, too, for his fiancée Judy (Jane Novak), breaks their engagement because of his callous act.

Despite this emotional scarring, Wingfoot learns to live with and respect his white overseers for the education and sustenance he would not have received at the reservation. Moreover, he is befriended in the hour of his humiliation by Cornblossom (Loraine Rivero), a six-year-old Pueblo girl. It is she who helps him retain his last vestige of pride as a redskin.

Wingfoot grows into a handsome, well-built man (Richard Dix) and enrolls at Thorpe University—a white man's college—where he continues his studies on a track scholarship. The now womanly Cornblossom (Gladys Belmont) also enrolls at Thorpe to be near him. Despite the accolades Wingfoot receives at Thorpe for his outstanding abilities as a runner, he still is considered a misfit, still perceived by his white classmates as a savage whose natural inclination is to do a war or rain dance at the first opportunity. Realizing he will never fit into white society, Wingfoot returns to Enchanted Mesa and to his cultural roots.

His father, Chief Notani (George Rigas) disavows him on sight when he arrives at the reservation dressed in the white man's uniform: a double-breasted suit and tie. Wingfoot remains an Indian at heart, but all Notani can see is a tailored traitor. Wingfoot's sickly grandmother, Yina (Augustine Lopez), persuades him to don his father's old costume and appear in it at the tribal rites scheduled for the next day. He does so, engendering so much pride in his father that he is appointed as successor to the aged and faltering medicine man, Chahi (Bernard Siegel), who has collapsed while dancing.

Much as Wingfoot wants to be accepted back into his tribe, however, he can no longer accept their superstitious ways, the fearful rituals by which they live, die, and harvest the land. "Your witchcraft killed my mother," he angrily retorts, "it is killing my grandmother, and now you want *me* to preach such nonsense." White society may have oppressed him but it has also given him a practical, scientific education from which there is no return to tribal ignorance.

This renunciation of tribal customs enrages Notani and the other Navajos, who immediately ostracize Wingfoot from the tribe. He flees to the Pueblo reservation to be with Cornblossom, who he learns is unwillingly betrothed to a brute named Pueblo Jim (Noble Johnson). Again, he is forced to run for his life, trekking for days across the parched Arizona desert.

Up to this point, *Redskin* is a competently written, well acted, although racially superficial drama. In fact, it reads more dramatically in synopsis than it plays onscreen. Richard Dix looks too old to be playing a man eighteen to twenty years old, but he brings a glowering intensity to the role of Wingfoot that mitigates the miscasting. Sound would have added immeasurably to the film's impact, enhancing Victor Schertzinger's workmanlike direction and enriching it with Dix's distinctive baritone. Conversely, the fluid editing and camerawork that propel the narrative would have been lost had it been made as a talkie. Still, one wonders why Paramount filmed it as a silent with synchronized score during the very time that the studio was converting to sound.

What ruins *Redskin* as an effective racial statement are its last twenty minutes. Instead of taking the scenario to its logical conclusion—a head-on confrontation between Wingfoot and the feuding tribes that will result either in bloodshed or grudging compromise—screenwriter Elizabeth Pickett gives the character of Wingfoot an easy way out: the discovery of an oil reserve on Navajo land that will make him rich and powerful. It is a blatant contrivance for a happy ending because once it is learned that the Whipped One has laid claim to a literal pool of wealth and is willing to share it equally with the two tribes in order to bring them to heel, he is acclaimed a hero and allowed to intermarry with Cornblossom. Pueblo Jim conveniently is shot to death in the last reel by Navajo Jim, a corny comic relief character played by Tully Marshall.

The last shot in the picture seems ludicrous by modern standards. Wingfoot and Cornblossom are united in marriage before the tribes and are faced to the camera at a right angle that looks posed and therefore unnatural. The effect is meant to be sentimentally uplifting but succeeds only in emphasizing the artificiality of the finale.

It is an implausible resolution because the interracial hatred of the tribes runs too deep to be assuaged by a material go-between. At best, there would be an uneasy truce for a few days before Wingfoot would be cast out again and the tribes would go to war for possession of the oil deposit. Either that or the white government would intervene and claim the oil for itself as it had done frequently with Indian property.

Redskin's denouement is ineffective because it relies on a plot device, a *deus ex machina* evasion, that assumes the power of money as an all-healing barter to end interracial squabbling. Without this crutch, Pickett's script would have had to face Wingfoot's ironic predicament honestly; in his own words that he is "not a white man or an Indian, but a redskin." Perhaps the filmmakers felt it was enough that they were going against the grain of Indian stereotypes by making a film that attempted to depict them as a proud, dignified people, and that delving even deeper into the societal schisms that exist between the white and red cultures, and between the tribes themselves, would have raised more questions than they cared to answer.

Whatever the case may have been, Paramount at least had the courage to make a pro-Indian film and a Technicolor one at that, considering the expense of the process. The color is also used for dramatic counterpoint because the second and third reels—the sequences taking place at the Indian school and the white college—are olive tinted, effectively contrasting the literally colorful life at the mesa with the drab, mundane one away from it.

Aside from Dix and Marshall, the cast is an unfamiliar one. Apparently no one in the cast is actually an Indian (the extras are Oriental), although Gladys Belmont is convincing as the Indian maiden Cornblossom, especially in her love scenes with the equally tender Dix.

Larry Steers does what he can with his cardboard role as the militaristic schoolmaster. His general blandness and matinee-idol looks (with his chiseled nose and trimmed moustache, he resembles a young Clifton Webb) undercut his attempts at dramatic depth, although he does have a few good scenes, especially when he punishes young Wingfoot and later apologizes to him for the uncalled-for whipping. Belmont and Steers aside, the rest of the supporting cast is serviceable but not at all memorable.

How much money *Redskin* made is impossible to say more than fifty years later. Today it is a forgotten film, although certainly deserving of mention as one of the few films of its era to address the problem of Indian assimilation into white culture. Two years later, in 1931, Paramount would again address the problem, although fleetingly, in the Oscar-winning *Cimarron*. Dix again starred, but this time as a white landowner who believes the Indians have been mistreated. This venture aside, it would not be until 1950, with the release of *Broken Arrow*, that Hollywood would again seriously confront the Indian issue. Considered in this context, while only above-average drama at best, *Redskin* is notable for presenting the Indian in a semi-favorable light.

Sam Frank

REGENERATION

Released: 1915
Production: William Fox
Direction: Raoul Walsh
Screenplay: Raoul Walsh and Carl Harbaugh; based on the book *My Mamie Rose* by Owen Kildare
Cinematography: George Benoit
Length: 5 reels

Principal characters:
Owen	John McCann
Jim Conway	James Marcus
Maggie Conway	Maggie Weston
Owen at seventeen	H. McCoy
Owen at twenty-five	Rockliffe Fellowes
Skinny	William Sheer
Ames	Carl Harbaugh
Marie "Mamie Rose" Deering	Anna Q. Nilsson

Regeneration is the earliest surviving feature film directed by Raoul (or, as he was then known, R. A.) Walsh (1887-1981), and, in addition, it was Walsh's first feature for the William Fox Company. Although it is questionable, as Walsh claims in his autobiography, that *Regeneration* was the first feature-length gangster film, the production is certainly the first of the gutsy, virile works with which its director was to become closely associated. The influence of D. W. Griffith is very apparent, not only because *Regeneration* has its origins in Griffith's 1912 one-reeler *The Musketeers of Pig Alley*, but also because it has a strong flavor of coy sentimentality running through the production, the same element present in many Griffith features. In fact, *Regeneration* looks very much like a Griffith-supervised Fine Arts production from the same period.

Regeneration was based on the book, *My Mamie Rose*, by Owen Kildare, which much mirrored the author's own life. Kildare did not learn to read or write until he was thirteen, and *My Mamie Rose* was his tribute to the young schoolteacher who had inspired in him a desire for knowledge and saved him from the life of a criminal. The book, it was not strictly speaking novel, had already been dramatized for the stage, as *The Regeneration*, in 1909.

The film utilizes exteriors shot on New York's Bowery and in Fort Lee, New Jersey, and successfully captures the spirit and vigor of life on the city's lower East Side. Yet again, it harks back to Griffith's American Biograph one-reelers in its use of real locations and nonactors. Walsh has also successfully managed to re-create the exterior scenes of the hideouts of the criminal element, demonstrating an attention to detail not only in the sets but also in the mannerisms of the performers. *Regeneration* has a documentary quality, without the coldness which is so often associated with documentary realism. Its characters come through as living and breathing entities in a film which is at times little more than a simple melodrama.

Regeneration is the story of Owen (Rockliffe Fellowes), who lives in the New York slums and obtains an education through the efforts of a society woman turned social worker, Marie Deering (Anna Q. Nilsson). Miss Deering is a woman "whose butterfly existence has hidden, even from herself, the knowledge of her nobler qualities." Owen is seen at three stages of his life, and it is quite remarkable that the other two actors playing the part bear a strong resemblance to Fellowes. After Owen (John McCann) has helped a gangster, Skinny (William Sheer), escape the law, Marie Deering has a confrontation with him, and she is shot when the gangster fires at Owen. Dying, she begs Owen not to seek revenge of her killer, who is, in fact, shot by a fellow gangster. With her death, Miss Deering's work in reforming Owen is complete; he is totally regenerated. Owen stands at the grave of Miss Deering, whom he has long affectionately called Mamie Rose, and says,

> She lies here, this girl o' mine, but her soul, the noblest and purest thing I ever knew, lives on in me. It was she, my Mamie Rose, who taught me that within me was a mind and a God-given heart. She made of my life a changed thing and never can it be the same again!

There is much that is remarkable about *Regeneration*, not the least of which is the unusual tragic ending, totally unpredictable and out-of-the-ordinary for films of the teens. The camerawork is also worthy of mention; at the beginning and end of each scene, the camera moves automatically (or so it seems) into or out of a medium shot.

The most spectacular sequence in *Regeneration* concerns a fire on board a ship on the Hudson River which is taking the residents of the slums for a day's outing. There are well-handled sequences of the crowd panicking, lifeboats overturning, and the like; but dramatic as this episode may be, it has no particular relevance to the plot and appears to have been inserted to expand the action away from the two dimensional scenes between the principals.

Walsh discusses the filming of this sequence in great detail in his 1974 autobiography, *Each Man in His Time*. He hired two Hell's Kitchen inhabitants to round up an assortment of men and women to portray the slum residents on the boat. All were expected to know how to swim and all were required to leap from the burning boat. The problem was that the women, many of whom were prostitutes, wore nothing under their dresses, as was very apparent when they jumped into the water. A "negative doctor" was hired to paint underwear onto the women's naked bodies. "We ran the doctored reels next evening and it was perfect," wrote Walsh, "except some of the women looked as though they were wearing diapers." It is an amusing story, but, of course, its authenticity cannot be verified. In that same auto-biography, Walsh inaccurately recalls that *Regeneration* ends with the heroine standing by the grave of the dead hero and even quotes an epitaph he claims to have written for the dead man.

Regeneration was well received by the trade paper critics. In *Motion Picture News* (October 2, 1915), Peter Milne wrote,

> This latest production of William Fox's is as different from the old time melodrama as night is from day. There are dozens of realistic touches in every reel comprising the feature. Life of the Lower East Side is depicted with a weird mixture of realism and the choicest humor. There are any number of laughs in the picture, but through it all runs the underlying touch of pathos, so elusive to the picture director. . . .

In *The Moving Picture World* (October 2, 1915), Lynde Denig commented, "A more sympathetic and stirring picture of slum life . . . need not be desired. . . . There is a grim sort of humor in many of the scenes; there is an abundance of excitement in others, and throughout, the picture carries a genuine heart interest that cannot fail to move an audience."

The career of Walsh probably reached its zenith in the 1930's, but films such as *The Bowery* (1933) and *The Roaring Twenties* (1939) only carried on a tradition and a directorial image, the groundwork for which had been laid with *Regeneration*. The 1915 film was long considered lost until the late 1970's, when a print was donated for preservation to the Museum of Modern Art.

Anthony Slide

REMODELING HER HUSBAND

Released: 1920
Production: New Art Film Company for Paramount-Artcraft Films
Direction: Lillian Gish
Screenplay: Dorothy Elizabeth Carter
Cinematography: George W. Hill
Length: 5 reels/4,844 feet

> *Principal characters:*
> Janie Wakefield .... Dorothy Gish
> Jack Valentine .... James Rennie
> Mrs. Wakefield .... Marie Burke
> Mr. Wakefield .... Downing Clarke
> Mr. Valentine .... Frank Kingdom

There are many "lost" films which are sought by both archivists and enthusiasts, but few have the appeal of *Remodeling Her Husband*, which is not merely a film directed by a woman, but a film directed by one of the most famous women and consummate actresses of the silent screen, Lillian Gish. *Remodeling Her Husband* was the only film that Gish ever directed, but, by all accounts there is no reason why she should not have continued as a director had not her urge to act been so strong.

It was Gish's mentor, D. W. Griffith, who suggested that she try her hand at directing. He had recently acquired a Mamaroneck, New York, estate, which he was converting into a studio, and while he was in Florida filming *The Idol Dancer* (1920) and *The Love Flower* (1920), Griffith suggested that Lillian take over the partially completed studios. "You know as much as I do about making pictures," said Griffith. "If you work with Dorothy, it would free her director, Elmer Clifton, to help me in Florida." According to Lillian the idea for the story of *Remodeling Her Husband* came from a magazine cartoon that her actress sister Dorothy had come across. In most interviews, Lillian has credited the authorship of the story to Dorothy Parker. This is obviously untrue, and the director is confusing literary wit Dorothy Parker with the name of Dorothy Elizabeth Carter, which appears with the screenplay credit in all contemporary writings on the film. Paramount's studio records contain no reference to Dorothy Carter, but, instead, indicate that the author of the screenplay is anonymous. There does appear to be a certain amount of evidence, however, to suggest that perhaps Dorothy Elizabeth Carter was a pseudonym for Dorothy and Lillian Gish.

Of the making of *Remodeling Her Husband*, Gish recalls that "Griffith left Harry Carr—he was the *Los Angeles Times* editorial writer—and me to do the film." Gish, according to her own account, had to do everything from having telephone poles put in to supply electricity to the studio on Mamaroneck Point to designing her own scenery. The weather was exceedingly cold in mid-December when they were filming, which caused additional problems, including love scenes between Dorothy Gish and James Rennie which looked as if the two stars were blowing smoke into each other's faces.

Gish had only fifty thousand dollars with which to make the film and through her own wits and some cooperation from a friendly New York City policeman who let the company film without city permits, she brought the picture in for only fifty-eight thousand dollars. As Gish said later, ". . . it made, I think, ten times what it cost."

The heroine of *Remodeling Her Husband* is Janie Wakefield (Dorothy Gish), a child at heart, who puts away her dolls and playthings when it comes time to marry Jack Valentine (James Rennie). After their marriage, she is little more than a trusting, innocent pet, until one day she sees her husband in a taxicab with a former girl friend of his. Later, she sees Jack entering the apartment of an attractive young widow, living across the hallway from them. When Janie discovers her husband making a date with a manicurist, she considers he has gone too far and leaves him.

Janie goes to work for her father, a wealthy importer, and soon becomes entrusted with most of the company's important business. In time, Jack decides to seek a reconciliation with his young bride. She will not see him at her father's home, but does agree to grant him an appointment at the office. Jack is outraged when he discovers that he must wait his turn for an interview with his wife, but her aloof attitude helps to rekindle his love. She ignores his letters and his personal pleadings, but eventually returns to Jack when it appears that he will destroy himself. A reconciliation is arranged, and thus does Janie remodel her husband.

From all accounts, *Remodeling Her Husband* proved a perfect vehicle for Dorothy Gish (1898-1968), who was an accomplished comedienne, as witnessed in her work in *Hearts of the World* (1918) and *Nell Gwyn* (1926). At the time of *Remodeling Her Husband*, Dorothy was starring in a series of comedies for Paramount, none of which appears to have survived. Her work has been eclipsed by the career of her sister, which is perhaps not entirely unfair because Dorothy never really reached the heights of acting demonstrated by Lillian, although she came fairly close with her portrayal of the blind Louise in *Orphans of the Storm* (1922). Playing opposite Dorothy in *Remodeling Her Husband* was James Rennie, whom the actress married later in 1920, but divorced a few years later.

Critical reaction to *Remodeling Her Husband* was somewhat mixed. *The New York Times* (June 7, 1920) commented,

Miss Gish's antics cannot enliven five or six reels of film otherwise dull, and *Remodeling Her Husband* is not, therefore, continuously amusing. There are long stretches of it that fail to win a smile. One reason is the subtitles. The spirit of most of the picture is one of mockery, but the words are labored and self-conscious. They slow down the action below farce-speed. . . . Also the others in the cast do not catch and convey the necessary speed and spirit. . . . Altogether one gets impatient with the story except when Miss Gish is at some of her foolishness.

Laurence Reid in *Motion Picture News* (June 19, 1920) agreed with *The New York Times*:

Only the presence of Dorothy Gish, with her undeniable charm and inimitable comedy, saves this piece from becoming a tiresome entertainment. . . . Lillian Gish shows her versatility as the director and her ability to make the most of the story is a creditable achievement.

Many critics expressed interest in the feminine aspect of the production. *Photoplay* (September, 1920) wrote,

This is a woman's picture. A woman wrote it, a woman stars in it, a woman was its director. And women will enjoy it most. It does an unusual and daring thing; it presents the feminine point of view in plot, in captions, in sets and acting. . . . Lillian Gish has gone back to acting, but we'd like to tell her that she is almost as good a directress as she is an actress—and that's going some.

In *The Moving Picture World* (June 19, 1920), Louis Reeves Harrison wrote,

Written, acted and directed by women, *Remodeling Her Husband* is a costume display, is dainty neat and pure of spirit. It is a cause of "Oh, Girls!" almost an Adamless Eden, the supposed men merely a befogged lot of creatures, whose sole reason for existence is their contribution to the economic situation of womankind.

Frederick James Smith wrote in *Motion Picutre Classic* (October, 1920) that "After observing Dorothy Gish's *Remodeling Her Husband* we are confident that Lillian Gish could easily develop into a director of fine originality." There were, of course, many women directors at work in the American film industry during the teens—the most important of whom was Lois Weber—but few women's films have evoked the interest shown *Remodeling Her Husband*. Its importance lies not merely in the name of its director but in the obviously feminist viewpoints expressed in the story.

Anthony Slide

ROBIN HOOD
(DOUGLAS FAIRBANKS IN ROBIN HOOD)

Released: 1922
Production: Douglas Fairbanks Pictures; released by United Artists
Direction: Allan Dwan
Screenplay: Based on a story by Elton Thomas (Douglas Fairbanks); scenario edited by Lotta Woods
Cinematography: Arthur Edeson
Art direction: Wilfred Buckland, Irvin J. Martin, and Edward M. Langley
Length: 11 reels/10,680 feet

Principal characters:
The Earl of Huntington/
Robin Hood .... Douglas Fairbanks
Richard the Lion-Hearted .... Wallace Beery
Prince John ....Sam De Grasse
Lady Marian Fitzwalter .... Enid Bennett
Sir Guy of Gisbourne .... Paul Dickey
The High Sheriff of Nottingham ...... William Lowery
Friar Tuck .... Willard Louis
Little John .... Alan Hale
Will Scarlett ....Maine Geary

Robin Hood, or *Douglas Fairbanks in Robin Hood* as it is sometimes called was one of a group of films made in the late teens and early 1920's which boasted of being "the most expensive film ever produced." Figures about the cost, profit, or loss of a film are very nebulous, however, as there are myriad ways in which one could measure such things. Also, an interpretation of figures does not take into account the natural inclination to exaggerate (or hide) the truth.

Yet, if one looks at *Robin Hood*, it is easy to see that it was indeed a lavish production. It had the largest single set ever built in Hollywood, it had spectacle, romance, action, and most important, it had Douglas Fairbanks. Fairbanks was born in 1883 as Douglas Elton Ulman. He began acting in the theater in the 1890's and was an established stage star by the early teens. His handsome face, athletic build, and contagious *joie de vivre* made him a natural choice for motion pictures, and he began in films in 1915 with the feature *The Lamb*, made for Triangle Fine Arts. The film was immediately successful, despite dire predictions made by the film's general supervisor D. W. Griffith, who did not appreciate what was the immutable Fairbanks style.

During the next few years, Fairbanks appeared in a large number of films, mostly features, and his popularity became almost unprecedented. Rudolph Valentino excepted, Fairbanks was the most popular male star in American films (probably the world) from the late teens through the late 1920's. The only female actress who approached Fairbanks in popularity (or possibly even surpassed him) was Mary Pickford. Pickford and Fairbanks met in late 1915, and although both were married at the time, they became almost immediately interested in each other. Because they feared the public's shock if they should divorce their respective spouses and marry, however, they did not wed until 1920.

Whatever fears that Pickford and Fairbanks or their friends had about the effect that their marriage would have on their respective careers were quickly dispelled. If anything, the marriage of "America's Sweetheart" to the flamboyant Fairbanks increased their popularity. "Doug and Mary," as they were known to virtually everyone, became the most popular couple in America, with their every move chronicled in the newspapers and magazines of the time. They bought a huge estate on Summit Drive in Beverly Hills and called it Pickfair. The estate still stands, now the home of a millionaire sprouts entrepreneur.

Although the fame and glory for both Pickford and Fairbanks would fade in the late 1920's, and their marriage would eventually end in divorce and remarriage for both, there has never again been a couple more popular than "Doug and Mary" in film history.

It was during the halcyon days of the early 1920's that Fairbanks first got the idea of making a film about Robin Hood. After the huge success of Fairbanks' first real swashbuckler, *The Mark of Zorro* (1920), Fairbanks was in the mood to make greater spectacles with more historical settings and swordplay. Initially to be called "The Spirit of Chivalry," the project started out to be a class-A, spare-no-expense production, and that tenet was kept throughout the filming. Because Hollywood was in the middle of a slack period for the film industry, Fairbanks himself decided to put up the proposed one million dollars in capital needed.

Fairbanks, along with Mary Pickford, Charles Chaplin, and D. W. Griffith, had started the United Artists releasing company in 1919, and all of his and Pickford's subsequent films were produced by their own production companies and released through United Artists. Thus, Fairbanks owned all of the rights to his films and became enormously wealthy.

Work on *Robin Hood* began in January, 1922, with background materials and research under the supervision of Dr. Arthur Woods. Fairbanks was enthusiastic about this project, as he was with everything, and the researchers, artists, and designers were hard at work almost immediately. The undisputed triumph of the project was the enormous castle set built on Fairbanks' new studio lot, under the supervision of director Allan Dwan and art director Wilfred Buckland. Fairbanks was reportedly away from California on business when the set was built and returned to Hollywood to see the largest set ever constructed before him. According to film historian Kevin Brownlow, Dwan was surprised by Fairbanks' initial reaction: the star felt that the castle was so big that no one would notice him on the screen. Dwan craftily changed Fairbanks' opinion, however, when he rigged up some slides and stairways to show Fairbanks what fantastic stunts could take place in such a set.

Never one stubbornly to refuse to change his mind about something, Fairbanks proceeded to make the film with enthusiasm. The production was so lavish and entertaining, in fact, that bleachers were built on the lot to accommodate the tourists who thronged to the studio to watch the filming.

With the popularity of Fairbanks, coupled with the advance publicity on the film, it could hardly fail, and it was indeed a huge success. It made an estimated five million dollars (some sources say two-and-a-half million), not an unsubstantial sum for 1922. The critics were generally very favorable in their reviews, but many felt that the division in the story between the early historical background and the Fairbanks sequences was detrimental to its overall merits. Most, however, did praise Fairbanks himself. In *The New York Times*, for example, in one of its two reviews of the film, the reviewer stated "To Zorro and D'Artagnan, Douglas Fairbanks has added Robin Hood, and Robin Hood is the greatest of the three." Other reviews were equally laudatory of Fairbanks, although in historical hindsight, the film is not of the caliber of the other spectacles he made.

In large measure, the drop in prestige of the film is due to exactly what bothered some contemporary reviewers: the first part of the film does not include any footage of the star as the public had come to know him. In the beginning of the film, the staid Earl of Huntington (Douglas Fairbanks) is asked by King Richard (Wallace Beery) to come with him on the Crusades. In the absence of King Richard, as any student of legend and film knows, the King's brother, John (Sam De Grasse), becomes an oppressive tyrant and attempts to usurp his brother's throne. When the Earl of Huntington returns to England and learns what has happened, he assumes the guise of Robin Hood, who "takes from the rich, to give to the poor."

In his element as the flamboyant Robin Hood, Fairbanks is able to fence, shoot (with bow and arrows), and romp his way through the rest of the film with all of the boyish charm and enthusiasm which made him one of the most popular stars of all time. Added in the fight against Prince John and his evil henchman the Sheriff of Nottingham (William Lowery) are the usual familiar supporters, Little John (Alan Hale), Friar Tuck (Willard Louis), and Will Scarlett (Maine Geary). As *The New York Times* aptly states, the second half of the film is ". . . a quick succession of starts and skirmishes and escapes, with Robin Hood darting and sending darts everywhere. . . ."

Lady Marian Fitzwalter (Enid Bennett) served as Robin Hood's romantic interest and is rescued by Robin Hood in time to end the film in his arms. As Bennett noted years later, she did not have much to do, or know exactly what she was supposed to be doing, but she did enjoy doing it.

Of the supporting cast, Wallace Beery made quite a good King Richard and, in fact, is better than some of the later, less robust Richards on film. Alan Hale was also good in a smaller role as Little John. He became in the minds of many filmgoers the definitive Little John, when he re-created the role more than fifteen years later for *The Adventures of Robin Hood* (1938) starring Errol Flynn.

Many film historians have argued the merits of *Robin Hood* as a whole, but Fairbanks seemed to be born to play Robin Hood just as he seemed born to play Zorro or D'Artagnan. Never taking himself seriously, his scenes which could border on corniness are nevertheless enjoyable because he pokes fun at himself. The Errol Flynn Robin Hood perhaps comes closest to the enthusiastic portrayal of Fairbanks in the 1922 version.

The film makes little or no attempt to be factual (despite the extensive research which helped to evoke the period and helped to perpetuate the myth of a good King Richard and a bad Prince John). No credit is given to any written source for the screenplay, with only the story attributed to Elton Thomas, Fairbanks' pseudonym. It certainly owes much of its "background," however, to Sir Walter Scott's *Ivanhoe*. Subsequent versions of *Robin Hood* actually are closer in spirit to the nineteenth century Scott novel and the 1922 film than actual historical fact.

History, though, does not need to be served by cinematic entertainment, and as entertainment, *Robin Hood* is very good. Although the film was thought to be lost for many years, it was rediscovered, and it was announced in 1982 that a new print was being prepared for re-release. The new release will be accompanied by a new score written especially for it, following in the wake of the success of Francis Ford Coppola's revival of *Napoleon* (1927) in 1981.

Patricia King Hanson

ROMEO AND JULIET

Released: 1916
Production: Fox Film Corporation
Direction: J. Gordon Edwards
Screenplay: Adrian Johnson
Cinematography: Philip Rosen
Length: 7 reels

> *Principal characters:*
> Juliet .... Theda Bara
> Romeo .... Harry Hilliard
> Mercutio .... Glen White
> Frair Lawrence .... Walter Law
> Tybalt .... John Webb Dillion
> Paris .... Einar Linden
> Montague .... Elwin Eaton
> Capulet .... Edward Holt
> Nurse .... Alice Gale
> Lady Montague .... Victory Bateman
> Lady Capulet .... Helen Tracy

Two film versions of William Shakespeare's immortal play *Romeo and Juliet* were produced in 1916, one by Metro and the other by Fox, both of which proved to be admirable attempts at translating to the screen perhaps the greatest romance of all time. The Metro version starred Francis X. Bushman and Beverly Bayne. Bushman was praised highly by critics for his interpretation of Romeo and Bayne was labeled the "sweetest" of Juliets. Naturally, comparisons between the Metro and Fox versions were made by the critics. Since Metro seemed to have the idea first, Julian Johnson, in his 1916 *Photoplay* review quipped,

> Not a nice thing this foxy faculty of pinning himself to everybody's coattails, yet he at least gives all his imitations with profound energy and prodigal extravagance. . . . While Metro's is the one entertainment worth perpetuity, Mr. Fox will carry the gospel of real drama far.

The Fox version was, as usual, a glittering spectacle with passion and a great deal of punch. A small street fight is blown into a civil war, and the Capulet mansion resembles an expensive bordello. Also, Fox's great chain of theaters would provide many people with the chance to view the classic who would not be able to afford to see the Metro version in other theaters.

It would be difficult to say that one film excelled as each had points of excellence in common and certain qualities in particular. Both Metro and Fox steered clear of the presentational, stage style of acting which was popular at the time, particularly when it came to projecting the emotion of love. The Metro picture was a bit more elaborate in evoking traditional decor and sticking to the original story, while the more condensed Fox version took more liberties with the text. "Fox had the notion to improve Shakespeare," one critic chided when discussing Fox's altered ending. In Shakespeare's play, Romeo comes to the tomb, and after assuming that the motionless Juliet is dead, he drinks a poison and dies instantly. A moment afterward, Juliet wakes to see her young husband dead and subsequently commits suicide with a dagger. In the Fox version, however, upon awakening from her coma, Juliet (Theda Bara) discovers Romeo (Harry Hilliard) and is overjoyed when he tells her that he has come to take her to Mantua. She learns in a moment, however, that he has taken the poison and is about to die, so she kills herself at the same time. The result is the same, but the newly written brief encounter between the two living lovers is highly dramatic and effective.

There are many points of merit in both films. The interior scenes of the Fox film were better than Metro's, while the outdoor scenes of the Metro version were superior to those of Fox. Metro handled the crowd scenes better, but the ball sequence where Romeo meets Juliet was much better done in the Fox version, which contained many wonderful sets as well as many locations of enchanting beauty. The Fox version also tells the story clearly and is full of suspense which remains throughout the picture. No stage production of the play could compete with the film, if only for the wealth of detail and superb settings.

Critical comparisons were also made between the actors of each production. All critics agreed that it was better to have a young Juliet than to have an actress such as Sarah Bernhardt trying to be young when the scrutinizing motion-picture screen refuses to be deceived. *Motion Picture Magazine* referred to Harry Hilliard as the "perfect lover" and praised Theda Bara for her range of dramatic ability by first playing Juliet as an ingenue and later as a "tragedienne." In the Metro version, Bushman was considered an "ideal" Romeo in physique, grace, and conception. "There is no strutting or posing," and he plays with ". . . a delicate, yet passionate appreciation." His dueling scene with Tybalt was also a remarkable display of fencing. Bayne was ". . . a winsome and lovable Juliet." In a final analysis, Bara was thought to be a better Juliet than Bayne since she brought to the part "all the steam-heat that the cool Beverly lacks." It was said that Bara had Bayne standing still while she ". . . sweeps by like a whirlwind." Additionally, Glen White's Mercutio is excellent and John Webb Dillion is highly effective as Tybalt in the Fox version. Alice Gale as the nurse was especially efficacious, while Walter Law gives the conventional portrayal of Friar Lawrence. The scenario by Adrian Johnson is economical, clear, and skillful, and although it departs from the Shakespearean ending, it adheres more closely to the original Italian version of the story on which Shakespeare's play is based. Metro's goal was the artistic perpetuation of a great story, while Fox's goal was to be exciting and entertaining. To that extent, then, they both succeed.

Tanita C. Kelly

ROSITA

Released: 1923
Production: Mary Pickford Company; released by United Artists
Direction: Ernst Lubitsch
Screenplay: Edward Knoblock and Hans Kraly; based on Edward Knoblock's
   adaptation of the play *Don César de Bazan* by Adolphe d'Ennery and
   Philippe François Pinel and a story by Norbert Falk and Hans Kraly
Cinematography: Charles Rosher
Art direction: William Cameron Menzies
Music: Louis F. Gottschalk
Length: 9 reels/ 8,800 feet

Principal characters:
Rosita, a street singer .... Mary Pickford
The King .... Holbrook Blinn
The Queen .... Irene Rich
Don Diego .... George Walsh
The Prime Minister .... Charles Belcher
Rosita's mother .... Mathilde Comont
Rosita's father .... George Periolat
Prison Commandant .... Frank Leigh

When Mary Pickford was visiting Europe in the early 1920's, she signed the eminent German director Ernst Lubitsch to come to Hollywood and direct her in a feature film. She was very anxious to get out of the little girl mold which had made her famous, and she decided that a popular novel of the time, *Dorothy Vernon of Haddon Hall*, the screen rights for which she had acquired from silent star Madge Kennedy, would be the vehicle to ease her into adult parts. Dorothy Vernon had been a fictitious heroine of the Elizabethan period who was not above sharing a bawdy joke with Queen Elizabeth and giving Mary, Queen of Scots, a helping hand when she was trying to get out of England.

Pickford looked forward to Lubitsch's arrival in Hollywood and was dismayed when Edward Knoblock, her writer, told her that Lubitsch was not going to make *Dorothy Vernon of Haddon Hall*. Lubitsch, instead, wanted her to play Marguerite in his version of *Faust*, and she went so far as to make a test with Conrad Nagel playing Marguerite's brother Valentin. When Pickford found out that Marguerite goes mad in her prison cell and kills her baby, she said firmly: "Mary is not going to do that."

Lubitsch and Pickford finally compromised on *Rosita*, which had been adapted from a popular play of the last century, *Don César de Bazan*, which had once served as a script that was never made, but was intended to star Rudolph Valentino as Don César. The role of Don César, called Don Diego for the film, was still a very romantic one, but Pickford's part as Rosita, the fair little street singer of Seville, who makes up funny, salacious songs about the King of Spain, which are being sung everywhere, was mischievous and delightful.

Production had no sooner been started on *Rosita* than word came that the new Pola Negri story, which Paramount was filming, was also a rewrite of *Don César de Bazan*. Pickford applied herself to the shooting at hand and determined that her version would at least be released first. It was released in September, 1923, and the next month the Negri version, *The Spanish Dancer*, opened. It was a draw, the critics decided. Both versions were good and were not so much alike, after all, for the Pickford one deviated clearly from the novel and took on a decided likeness to the plot of the opera *Tosca*, with variations.

Pickford hated *Rosita*. She was glad that the books showed some modest profit, but she very quickly withdrew it from circulation, concentrating her efforts on making *Dorothy Vernon of Haddon Hall* a success. She was directed in that film by her old friend Marshall Neilan. Today, *Rosita* is remembered fondly, and most fans who can remember it, classify it as one of Pickford's best. She was always quick to explain that she disliked Lubitsch, not *Rosita*. It was a beautiful production to look at, and Pickford and Holbrook Blinn, who played the King, won great acclaim. Fans also like her handsome leading man, George Walsh (Raoul's younger brother), and Irene Rich as the lovely but unloved Queen. Pickford has gone on record as saying that she hoped the film was disintegrating in some vault. She forbade showings of it, but there is a print of it in mint condition in the Soviet Union, and several film museums have, but do not like admitting that they have, prints of it. She is better in it than in any of the talking films she made, for example, except perhaps *Secrets* (1929). It should be shown because modern audiences would love it.

The first entrance of Rosita (Mary Pickford) in the story is well hearlded. The fun-loving citizens of Seville see her approaching off camera, and their faces and shouts of "bravo" indicate how fond they are of her. "I know a King," she sings, accompanied by her guitar, and goes on to sing that he is a royal rake who rakes in all that his subjects make. King Carlos (Holbrook Blinn) is introduced by a subtitle indicating that his affairs are heavy on his hands, while he plays a game of hand-smacking with three courtesans that is great fun.

Carlos hears about Rosita and summons her to the palace to sing for him. She dazzles him, and he gives her fine jewels, even though she is deeply in love with a penniless nobleman, Don Diego (George Walsh), who tries to defend her physically when the King's guards arrest her for lampooning the King. Don Diego is imprisoned for defending her, and he is sentenced to be shot. Rosita, however, is summoned to the King's chambers and given beautiful silk gowns as well as a luxurious villa in the countryside.

King Carlos makes a deal with her; he arranges a marriage between her and Don Diego in which they will each be blindfolded before the order is given to kill him. Thus, she will become a countess before she becomes a widow. Thanks to orders from the Queen (Irene Rich), however, blank cartridges are put in the executioner's weapons. Don Diego, pretending to be dead, is brought to Rosita's villa. He jumps to his feet and stays her hand holding a dagger as she is about to stab the King. Carlos, seeing that the two are really in love, pardons Don Diego, and they are freed to live as one.

When the annual box-office results were in, both versions of the story were among the big moneymakers of the year, particularly interesting because *The Spanish Dancer* was the first of Negri's American films to be well liked, and Pickford fans loved her with her hair tied up in *Rosita* and a saucy look in her eyes as she sang slightly naughty verses.

An interesting fact about the film concerns a contest held at the time by Pickford's unit for a theme song. Irving Berlin won, but for a song that remains unknown. Victor Schertzinger had submitted one, too, called "Rosita"; he then simply changed the title "Rosita" to "Marcheta" and the song in no time at all became a standard.

DeWitt Bodeen

SADIE THOMPSON

Released: 1928
Production: Gloria Swanson Productions; released by United Artists
Direction: Raoul Walsh
Screenplay: Raoul Walsh; based on the short story "Rain" by W. Somerset Maugham and the play *Sadie Thompson* by John Colton and Clemence Randolph
Cinematography: George Barnes, Robert Kurrle, and Oliver T. Marsh
Editing: C. Gardner Sullivan
Art direction: William Cameron Menzies
Length: 9 reels/8,600 feet

Principal characters:
Sadie Thompson	Gloria Swanson
Alfred Atkinson	Lionel Barrymore
Mrs. Atkinson	Blanche Frederici
Dr. McPhail	Charles Lane
Mrs. McPhail	Florence Midgley
Joe Horn	James Marcus
Ameena	Sophia Artega
Sergeant Tim O'Hara	Raoul Walsh
Quartermaster Bates	Will Stanton

W. Somerset Maugham's short story "Rain" was first published in 1921, in the collection *The Trembling of a Leaf.* Its subsequent success inspired Maugham and his publishing house to reissue it in 1928 in a collection entitled *Sadie Thompson, and Other Stories of the South Seas.* The stage version of the story was adapted by John Colton and Clemence Randolph and it became a personal triumph for Jeanne Eagels in 1922. Later stage versions starred Tallulah Bankhead (1935) and June Havoc (1945), the latter an unsuccessful musical adaptation (which was to have starred Ethel Merman) produced by the great film director Rouben Mamoulian.

As a potential screen property, it numbered among those more than 150 plays and novels which were condemned by the Will H. Hays-headed Motion Picture Producers and Distributors Association of America which, in a self-imposed effort to stave off national censorship, devised "The Formula," a decency code of motion-picture production ethics, and listed certain plays and novels as objectionable for presentation on the motion-picture screen.

In 1926, M-G-M's Irving G. Thalberg had confronted the Association with the argument that Nathaniel Hawthorne's *The Scarlet Letter*—one of those "objectionable" works—was of an entirely moral purpose even though it dealt with adultery. He was thereby able to gain permission to make the film starring Lillian Gish in what is one of her truly great performances.

That same year, Gloria Swanson's contract with Paramount expired, and despite the enticement of eighteen thousand dollars as a weekly salary offer, Swanson did not renew with Paramount but instead chose to form her own Gloria Swanson Productions, Inc., for release through United Artists. Her first independent production had been *The Love of Sunya* (1927), after which she set out to convince the Association to grant her permission to make *Rain* with Raoul Walsh directing.

Fully aware that the story was not acceptable as it stood, she nevertheless was confident that she had a chance of skirting the censors' objections if they made two vital changes. First, the "Reverend" Davidson would have to be changed to simply "Mr." Davidson and described as being an evangelist of no particular denominational association. (His name was eventually changed to Mr. Atkinson in the released version). Second, was the matter of the heroine's language which would entail whitewashing the titles.

With the help of United Artists' Joseph Schenck she was able to purchase the rights to both the play and the short story for sixty thousand dollars (the original asking price had been $100,000), and after mountainous letters and telegrams among all of the concerned parties, it was announced that the project would be filmed.

The first item to which the fashion trend-setting Swanson addressed herself was to update Sadie's wardrobe to 1928, casting aside the high-button shoes which had been the mode during World War I, replacing them with black patent ankle strap pumps with white bows. Her costume, to create a Sadie of cheap finery and gaudy jewels, consisted of a black and white vertically striped two-piece dress. The skirt was wraparound to show off her legs and the camisole underneath was white with a black "ST" embroidered over the left breast pocket. She wore two strands of crystal beads; a large black and white hat which framed her face and which sported a huge bird of paradise on the brim. She carried a drawstring fishnet handbag and a lace parasol and topped it all off with an Iceland fox scarf. This outfit, plus garish makeup and a ubiquitous cigarette, transformed Gloria Swanson into Sadie Thompson.

The film opens with an odd assortment of passengers disembarking from a tramp ship at Pago Pago, the only port in American Samoa. The ship is forced to dock there because of a smallpox quarantine, but its ultimate destination is Apia, the chief port of the West Somoans on the volcanic island of Upolu. The first title reads: "It was too hot in Pago Pago to need bedclothes but the rain came down in sheets," which must have made Maugham turn pale.

The passengers include the sanctimonious moralist Alfred Atkinson (Lionel Barrymore), his wife (Blanche Frederici), Dr. and Mrs. McPhail (Charles Lane and Florence Midgley), and Sadie Thompson (Gloria Swanson), the prostitute who is fleeing from a police indictment and penitentiary sentence for what she maintains is a trumped-up charge.

As Sadie steps off the gangplank she is greeted by several Marines and quips: "Where can I park my body?" Quartermaster Bates (Will Stanton) introduces her to Sergeant Tim O'Hara (Raoul Walsh), and they escort her to the rooming establishment run by trader Joe Horn (James Marcus) and his native wife Ameena (Sophia Artega).

Sadie settles in the cheap room and becomes the belle of the island. She plays her phonograph too loud, and laughs, drinks, and dances with the Marines to the distraction of the other staid guests. Sadie acknowledges their disdain of her and her behavior by saying: "I guess they think I'm Mr. Halitosis."

The self-righteous and subliminally lecherous Atkinson accuses Sadie of being from the vice district of Honolulu and implores Horn to evict her. When Horn refuses to throw her out in the rain, Atkinson goes to visit the governor of the island. When he returns, he pleads with her to reform and hints that he can prevent her from continuing on to Apia. Tim O'Hara ignores the rumors about Sadie's past and proposes to her saying he will take her with him to Sydney when the next boat comes through. His proposal is spoiled by the arrival of a letter from the governor saying she must leave the island on the next available boat. Sadie begs Atkinson to let her stay and continue with them on to Apia and confesses to him her reason for running away from the San Francisco police. He says she must go serve her sentence and repent, and he jealously has O'Hara confined to the guard house on false pretenses.

He then convinces Sadie to reform and leads her in hours of prayer, not leaving her room until three in the morning. His lust for her and his repressed passion are more than he can contain, and he rapes her and ultimately shoots himself. Sadie feels she is unfit to marry O'Hara, but in the end she and O'Hara head off to Australia and a new life.

Swanson gave her best performance to date in this film and received an Academy Award nomination in that first year of the Oscars, but she lost out to Janet Gaynor. Her performance revealed a talent of a depth that she heretofore had not displayed on screen and once again critics were remarking on her ability to change her image and on her versatility.

Lionel Barrymore was splendid as the overzealous and sadistic Atkinson and Raoul Walsh made a masculine and forthright O'Hara. As director, Walsh was commended for being properly restrained here in comparison to his lusty, gutsy, and animalistic *The Thief of Bagdad* (1924), *What Price Glory?* (1926), *Klondike Annie* (1926), and *The Loves of Carmen* (1927), and, later in his career, such works as *High Sierra* (1941), and *White Heat* (1949).

The film also received an Academy Award nomination for George Barnes's cinematography (although his conflicting schedule with another project required part of the film to be finished by first Robert Kurrle, and then Oliver T. Marsh), and his camerawork pictorially captured the heat, wetness, and tropical languor of this richly colored story which was shot on Catalina Island.

The only negative criticism was for the titles, especially that "halitosis" line, which one critic called vandalism on such a good film. Another title has Swanson saying "And be hanged," when on screen one can read her lips saying "Hang me and be damned," but such were the inanities imposed by censorship.

One revealing scene cut from the script entirely, but which had been one of the highlights of the stage version was where Mrs. Atkinson (Hamilton in the play) confesses her all-consuming and earthly love for her husband but says that she has never been allowed to express that love in any manner. She is but a "spiritual companion" to her husband. Blanche Frederici played that role on both stage and screen, and she was singled out in the theater reviews for making this a memorable scene.

That kind of character analysis is what some Maugham purists missed in this screen version of "Rain," for in Maugham's story, Sadie is not the central attraction. It was the Reverend Atkinson (Hamilton) and his moral downfall which Maugham emphasized. Also, *The New York Times* remarked that after seeing the beautiful Eagels and Swanson portray Sadie, the public would now be disappointed if Maugham's *real* Sadie were presented—Sadie, the weary sophisticate who harbored a hatred of all men, who had fat legs encased in white cotton stockings, and who was neither young nor old.

There have been two subsequent screen versions of "Rain." The second, *Sadie Thompson* (1932), directed by Lewis Milestone and starring Joan Crawford, incorporated more of the angst of Maugham's characters, but arriving only four years after the original, it took years for it to be appreciated. The second version, entitled *Miss Sadie Thompson* (1953), was directed by Curtis Bernhardt and starred Rita Hayworth. It was lukewarm Maugham tailored to the lovely Hayworth's modest talents and hers was a more likable Sadie who dances erotically as only Rita could dance, but it was not Maugham. There was a snippet of *Sadie Thompson* in the 1957 film biography *Jeanne Eagels*, wherein Kim Novak portrayed Maugham's harlot, but its dramatic value is best left undiscussed.

Swanson's version remains the best of the Sadies on film and for reasons best described by herself: "I had better luck with *Sadie* than any other movie star because I had the advantage of making a good silent of it. If you have to censor Sadie's language, how can you really portray her?"

Ronald Bowers

SAFETY LAST

Released: 1923
Production: Hal Roach Studios; released by Pathé
Direction: Fred Newmeyer and Sam Taylor
Screenplay: Hal Roach, Sam Taylor, and Tim Whelan
Cinematography: Walter Lundin
Length: 7 reels/6,300 feet

> *Principal characters:*
> The Boy (Harold Lloyd) .... Harold Lloyd
> The Girl (Mildred) .... Mildred Davis
> The Pal (Limpy Bill) .... Bill Strother
> The Law .... Noah Young
> The Floorwalker (Mr. Stubbs) .... Westcott B. Clarke

The figure of a bespectacled young man in a straw hat, suspended perilously above city streets, clutching desperately to the hands of a huge clock, is one of the major cultural icons of twentieth century American culture. To the millions who have seen it, including many who could not identify the man, Harold Lloyd by name, it is an unforgettable image that has come to epitomize silent-film comedy. Even discounting the universality of this frozen moment, however, it is likely that *Safety Last* (1923) would still be Lloyd's best-known film. It represents perhaps the purest expression of his screen character, contains one of the most spectacularly hair-raising and hilarious sequences in all of film history, and marks a significant milestone in the development of the feature-length comedy film.

The latter point is often neglected. In focusing on the comic masterpieces of the 1920's—such as Charles Chaplin's *The Gold Rush* (1925) and Buster Keaton's *The General* (1926)—it is easy to forget that the development of the feature-film comedy was nearly as tentative as the growth of the feature film itself. Physical comedy, or slapstick, had entered the cinema and thrived in one-reel films. Its aesthetic revolved not around narrative principles but around the visual unit of the "gag," or individual joke; while short comedies could easily get by as an aggregation of gags tied together by a location, a situation, or a rudimentary plot, such a haphazard structure could not be effectively extended to feature length.

Years after *The Birth of a Nation* (1915), the great masters of screen comedy—Chaplin, Keaton, Roscoe "Fatty" Arbuckle, and Lloyd among them—were still refining their art in one- and two-reelers. Feature-length comedies were being made, but they were almost exclusively of the "genteel," or socially oriented, variety. Mack Sennett's six-reel *Tillie's Punctured Romance* (1914) was an aberration, and the early films of Douglas Fairbanks merely injected the genteel formula with a dose of athleticism. The first truly important comedy feature did not appear until 1921, when Chaplin produced *The Kid* in six reels. Although it was one of his most important films, *The Kid* was not the breakthrough it might have been, for Chaplin hedged his bets by structuring it as a melodrama rather than a full-fledged comedy. Even Chaplin must have recognized its tentative nature, for he retreated into the familiar realm of the short film until *The Gold Rush* in 1925. Keaton, apart from *The Saphead* (1920), an adapted play in which he had no creative hand, made two-reelers exclusively until mid-1923, and his "first" feature, *Three Ages* (1923), composed of three two-reel variations on a theme, proved equally tentative. The feature-film career of Arbuckle (which in any case involved a considerable compromise of his knockabout style) was cut short tragically in 1921 by the Virginia Rappe scandal. Lloyd, therefore, working his way up methodically from the short-subject field, found himself rather unexpectedly in the forefront of feature comedy production.

Lloyd had entered motion pictures in 1913 as an extra; he began his rise to stardom in 1915, when he began appearing in short comedies as a character named "Lonesome Luke," conceived as a sort of reverse variation on Chaplin's tramp. In the sixty or so one- and two-reel films he made featuring this character from 1915 through 1917, Lloyd learned the basics of film comedy, but he also became aware of his character's limitations. Late in 1917, he took the first step toward a more flexible screen image when he donned a pair of lensless horn-rimmed glasses; for a brief period, he alternated between Lonesome Luke films and those with this new costume, but by the beginning of 1918, he had completely abandoned the Luke character. Over the next few years, he gradually filled in the image he had adopted, crystallizing the traits of his new screen *persona*, which he referred to as the "glasses character." Its development was largely complete by the time Lloyd took his first tentative steps toward longer films.

Lloyd's bridging of the gap between shorts and features was gradual, befitting his style of carefully thought-out comedy construction. By late 1919, he had advanced from one- to two-reelers, a format to which he adhered throughout the following year. In 1921, he made four three-reel films (one of which was cut to two reels for release after unsuccessful preview reactions) and one film in four reels; the latter, *A Sailor-Made Man*, is usually regarded as his first feature film, although four reels was obviously an interim length. *Grandma's Boy* and *Doctor Jack*, his 1922 releases, each ran five reels and exhibited an increasing narrative sophistication. *Safety Last*, his next film, was seven reels long—one reel more than *The Kid* and considerably more progressive in terms of adapting the sight-gag tradition to the longer narrative format. The concurrent evolution of Lloyd's screen character, the earnest young man in the horn-rimmed glasses, had given him a firm foundation on which to build more complicated stories. The qualities of Lloyd's character made him easily adaptable to narratives involving more than a simple string of interconnected gags.

The commonly held notion of Lloyd's character as a Horatio Alger-type "All-American boy," eternally striving to "make good," while fundamentally true, has tended to obscure its adaptability to the wide variety of situations necessary for an extended career of feature films. Lloyd recognized this adaptability as one of the character's main strengths and made full use of it. "Sometimes he was a brash character," Lloyd once said,

> sort of a go-getter like we have in *Safety Last*; another time . . . he was a bashful, shy type of character. Sometimes he was rich, sometimes he was poor, sometimes he was a sophisticate, sometimes he was a dreamer, and each quality would motivate a lot of gags we'd do.

Lloyd's "glasses character," in fact, was not so much a character as an attitude, embodied in a particular comic style. Like that of Harry Langdon's "baby adult," the essence of Lloyd's *persona*—ambition, optimism, and ingenuity—shone through the veneer of whatever role he played, and his aggressive approach to life and its problems varied little, whatever his ostensible character traits. This spiritual, rather than actual, one-dimensionality of Lloyd's character has led some critics to assert that Lloyd himself was not "funny," but that he relied largely on the success of his material. Lloyd was certainly aware of the importance of strong gag material, but to claim, as some have, that this material would have been just as effective in the hands of another comedian is absurd. Such an attitude is not only unfair to Lloyd's abilities as a comic performer but also fails to acknowledge his greatest achievement— the fusion of the slapstick and genteel comedy traditions, through the integration of gag comedy with a middle-class American ethos. Lloyd was quintessentially a man of his time, a brash and optimistic figure for a brash and optimistic age. Audiences strongly identified with his image, which was lent further credibility by the fact that Lloyd's personal life closely paralleled the success stories that he acted out on the screen. It was no accident that his character in virtually all of his silent features is named "Harold."

In *Safety Last*, his name (shown on his payroll slip) is actually "Harold Lloyd," although the credits identify him as "The Boy." The film opens as he is bidding farewell to his sweetheart, the Girl (Mildred Davis, Lloyd's wife in real life), as he departs his hometown of Great Bend, bound for the big city to seek his fortune. Mildred has promised to come to the city to marry Harold just as soon as he makes good, a goal about which she is adamant: "it would just break my heart if you failed," she tells him.

In the city, Harold rooms with his pal Limpy Bill (Bill Strother) and works as a clerk in a department store. He makes only fifteen dollars a week, but scrimps and saves to be able to send Mildred gifts to support his assertions of his "wonderful success." In reality, he is constantly on the verge of losing his job, having incurred the antagonism of the pompous and self-centered floorwalker (Westcott B. Clarke). Departing work one day, Harold bumps into an old buddy from Great Bend who is now a city policeman; showing off for Bill, Harold engineers a prank on the cop, but a last-minute switch results in his pal incurring the enmity of a different cop (Noah Young). Taking flight, Bill eludes the cop by climbing the side of a building—thus revealing his abilities as a "human fly."

Meanwhile, Harold's protestations of success have proven so persuasive that Mildred decides to surprise him with a visit. When she shows up unexpectedly at the store, Harold is obliged to orchestrate an elaborate series of deceptions to keep her from discovering the truth about his position. He winds up convincing her that he is the store's general manager, and they make plans to be married the following day. Faced with the immediate necessity of achieving his until-now illusory success, Harold overhears the general manager make an offer of one thousand dollars to anyone who can come up with an idea to draw attention to the store. Harold proposes that a human fly scale the building and offers Bill half of the prize money to make the climb. The morning newspapers herald the climber as a "Mystery Man," arousing the suspicions of the policeman who had pursued Bill the day before. At the appointed time, the cop is standing watch and Bill is unable to show his face. He and Harold concoct a scheme whereby Harold will climb the first floor of the building, then duck inside and change clothing and places with Bill; the cop spots Bill, however, rendering the entire plan contingent on Bill shaking off the cop. He leads him a merry chase through the building, but is unable to lose him, and Harold is forced to make the climb himself. During his ascent to the top, he encounters an incredible variety of obstacles and difficulties, as Bill keeps popping out of windows, urging him to climb "just one more floor." Bill never does shake the cop, but Harold makes it on his own to the very top of the building, where he finds Mildred waiting for him.

Even in 1923, much of the basic fabric of *Safety Last* was not new to Lloyd. He attributed the film's conception to his uneasiness while witnessing a building ascent by Bill Strother, a real-life human fly whom he subsequently hired to play his pal; this may be true, but Lloyd was already well-known as a purveyor of what he called "thrill" comedy. Prior to *Safety Last*, he had made three films which used perilous height for comic effect—*Look Out Below* (1919), *High and Dizzy* (1920), and *Never Weaken* (1921), in the respective lengths of one, two, and three reels. What was innovative about *Safety Last* was his integration of this type of comedy into a feature-length narrative. The notoriety of the building-climbing sequence in *Safety Last* has fostered the assumption that Lloyd's comedy revolved largely around similar dangerous predicaments (which again contributes to the critical emphasis on the importance of his gag material). Lloyd himself, however, tended to divide his comedies into "character" films and "gag" films, with thrill comedy being a sort of subcategory of the latter. In fact, the division is not so clear-cut, being more a matter of emphasis than of actual content. It is no injustice, however, that Lloyd is best known for his thrill comedy, for he did it better than anyone else, and its basic underlying notion of life as a series of crises was central to most of his films.

Because of the extensive attention devoted to the climb in many books, both on Lloyd and on film comedy in general, this article will eschew a detailed dissection of the sequence. There are a few long-standing myths about the climb, however, that should be dispelled. The first, and most important, is the notion that Lloyd "actually" climbed a "real" building, with only an inadequate platform several floors below him. This is an elaborate fiction maintained largely by Lloyd himself until his death in 1971. In fact, the portions of the climb performed in medium long shot by Lloyd himself were done on false building sections constructed on the rooftops of other buildings, with camera angles carefully chosen to make it appear that he is dangling far above street level; extreme long shots of a figure undeniably scaling a real building were done by a double. Furthermore, if one watches the film closely, it can be seen that Lloyd passes in front of three distinctly different backgrounds on his way up the building—indicating that the various facades were built on the tops of three different buildings (or at least facing in three different directions). The most remarkable indication of the tenacity of this legend is perhaps the fact that, cutting across the lower right-hand corner of the ubiquitous still of Lloyd hanging from the clock are the letters of a see-through sign, seen from behind. The presence of this sign in this position is completely inconsistent with the assertion that Lloyd was hanging unprotected above city streets—yet it has never been remarked upon, even though the still frequently appears alongside textual material describing the "authenticity" of the climb.

One other point to refute about the climb, relatively minor but nevertheless irritating in its persistence, is the absolutely consistent description of its setting as being twelve stories tall, as stated in one of the film's titles. A simple count during Harold's ascent reveals only nine stories, consistent with long shots of the building. This may seem insignificant, since the "building" is in a sense illusory, but Lloyd was careful to maintain continuity from each shot to the next. Both the alleged actuality of the climb and the mistaken height of the building are clear examples of the tenacious prevalence of myth over fact in the course of film history, even when the evidence clearly contradicts the myth. It should also be noted, however, that neither of these considerations is in the least bit relevant to the effectiveness of the sequence. The illusion is so well maintained (largely because of the intelligent decision always to keep the busy street below in view) that the necessity for suspension of disbelief, even when one is aware of the techniques involved, is minimal.

The critical emphasis on this sequence is easily understandable and is, in a sense, encouraged by the film's clear division into two sections, which might be designated "the climb" and "the events leading up to the climb." This narrative dichotomy has led many critics to dismiss the film's first section— to praise the execution of the climb itself while failing to appreciate it in the context of the entire film. The film's first five reels are not merely exposition, but provide an indispensable narrative and thematic setup for the climb; to divorce the two parts is to divest the latter sequence of its metaphorical function. Most simply put, the climb is a comic expression of Harold's desire for success, couched in terms of a task that is as physically perilous as his prior sham existence was socially perilous. The danger of failing which is the central crisis of the film's first section is transmuted into the danger of falling. Contemplations of mortality are not Lloyd's stock in trade, however—his fear is not of death, but of falling back into the common crowd above which he has temporarily risen. This crowd is presented throughout the film as a mob, alternately uncomprehending (the spectators to his climb, who cheer his "antics" without acknowledging his peril) and malevolent (the female customers who threaten to tear him limb from limb in their lust for bargains).

Robbed of its resonances with the film's first section, the climb would be simply a mechanical exercise in laughmaking—a criticism often leveled unjustly at Lloyd's films. Yet, for all its darker undertones, *Safety Last* proceeds unencumbered with thematic baggage. Lloyd's style is too straightforward to accommodate any "message" that is not inherent in the material itself. The intent as he ascends the building is not that the audience contemplate the ethical infrastructure of American capitalism but rather be thrilled and amused. As his "social climbing" becomes manifest, the film's thematic concerns are pushed even further into the realm of abstraction. Viewers understand intuitively, for example, that the top of the building represents success for Harold, but as he dangles from the hands of the clock, the tense audience no more thinks of the one-thousand-dollar prize money, or of the girl, than he does. The focus, as it is throughout the film, is on the particular crisis at hand and on Harold's manner of dealing with it.

Considered apart from this famous sequence, *Safety Last* is quite simply a very good comedy. It is fast paced, well constructed, packed with gags, and shows Lloyd's "go-getter" *persona* to full effect. Most of the individual gags are clever, and Lloyd's sense of pacing keeps the plot moving along with few dead spots. The best extended sequence is the one which begins when Harold is inadvertently locked in a linen supply delivery truck and deposited miles away from the store, with only a few minutes remaining before he is late for work. He first tries and fails to board an impossibly crowded streetcar then finds another one that is completely empty; after taking a seat, however, he discovers that it's heading in the wrong direction. Returning to the overloaded one, he manages to find a place clinging to another man's back—but when the streetcar departs, the man is revealed to be simply standing there, Harold on his back. Harold runs after the streetcar and jumps on; it is not going fast enough for him, however, and as he attempts to climb aboard an automobile traveling alongside, the two vehicles' paths diverge and Harold is dumped in the middle of the street. The driver stops his car and walks back to help Harold up; they return to the car, and Harold is handed a ticket, for the man has parked in front of a fire hydrant; Harold hands the driver the ticket and gets out of the car. He hitches another ride, but the car swings around to head in the wrong direction. Finally, he spots an ambulance across the street, with the attendants having no luck convincing an argumentative patient to accompany them; seizing the opportunity, Harold lies down next to their stretcher and feigns unconsciousness. The astonished attendants load him into the ambulance and drive pell-mell through the crowded streets; at the proper corner, Harold "regains consciousness" and asks to be let out.

As he approaches the employees' entrance, however, he sees a co-worker admonished for clocking in late and threatened with dismissal. He manages to sneak into the store by disguising himself as a dress dummy; when the man carrying him pauses in front of the time clock, Harold turns it back to eight o'clock and punches in, unseen by the supervisor. Once inside the store, however, he still must get to his post without alerting the floorwalker. He duck-walks along, head between his knees, hidden behind a box being pulled along the floor; but when the man pulling it makes an unexpected turn, Harold is left waddling all alone in the middle of the aisle. The floorwalker spots him, but as he is trying to get a look at his face, Harold maneuvers him in front of an elevator, then suddenly springs up and down; the floorwalker, startled, staggers back into the elevator just as its doors close, and Harold is saved. This lengthy sequence, like much of the film, including the building ascent, is structured as a series of crises, each of which is overcome by Harold through sheer inventiveness and, it seems, force of will. He *must* get to work on time to avoid losing his job, and he does. Lloyd's pacing is relentless, however; no sooner has he gone through the above ordeal than he must face an overly particular lady customer—who keeps him in the store until two hours past closing time on Saturday afternoon.

As the above sequence illustrates, the whole of *Safety Last* is, in a sense, thrill comedy. Harold must cope with a constant stream of threats to his facade of success, the collapse of which would thwart his life's desire to make good and marry his girl. His life in the workplace is a harried effort simply to keep from losing ground; when Mildred appears, the level of crisis is heightened, as he must now engage in an even more complex subterfuge in order to maintain the fiction he has created. In this context, the final climb not only concentrates the issue and ups the stakes, but it also offers for the first time a ray of hope. In the earlier sections, Harold makes no real progress, nor is any in sight—he is tenuously clinging to a menial job, struggling to maintain the illusion of success. Once the climb has begun, however, and illusion gives way to hard reality, there is a sense of achievement, however incidental. Each obstacle overcome, each additional ledge attained, is another step upward—although the emphasis is primarily on simple survival.

Safety Last, while certainly demonstrating Lloyd's skills as a comedy maker, also provides ammunition for critics of the values embodied in his character. The film provides a particularly vivid expression of the nightmare of middle-class ambitions, expressed via the contrast between the pretensions Harold adopts and the air of desperation that characterizes his daily life. His ingenuity and wholesomeness do not completely mask the fact that he is constantly taking advantage of others (friends included), lying and bluffing in his quest to avoid failure. The methods he employs are standard business practice; it is entirely appropriate that his springboard to success is his conception of a brilliant advertising stunt. Significantly, Harold does not regard his actions as sinful because of his fervent belief that he *will* be successful. He acts as he does not out of mean-spiritedness but out of necessity; he sees the deception as only temporary and morally justified as a means of keeping his goal—the girl—from being lost. As he states to Bill at one point, "She's just got to believe I'm a success—until I am." The climb thus serves as both a come-uppance for his manipulation of others and a spiritual trial of sorts, a challenge to rely on himself to reach the top—to "put up or shut up." There is also a racist undercurrent to Lloyd's philosophy, manifested in *Safety Last* by unfortunate caricatures of both Jews and blacks. In criticizing Lloyd's values, however, it is well to remember that in the 1920's, they were shared by the vast majority of his audience; in any case, as critic and film historian Andrew Sarris wrote of Lloyd, it is possible to question his values without questioning his worth.

Lloyd's filmmaking has often been called "mechanical," but there is a danger in applying this term pejoratively. Lloyd's comedy was mechanical, in the sense of well constructed and efficient. As James Agee wrote: "If great comedy must involve something beyond plain laughter, then Lloyd was not a great comedian. If plain laughter is any criterion . . . few people have equaled him, and nobody has ever beaten him." Lloyd wanted to make people laugh, and he was constantly striving for the techniques to accomplish this. More, perhaps, than any other comedian before or since, Lloyd recognized the audience as a valuable part of his filmmaking equipment, and during his silent period, he knew his audience—and how to manipulate it—thoroughly. Lloyd is often credited as one of the earliest practitioners of the "sneak preview"—the testing of an unfinished film before an audience and its subsequent retailoring to their responses—and his films show the care with which he went about his business. *Safety Last* is an excellent example of Lloyd's methods of comedy construction, and seen today under proper conditions, with a large audience, it fully retains its power to thrill and amuse—just as it did in 1923.

Howard H. Prouty

SALLY OF THE SAWDUST

Released: 1925
Production: D. W. Griffith for Paramount; released by United Artists
Direction: D. W. Griffith
Screenplay: Forrest Halsey; based on the play *Poppy* by Dorothy Donnelly
Cinematography: Harry Fischbeck and Hal Sintzenich
Length: 10 reels/9,500 feet

Principal characters:
Sally	Carol Dempster
Professor Eustace McGargle	W. C. Fields
Peyton Lennox	Alfred Lunt
Judge Henry L. Foster	Erville Alderson
Mrs. Foster	Effie Shannon
Lennox, Sr.	Charles Hammond
Detective	Roy Applegate
Miss Vinton	Florence Fair
Society Woman	Marie Shotwell
Leon, the Acrobat	Glenn Anders

The cinema of D. W. Griffith is conservative, moralistic, and sentimental, with heroines who are pure and self-sacrificing. The screen *persona* of W. C. Fields is, on the other hand, quite eccentric—a selfish, cowardly, alcoholic funnyman about as gallant as Attila the Hun. Once, when Fields was on the threshold of his film career and Griffith was past his glory, they collaborated on a feature, *Sally of the Sawdust*, a curious union between two very different cinema legends.

Fields stars in *Sally of the Sawdust* as Professor Eustace McGargle, a slick, sly, egotistical sideshow fakir. McGargle believes that work is for losers, jerks, and suckers. He will happily cheat one and all, and he will "never give a sucker an even break." The film opens, however, with a sequence presenting a theme that runs through Griffith's filmography—the separation of parents from child, the denial of familial love. Despite the protests of his sweet wife (Effie Shannon), mean old Judge Henry L. Foster (Erville Alderson) kicks his daughter out of his home because she has married a circus performer, a man beneath their station. The young couple are conveniently killed by some vague affliction, and their daughter, Sally (Carol Dempster), is left in the care of McGargle.

The professor becomes Sally's surrogate father. He loves her and cares for her, yet still teaches the child to dance and perform acrobatics to warm up the crowds for his own act—which, of course, includes juggling. McGargle is adept at hustling his audiences in shell games and picking their pockets, but at the same time, he realizes that perhaps a carnival is not the best environment for Sally—particularly after she is almost raped by an acrobat (Glenn Anders).

McGargle decides to take Sally to Connecticut, to the hometown of her grandparents, the Fosters, where he has been offered a carnival job. They have no money and spend their last quarter on a hot dog for Sally and a cigar for McGargle, and they travel to the town on the steps of a railroad car. When they arrive, they are sopping wet, having been washed off the train by a water-tank spout. They spend an afternoon in a bake shop, where the proprietor allows them to shelter in return for minding the premises while he is away.

McGargle performs at a charity bazaar. He is applauded for his work, yet it is clear that the town scions—including the Fosters, who have become wealthy in a real estate boom—look down on circus performers. Sally meets and falls in love with Peyton Lennox (stage star Alfred Lunt, in a very rare screen appearance), son of one of the town's leading families. Their love scenes, shot outdoors, are pastoral—pure Griffith.

Meanwhile, McGargle unsuccessfully attempts to introduce Sally to her grandparents. They visit the Foster mansion, where McGargle's pants are accidentally sprinkled by the gardener, and he inadvertently thinks a friendly puppy is responsible. Sally is about to hurl a stone at the residence when McGargle admonishes her, forcing her to drop the weapon; then, he hands her a brick to throw. With Lennox's assistance, Sally is hired to dance at a party, and Mrs. Foster, still pining for her lost family, is touched by her. Lennox's father disapproves of his son's affection for Sally, however, and sends him out of town.

McGargle has again taken up the shell game. Although completely innocent, Sally is jailed while the professor makes his getaway. He then becomes the prisoner of bootleggers, who think he is a tax agent. He escapes in an old car and is chased in the direction of the town while Sally is on trial. Now, it is Sally's turn to escape. After leaping out of the courtroom window and climbing down a tree, she is pursued by the police and captured. McGargle's jalopy finally crashes, and he stumbles into the courtroom and reveals Sally's identity. The charges are dropped; Sally is taken in by her grandparents and reunited with Lennox. At the finale, McGargle, in the style of Charlie Chaplin, walks by himself down a country road, but is invited to stay with Sally. He becomes a successful real estate tycoon, with the profession depicted as merely another shell game.

There are several entertaining comedy bits in *Sally of the Sawdust*. In one, McGargle steals a wallet and places it in his pocket; an elephant then hustles the hustler, purloining it from the professor. In another, McGargle takes a quick snooze in a warm kiln in the bake shop, and Sally, unaware that he is inside, piles coals on the fire. After an uneasy nap, McGargle is unable to stand upright as he hops around until he is rescued. Sally stuffs some rolls down the front of her dress; McGargle is befuddled that she has "matured" so quickly. Although uncertainly directed, the final car chase, with McGargle completely out of control of the vehicle, is still funny and a fine example of simple screen mirth. Also, McGargle/Fields' juggling is a visual delight, particularly when he fakes dropping a ball and knocks it back up into the air with his elbow.

The key role in *Sally of the Sawdust* is not the title character—although Griffith was in love with Dempster and hoped to make her into another Lillian Gish or Mae Marsh, and perhaps wished that all eyes would focus and remain on her. Instead, Eustace McGargle, impersonated by Fields in flashy checkered pants and a fake mustache, dominates the film. Previously a vaudeville headliner, Fields appeared in every version of the Ziegfield Follies from 1915 to 1923, and at one point, earned more than one thousand dollars a week. He played McGargle on Broadway in 1923 in Dorothy Donnelly's hit musical comedy *Poppy*. The part was not written for him, yet it was as much his creation as Donnelly's by the time the show opened at the Apollo Theater.

Fields played McGargle for more than a year and then made the film. Despite his success on the stage, he was then unknown to film audiences and was lucky to have been signed for the part; previously, he had appeared in a few one-reel comedies and in a bit as a drunken British sergeant in *Janice Meredith* (1924), starring Marion Davies. *Poppy* and *Sally of the Sawdust* established for Fields the con man character that he played so wonderfully for the rest of his career. Although acknowledged as one of the great comedians of sound films, Fields made eight silent features after *Sally of the Sawdust*: *That Royle Girl* (1926), *It's the Old Army Game* (1926), *So's Your Old Man* (1926), *The Potters* (1927), *Running Wild* (1927), *Two Flaming Youths* (1927), *Tillie's Punctured Romance* (1928), and *Fools for Luck* (1928).

Griffith's films had been steadily losing money when he directed *Sally of the Sawdust*, a commercial property he hoped would resuscitate his career. He could no longer obtain bank credit, and he was unable to fulfill his contractual obligations to United Artists, the company he had founded in 1919 with Charles Chaplin, Mary Pickford, and Douglas Fairbanks—an agreement which allowed him creative independence. He signed a contract with Paramount as a staff director, accepting $250,000 from Adolph Zukor, the studio's top executive, against his own commitment to direct three films for Zukor. To clear the director of his legal obligations to United Artists, Zukor arranged for the distribution of *Sally of the Sawdust* with that studio. Griffith still refused to conform to public taste and make the kind of features that were then popular, notably snappy comedies featuring jazz babies and bootleg liquor. That simply was not Griffith's style—*Sally of the Sawdust* was his concession to the changing times.

The film was made at Paramount's Astoria, New York, studio, and the shooting was not without conflict. Fields constantly defied Griffith, performing in one part of a scene in one costume and changing into another for the rest. He also insisted on wearing the same clip-on mustache he used on stage, and could not be convinced that the artificiality would show on the screen. Fields and Griffith were to make one more film together, however; a year later, they and Dempster worked on *That Royle Girl*, a poor melodrama with Fields wasted as Carol Dempster's crooked father.

Sally of the Sawdust was fairly well received by the critics, a rarity for Griffith at this point in his career. It is, however, haphazardly directed. The editing is shabby, particularly during the final chase sequence. Time lapses are illogical, and the bootleggers mysteriously disappear at the end. Griffith regularly cuts away to develop the story during Fields' comedy and acrobatic routines, which diminishes their effect. It is quite clear that Fields and his shenanigans are the redeeming feature of the film.

The property was remade in 1936 by A. Edward Sutherland under its stage title, with Fields toplined as McGargle and Rochelle Hudson replacing Dempster. The film is not one of the comedian's more successful sound efforts: the stress is on the romantic subplot, with Fields present for perhaps twenty-five percent of the story. The original, despite its flaws, is far superior.

Sally of the Sawdust is far from Fields's best film, but it is his first major work on celluloid, and his character, Eustace McGargle, is the model from which the comedian developed his screen *persona*.

Rob Edelman

SECRETS OF A SOUL

Released: 1926
Production: Hans Neumann for Ufa
Direction: G. W. Pabst
Screenplay: Colin Ross and Hans Neumann, in collaboration with Dr. Hans Sachs and Karl Abraham
Cinematography: Guido Seeber, Kurt Oertel, and Robert Lach
Technical adviser: Dr. Nicholas Kaufmann
Art direction: Erno Metzner
Length: 8 reels/7,263 feet

> *Principal characters:*
> Martin Fellman .... Werner Krauss
> His wife .... Ruth Weyher
> Dr. Charles Orth ....Pawel Pawlor
> Erich, the cousin ....Jack Trevor
> The mother .... Ilka Gruning

In 1926, the work of Sigmund Freud in the field of psychoanalysis was still new and revolutionary, and in cinema, the surrealistic experiments of Fernand Leger, Jean Cocteau, Salvador Dali, and Luis Buñuel were still to come, beginning at the end of the decade. The two were first united on film by G. W. Pabst in *Secrets of a Soul* (originally released as *Geheimisse Einer Seele*). Based on an actual case history reported by Freud, the film combined the narrative of a troubled chemist who gains an understanding of his life and fears through psychoanalysis with symbolic sequences representing the patient's dreams.

The film begins with a long title, necessary for audiences totally unaware of Freud and unprepared for its content:

> In every man's life there are wishes and desires in the unconscious mind. In the dark hours of mental conflict these unknown forces struggle to assert themselves. Mysterious disorders result from these struggles, the explanation of which is the actual work of psycho-analysis. The doctrine of Dr. Sigmund Freud. . . .

After the initial title card, Dr. Charles Orth (Pawel Pawlor), a disciple of Freud, is first introduced. Then, the action switches to the home of Martin Fellman (Werner Krauss), the chemist who lives with his wife (Ruth Weyher) in Vienna. Fellman fears knives, razors, and other sharp objects. At first, while giving his wife a haircut, he accidentally cuts her upon hearing the sudden scream of a woman on the street. As the woman is taken away on a stretcher, a bystander remarks, "He did it with a razor."

Fellman is also impotent. At his laboratory, he is clearly not attracted to his pretty assistant and a young visitor. He is asked to explain the events which occurred outside his house; then he becomes anxious when learning that his dashing cousin Erich (Jack Trevor), an explorer, will soon be arriving.

That evening a storm commences as the chemist is about to retire. In the film's highlight, he dreams first of Erich as a child in a safari outfit. The cousin fires a gun in his direction, and he runs away, falling through space. Then, he exits from what appears to be a cave and walks through objects as he enters a temple. Trains are superimposed over one another. Fellman then appears in front of a bell tower, surrounded by a staircase. As he climbs the stairs, his wife, assistant, and others are seen laughing at him. He is in jail, behind bars, and is powerless to prevent a murder he observes. Erich blames him for the crime. An accusing finger and the shadow of a drummer symbolize his "trial," as well as a triangular composition of him, his wife, and his cousin. He is guilty. From his prison cell, he watches helplessly as his wife and cousin romance each other near a lake. His anger overcomes him as he begins to harass his wife. Finally, he is awakened by his wife, who has been sleeping innocently nearby. He cannot remember the nightmare.

In the morning, Fellman nervously shaves. He visits a barber shop and becomes agitated after seeing a newspaper report of the crime near his house. Later, he is unable to use a letter opener and drops a test tube in his laboratory when learning that Erich has finally arrived. A fertility doll and sabre, gifts from the explorer, make the chemist feel uneasy. All goes well that evening as he is reunited with his cousin, until he is called on to use a knife during a meal. He excuses himself and leaves.

Fellman and Orth then are seen at different tables in a café. The chemist cannot find his key when he arrives home, and the doctor, who has followed him, explains that he has left the key elsewhere on purpose, and that he has some reason for not wanting to enter his house. Soon after, Fellman becomes angry upon seeing the fertility doll and sublimates his desire to murder his wife with the sabre. His desire to kill becomes so strong that he feels he must leave his house. He visits his mother and admits to her his fears and feelings and tells her of his meeting with the doctor. She cuts his food for him, which he eats with a spoon.

Fellman's mother also suggests that he visit Orth, and Fellman complies. Finally, with Orth's help, the chemist is able to recall the events that led to his dream and its actual highlights. He then comprehends its symbolic meaning. Various parts of the dream are then "played back," with an analysis of the symbolism. Fellman is impotent, while his wife desires children; thus, he is jealous of his cousin. He visited a bell tower on his honeymoon, and this image is phallic. He once was rejected during the Christmas holidays when he was younger and has destructively held on to his feelings of anger and loneliness. He also acts out the murder he has wanted to commit to redeem himself, to feel a sense of power. Through psychoanalysis, Fellman is able to reconcile his feelings toward his cousin and have a child with his wife.

Throughout *Secrets of a Soul*, Pabst most effectively visualizes the unconscious by superimposing images. For example, Fellman's head dominates one shot as he sleeps; it is framed by what appears to be a staircase and surrounded by several complete or upper torsos of himself. A practically leafless tree covers the left half of another shot, with an upper torso protruding from its top: in the upper right, a figure dives into darkness, in the lower right is the miniature of a house. As Fellman falls through space, Pabst uses subjective camera movement. He also uses slow motion, optical distortion, split screen, and miniatures during the sequence—which took six complete weeks to shoot.

While Pabst was not the first filmmaker to attempt to cinematize dreams or utilize these effects, he was the only one to examine the psyche, the workings of the unconscious in relation to his images. The actors in *Secrets of a Soul*—particularly Pawel Pawlor, a Russian—give fine performances. In addition to Pabst, however, the real stars of the film are cinematographers Guido Seeber, Kurt Oertel, and Robert Lach, and set designer Erno Metzner.

Secrets of a Soul was the brainchild of its producer, Hans Neumann, who for a long while had wanted to make a film about Freud. Pabst had kept up an interest in psychoanalysis and Freud's dream theories in particular. Through Dr. Nicholas Kaufmann, the film's technical adviser, the director met Dr. Hans Sachs and Karl Abraham, assistants to Freud, who collaborated wtih Neumann and Colin Ross on the scenario.

The film received mixed reviews, with some critics finding it too abstract and passionless. It was still a box-office success, however, opening in the United States a year after its release in Germany. A later German import, also entitled *Secrets of a Soul*, played in New York in 1950, with the character of Martin Fellman changed to Johanna Stegen, and the specifics of her case altered. The film, however, was boring and confusing.

Rob Edelman

SENTIMENTAL TOMMY

Released: 1921
Production: Famous Players-Lasky; released by Paramount
Direction: John S. Robertson
Screenplay: Josephine Lovett; based on the novel of the same name by James M. Barrie
Cinematography: Roy F. Overbaugh
Length: 8 reels/7,575 feet

Principal characters:
Tommy Sandys .... Gareth Hughes
Grizel .... May McAvoy
Dr. McQueen .... George Fawcett
Elspeth Sandys .... Leila Frost
Dr. David Gemmell .... Kempton Greene
The Painted Lady .... Mabel Taliaferro
Lady Alice Pippinworth .... Virginia Valli

Sir James Matthew Barrie's plays and novels were the basis of seven particularly fine films during the 1920's. Cecil B. De Mille's box-office success *Male and Female* (*The Admirable Crichton*, 1919), was the first picturization and was followed immediately with two competing versions of *The Little Minister* (1921 and 1922) from Paramount and Vitagraph in succession. In 1921, Paramount carefully produced two more Barrie works, *What Every Woman Knows* and *Sentimental Tommy*. The year 1924 saw the production of Barrie's most famous play, *Peter Pan*, and then, in 1926, his most charming, *A Kiss for Cinderella*. By 1927, the film rights to *Quality Street* were so costly that only Marion Davies with William Randolph Hearst's financial backing could afford them, and it gave her one of her best roles.

Sentimental Tommy was first published as a novel in 1896, but was not dramatized by Barrie, as were the other six novels. *Sentimental Tommy* has been called autobiographical by more than one critic, so it was only natural that the author was concerned about who should portray Tommy in the film. When Paramount announced, in 1921, that a young Welsh actor named Gareth Hughes would play the lead, the author was quite happy, for Gareth had won critical acclaim in Barrie's wartime play, *The New Word*, in 1917. He played a soldier spending his last night with his family before going away to fight. Paramount's film of *Sentimental Tommy* was an unqualified success when released, and it made Hughes one of the most critically acclaimed and sought after young actors in America.

Barrie was born in the small Scottish village of Kirriemuir in 1860. His family left the little town when he was eight and moved to Glasgow. Kirriemuir became a shining memory for Barrie as he grew up in the busy and dirty streets of Glasgow, and it became an elusive symbol of happiness forever lost. His earliest writings were reflections on that little Scottish town, only he changed its name to Thrums.

Sentimental Tommy is about the son of a poor widow in London, whose tales of her hometown, Thrums, turn it into a magical place in her son's imagination. When she dies, leaving him and his young sisters orphans, they travel there to live with the man their mother had spurned years before. Tommy (Gareth Hughes) tightly holds the hand of his sister Elspeth (Leila Frost) as they enter the town they had heard tales of since birth, and the title cards indicate that Elspeth asks, "Where are the stairs that are so grand that houses wear them on the outside?" All they see is a row of little stone dwellings, but Tommy, undaunted, answers, "They are certainly beauties. We are not used to such grand sights, that's all!" Little Elspeth, however, can only sob, "But I thought it would be bonnier."

Soon they reach the little village well which their mother had told them delivers a fairy with each bucketful, but all they see in the bucket which a woman brings up is water. As they walk on, one woman turns to another and says, pointing at them, "Their mother was a strange one, writing here and telling about her carriages and mansions, while all the time she was starving and slaving. It is good of Aaron to take in her kids after she jilted him like she did." Ahead, Tommy and Elspeth see a group of village children taunting a young girl who is doing her best to ignore them. The mean children yell over and over, "The Painted Lady's brat!" Tommy runs up to the biggest boy and throws all the weight of his slight body against the bully. A fight ensues, but Tommy soon comes up on top and pins the boy down. When he asks the boy why he is tormenting the girl, he replies, "She's the Painted Lady's brat." When the girl, Grizel (May McAvoy), hears this, she runs up and screams down at the bully, "You lie! My mother is sweet." Then she runs off. Tommy is up in an instant and runs after her. When he catches up, she suddenly stops, turns around, and smiles at him—her prince in shining armor.

They politely exchange names, and she invites him and his sister to come to her house and visit. Tommy, Elspeth, and Grizel spend a lot of time playing together, and one of their favorite games is "Dress-up." Tommy puts on an old plaid kilt of Aaron's and with a wooden sword he slays the dragon. Grizel is always the princess, and Elspeth is Tommy's devoted slave.

One night, Grizel's mother, the Painted Lady (Mabel Taliaferro), dies, and the village women wait around outside for the doctor to come out of her cottage. When Doctor McQueen (George Fawcett), an old bachelor, comes out, shaking his head, he looks at the women and asks, "Who will take the child?" None of the women will take Grizel, for they fear her blood is bad, so the doctor decides to take care of Grizel himself.

From then on, Grizel lives with the doctor. When Tommy is twenty, he and his sister leave Thrums and go to London, where Tommy is to pursue a career as a writer. The townspeople laugh behind his back when he leaves and call him a dreamer. Only Grizel is sure that Tommy will succeed. A year passes with no news of Tommy, and then a little London newspaper story tells that he has run off with a lord's wife to Switzerland. Grizel becomes strange after that, and village people say that her bad blood is surfacing.

Tommy comes back to Thrums a successful author and feels guilty when he sees how Grizel has changed. He marries her and nurses her back to happiness. When they have a child, their joy is complete, and the story ends.

One of the best things to come out of *Sentimental Tommy* for Paramount was May McAvoy, for they quickly signed her to a contract after they saw her rushes for the film. She went on to appear in some of Paramount's finest films in the 1920's and later starred at other studios in *The Enchanted Cottage* (1924), *Lady Windermere's Fan* (1925), *Ben-Hur* (1925), and *The Jazz Singer* (1927).

Hughes worked on through the 1920's in films and on stage. He became quite religious in the 1930's, and one day suddenly sold all his possessions and gave the proceeds to the poor. He joined a missionary church and was placed among the American Indians in Nevada, where he was known as Brother David. He ruined his health there after twenty years of deprivation and eventually entered the Motion Picture Country House with many physical ailments, and he died there in 1965.

Larry Lee Holland

SEVEN CHANCES

Released: 1925
Production: Joseph M. Schenck for Buster Keaton Productions; released by
   Metro-Goldwyn-Mayer
Direction: Buster Keaton
Screenplay: Clyde Bruckman, Jean C. Havez, and Joseph A. Mitchell; based
   on the play of the same name by Roi Cooper Megrue
Cinematography: Elgin Lessley and Byron Houck
Editing: Buster Keaton (uncredited)
Length: 6 reels/5,113 feet

Principal characters:
Jimmie Shannon .... Buster Keaton
Mary Jones .... Ruth Dwyer
Billy Meekin .... Ray Barnes
The lawyer .... Snitz Edwards

For each of his classic silent feature films Buster Keaton himself was truly in charge of the production and responsible for the final result. Besides being the principal actor, he was also the director (although he often shared the directing credit with someone else), the editor (although no editing credits are given in the films), and he made significant contributions to the story. There was, in fact, no script for these films; Keaton and his staff of writers simply worked out the plot in advance without writing down the detailed scenario that most other filmmakers used. The source or the inspiration for a Keaton film could be something as simple as the availability of an ocean liner that could be used as a setting (*The Navigator*, 1924), or it could be something as seemingly obscure as a civil war narrative (*The General*, 1926). The source of *Seven Chances* is a play written in 1916 that had achieved very little success on the stage and about which Keaton was initially unenthusiastic. Once Keaton and his staff worked on it and even added an exciting sequence after the film had been shown to a few preview audiences, however, the indifferent play had been transformed into a superior film.

As in many Keaton films, events of the first half are reversed in the second half; in this regard, *Seven Chances* can be considered Keaton's most symmetrical film because during the first half of the film Keaton is rejected by women and during virtually all the second half he is pursued by them. Indeed, film critic Daniel Moews reports that there are 216 shots in the first part of the film and almost exactly the same number—208—in the second part. The film also compresses its action into a limited span of time. Except for a prologue, the events depicted all take place within a period of less than eight hours.

Although the film as a whole is well integrated, with each part leading directly into the next, there is one sequence that is extraordinary whether it is considered alone or in the context of the film as a whole. This is the sequence that was added after the first version of the film had been completed. It was Keaton's practice to preview each of his films before several audiences so that he could see how people reacted to the various elements within the film. These previews often gave Keaton ideas for minor changes that made the film more effective.

When he previewed *Seven Chances*, he noticed that when the audience noticed a minor incident in one part of the film's long chase sequence they "sat up in their seats and expected more." As Keaton ran down a hill in the film, he accidentally dislodged a rock and that rock, as it rolled downhill, dislodged two more. After seeing the audience's expectant reaction, Keaton had a large number of rocks of all sizes constructed out of lightweight material. He then set up and photographed a sequence in which he was chased by rocks and boulders. The three "accidental" rocks of the first version of the film became fifteen hundred purposeful rocks in the final version. They chased him relentlessly down the hill no matter what he did to evade them. At one point, he climbs a tree to escape them, but a large boulder then demolishes the tree, and he must start running again. Later, he seeks shelter behind an unmoving boulder, but the landslide of smaller rocks accumulates and begins to move the boulder. Finally, however, the threat becomes his deliverance. The group of women that had been chasing him had taken a shortcut and now appear at the bottom of the hill surging toward him. He chooses to face the rocks rather than the women and deftly makes his way through the bounding rocks, which continue down the hill and rout the women. Then, when all seems peaceful, one rather small rock rolls by and knocks him down.

The events that lead up to the Keaton character's escape from a pursuing mob of women are also artfully comic, though generally less tumultuous. The film, in fact, begins very quietly with Jimmie Shannon (Buster Keaton) and Mary Jones (Ruth Dwyer) standing at the gate of a white picket fence in front of Mary's house. A title announces that Jimmie "wanted to tell her he loved her," but that scene is followed by three others in which the action is the same—only the seasons change—and Jimmie remains unable to express his love. After this prologue, however, the pace of the plot quickens.

Jimmie and his partner, Billy Meekin (Ray Barnes), need money quickly because they have been tricked into a deal that could result in disgrace or a prison term if they fail to raise the required amount. When a lawyer (Snitz Edwards) whom they do not know comes to their office, they assume he represents a creditor. They elude the lawyer and go to the country club, but the lawyer follows them and finally delivers his news—Jimmie will inherit seven million dollars if he is married by 7:00 P.M. on his twenty-seventh birthday. Since today is his twenty-seventh birthday, he realizes he can no longer hesitate. He goes straight to Mary and proposes, and she accepts.

Obviously, however, the problem cannot be solved that easily. Jimmie immediately blunders by explaining the terms of the inheritance in words that make Mary think he is interested only in the money and not in her. She then refuses him, and he returns to the country club where Bill convinces him that he must marry to obtain the inheritance and save them from shame or prison. Then begins a humorous sequence in which Jimmie proposes to and is rejected by a series of women. Keaton and his writers devised some seventeen or eighteen different variations on the theme of proposal and rejection. One time, for example, he speaks to one woman as he walks up a flight of stairs, and when he receives her refusal, he turns around without pausing and addresses another woman who is coming down the stairs. Most of his rejections are humiliating ones. He sends a note to a woman on a balcony, and she merely tears it to pieces and throws it down on him, for example. The title of the film comes from this sequence. Jimmie, Billy, and the lawyer look at a group of seven women sitting in the dining room at the country club. Billy writes down their names in his notebook and announces to Jimmie, "You have seven chances." Before long, however, all seven names have been crossed off of the list. Finally, his last proposal is rejected in a manner that is not only humiliating but violent; he unknowingly approaches a female impersonator offscreen, and when he reappears, he has obviously been beaten up.

Meanwhile, Mary has decided to accept Jimmie after all, but she is unable to contact him. Also, Billy has decided that desperate measures are called for and tells Jimmie to meet him at the Broad Street church at five o'clock: "I'll have a bride there if it's the last act of my life." Billy then visits the newspaper, and soon a front page story explains the inheritance and announces that the girl who appears in bridal costume at the church "will be the lucky winner."

The second part of the film begins with Jimmie entering the church and sitting down in the front pew. He then leans over and goes to sleep. Thus, he is not seen by the prospective brides who begin coming in the church. Dozens, perhaps hundreds, of women of all sizes and shapes—all wearing some sort of bridal headdress—come to the church on every imaginable type of conveyance. When Jimmie wakes up, he finds that his fortunes have reversed—a multitude of women will now accept him, but when the minister tells the women it must be a practical joke, they turn on him and he barely escapes from the church. Outside the church, he finds that Mary will marry him and most of the balance of the film shows his frantic efforts to get to Mary's house in time while he is pursued by a mob of angry women. Thus are combined two of the classic elements of film comedy: the chase and the deadline that must be met.

After the exciting chase that invokes such items as a brick wall, a football game, a Turkish bath, and a squad of policemen, as well as the rocks, Jimmie arrives at Mary's house—too late, according to Billy's watch. Jimmie sees that by the clock on the church steeple he has just enough time, however, so he and Mary are married.

Thus Mary is like most of the heroines in Keaton's films; she is the reward for the hero, but she plays little part in the action except as a stimulus. Only in two of his classic features, *The Navigator* and *The General*, does the Keaton heroine have a major role in the film. In fact, Keaton's producer reportedly believed that it was unimportant to hire top-quality actresses for Keaton's films, because the women's roles were not that important.

Seven Chances is also notable for one bit of photographic virtuosity. When Jimmie goes from the country club to Mary's house and back again early in the film, he simply sits still in his car while the background changes. Thus in the first shot, he walks from the country club to his car, sits in the driver's seat as the background changes, and then opens the car door and walks into Mary's house. Without moving, the car changes locations. The effect was accomplished with the use of surveyor's instruments.

All in all, *Seven Chances* is an entertaining and artistic mixture of subtle comedy and exciting action.

Marilynn Wilson

7th HEAVEN

Released: 1927
Production: William Fox
Direction: Frank Borzage (AA)
Screenplay: Benjamin Glazer (AA); based on the play *Seventh Heaven* by
  Austin Strong
Titles: Katherine Hilliker and H. H. Caldwell
Cinematography: Ernest Palmer
Editing: Katherine Hilliker and H. H. Caldwell
Music: Erno Rapee and Lew Pollack
Length: 9 reels/8,500 feet

Principal characters:
Diane	Janet Gaynor (AA)
Chico	Charles Farrell
Colonel Brissac	Ben Bard
Gobin	David Butler
Madame Gobin	Marie Mosquini
Papa Boul	Albert Gran
Nana	Gladys Brockwell
Father Chevillon	Emile Chautard

It is probably no overstatement to describe Frank Borzage as the screen's greatest romantic director. Critic Andrew Sarris has hailed Borzage as "that rarity of rarities, an uncompromising romanticist." So many of the director's films show the romantic side of existence, usually in an atmosphere or environment that is heavy with poverty and suffering. Borzage's best romantic works are *Street Angel* (1928), *The River* (1929), *Liliom* (1930), *A Farewell to Arms* (1932), and *Man's Castle* (1933). These films all propagandize a theory, which is stated in one of the titles in another Borzage great romantic creation, *7th Heaven*: "For those who will climb it, there is a ladder leading from the depths to the heights—from the sewer to the stars—the ladder of courage."

Borzage (1893-1962) began his film career as an actor in the early teens. He became a director—first of his own films—in 1916, and soon became one of the industry's top directors, working for all the major studios. He joined the William Fox Company in 1926 and was to remain there, as probably its highest paid director, until 1932. Although he continued to direct until 1959, the pinnacle of Borzage's success was undoubtedly the years with Fox, and his finest achievement with that studio was *7th Heaven.*

7th Heaven was one of the last great silent films, produced in the year that also saw the release of *The Jazz Singer*, and, like a number of other Fox films from this period, it was generally released with a musical score recorded, sound-on-film, by the Fox Movietone system. In fact, when 7th Heaven received its New York premiere, on May 25, 1927, it was preceded by a number of sound Movietone shorts featuring the likes of Raquel Meller and Gertrude Lawrence. The music score, composed by Erno Rapee and Lew Pollack, is an integral part of the film, and disproves the theory that silent films may be enjoyed in silence. Not only does it include its famous, and still popular, theme song, "Diane," but also, as Diane and Chico declare their love for each other, a soprano is heard singing "Oh Divine Redeemer" by Gounod, and there is nothing at all incongruous in this. The singing adds to the emotional intensity of the scenes. Similarly, a few moments later, as the couple learns of the outbreak of World War I, rousing martial music breaks into the soft love-tones of the score, interrupting the melodic score just as World War I will interrupt the young lover's lives together.

In the film, Chico (Charles Farrell) works in the sewers of Paris—he is first seen standing in the sewers looking out through a manhole cover which lets in the sunlight—but he dreams of one day becoming a street cleaner. As he describes himself, he is "a remarkable fellow." Diane (Janet Gaynor) is a poor waif, living in a slum with her vicious sister, Nana (played with superb cruelty by Gladys Brockwell). When an aunt and uncle arrive, who might take Diane out of the slums, she is unable to lie when they question her concerning her morality, and so she is left to live out her sordid existence with Nana. Diane is chased into the streets by the whip-carrying Nana, but Chico intervenes and threatens to throw Nana down the manhole into the sewer unless she leaves Diane alone.

As Chico, ignoring Diana, sits in the gutter and eats his meal, Father Chevillon (Emile Chautard) appears. Chico tells the Father that he does not believe in God; he had tested him twice, but God had failed him. In addition, Chico claims God owes him ten francs for the candles that he purchased when he prayed to be made a street cleaner and to be given a wife. In response, the Father gives Chico two medallions and a chit which will get him the sought-after job of street cleaner.

After the priest has left, Diane is about to leave, but the police arrive on the scene and are about to arrest the girl for prostitution until Chico says that she is his wife. Because the police will check Chico's address and see if he is really telling the truth, Chico is forced to take Diane back to his lodging, which is on the top, seventh floor, of the building. In a scene of brilliant technical ingenuity, the pair slowly climb from the street and its sewers to Chico's apartment and heaven. The apartment symbolizes Chico's outlook on life, "Never look down. Always look up." (Strangely enough, the stairs which rise straight up in the opening reels of film have suddenly become spiral for the film's close.) The couple's relationship—and at this point it is not even that—is a purely platonic one. Diane peers, from under the bedclothes of the bed she will occupy alone, at Chico, stripped to the waist and bathing himself.

Chico's outlook on life becomes even sunnier once he has become a street cleaner, and is working with his new friend Gobin (played by director-to-be David Butler), who lives with his wife in an apartment across the rooftops from Chico. Through simple episodes, such as Diane cutting Chico's hair, a loving relationship develops between the young couple. Diane tells Chico that "God brought me to you." Unable to express his love for Diane in words, Chico brings her a white wedding dress. He says the three words that symbolize their relationship, "Chico. Diane. Heaven." (In fact, lip-readers will note that the couple is speaking in French during the film's close-ups, and, actually, recite, "Chico. Diane. Ciel.") Chico teaches Diane courage, and she tells him she will never be afraid again.

At this point, the war intervenes, and Chico is ordered to mobilize. He decides to give God a chance by performing a marriage ceremony between the two of them, with the medallions given to him by Father Chevillon serving to sanctify their marriage vows. Chico tells Diane that each morning at eleven, the two will renew their vows with the words "Diane. Chico. Heaven," and the two will be spiritually joined together. Shortly ater Chico's departure, Diane's sister Nana reappears to try and re-assert her dominance over the girl, but, thanks to Chico, Diane is no longer afraid and this time it is Diane who takes a whip and drives Nana from the apartment.

While Chico is fighting at the front, Diane gets a job in an armaments factory, where she rejects the affectionate attentions of Colonel Brissac (Ben Bard); and each morning at eleven Diane and Chico come together through their overwhelming love for each other. Diane is in Paris, Chico is at the front, but they "are shoulder to shoulder—that is all that matters."

One incident of World War I is featured in *7th Heaven*, and that is General Galliene's marshaling of some one thousand Parisian taxicabs to rush troops of the 62nd Division twenty-five miles to the battlefront to prevent the German advance on the city. One of Diane and Chico's friends, Papa Boule (Albert Gran), drives his taxi, Eloise, to the front, where it is blown up leaving the tearful cabby with nothing but the horn as a memento of the taxicab's bravery. The special effects for the war scenes were created by Louis Witte and were filmed, as were all the street scenes, at the new Fox studios at what was then called Movietone City and is now called Century City in Los Angeles.

As the war ends, the audience quite clearly sees Chico killed. Father Chevillon visits Diane with the news, bringing Chico's medallion with him. First Diane will not believe him, pointing out that every morning at eleven she communed with Chico, but as she realizes the truth, she turns her anger on the priest, striking him across the chest and crying, "For four years I called this Heaven—prayed—I believed in God—I believed he would bring Chico back to me." Suddenly, there is a sharp cut to the crowds outside celebrating the armistice, and in the midst of the crowd, Chico is seen, blinded but struggling to return to Heaven and to Diane. As he mounts the stairs, it is eleven o'clock and the two lovers call out to each other. "They thought I was dead, but I'll never die," says Chico, and, as the two embrace, a flood of sunlight pours in through the window. Love has conquered all, even death. It is an extraordinary ending, so heavy with emotion and spirituality that it totally overwhelms the audience and enables us to suspend all disbelief.

7th Heaven created a new romantic film team with Charles Farrell and Janet Gaynor, and for several more years, the two were to delight audiences in light comedy-dramas (often with interpolated musical numbers), such as *Christina* (1929), *Sunny Side Up* (1929), *Lucky Star* (1929), and *Delicious* (1931). Only the film *Street Angel*, however, approached the emotional intensity of *7th Heaven*, and that was also directed, a year later, by Borzage.

The film was as much of a critical success as the original stageplay, with Helen Menken, had been in 1922. *Photoplay* (July, 1927) commented,

> One John Golden play plus one talented director plus two brilliant young people equals one fine picture. . . . It is permeated with the spirit of youth, of young love, of whimsy. . . . It's tender and tragic and wholly appealing, splashed now and then with that grandly human comedy for which Director Frank Borzage is known.

In *The Film Spectator* (May 28, 1927), Welford Beaton wrote, "It's the soul of *7th Heaven* that gets you, the soul put into it by an understanding script, sympathetic direction and superb acting."

The film industry agreed with its critics, and at the first Academy Awards ceremony on May 6, 1929, *7th Heaven* was honored with three awards: Best Actress to Janet Gaynor, Best Direction to Frank Borzage, and Best Writing (adaptation) to Benjamin Glazer. In addition, *7th Heaven* was nominated for Best Picture and Best Art Direction.

In 1937, *7th Heaven* was remade, under the direction of Henry King, and starred James Stewart and Simone Simon. Neither artistically nor commercially did it match the success of its silent predecessor

Anthony Slide

SEX

Released: 1920
Production: J. Parker Read for Hodkinson/Pathé
Direction: Fred Niblo
Screenplay: C. Gardner Sullivan
Cinematography: Charles J. Stumar
Length: 7 reels

> *Principal characters:*
> Adrienne Renault .... Louise Glaum
> Philip Overman .... William Conklin
> Mrs. Overman .... Myrtle Stedman
> Dave Wallace .... Irving Cummings
> Daisy Henderson .... Peggy Pearce

In the film *Sex*, Adrienne Renault (Louise Glaum) is the reigning dance queen of the Midnight Frivolities. She believes in getting everything she wants, regardless of what the effect may be on others. She has lured a husband, Philip Overman (William Conklin), from his wife (Myrtle Stedman) and has been set up in a huge, lavish apartment.

Adrienne's best friend and her protégée is Daisy Henderson (Peggy Pearce), an innocent country girl who works in the chorus at the Midnight Frivolities. Daisy is surprised at Adrienne's morals, but Adrienne tells her never to worry about another woman's husband because he would not wander if he was happy. Daisy argues, but Adrienne proves a good teacher, and Daisy slowly grows to be like her mentor.

One night, as Daisy visits Adrienne in her lavish apartment, and as the older girl teaches the younger one how to smoke cigarettes, there is a knock at the door. When Adrienne finds out that it is her sugar daddy's wife, she tells Daisy to wait in the bedroom and listen. Adrienne lets in the wife, and, with an amused expression, listens to the wife plead for her to leave the husband alone. Adrienne only laughs at Mrs. Overman, but just then Philip Overman makes a surprise visit and is horrified to see his distraught wife. She screams at him that she is getting a divorce and storms out. Adrienne tries to cheer the shocked husband by opening a bottle of champagne. Daisy comes out of the bedroom, and soon the three are having a gay little party.

Not long afterward, Adrienne meets a millionaire, Dave Wallace (Irving Cummings), at the supper club and finds herself falling in love for the first time. She soon marries him and is very happy being a wife who stays at home. Dave, however, likes to go out to the nightclubs, and Adrienne spends many evenings at home alone.

Daisy, meanwhile, has taken Adrienne's place as the star dancer at the Midnight Frivolities. Adrienne's job, however, is not the only thing Daisy has taken, for she also is being kept by Adrienne's husband. When Adrienne finds out, she is sick at heart, and asks Daisy how she can do that to her. Daisy only laughs and tells her that she has no right to question her conduct, for Adrienne taught her everything herself. Adrienne leaves her husband and books passage for Europe. On the steamer, she sees Philip Overman and his wife on their second honeymoon, and she spends the entire voyage suffering for her past sins.

The plot, although moralistic and trite, was a showcase for Louise Glaum's particular style of filmmaking. She, like Theda Bara, was an important screen vamp. *Sex* opens at a midnight supper club with a spectacular floor show where Glaum, as Adrienne Renault, is lowered to the stage on a giant spider web. She is clad in a black sequin gown and draped in a spider web of pearls. A male dancer with a feather headdress joins her, and they perform a ballet of the spider and the fly fable. Costumes were very important for the film vamps, and Glaum was the most lavish and bizarrely dressed of all of them. Bara may have had her breasts encircled with golden asps in *Cleopatra* (1917), but Glaum had the nipple of one exposed breast covered with a realistic black widow in *The Wolf Woman* (1916). Those elaborate costumes have long since decayed and are not to be found among the later wardrobe artifacts the public views in museums. In 1975, however, a little junk store in Hollywood had a chipped mannequin in its window dressed in a black sequin gown and draped with a spider's web of silvered glass beads. It was the original costume from *Sex*. After Glaum's death in 1970, the proprietor had purchased it, along with many boxes of other costumes from the vamp's sister, who told him proudly that she had made all of Louise's costumes herself.

Glaum was born in Baltimore in 1894 and moved to California as a child. As a teenager, she worked in stock, playing ingenue parts, then in 1912, she began working in films for Al Christie in his Nestor brand comedies. She was offered more money by Bison Films and began her acting stint there when asked by the director to hang from a second-story window sill by her teeth until the hero rescued her. She quickly gave up working for Bison when Thomas Ince offered her work with his Broncho and Kay-B units. Next, Universal asked her to be a leading lady in flounces and ribbons for a popular comedy star they had just stolen from Essanay, Alkali Ike. The director of the series was Harry Edwards. She married him, then six months later she was back at Ince, where she starred with William S. Hart and Charles Ray. Hart features such as *The Iron Stain* (1915) and *Hell's Hinges* (1916) gave her strong roles as "bad" women.

Glaum became typed in vamp roles by the public after *The Toast of Death*, a four-reel picture released by Ince in August, 1915. In that film, she played the faithless wife of an English Army officer stationed in India.

The Wolf Woman (also called *Dust*) made her an important competitor to Fox's Bara. In that film, she made the fool totally forget his wife and eight children, possibly on the strength of her provocative spider gown alone. At the end, however, she got her comeuppance when her vanity caused her to walk into a full-length mirror and shatter her beauty.

Separated from her husband, Harry Edwards, shortly thereafter, Glaum was greatly influenced by producer and director J. Parker Read. She left Ince in early 1918 and joined the newly formed film company, Paralta. For a year she turned out that company's most successful features, but, by the end of the year, Paralta ceased production, and Read began releasing her features through Hodkinson and, later, Associated Producers. Her films became more elaborate and were specials in every sense of the word. *Sahara* (1919), *Lone Wolf's Daughter* (1919), *Love* (1920), *Love Madness* (1920), *The Leopard Woman* (1920), and *I Am Guilty* (1921) were all big moneymakers. Their film *Sex*, however, set the money record.

In the summer of 1921, Glaum traveled through Mexico extensively to see if she could possibly produce her films there, but after contracting a serious case of dysentery, she had to return to Hollywood, where she spent a year recovering. After gaining excessive weight after her illness, however, she was unable to regain her figure. She retired from films, and never made another before her death in 1970.

Larry Lee Holland

THE SHEIK

Released: 1921
Production: Famous Players-Lasky; released by Paramount
Direction: George Melford
Screenplay: Monte M. Katterjohn; based on the novel of the same name by Edith Maude Hull
Cinematography: William Marshall
Length: 8 reels/8,963 feet

Principal characters:
Diana Mayo	Agnes Ayres
Sheik Ahmed Ben Hassan	Rudolph Valentino
Raoul de Saint Hubert	Adolphe Menjou
Omair	Walter Long
Gaston	Lucien Littlefield
Aubrey Mayo	F. R. Butler
Yousaf	George Waggner
The serving girl	Patsy Ruth Miller

The Sheik is one of the few films ever made that affected daily life for more than a decade. Based on what was a current best-selling novel by Edith Maude Hull, the controversial story answered escapist needs of a society in a state of moral and emotional flux brought on by World War I, a vacillation which resulted in the dichotomy of Prohibition and the Jazz Age. The raciness of the story caused some people to want to censor the film, but that idea met with little success. The film's popularity won out, and the word "sheik" entered the American vocabulary. Women wanted their boyfriends and husbands to be "sheiks," to act with the omnipotence of the sheik, but with his sensitivity as well. Popular songs, such as "The Sheik of Araby" and "The Sheik of Avenue B" told of the love of a sheik and his woman (or women). Films such as *She's a Sheik* (1927), *The Shreik of Araby* (1922), and *The Son of the Sheik* (1926), satirized the love story.

Fashions reflected the desert capes and headdresses, and the Arabian look touched the interior design of theaters and homes. Film historian William K. Everson, in making a point that art direction in Universal studio films mirrored trends of the day, writes in *American Silent Film*, "When everybody goes to a party in *Skinner's Dress Suit* (1925), the night-club is decked out Egyptian style, with tent motif and Nubian slaves, an acknowledgement of the enormous influence of Valentino and *The Sheik* on day-to-day living."

As popular as the novel was at the time the film was released, one doubts that the motion picture would have been such an outstanding success without Rudolph Valentino in the title role. Valentino was an Italian immigrant who had worked in New York as a taxi dancer, a nightclub dancer, and then chorus boy in a musical show which brought him to the West. In the late teens, he appeared in Hollywood films as an extra, a dancer and gangster. In early 1921, his tango dance in Metro's *The Four Horsemen of the Apocalypse* was so torrid that it won the attention both of critics and the female audience. Following that role came the part of Armand in *Camille* (1921) with Nazimova. Again, his ability to arouse the passions of the women in the theater worked in his favor, and he was establishing himself as a romantic lead.

Valentino's swarthy looks, his muscular build and flashing eyes, made him a perfect choice for *The Sheik*. Even though it was Agnes Ayres who received star billing, it was Valentino who made the film a box-office sensation. He became the symbol of male eroticism and gave interviews to *Photoplay* and other fan magazines about the women of his dreams and how to make love to a woman.

Much of the analysis of *The Sheik* rightfully deals with its impact on American society rather than its worth as a motion picture; however, it should be noted that *The Sheik* is a well-constructed and well-produced dramatic film. George Melford had directed as many as nine feature films per year during the teens and was an expert storyteller, as was veteran screenwriter Monte M. Katterjohn.

The opening title places the viewer in the exotic atmosphere: "In this world of peace and flame lies a palm garden of the Sahara—a blessed oasis of the sands." The scene is a marriage market, where wives are bought by wealthy men. Yousaf (George Waggner), a tribal chieftain, protests the sale of his sweetheart Zilah, and Sheik Ahmed Ben Hassan (Rudolph Valentino) settles the situation in Yousaf's favor, which is also in love's favor.

In Biskra, gateway to the desert, Diana Mayo (Agnes Ayres) holds a dance to celebrate her farewell to Biskra. Against the wishes of the older British women of the community and her brother Aubrey (F. R. Butler), she will travel through the desert accompanied only by Mustapha Ali, an Arab guide. As the orphaned daughter of English poetess Lady Diana Mayo, the younger Diana lives for adventure and considers marriage as "captivity—the end of independence. I am content with life as it is."

That evening, the Sheik arrives at a casino where only Arabs are allowed. Diana is standing outside, and their eyes meet. Protesting her inability to enter the casino, she asks why "a savage desert bandit" can keep her from entering a public place. An officer corrects her, informing her that the Sheik is a rich tribal prince who was educated in Paris and that his word is law in Biskra.

Diana catches a glimpse of a dancing girl entertaining the Arab men in the casino and decides to borrow one of her costumes as a disguise. Inside the casino, men gamble for brides. Diana sneaks inside wearing the dancer's garb and a cloak. She watches the dancer and the gamblers and thinks them barbarous. Then, she is called upon to dance. When she hesitates, the Sheik notices that she is a white woman. He asks her the reason for her presence, and she answers, "I wanted to see the savage who would bar me from this casino." The Sheik smiles and leads her to the door. Mustapha Ali tells the Sheik that he will be escorting Diana into the desert tomorrow morning, and the Sheik grins.

Early the next morning, Sheik Ahmed climbs the trellis to Diana's balcony to serenade her with "Beautiful Dreamer." She listens and smiles, but the Sheik rides away before she can identify the songster. Shortly afterward, Diana and Aubrey enter the desert with Mustapha Ali. From another part of the desert, through binoculars, the Sheik watches Diana say farewell to her brother as she and her guide embark upon their desert journey. Soon after their journey begins, a party of one hundred Arabs start chasing her, and she drops her gun. Suddenly, only the Sheik is chasing her. He snatches her from her horse and onto his, and as he warns her "Lie still, you little fool," she collapses in his grasp.

Diana is brought to the Sheik's camp as his captive. He shows her his tent and, with his eyes, commands her to enter. He claps his hands and a serving girl (Patsy Ruth Miller) enters to take Diana's hat and gloves, then the title cards read, "Why have you brought me here?" "Are you not woman enough to know?" These two lines have become classic screen dialogue, and, even though they often have been satirized, they work powerfully in the film.

Sheik Ahmed tells Diana that she is beautiful and that she must obey him. At first, she fights him but then obeys and enters the boudoir. Gaston (Lucien Littlefield), valet to the Sheik, assists her and then the girl enters to "serve my master's bride." Outside, a sandstorm is raging, but inside the tent, the Sheik and Diana dine together. She warns Ahmed that her friends in Biskra will miss her, but he says that by that time it will be too late. The desert is big, and nobody will learn their whereabouts. She runs out into the storm, but he retrieves her, telling her that she would die in an hour in such a storm. She grabs a knife and threatens to kill herself, but he stops her. "You are so pretty and if I choose, I can make you love me." She answers, "I would rather you kill me," but he only laughs and embraces her.

A man then enters the tent to report that the horses have broken loose, and after the Sheik leaves, she prays. Ahmed returns to find her lying on the floor. Noting her distress, he leaves her alone. The serving girl offers comfort, and the two women embrace. The next morning, the serving girl unpacks Diana's valises, and Gaston prepares the breakfast. Diana is awakened by a sprinkling of rose petals. She is brought Arab clothes to wear, on the Sheik's orders. Gaston serves breakfast with a rose from Ahmed, and Diana thrusts it to the ground.

Weeks of "sullen obedience" pass, then word arrives that Raoul de Saint Hubert (Adolphe Menjou), Ahmed's novelist friend from Paris, will be visiting the camp. Diana overhears the Sheik singing "Beautiful Dreamer" and realizes that he was the mysterious serenader in Biskra. He tells her he sings when he is happy and that he is elated over Raoul's upcoming visit. She becomes distressed at the thought of a white man seeing her living as an Arab woman in Ahmed's tent. Ahmed expects her to act cordially to his friend, and he permits her possessions to be returned to her. Diana is so pleased by Ahmed's gesture that she embraces him, but she cannot manage to enjoy his kiss. His feelings hurt, he leaves for Biskra to meet Raoul.

Diana dreads "the humiliation of meeting a man from her own world," so she runs away while horseback riding with Gaston. Meanwhile, Ahmed discusses Diana with Raoul who tells the Sheik he is acting badly. "When an Arab sees a woman he wants, he takes her," the Sheik responds. Back on the desert, Diana has become lost. Having become separated from her horse, she is nearly captured by Omair (Walter Long) the bandit and his men but is rescued by Ahmed and Raoul. They find Gaston and return to camp. The three dine together and then she retires, with the permission of the Sheik. Raoul becomes angry with Ahmed for humiliating Diana, but Ahmed insists, "She is content."

The next day, Diana and Raoul start to discuss the situation, but she feels as though he is only interested in her as material for another novel. To clarify his feelings, Raoul kisses Diana's hand and asks for her friendship, but the Sheik eavesdrops on the scene and misreads its meaning. Then, Raoul is called to help a man whose gun has exploded in his hand.

Omair the bandit sends a spy to Ahmed's camp in order to bring information of the white woman back to him. Fearing another attempt on Omair's part to capture Diana, Ahmed gives Diana back her gun, telling her that he trusts her. Ahmed captures Omair's spy and has the man tortured. Seeing this, Raoul decides to take Diana to Biskra, but the Sheik thinks Raoul wants Diana for himself. After a row with his friend, Ahmed is full of regret. "How I have made her suffer. Merciful Allah, why does it give me so much pleasure?" Out on the desert for a ride with Gaston, Diana stops to write in the sand, "Ahmed, I love you."

The Sheik makes up his mind to give her up and have Raoul ride with her to Biskra. Then, Raoul will return to camp to console Ahmed on his loss. While the friends make plans, Omair and his gang of bandits battle with Gaston and Diana, wound Gaston, capture Diana, and take her back to their camp. When Ahmed looks for his woman and valet, he finds "Ahmed, I love you" written in the sand, and then locates Gaston who has been shot by Omair's men. Revived, Gaston describes the battle and the capture of Diana.

When night falls, the Sheik and his men approach Omair's walled camp to rescue Diana. Inside Omair's tent, Diana is held under armed guard and ordered to prepare herself for the bandit chieftain. Omair begins to make love to Diana, when a jealous mistress rushes in to stab him. In a fury, Omair overpowers the woman. As the Sheik and his forces draw nearer, Diana struggles with Omair. The Sheik and his men climb over the wall and wage war on the bandits. Ahmed arrives at Omair's boudoir in time to save Diana, but he is shot by one of Omair's men. Victorious, the Sheik and his tribe return with Diana to their camp, where the health of Ahmed "rests with Allah."

The Sheik's tribe prays to Allah as Raoul tends his wounded friend. Raoul tells Diana there is still hope, and she is relieved. She sits at Ahmed's bedside to watch over him and to fondle his hand.

"His hand is so large for an Arab," she says. "He is not an Arab. His father was an Englishman, his mother a Spaniard," Raoul explains. The old Sheik found him as an infant whose parents had died on the desert. He was reared as the Sheik's son and succeeded his stepfather as ruler of the tribe.

When Diana offers God her life instead of his, the Sheik overhears her prayer and smiles. She leans close to him, as Raoul leaves the room to report the Sheik's recovery to the tribe. Realizing their mutual love, Diana and the Sheik embrace, and an elderly tribesman adds, "All things are with Allah."

Even sixty years after this film was released, the sincerity of Valentino's performance makes this a most powerful and erotic adventure. It is psychological drama played with no pretenses, and contemporary critics recorded that some women viewers even fainted during the love scenes. In an age of female "vamps," such as Pola Negri and Theda Bara, this film proved that women, too, had an urge for forbidden fruit. The tremendous popularity of the film caused local censorship boards to complain about the kind of motion pictures the public was being fed by Hollywood—a Hollywood currently in the throes of the Fatty Arbuckle scandal—but *The Sheik* was a film that touched people beyond a two-hour experience in a darkened theater. Its theme entered the popular culture and helped to expand women's awareness of themselves as sexual human beings.

Audrey E. Kupferberg

SHERLOCK, JR.

Released: 1924
Production: Joseph M. Schenck for Buster Keaton Productions
Direction: Buster Keaton
Screenplay: Clyde Bruckman, Jean C. Havez, and Joseph A. Mitchell
Cinematography: Elgin Lessley and Byron Houck
Editing: Buster Keaton (uncredited)
Length: 5 reels/4,065 feet

Principal characters:
The boy/Sherlock, Jr. .... Buster Keaton
The girl .... Kathryn McGuire
Her father .... Joe Keaton
The sheik/villain .... Ward Crane
The butler/handyman .... Erwin Connelly

Buster Keaton's *Sherlock, Jr.* is a film about film, about reality and illusion, about dreams and fantasies. Containing another film within itself as well as perhaps a dozen instances of one character being transformed into another, through cinematic devices or through disguises, *Sherlock, Jr.* is so technically impressive that film craftsmen of the time went to see it repeatedly to marvel at its effects and to attempt to understand how they were done. In this film, Keaton drew upon both his early background in vaudeville and his quite rapid mastery of the effects and the artistry of motion pictures to create a film which is impressive on many different levels. Keaton himself directed the film, but he may have worked with Roscoe "Fatty" Arbuckle on some of the early sequences, although the latter is uncredited.

Sherlock, Jr. both begins and ends in a small-town film theater and concentrates upon the real and fantasized adventures of a character designated simply as "a boy" (Buster Keaton). Indeed, most of the characters in the film are not given names but are merely identified by such descriptions as "the girl," "the girl's father," and "the sheik."

After the opening sequence which establishes that the boy works in the theater and is "studying to be a detective," the story begins with the boy's visit to the girl (Kathryn McGuire) at her house. He presents her with a box of chocolates, but he is soon outmatched by his rival, the sheik (Ward Crane), who appears with a larger box of candy. Then the girl's father (Joe Keaton, Buster's father) announces that someone has stolen his watch. The audience knows that the sheik has stolen the watch and pawned it to buy the large box of candy, but the boy does not. He promptly decides to solve the case himself and, after consulting his book on how to be a detective, he begins searching everyone. His search reveals nothing, but when the father searches the boy, he finds a pawn ticket for the watch. The ticket was, of course, planted on him by the sheik, but the damning evidence causes the father to order the boy out of the house, and the sheik's success is complete.

The boy does not give up trying to solve the case, but after a fruitless (but decidedly eventful) attempt to find out something by following the sheik, he returns to the theater for his job as projectionist. The film he begins projecting is entitled *Hearts and Pearls* or *The Lounge Lizard's Lost Love*. The boy then quickly falls asleep and begins to dream. It is at this point that *Sherlock, Jr.* opens into another dimension; a dimension in which the character in *Sherlock, Jr.* becomes entangled with those in *Hearts and Pearls*. A transparent figure of the boy separates itself from the sleeping boy and looks at the film being projected in the theater. Soon, he sees that the people in his life have become characters in *Hearts and Pearls*, and that the sheik is the villain of the film and is threatening the girl. He runs down the aisle of the theater, now no longer transparent, and attempts to save her by jumping into the picture on the screen. The villain, however, throws him back out of the film. He then reenters the film and stays there, but he is not completely allowed into the world of the film. For example, when he sits down on a garden bench, the film cuts to a city scene and the disappearance of the bench causes him to fall down in the street. As the film changes to other settings, he continues to have trouble with the abrupt transitions; a dive into the ocean, for example, becoming a dive into a snowbank.

Finally, though, the boy becomes completely integrated into the film within the film. In *Hearts and Pearls*, the characters are members of the fashionable upper class, and there is a theft, but it is the theft of a pearl necklace by the sheik/villain and his accomplice the butler (Erwin Connelly, who plays the father's handyman in the other story). The boy's importance is also increased considerably in the transition from one story to the other. After the father makes a telephone call, the sheik exclaims, "We are lost! He is sending for the world's greatest detective—Sherlock Jr.!" Presently Keaton enters as Sherlock, Jr., elegantly dressed and completely confident. He skillfully eludes the traps the villains have set for him—an exploding billiard ball, a booby-trapped chair, and a poisoned drink. Then, just as he did in the other story, he follows the sheik to try to solve the crime. At first, this shadowing echoes that of the other story, but it then continues into a wildly exciting and diversified chase in which Sherlock receives essential help from his assistant Gillette (played by the same man who plays the theater manager in the other story), who uses several disguises to fool the villains.

Sherlock retrieves the pearls from a group of villains and rescues the girl from the butler, finally ending up in an automobile that is sinking in a river. As he begins to swim, viewers are returned to the original story and see Keaton as the boy waking up in the theater projection booth. The girl, who had gone to the pawn shop and found out that it was the sheik who pawned the watch, comes to see him. "Father sent me to tell you that we've made a terrible mistake," she says. The boy does not know how to respond until he looks down at the screen and sees the conclusion of *Hearts and Pearls*. The man in that film kisses the woman's hand; the boy then kisses the girl's hand. The man gives the woman a ring; the boy does the same. The onscreen couple embrace; the boy kisses the girl rather tentatively. Then the other film has a fade out and fade in to the couple sitting side by side, with two babies on the man's lap; the boy turns, scratches his head, and *Sherlock, Jr.* ends.

Thus, there are many levels in *Sherlock, Jr.* and much interaction between "real" life and cinema, as well as some parodies of conventions of the cinema and of specific films and types of films. For example, Daniel Moews—in his excellent study of Keaton—suggests that *Hearts and Pearls* is a parody of Cecil B. De Mille's films about the very rich as well as of John Barrymore's *Sherlock Holmes* (1922), and that the girl's resemblance to Mary Pickford is a comment on the many people who used film stars as their models. In any case, the last scene is certainly an explicit treatment of the theme of the influence of film on its audience, a topic that is still discussed and debated today.

In addition to the witty treatment of the nature of cinema, including effects and implied commentary that have not been surpassed in the succeeding decades, *Sherlock, Jr.* has many delightful and impressive scenes that need little or no help from the camera. For example, to escape the villains in one instance, Keaton dives through a window that he has previously prepared. As he jumps through the window, he also jumps into a woman's dress and emerges on the other side disguised as a woman. This is shown in one shot so that the audience can see that no camera trickery was used. Soon after that scene, Keaton is still pursued. He sees an old woman selling ties from a case suspended from a strap around her neck. Keaton heads straight for the case and jumps through it and seemingly through the body of the old woman. (The supposed woman is actually the detective's assistant, who has cleverly arranged himself and a dummy lower body and a trap door to make possible the escape.) Keaton also rides on the handlebars of a motorcycle that has lost its driver. These stunts were not without their dangers. In one of them, Keaton fractured his neck, but he continued working and only learned the seriousness of the injury when he was X-rayed many years later. All in all, *Sherlock, Jr.* is a continually surprising and exciting film that is amazing and enjoyable throughout as well as being thought-provoking.

Timothy W. Johnson

SHE'S A SHEIK

Released: 1927
Production: Paramount
Direction: Clarence Badger
Screenplay: Lloyd Corrigan and Grover Jones; based on an original story by
 John McDermott
Titles: George Marion, Jr.
Cinematography: J. Roy Hunt
Length: 6 reels/5,931 feet

> *Principal characters:*
> Zaida ....Bebe Daniels
> Captain Colton .... Richard Arlen
> Kada .... William Powell
> Wanda Fowler ....Josephine Dunn
> Jerry ....James Bradbury, Jr.
> Joe .... Billy Franey
> Sheik Yusiff ben Hamad ....Paul McAllister

For ten years, from 1919 to 1929, Bebe Daniels was a Paramount player, starting as a featured actress in Cecil B. De Mille productions, then going on to play leading roles opposite male stars such as Wallace Reid. By 1920, she was a star in her own right at Realart, a subsidiary of Paramount, and she then moved over into the first line of Paramount stars, in dramas such as *Pink Gods* (1922), *The World's Applause* (1923), and *Sinners in Heaven* (1924). That same year she was one of three leading ladies playing opposite Rudolph Valentino in his comeback film, *Monsieur Beaucaire*. By 1926, she was concentrating on feature comedies. She had said once in her early days when she was Harold Lloyd's leading lady, "When you know how to play comedy, you know how to play anything." She played everything by this time as if she were born to play it.

Two of the features she did in this era were satires on two of the big moneymakers of the day, and they were themselves box-office hits—*Señorita* (1927), a take-off on the Douglas Fairbanks style of zany Zorro comedy, and *She's a Sheik*, a very funny burlesque of *The Sheik* (1921), the picture that made Valentino the top Hollywood star of his time.

She's a Sheik opens with two serious old cronies discussing the charms of Zaida (Bebe Daniels), the Spanish-Arabian granddaughter of the Sheik Yusiff ben Hamad (Paul McAllister). One of them admits he is going to buy permission to wed Zaida, whom he describes as "a hot number."

Like Valentino in *The Sheik*, Zaida's motto is "When I see a man I want, I take him." She is very particular about the man she wants. He must be a Christian; no swarthy desert chieftain will do. When she sees the handsome

Captain Colton (Richard Arlen), a legionnaire who appears to be about to fall in love with a blond girl, Wanda Fowler (Josephine Dunn), Zaida arranges to have Colton kidnaped and brought to her tent, where he is put into a cage formerly occupied by her pet leopard. A few days later, he is sufficiently tamed, and so he is tidied, freshly barbered, and brought to Zaida. The two instantly fall in love with each other, with Zaida the aggressor, and Colton not averse to being wooed by a lady sheik, especially when she is as attractive as Zaida.

There is a fierce bandit who also is anxious to win Zaida; however, she is uninterested in him. He is named Kada (William Powell), and he serves not only as the comic suitor who loves Zaida hopelessly but also as a menace. He does not frighten Zaida, however, in the least. She knows how to fence and skillfully rips off Kada's flowing garments with her rapier before having him thrown out.

There are two traveling showmen, Jerry (James Bradbury, Jr.) and Joe (Billy Franey), who travel the desert oases, exhibiting films to the tribesmen, and when they are mistreated by Kada, Zaida drives him off at swordspoint and takes in the showmen at the garrison.

Kada, however, sells out to the renegade tribesmen and leads them in a night attack upon the out-numbered French garrison forces. Zaida defends her unit brilliantly. Jerry and Joe help her save the day and the garrison when they project a film they have of attacking Arabs, terrifying the tribesmen and causing them to retreat in disorder. Kada and the attacking regulars are completely routed, and Zaida is ready for her own conquest of her handsome captain.

In 1928, when it was obvious that talking features were going to stay, Daniels was only twenty-seven and had every intention of going on as a talking actress. Paramount, however, did not see things her way. They let her buy up the remaining year of her contract. She knew William Le Baron well from his days as a producer at Paramount, and when she learned that RKO/Radio, where he had gone as production head, was going to film a big musical version of *Rio Rita* (1929), she asked Le Baron to give her a test, not only speaking but singing. She had been studying voice for some time and proved to have a lovely lyric soprano, so Le Baron gave her the role of Rita.

Publicity was deliberately curtailed during the picture's production, and suddenly it was announced as the next attraction of the big theater at Carthay Circle in Beverly Hills. Firstnighters were stunned by Daniels' display of a talent that had never even been expected, and her career as a talking and singing actress was assured. She made five films for RKO, then co-starred with Fairbanks at United Artists in *Reaching for the Moon* (1931). She signed a new contract at Warner Bros., where she started off with films such as the first version of *The Maltese Falcon* (1931) and a big drama of *Silver Dollar* (1932), starring Edward G. Robinson, based upon the life of Horace A. W.

Tabor, the "Silver King," in which she played a character that was very much like the legendary "Baby Doe." Her most successful film at Warners was *42nd Street* (1933), in which she sang and danced the lead. That same year, she moved over to Universal to play her best dramatic role with John Barrymore in what some critics feel was his best picture, directed by William Wyler, *Counsellor at Law*.

She had married Ben Lyon, and they did a play together, *Hollywood Holiday*, moving East first and then finally to London, where they had a tremendous popularity in films, theater, radio, and eventually television. They stayed abroad during World War II and entertained the troops. Daniels was the first woman to land with the troops on D-Day. For her work during the war, the United States gave her the Medal for Freedom, which is awarded only for service under fire.

Daniels and Lyon, and their daughter and son, played on radio and then television as a unit, and their shows *Life with the Lyons* and *The Lyons in Paris* became popular situation comedies of the time, and they made feature-film versions of them. Daniels died in 1971. Lyon married actress Marian Nixon after Daniels' death, and they returned to the United States, where he died in 1979.

When the National Film Theater in London honored Daniels with a screening of one of her past successes, she chose *She's a Sheik* because it most nearly approximated what she had been trying to achieve in the field of silent comedy. She was well enough to attend the picture's screening and spoke to the audience from her wheelchair. She sat through the screening, entertained, as was the audience, with *She's a Sheik*.

DeWitt Bodeen

SHOES

Released: 1916
Production: The Smalleys for Universal/Bluebird
Direction: Lois Weber
Screenplay: Lois Weber; based on a magazine story by Stella Herron
Cinematography: Norton A. Ziegler
Length: 5 reels

Principal characters:
Eva Meyer .... Mary MacLaren
Her father .... Harry Griffith
Her mother .... Mrs. Witting
Lil .... Jessie Arnold
"Cabaret" Charlie .... William V. Mong

There were several groups of sisters who were stars in silent films and inevitably they were opposites, almost as if this were an unwritten law. Lillian Gish was a dramatic actress, while Dorothy, her sister, was a comedienne. The same was true with Norma Talmadge and her sister, Constance. No two sisters, however, could have been more different than Mary MacLaren from Katherine MacDonald. MacLaren's screen image was that of a wistful and simple girl, while MacDonald's *persona* was that of an icy society beauty.

Katherine was born in Pittsburgh on December 14, 1892, and Mary was born in the same city eight years later on January 19, followed several years later by another sister, Miriam. Their father deserted the family when they were children and the mother and children struggled to preserve their dignity as best they could. Katherine, however, had always fancied herself to be a debutante and diligently pursued all the frivolous pleasures of the rich. She exhibited prize French bulldogs in order to mingle with the elite. Yet, Mary was true to herself and lived most simply. One could have called her a shy child possessing an abundance of modesty. She was easily led by her sister Katherine, who managed her career with the skill of an experienced agent.

Mary, Miriam, and their mother moved to Hollywood in late 1915, leaving Katherine in New York, where she was working as an artist's model. Mary's first film was a bit part in Universal's *Where Are My Children?* in early 1916, directed by Lois Weber, who discerned great sensitivity in Mary and made her the lead in her next feature, *Shoes* (1916). Her performance was so moving and Mary was so perfect in the role of the poor working girl that Universal gave her her own company and star billing before the picture's title. Additionally, Louella O. Parsons called *Shoes* "one of the best moving pictures of 1916."

The film covers a month in the life of a five-and-dime store salesgirl named Eva Meyer (Mary MacLaren), who toils for the meager sum of five dollars a week. At home, her mother (Mrs. Witting) takes in washing to support two smaller children and an unemployed, beer-drinking husband (Harry Griffith).

Eva turns all her wages over to her family and keeps nothing for herself. She desperately needs new shoes, because her only pair are extremely shabby and have holes in the soles. The floor behind the counter where she works is of rough boards, and she constantly gets splinters in her feet. She tries repairing her shoes by cutting out cardboard insoles and inserting them which helps for a while until a rainstorm comes.

Each day, as she walks home after work, she passes a shoe store, which has a pair of shoes in the window that she particularly desires. Yet, when Eva asks her mother for money for a new pair of shoes, the poor woman always has some pressing bill that must be paid.

Lil (Jessie Arnold), the girl who works next to Eva at the five-and-dime, is better dressed, and Eva wonders why. She then notices that Lil has a large acquaintance of sporty young men. When Lil introduces Eva to an entertainer at a nearby cabaret named Charlie (William V. Mong), he repeatedly asks Eva to come to the cabaret, but she always declines.

One evening, as Eva watches her father sit and drink beer while she soaks her feet, as she usually does, in hot water, she makes a resolution. She puts on her best clothes and tells her mother that she is going to spend the night at Lil's house.

Eva goes to the cabaret, where she meets Charlie, and he takes her into a private room. The next day Eva returns home, wearing a new pair of shoes. Her mother holds Eva to her breast, and with a horrified expression says, "Sold out for a pair of shoes."

With the great success of *Shoes*, Lois Weber and MacLaren were told by Universal to continue together. Their next film was *Saving the Family* (1916) and then *Idle Wives* (1916), *Wanted—a Home* (1916), and *The Mysterious Mrs. M* (1917). At this point Katherine came to Hollywood where she spent a few weeks watching Mary work and then announced one night at the family dinner table that Mary should get more money. Furthermore, she decided that she would negotiate for Mary.

Katherine demanded of the rather cheap Universal that they increase Mary's salary about ten times. Universal refused, however, and Mary stayed home. Mary spent all of 1917 off the screen, as Katherine dickered with the studio. Yet, Katherine was able to get herself work at a fabulous salary and had her first acting assignment with Jack Pickford in *The Spirit of '17* (1918).

Katherine was Douglas Fairbanks' leading lady next in two subsequent films, *Headin' South* (1918) and *Mr. Fix-it* (1918), and William S. Hart's heroine in *Shark Monroe* (1918) and *Riddle Gawne* (1918). Cecil B. De Mille gave her the starring role in his 1918 remake of *The Squaw Man*.

Mary finally went back to work at Universal and began turning out a steady stream of charming pictures such as *The Model's Confession* (1918), *The*

Amazing Wife (1919), *The Unpainted Woman* (1919), *The Weaker Vessel* (1919), *Bonnie Bonnie Lassie* (1919), and *Rouge and Riches* (1920). Yet, Katherine again decided that Mary needed more money from Universal and kept her at home for another year. Mary never did return to Universal and instead drifted about as an independent player with her best role being the Queen opposite Douglas Fairbanks in *The Three Musketeers* (1921). Katherine, however, negotiated herself a million dollar contract at Associated First National and turned out a steady stream of hits from 1920 to 1923.

Katherine married two multimillionaires in succession after she retired. Mary married an English soldier in 1924 and lived with him in India until the early 1930's. She returned to Hollywood and worked as a bit player and lived in the same bungalow that she had bought in 1916 with her wages from *Shoes*, while Katherine lived less than a mile away in a huge mansion in Hancock Park, where she died in 1956. Mary still lives in her bungalow, even though it has been partially destroyed by a fire, and the city of Los Angeles is pressing her to vacate it.

Larry Lee Holland

SHORE LEAVE

Released: 1925
Production: Inspiration Pictures for Associated First National
Direction: John S. Robertson
Screenplay: Josephine Lovett; based on the play *Shore Leave: A Sea-goin'*
Comedy in Three Acts by Hubert Osborne
Titles: Agnes Smith
Cinematography: Roy F. Overbaugh and Stewart Nelson
Technical adviser: Commander Fitzhugh Green
Length: 7 reels/6,856 feet

Principal characters:
Bilge Smith	Richard Barthelmess
Connie Martin	Dorothy Mackaill
Bat Smith	Ted McNamara
Captain Martin	Nick Long
Mrs. Schuyler-Payne	Marie Shotwell
Mr. Schuyler-Payne	Arthur Metcalfe

Richard Barthelmess became a star while working for D. W. Griffith in, most significantly, *Broken Blossoms* (1919) and *Way Down East* (1920). He was the perfect Griffith hero: attractive without being starkly handsome, quiet and modest, yet still virile. In 1920, Barthelmess left the director to establish his own production company, Inspiration. He began this new phase of his career by starring in what is arguably his greatest role, the country boy who bests a trio of heavies and successfully delivers a load of mail, in *Tol'able David* (1921). While none of his subsequent films approached the stature of *Tol'able David*, most were slick, well-made audience pleasers, a typical example of which is *Shore Leave* (1925).

The film is based on Hubert Osborne's play *Shore Leave: A Sea-goin' Comedy in Three Acts*, which played on Broadway in 1922 with James Rennie and Frances Starr in the leading roles. The play was also the basis for the Fred Astaire-Ginger Rogers film *Follow the Fleet* (1936). Its plot, though, is as much a fairy tale as a comedy. In the story, Connie Martin (Dorothy Mackaill), an orphan, is a dressmaker in a small New England seaport. Her mother was an elephant trainer with a circus and her father a sea captain. She has inherited from the latter a love of the ocean. Bilge Smith (Richard Barthelmess), a carefree sailor, is on leave from his battleship. He and Connie meet, and the sailor flirts with the girl. Connie, who has never had a boyfriend, naïvely takes Bilge's attention seriously, and falls in love; but to the sailor, she is merely another girl like those found in every port.

Before his ship sails, Bilge promises to return to Connie, adding in passing that he someday hopes to be captain of his own vessel. Coincidentally,

Connie's father has left her the *Zanoma*, an old, broken-down schooner lying in the mud somewhere near the Ganges. The girl decides to transport it back to America and have it remodeled for Bilge. For capital, she sells a necklace given her by her mother that was originally a wedding gift from P. T. Barnum. She sends Captain Martin (Nick Long), an old friend of her father, to retrieve the *Zanoma*.

Unfortunately, Bilge never did tell Connie his first name. She does know that his surname is Smith, however, so she sets out to locate him, at first without success. Connie writes the Navy Department, only to learn that there are more than 2,600 Smiths in uniform. In fact, even Bilge's best friend, (Ted McNamara), has the same surname. Captain Martin arrives with the *Zanoma* and a valuable cargo, and Connie becomes instantly wealthy. The Atlantic fleet returns to port, and she decides to sponsor a party on board her ship for all the Smiths in the fleet. Bilge attends but hardly remembers Connie. When she tells him of her plans, he refuses to become involved with this "rich skirt." His pride will not allow him to be supported by Connie's wealth, and again, he sails away.

A few years pass, but Connie is still positive that Bilge will someday return to her. She places her schooner in trust for her first child—who can eventually own the property only if its name is Smith. She now no longer has title to the ship, and she is penniless. Bilge is discharged from the Navy after learning about Connie while in South America. He has lost all his pay, however, and arrives at the seaport on a stoker. Bilge ultimately discovers that he loves Connie, and they live happily ever after.

Shore Leave may be predictable and corny, but it is still a pleasant, well-directed and well-acted film. It was produced in cooperation with the United States Navy, with sequences shot aboard the U.S.S. *Arkansas*; forty sailors, commanded by two petty officers, appeared off the battleship in studio-shot scenes. *Shore Leave* received adequate reviews: while not an outstanding film, there is nothing in it really to criticize. Barthelmess is especially at ease as Bilge and is ably matched by Dorothy Mackaill's snappy performance.

The English-born Mackaill began her career as a London showgirl and came to Hollywood after appearing in the Ziegfeld Follies. She played leads in many silents, most memorably opposite Jack Mulhall, and also in a number of early sound films. She never became a top star, however, and retired from filmmaking in the late 1930's. Her name is known today only to film historians and buffs. The director of *Shore Leave*, John S. Robertson, is as equally obscure as Mackaill. His most famous credit is easily John Barrymore's memorable *Dr. Jekyl and Mr. Hyde* (1920). He also directed Barthelmess and Mackaill in *The Fighting Blade* (1923) and *Twenty-One* (1923). Robertson was signed by Barthelmess to an Inspiration contract and directed the actor in a series of features beginning with *The Bright Shawl* in 1923. Previously, he had appeared on the stage with Maude Adams and others and began his career in films in front of the camera as a villain at Vitagraph. He also directed Mary Pickford in the remake of *Tess of the Storm Country* (1922), Lillian Gish in *Annie Laurie* (1927), and Greta Garbo in *The Single Standard* (1929). Noted by contemporaries for his craftsmanship, his career lasted into the mid-1930's.

Barthelmess remained a star throughout the 1920's, with films such as *Shore Leave* assuring his popularity; the actor even won an Academy Award nomination in 1927/1928 for his performances in *The Patent Leather Kid* (1927) and *The Noose* (1928). He starred in films into the early 1930's, but his projects were no longer prestigious. Eventually, Barthelmess drifted into supporting and character roles, often playing heavies; perhaps his best-recalled film in the later part of his career was *Only Angels Have Wings* (1939). He retired from the screen in 1942. Most appropriate to his characterization in *Shore Leave*, he joined the Naval Reserve.

Rob Edelman

SHOW PEOPLE

Released: 1928
Production: Metro-Goldwyn-Mayer
Direction: King Vidor
Screenplay: Agnes Christine Johnston, Laurence Stallings, and
Wanda Tuchock (continuity)
Titles: Ralph Spence
Cinematography: John Arnold
Editing: Hugh Wynn
Length: 9 reels/7,453 feet

Principal characters:
Peggy Pepper	Marion Davies
Billy Boone	William Haines
Colonel Marmaduke Oldfish Pepper	Dell Henderson
André Telefair	Paul Ralli
Casting director	Tenen Holtz
Comedy director	Harry Gribbon
Dramatic director	Sidney Brace
Producer	Albert Conti
Peggy's maid	Polly Moran
Special guest appearances	John Gilbert
	Mae Murray
	Charles Chaplin
	Douglas Fairbanks
	Elinor Glyn
	William S. Hart
	Lew Cody
	Louella Parsons

"I couldn't act," Marion Davies once remarked, "I couldn't act, but the idea of silent pictures appealed to me because I couldn't talk either." The woman's charmingly phrased but harsh assessment of herself (although in reality she did stutter) was a view shared by many critics and film historians for quite a long time. In recent years, however, this opinion has been challenged by a critical assessment of Davies' career.

This reevaluation was necessary because Davies' screen work has been overshadowed by her offscreen role as mistress to one of America's most powerful men, newspaper magnate William Randolph Hearst. This offscreen relationship which lasted more than thirty years adversely affected critical views of her work. It was understandably difficult to be critically objective about a woman whose films were provided with consistently appreciative reviews by the Hearst newspapers. The critical shenanigans by the Hearst chain, combined with the fact that many of her films were unavailable for viewing for years, led to the impression that Davies was without talent. It also seemed that her personal life made infinitely more interesting copy than her films.

Her life was truly the stuff of which dreams (and films) are made. The daughter of an ambitious mother, she became a chorus girl, a film star, and "friend" of Hearst. She lived out a rags-to-riches story, a female Horatio Alger tale with an unfortunately realistic twist. Young male Horatio Algers might be expected to advance themselves through hard work and business sense, but young women were likely to be dependent on good looks and a winning personality to ensure that Prince Charming would recognize his Cinderella. In Davies' case, Prince Charming was royalty by American monetary standards, but he was also old, married, and the father of several children. Davies' Cinderella turned into a benign version of Madame de Pompadour. She became the object of public wonder, envy, and moral indignation.

If this were not sufficient to make any career dim beside the interest inherent in her private life, another event occurred that would make the popular conception of Davies take a turn for the worse. Orson Welles, RKO's newly acquired *enfant terrible*, decided to transform Davies' and Hearst's lives into the film *Citizen Kane* (1941). Welles amusingly, if somewhat perversely, denied the film's connection to their lives, although the RKO legal department was no doubt grateful to him for that small courtesy. Yet Welles knew, Hearst knew, and Davies knew, what everyone else in America knew, that Citizen Kane was Hearst, and that Susan Alexander Kane, an untalented opera singer and common-born attractive blond, was Welles' interpretation of Davies, from the "fixed reviews" to the misdirected ambition of her aging lover. Davies the actress was trapped by the legends emanating from *Citizen Kane* and from her own not so private life. Thus, the legends became fact.

Although some critics, such as Walter Kerr, do not view *Show People* (or other recently revived Davies' films) as providing sufficient revelation of her talent, others, such as Molly Haskell, strongly disagree. Even if *Show People* cannot be said to reveal Davies as a mature comic performer, it does offer a glimpse of what her talent was and what the future promise of that talent might have been had it been sufficiently nurtured. *Show People* decidedly refutes the position that Davies was as untalented as portrayed in *Citizen Kane*, or as incompetent as her severest critics, or she herself, declared her to be.

In 1928, the year that marked two of her best films, *The Patsy* and *Show People*, Davies was M-G-M's fifth biggest female star. Her half-million-dollar-a-year salary was picked up by Louis B. Mayer, in exchange, so it was rumored, for the Hearst empire's promotion of all M-G-M films and stars. The rumor was true; Hearst wanted Davies to be a great star. He also wanted her to be a very specific kind of star, one clearly in the tradition of Mary Pickford—demure, innocent, and unreproachably pure. His vision of Davies' screen *persona* was the opposite of the real Davies. The offscreen Davies was knowing but good-natured. She was an unpretentious, overimbibing, adored prankster and good time girl. It is one of the great tragedies of her career that the King Vidor comedies and a few moments in other films were her only opportunity to reveal some of the delightfully uninhibited and likeably off beat aspects of her personality. Hearst provided her with film vehicles such as *The Young Diana* (1922) and *When Knighthood Was in Flower* (1922), which he somehow reasoned would insure the purity of her image, in spite of the fact that a whole nation knew that she was his mistress. Davies' natural talents were comedic. She had a superb gift for mimicry. Her round, appealingly pretty but imperfect face and the loose plasticity of her body were the perfect raw material from which to shape a mature comic performer—but this was never to be. Davies was compliant to Hearst's wishes, and so she condemned herself to personal frustration, professional mediocrity, and a lingering sense of incompetence.

In 1928, Hearst persuaded Vidor to direct Davies. He had admired Vidor's direction of *The Big Parade* (1925) and certainly must have admired that film's enormous popularity as well. Davies was never at a loss for talented collaborators. Hearst always got the best, or at the very least, the cooperative second best. Metro executives and Vidor pleaded with Hearst to allow Davies to do comedy. Frances Marion, screenwriter on a number of Pickford and Davies films, had warned Hearst on more than one occasion that he was going to ruin Davies' career if he persisted in putting her in films that ignored her comic talents. Fortunately, this time Vidor and M-G-M were successful in their arguments, and Davies made *The Patsy*. The film was a box-office hit and Davies received good reviews, even in the non-Hearst papers. Following this triumph, Laurence Stallings, scenarist for the film, took a rather lackluster play owned by M-G-M and reworked it into a screenplay for *Show People*.

Show People satirizes Hollywood's mores and manners during the golden age of silent film. It is accurate, but too affectionate toward its subject to be very incisive. The film centers around a country girl's rise to fame and fortune in Hollywood, a topic utilized in many other films, most notably in the several versions of *A Star Is Born* (1937, 1952, and 1978). The film's opening title, "To hopeful hundreds there is a golden spot on the map called Hollywood," stands as the summation of the grand fantasy that Hollywood represented to America, and which Hollywood tried very hard to keep affixed to the American psyche. The Hollywood of *Show People* is the milieu of the Keystone cops, Mack Sennett bathing beauties, and unprepared innocents transformed into *nouveau riche* screen idols.

Silent film encouraged the expectation that anyone could be a star. Any shop girl from Brooklyn could dream of being one without worrying that her speech would alter her romantic film image. *Show People* reinforces the Hollywood myth that even the most untalented amateur can become a star through sheer strength of desire. The film's heroine, Peggy Pepper (Marion Davies) goes to Hollywood from the Georgia countryside. She is very green, but determined to be a serious dramatic actress. Her first audition at a studio casting office, however, results in the misinterpretation of her "serious moods" as a comic routine.

Peggy first arrives in Hollywood with her father, Colonel Marmaduke Old-fish Pepper (Dell Henderson), the stereotypical Southern Colonel. After her successful "comedy" audition at a studio, Peggy and her father lunch in the studio commissary with their last fifty cents. There, they meet an amiable young comic, Billy Boone (William Haines), who arranges for Peggy to meet a casting director at Comet Studios, a Mack Sennett-like enterprise where comedy reigns supreme. Peggy is hired and shows up for work unprepared for her role as second banana in a slapstick comedy. The director (Harry Gribbon) tells her she should not anticipate her acting. She learns the meaning of that instruction when she is greeted by seltzer water in the face (Hearst forbade the humiliation of Davies being pelted by pies). After her initial shock and anger, Peggy is comforted by Billy, who assures her that she was fine. Soon, she is making her way up the ranks of the studio's comedy performers, and her first big film is a hit. At the premiere, she absentmindedly snubs a little man who asks for her autograph, and when she discovers that he was Charlie Chaplin, she faints. Davies told of a similar real-life incident in which she once threw her mink to a doorman at a party. The "doorman" turned out to be the party's guest of honor, the King of Siam.

High Art Studio offers Peggy an opportunity to do "serious" drama, and Peggy accepts, despite her pact with Billy that they will advance to stardom together. At High Art she stars in costume dramas (just as Davies did) and takes advice on how to behave like a star from her leading man, André Telefair (Paul Ralli). André claims he is a count, but he is really an exwaiter. (It has been suggested that André bore a striking resemblance to John Gilbert in mannerisms and looks, but this may be an unfair observation as he also had some of the characteristics of other Hollywood leading men of the time.) Like Lou Telegen, whom he resembles in name, André has a fabricated autobiography. His claim to be royalty was a proliferating tendency in the Hollywood of the 1920's. There were hardly enough counts to go around for all the leading ladies who wanted to add a title to their names through marriage.

André convinces Peggy that she must assume a "new personality" with a "superior manner" to fit her new status as a dramatic star. Peggy changes her name to Patricia Pepoire, and André tells a reporter that she is a direct descendant of Robert E. Lee. Patricia affects the peculiar facial mannerisms of both Mae Murray and Gloria Swanson and takes up residence in a mansion complete with maid (Polly Moran). Her old friends and her father now are forgotten.

Peggy's transformation from comedy player to leading lady parallels the career of Swanson. Swanson started as a Sennett bathing beauty, graduated to Cecil B. De Mille class-"A" productions, and acquired the refined (by Hollywood standards) tastes and manners expected of a star. Along the way she divorced the husband she had acquired in her comedy days (the very plain Wallace Beery) and became the Countess de le Marquis de la Falais, the first Hollywood star to marry "royalty." Swanson, unlike Peggy, however, never gave up her acquired elegant *persona*. *Show People* assumes that audiences would rather be reassured that the original middle America values of family, hard work, and simplicity, are not lost in the glitter world of filmmaking. Peggy Pepper cannot remain Patricia Pepoire.

In one of the film's best scenes, the Hollywood of silent film is shown at its most appealing. In the open air, under the trees, productions grind away within a mere few feet of each other, a luxury allowed by the silence of the medium. Peggy is making a costume epic with André, when Billy, trailing a car filled with Keystone cops, drops behind his company and sights Peggy, whom he still loves. As he approaches, he is warned by a crew member that "Miss Pepoire's nerves ain't right today." While the prima donna prepares for a scene, Billy asks her to return to the Comet Studio troupe and to him, but Peggy cruelly dismisses him as "a cheap clown."

In accordance with viewers expectations, Peggy must get her comeuppance and she soon does, at a studio luncheon attended by many of Hollywood's most famous. (The luncheon resembles those Davies hosted in her fourteen room, seventy-five thousand-dollar "bungalow" that Hearst built for her at M-G-M.) Peggy is called into tne office of the producer (Albert Conti). He tells her that the exhibitors are complaining that the public does not want to see this new personality of hers—they want the old Peggy. Ironically, Davies faced a similar situation at M-G-M when exhibitors complained that they could only obtain a Greta Garbo film if they agreed to take a Davies picture. Peggy tells André of her problem, and he suggests that she marry him as a publicity stunt to boost her waning popularity. On the day of the wedding, Billy covertly enters Peggy's mansion. After a frantic encounter, Billy squirts Peggy (and André) with seltzer and manages to restore, not only Peggy's old sense of humor but also her common-clay personality. In the final scene of the film, Vidor directs Peggy and Billy in a romantic moment from a doughboy film much like *The Big Parade*. Peggy has learned her lesson.

Although Peggy is guilty of snubbing her old friends and adopting pretentious new habits, she is never accused of anything more serious than being a silly snob. *Show People* avoids dealing with the more unpleasant aspects of the Hollywood get-rich-quick syndrome. The film's view of Hollywood is really quite Pollyannaish, unlike that of Blake Edwards' recent scathing appraisal of Hollywood in *S.O.B.* (1981).

As often happens in life, the lessons offered by *Show People* were ignored by those who made the film. Hearst continued to push Davies into boring romantic dramas, even though *Show People* was a hit both critically and at the box office. In the 1930's, Hearst unsuccessfully tried to obtain *Marie Antoinette* and *The Barretts of Wimpole Street* as vehicles for Davies, but after both went to M-G-M production head Irving Thalberg's wife, Norma Shearer, Hearst decided that Davies had had enough of M-G-M, and he moved her to Warner Bros.

Hearst certainly was responsible for part of the reason for Davies' insecurity as a performer. She was incapable of fulfilling Hearst's dream of her becoming Pickford's successor. Davies' pronouncements that she "had no talent" and her recollection that "people got so tired of the ham Marion Davies that they would actually insult me" show that she wrongly assumed the entire burden of responsibility for her failures. She did not have the kind of talent that Hearst wanted her to have, and to Davies, that meant she had no talent at all. Davies was correct when she said she was "no Sarah Bernhardt," but *Show People* reveals that she had the potential to be something just as valuable in its own way—a very funny lady.

Gaylyn Studlar

THE SIN FLOOD

Released: 1921
Production: Frank Lloyd for Goldwyn Pictures Corporation
Direction: Frank Lloyd
Screenplay: J. G. Hawks; based on the play *The Deluge* by Frank Allen and
the Swedish play *Syndafloden* by Henning Berger
Cinematography: Norbert Brodin
Length: 7 reels/6,500 feet

Principal characters:
Billy Baer, the Broker's Clerk	Richard Dix
Poppy	Helene Chadwick
O'Neill	James Kirkwood
Swift	John Strippling
Fraser	Ralph Lewis
Sharpe	Howard Davies
Stratton	Will Walling
Nordling	William Orlamond
Charlie	Darwin Karr
Higgins	Otto Hoffman
The Drunk	L. H. King

Writing about *The Sin Flood* revives interest in one of the most proficient and most forgotten of Hollywood directors, Frank Lloyd. To describe a director as proficient is not necessarily the highest praise, for somehow proficient implies that the director's work lacks entertainment or excitement values. Part of the lack of interest in Lloyd's career is that many of his contemporaries felt his films did indeed lack both entertainment and excitement.

The great opera singer and actress Geraldine Farrar, whom Lloyd had directed in *The World and Its Women* (1920), once remarked that Lloyd "was better with ships than with people," and among Lloyd's prolific output are numerous films involving ships and battles at sea. The egocentric but critically acclaimed director Josef von Sternberg once patronizingly called Lloyd "a usually good commercial director." Both criticisms lack insight and, if not malicious, are certainly condescending and short-sighted. Yet Lloyd, a director who received two Academy Awards, one each for *The Divine Lady* (1928-1929) and *Cavalcade* (1932-1933), remains one of Hollywood's forgotten men.

Lloyd was born in Glasgow, Scotland, in 1885, and developed a love of the sea at an early age since his father was an engineer who installed turbine engines in ships. In 1909, Lloyd sailed for Canada where, for reasons never quite clear to him, he joined a traveling acting group which eventually brought him to the United States and California. From there, it was a natural progression to acting in films.

He turned to directing one-reelers in 1915 and in 1917 directed a much-praised feature—an authentic version of Charles Dickens' *A Tale of Two Cities*. That film and his subsequent production of *Les Miserables* (1918) earned Lloyd a reputation as a literary director and prompted his move to the Goldwyn Studios where he headed his own production unit. For Goldwyn, he directed *The World and Its Women* starring the beautiful Farrar. Although she did in later years make that crack about ships versus people, at least in her autobiography, *Such Sweet Compulsion* (1938), Farrar wrote: "My director was to be a distinguished gentleman who is still making fine and beautiful pictures today, Frank Lloyd."

In 1920, he directed the memorable *Madame X*, which contains Pauline Frederick's greatest screen performance. In 1921 came *The Sin Flood*, a film based on a play entitled *The Deluge*, which was an English translation of the Swedish play *Syndafloden*. The English version was presented on Broadway in 1917 by Arthur Hopkins and starred Pauline Lord, Henry E. Dixey, and a young Edward G. Robinson. Its run was a brief one and it was labeled an "artistic failure." *The Sin Flood* is a very somber psychological drama of regeneration very realistically directed by Lloyd. The story takes place in one set, basically: the claustrophobic atmosphere of a basement-level bar in a small saloon town on the Mississippi River. Gathered inside is a motley group of rapacious human beings—the dregs of mankind.

Comprising the group is Billy Baer (Richard Dix), the young broker's clerk who has graduated to the high finance world of cotton speculation by stealing money from his former employer. With him is his chorus-girl friend Poppy (Helene Chadwick), whom he has abandoned romantically now that he has risen in station and means. Also included is O'Neill (James Kirkwood), the unfrocked preacher who drinks too much; two unscrupulous cotton traders who hate each other, Fraser (Ralph Lewis) and Swift (John Strippling); Higgins (Otto Hoffman), a ham actor; and a drunken waterfront bum (L. H. King).

While they are in the cellar café, a severe storm comes up, causing the river to rise and threatening to burst the levee and flood the town and the cellar café. The telephone service is disconnected because of the storm and the ticker tape machine—so important to Billy and the cotton traders—stops working. Finally, the electricity goes off and they have only candlelight by which to see.

The bar owner closes the vault-like doors in an effort to protect the ten men and one woman inhabiting the shabby little bar, but all of them realize that the doors offer little protection if the levee breaks—the bar will be flooded and they will drown. If not, there is the good possibility of their dying from asphyxiation.

These dire circumstances awaken this dissolute group to their senses, and they begin to confront the fact that the end may be near. All they have is each other now, and it is time to repent. In this close-quartered, talky, and very theatrical situation—with director Lloyd carefully focusing the camera from face to face to create a sense of space and movement—the characters begin to go through a transformation. Billy and Poppy make up, pledge their love, and cling to each other; the two traders stop their quarreling and respond to each other as if they were long-lost brothers; the mercenary barkeeper serves free drinks, and the stingy bartender opens a free lunch counter. The reformed group joins hands in the brotherhood of love and awaits its fate.

Morning arrives, along with the quiet which marks the end of the storm. The barkeeper opens the heavy doors to let the sunshine in, and they discover that the levee did not burst and the streets are only flooded from the tumultuous storm. The rejoicing group celebrates its rebirth while the minister without a church marries the young couple.

This was heavy fare for the filmgoing public, and thus it was not a successful film, although the critics commended the performers. Helene Chadwick was cited for her portrayal of the doxy, but it was noted that the part was considerably "cleaned up" from that which it had been in the play. Richard Dix was especially complimented as he was an up-and-coming and promising newcomer. This was the sixth film appearance for Dix and his first important role. Critics praised his work, and he went on to become a popular leading man who was nominated for an Oscar for his performance in *Cimarron* (1931).

Ironically, *The Sin Flood* was the film chosen to open at the Capitol Theater in New York City on October 22, 1921. That date celebrated that theater's third anniversary, and in honor of the occasion, the stage show presentation was a musical extravaganza—a welcome respite for most of the audience.

Following *The Sin Flood*, Lloyd took his unit to Associated First National where his next film was the much more accessible *The Eternal Flame* (1922), a screen adaptation of Honoré de Balzac's *La Duchesse de Langeais* starring Norma Talmadge. He followed that with another interpretation of Dickens, *Oliver Twist* (1922), starring Jackie Coogan in the title role. In 1929, he directed the exquisite *The Divine Lady*, the story of Lord Nelson (Victor Varconi) and Lady Hamilton (Corinne Griffith), and while he did direct impressive sea-battle scenes, he emphasized the romance more than the French Revolutionary Wars and his direction earned him the Academy Award.

His second Academy Award came from directing *Cavalcade*, a sentimental tribute to the English spirit based on the play by Noel Coward. This was a dynastic saga of the Marryot family from the Boer War in 1899 through the death of Queen Victoria, the sinking of the Titanic, World War I, and on into the 1930's. Today the film seems a bit stodgy and dated but it nevertheless is representative of Lloyd's versatility.

Possibly his versatility, his ability to handle most any subject on the screen, is one of the reasons for Lloyd's obscurity. The remainder of his career is an astonishing testimony to his versatility and his craftsmanship. After *Cavalcade* he directed an excellent version of *Berkeley Square* (1933) starring Leslie Howard and Heather Angel and the same year directed *Hoopla* with Clara Bow. He was once again nominated for an Academy Award for his expert "entertaining and exciting" direction of *Mutiny on the Bounty* (1935) starring Charles Laughton, Clark Gable, and Franchot Tone. This is considered his best film by many; it is certainly his most popular, and it remains a favorite even today.

Lloyd's output continued to vary and please: *Under Two Flags* (1936) starring Ronald Colman and Claudette Colbert; *Maid of Salem* (1937), starring Claudette Colbert and Fred MacMurray; and *If I Were King* (1938), starring Ronald Colman and Frances Dee. His last exceptional film was the wartime programmer *Blood on the Sun* (1945) starring James Cagney and Sylvia Sidney. Lloyd's legacy is full of artistic merit and value and not a few great films. He is a director who should not be forgotten.

Ronald Bowers

THE SINGLE STANDARD

Released: 1929
Production: John S. Robertson for Metro-Goldwyn-Mayer
Direction: John S. Robertson
Screenplay: Josephine Lovett; based on the novel of the same name by Adela
    Rogers St. Johns
Titles: Marion Ainslee
Cinematography: Oliver T. Marsh
Editing: Blanche Sewell
Art direction: Cedric Gibbons
Costume design: Adrian
Music: William Axt
Length: 8 reels/6,574 feet

> *Principal characters:*
> Arden Stuart .... Greta Garbo
> Packy Cannon .... Nils Asther
> Tommy Hewlett ....Johnny Mack Brown
> Mercedes ....Dorothy Sebastian
> Ding Stuart .... Lane Chandler
> Anthony Kendall .... Robert Castle
> Mr. Glendenning ....Mahlon Hamilton
> Mrs. Glendenning .... Kathlyn Williams

The Single Standard is neither a great film nor Greta Garbo's best, but it is a curious one in her career for a variety of reasons. This was the twelfth of her thirteen silent films and was only the second one in which the enigmatic and mysterious Swede had played an American woman—an essentially good woman, as she had in *Wild Orchids* (1929), the film she made prior to *The Single Standard*.

Another point of interest is the manner in which screenwriter Josephine Lovett incorporated in her adaptation of the novel by Adela Rogers St. Johns, upon which the film was based, numerous subtle references to the real-life Garbo. Both Lovett and St. Johns were friends of Garbo and the film's heroine flaunts convention in ways not unlike the offscreen Garbo did in those early years in Hollywood and continues to do today. While she had only been in America three and a half years, Garbo's obsession with privacy had already become a substantial part of her myth, so much so that the name of the yacht owned by the character played by Nils Asther in *The Single Standard* is *All Alone*.

Still another factor regarding *The Single Standard* was the gradual "loosening up" which Garbo had been revealing in her most recent screen performances. In *A Woman of Affairs*, *Wild Orchids*, and *The Single Standard*, all released in 1929, critics were noticing that Garbo was beginning to appear relaxed on screen. One reason for her growing ease was the presence of her countryman Nils Asther, who was her co-star in *Wild Orchids* and *The Single Standard*.

The most significant aspect of this film in relation to Garbo's all-too-brief and unique career is that it might never have been made with her at all, because at this time, based upon many complications, including the death of her mentor Mauritz Stiller, Garbo had threatened to leave the Hollywood "factory" of M-G-M and return to Sweden and retirement. She did return to Sweden in late 1928, for the first time since arriving in this country, after having completed *Wild Orchids*, but not before M-G-M's Louis B. Mayer had ordered several retakes which she refused to do, resulting in her being suspended from M-G-M as she left the country.

Stiller was the director who cast Garbo as Countess Elizabeth Dohna in *The Atonement of Gosta Berling* in 1923, and from their very first meeting, they shared a close friendship which would last until his death. Stiller recognized the potential in this beautiful, shy, and then somewhat overweight girl, and Garbo was completely trusting in deferring to all decisions he made regarding her career.

When Mayer signed Stiller to come and direct in Hollywood, Garbo became a part of the package possibly because Stiller refused to leave without her. Unfortunately, Stiller's attempts at working in Hollywood were aborted— M-G-M took him off Garbo's *The Temptress* (1926) and replaced him with Fred Niblo—and when Stiller returned to his homeland, while Garbo's career flourished here, it was the beginning, say her friends, of her lifelong melancholia.

While nearing completion of *Wild Orchids*, Garbo received a wire informing her that her beloved Stiller had died on November 8, 1928, at age forty-five. Garbo had already made plans to spend her first Christmas in Sweden since coming to the United States in 1925, and now more than ever, she wanted to leave. She asked Mayer to allow her to stop work at once, but Mayer refused, saying she owed it to the studio. She responded by saying, "You will have something dead on the screen. It will have no life."

Asther recalls that on the day she received the wire informing her of Stiller's death, they were working on the set, and her reaction of shock was such that he thought she was going to faint. Garbo left the set and went to her dressing room. Several minutes later she sent word for Asther to come see her, and as he approached the dressing room, he heard a strange kind of laughter which was obviously Garbo. When he entered, she showed him a perfume bottle which contained a small amount of brandy (this was during Prohibition) and which was accompanied by a note which read: "Dear Greta, My sympathy in your sorrow. But the show must go on. Louis B. Mayer." Later, Mayer had the bad taste to tell her how he had painstakingly filled the bottle with a teaspoon.

Finally, on December 3, 1928, the day of her departure east on The Chief, Garbo received a telegram from Mayer in her train compartment demanding that she delay her departure for the few retakes on *Wild Orchids* or suffer the consequences. She refused to comply with his demands, left on her vacation, and was suspended, without salary.

During her visit in Sweden she visited Stiller's home and met with his executors to find that he had left one-half of his ninety-five-thousand-dollar estate to her. When she returned to the United States in March, 1929, she said she would like to play Joan of Arc or "something unusual, something that had not been done before." By this time, her contractual differences with M-G-M had been diplomatically resolved, but the assignment they gave her was not Joan of Arc, it was *The Single Standard*, co-starring Asther.

The character of Arden Stuart which Garbo portrayed in *The Single Standard* was that of an impetuous young San Francisco debutante who flaunts convention and seeks to live her life as a modern "free soul." Arden rebels against the strict code of the day which allows the male in society to have his married home life and yet have his romances on the side with no reprimand from his peers. This duplicity and hypocrisy angers Arden, and she embarks upon an affair with her chauffeur. He, however, is aware of the impropriety of their romance and commits suicide to avoid a scandal.

The disillusioned Arden takes a nocturnal stroll in the rain, and here again the writer inserts references to the offscreen Garbo as at one point she is asked by a passerby why she is alone, to which she replies in typical Garboese: "I am walking alone because I want to be alone."

To seek protection from the rain, Arden enters a Telegraph Hill art gallery where she meets Packy Cannon (Nils Asther), a handsome, ex-Navy heavyweight boxer, idealist, and painter. She leaves the gallery with him, and he takes her to his yacht in the beautiful misty San Francisco harbor. The yacht is named *All Alone*, and the next morning they sail off to an idyllic interlude in the South Seas.

Arden and Packy sun and swim (and kiss) underwater like two free spirits, and Arden finds love and contentment for the first time in her life. They return to San Francisco, but Packy now shatters Arden's reverie by saying that he must go to the Orient on business for an indeterminate length of time. Bidding her good-bye, he says, "If one doesn't want happiness to die, one must relinquish it voluntarily."

She returns to her old social set to find that most of her friends now think of her as an outcast. She goes about as if nothing has happened and is courted by her former beau, the rich Tommy Hewlett (Johnny Mack Brown). Tommy begs her to marry him but she says no, claiming that one day Packy will return to reclaim her. Tommy persists, however, and she reluctantly relents, marries him, and bears him a son.

Three years later, Packy returns, older, haggard, and weary from eating his heart out over the love he cannot forget. He pleads with her to run away with him again, and she at first agrees. Tommy, jealous of her love for Packy, threatens suicide if she goes, and Arden, aware of her obligations as a mother, changes her mind at the last minute, and the film ends with husband and wife rocking their son in his cradle.

This is a slight film but a well-acted one with its "new woman" message marred only by the mandatory happy ending. Garbo looks smashing in her Adrian gowns and loose flowing hair, and the love scenes on the yacht with Asther are exquisitely erotic and refreshing. This film also displays some of the screen's most breathtaking Art Deco set designs by M-G-M's Cedric Gibbons.

The year 1929 was the transitional year for sound films, and *The Single Standard* was played with a synchronized musical score by Dr. William Axt in those theaters so equipped. Future star Joel McCrea, who had doubled for Garbo on horseback in *The Torrent* (1926), had a small role in this film in which he dances briefly with Garbo. The handsome novice was so flustered that the scene had to be reshot several times.

The Single Standard was hardly a film to cause great critical praise, but Pare Lorentz, a rarely quoted serious critic, wrote a most curious review in *Judge*, which read:

> For the first time since she hit these shores, grim Greta Garbo has done a good piece of work. In *The Single Standard* she actually walks, smiles, and acts. I have never been able to understand the universal palpitation that has followed her slow but stupid appearance on the great American screen—sex appeal, unfortunately, is a matter of opinion. Nevertheless the lady can, and does, act in her latest movie, and the fact that she is homely and awkward while so engaged only makes me like her more.

Ronald Bowers

THE SINKING OF THE LUSITANIA

Released: 1918
Production: Winsor Z. McCay; released by Universal-Jewel
Direction: Winsor Z. McCay
Assistant: John A. Fitzsimmons
Screenplay: Winsor Z. McCay
Cinematography: Winsor Z. McCay
Animation: Winsor Z. McCay
Length: 1 reel

Although the filmmaking career of Winsor Z. McCay is shrouded in obscurity—partially because of the fact that McCay never sought commercial recognition for his work—there is no dispute concerning his position as a founding father of animation. The son of a lumberman, McCay was born in 1871, and as a child was said to have exhibited drawing skills. One of his earliest jobs found him painting posters and billboards for traveling carnivals and circuses, and before the age of twenty, he was a staff artist for the *Cincinnati Commercial Tribune*.

Impressed with his work, the *New York Herald* and *New York Evening Telegram* lured him away from Cincinnati and in 1903, McCay was working in Manhattan. At this point, he created his most memorable comic strips—some of which eventually were filmed—including "Hungry Henrietta," "Little Sammy Sneeze," "Dreams of a Rarebit Fiend," and what is generally regarded as his greatest comic strip, "Little Nemo in Slumberland."

The success of these strips and McCay's artistic format (including the positioning of the figures within the "frames" of the comic strip) gave impetus to the filmmaking that followed. Edwin S. Porter did a film version of McCay's "Dreams of a Rarebit Fiend" in 1906. By 1907, McCay himself was at work on an animation of *Little Nemo*, the first of his ten animated films that were released between 1911 and 1921.

Among these films are *Gertie* (1914), which features a beguiling brontosaurus who was, in effect, the first cartoon "star," and McCay's 1918 film *The Sinking of the Lusitania*. Perhaps McCay's most distinctive animation, because it is his only re-creation of a historical event (the other films were based on fantasy), *The Sinking of the Lusitania* also represents his first animation on celluloid.

McCay spent twenty-two months working on the film, which utilized twenty-five thousand drawings photographed one at a time against a "moving" sea. At the time of its release, on July 20, 1918, *The Sinking of the Lusitania* was the only existing documentation of the 1915 event that eventually assured United States involvement in World War I. The incident was not recorded by still cameras, and newsreels did not exist at the time.

When viewed today, *The Sinking of the Lusitania* is not without propagandist strains. Indeed, the closing title card reads: "The man who fired the shot was decorated for it by the Kaiser!—AND YET THEY TELL US NOT TO HATE THE HUN." Overriding the anti-German sentiment of its day, however, is the film's animation, which stuns with its artistry, especially considering that McCay's initial animation preceded Walt Disney's work by some two decades.

Opening with the title card, "An amazing moving pen picture by Winslow McCay," *The Sinking of the Lusitania* carries a brief live-action segment in which McCay (labeled the "originator and inventor of Animated Cartoons") decides to draw a record "of the crime that shocked humanity." He is given details about the ship and the sinking, as are the film's viewers.

On May 17, 1915, the English Cunard passenger liner *Lusitania* was en route to Liverpool from New York, when it was torpedoed by a German submarine. The tragedy occurred off the coast of Ireland. Within eighteen minutes, the ship had sunk, taking with it 1,198 lives, among them 124 Americans.

As the film's *Lusitania* sets sail, with the Statue of Liberty in sight, viewers are informed (via titles) that "Germany, which had already benumbed the world with its wholesale killing, then sent its instrument of crime to perform a more treacherous and cowardly offense."

Suddenly, a submarine appears (there are small figures moving atop it) and later submerges. It cruises near the *Lusitania*, its periscope ominously peering above the waves. The next scene takes place underwater, as two fish—bearing alarmed expressions—watch an approaching torpedo. It hits the ship, and the great sinking begins.

Through title cards, the viewer learns that those who perished included "men of worldwide prominence." Photographs accompany the names of some of the victims, among them Alfred G. Vanderbilt, "the multi-millionaire American sportsman," and Charles Frohman, "the world's foremost theatrical manager." Frohman, the audience is told, "faced death smiling and uttered to those about him, just before the end came, his immortal observation that 'Death is but a beautiful adventure of Life.'"

These literary dramatics are followed by another journey into the water, where the ship is struggling. The scene then moves above water, to find lifeboats being lowered. Just then, however, a second torpedo hits. "This was the death blow," the title reads. Now a massive explosion literally fills the screen, with belching smoke ballooning outward and bodies tumbling from the decks. There are myriad angles showing the ship making her descent, all of which are extremely impressive; there are effective glimpses of bodies bobbing helplessly against the waves.

In the aftermath of one last, angry explosion, the ship plunges downward. Viewers follow its course past bubbles and finally into total blackness. The last evocative scene is of a graceful woman, in flowing clothing, fighting unsuccessfully against the waters. There is a baby in her arms, and she holds it upward trying to prolong its life, but the sea soon envelopes them both. The symbolic mother and child gives the film its last, lingering image.

In creating *The Sinking of the Lusitania*, McCay used a stationary background which was not redrawn with every frame. Assisting him with the film was John A. Fitzsimmons, then a teenage neighbor of McCay, who was trusted with the job of "moving" the waves and water. Much of what is known about McCay's filmmaking techniques is derived from Fitzsimmon's memories. During the 1970's, a number of film historians attempted to trace the mysterious career of McCay and Fitzsimmons, who was then in his eighties, proved to be an agreeable interview subject.

As for McCay himself, he told *Cartoon and Movie Magazine* in the April, 1927, issue that

> The part of my life of which I am proudest is the fact that I was one of the first men in the world to make animated cartoons. . . . I went into the business and spent thousands of dollars developing this new art. It required considerable time, patience and careful thought—timing and drawing the pictures . . . this is the most fascinating work I have ever done—this business of making cartoons live on the screen.

A man who pursued filmmaking for the sake of the art, with no apparent moneymaking goals, McCay frequently appeared with his films on the vaudeville circuit. Prior to his days of filmmaking, McCay toured vaudeville with his presentation, "The Seven Ages of Man." Against a blackboard the artist revealed his skills as an illustrator, and, according to *Variety*, the show found him creating faces "from the cradle to old age, never once altering the original outline of his subjects' faces."

Because McCay liked to appear with his films on stage, he had contractual demands that ultimately impaired the possibility of wide distribution. For example, McCay's second film, *The Story of a Mosquito* (1912), could not be shown in the United States apart from his vaudeville act, but the film could be widely circulated in Europe. For this reason, McCay is better known in Europe than in his own country.

The most famous and novel vaudeville outing, for McCay, involved the film, *Gertie. The Moving Picture World* called *Gertie* "the greatest comedy film ever made! Gertie is a tango dancer—She is as big as the Flatiron building and eats 'em alive—from whales to elephants!" *Gertie* made use of a then-unique detailed background landscape and consisted of some sixteen thousand drawings. (Fitzsimmons also assisted on this project.) In showing this film, McCay worked in tandem with the mischievous dinosaur. Dressed as an animal tamer, and brandishing a whip, McCay would issue "commands" to his screen creation. To the delight of the audiences, Gertie followed his commands. Especially popular was the point at which McCay tossed an apple upward; it continues on the screen in animated form and is caught by the precocious Gertie. An undeniably charming screen character, Gertie winked at audiences and was even given to frequent laughing fits. At this point, she stands on her back legs and uses her forelegs to clutch at her shaking stomach. It is not difficult to see how this figure became the first "star" of animated films.

McCay's work on the vaudeville circuit was eventually affected by contractual disputes with the Hearst newspapers, for whom he was then working. Thus, the filmmaker pulled back from vaudeville appearances, and his films went into commercial distribution.

Noted for their advanced animation techniques (unlike other animation of the era, McCay's drawings did not have a "jerky" movement—instead the images flowed smoothly), McCay's fantasy works are also highly imaginative. They are dominated by fanciful creatures and wondrous happenings. In *The Pet*, for example, part of the *Dreams of a Rarebit Fiend* (1921) series, a pet grows into an out-of-control monster and devours everything in its path. McCay's film career, which began when he exhibited *Little Nemo* (1911) at New York's Colonial Theater, includes *The Story of a Mosquito, Gertie, The Sinking of the Lusitania, The Centaurs, Flip's Circus, Gertie on Tour* (1918), and three films from *The Dreams of a Rarebit Fiend* series: *The Pet, Bug Vaudeville*, and *Flying House*.

Although he never attained commercial merit for his innovative filmmaking, McCay was a recognized celebrity during his lifetime, which ended in 1934. He was sixty-three at the time of his death.

Pat H. Broeske

SMOULDERING FIRES

Released: 1925
Production: Universal
Direction: Clarence Brown
Screenplay: Sada Cowan, Howard Higgin, Melville Brown; based on a story
  by Margaret Deland, Sada Cowan, and Howard Higgin
Cinematography: Jackson Rose
Editing: Edward Schroeder
Art direction: Leo E. Kuter and E. E. Sheeley
Length: 8 reels

> *Principal characters:*
> Jane Vale .... Pauline Frederick
> Dorothy Vale .... Laura La Plante
> Robert Elliott .... Malcolm McGregor
> Scotty .... Tully Marshall
> Lucy .... Wanda Hawley
> Kate Brown .... Helen Lynch
> Mugsy .... George Cooper

Clarence Brown signed a contract to produce and direct feature films for Universal in 1923, he made five pictures before the end of 1925 that were all exceptionally good entertainment. The first three were *The Acquittal* (1923), a courtroom drama with Claire Windsor; *The Signal Tower* (1924), a very fast-moving, strong railroad melodrama with Virginia Valli; and *Butterfly* (1924), a romantic drama with Laura La Plante. He came to the attention of John Considine at Joseph Schenck's company with his next two in 1925, *The Goose Woman* and *Smouldering Fires*, both so exceptional that Schenck signed him to direct Rudolph Valentino in *The Eagle* (1925) and Norma Talmadge, Schenck's wife, in *Kiki* (1926). Offers came in from all the other studios, but Brown elected to go to M-G-M where his first assignment was *Flesh and the Devil* (1926), with John Gilbert, Lars Hanson, and Greta Garbo. From then on, he stayed exclusively at M-G-M, with one success after another until the 1950's when he retired to Palm Springs.

It was only by accident that Considine saw *Smouldering Fires* at the Forum in Los Angeles, California. He came in after the picture had started and missed the credits. He was so impressed with the film that he thought it must be an Ernst Lubitsch production. Then came the end-of-the-picture credit— "A Clarence Brown production directed by Clarence Brown." He telephoned Brown the next day. Brown was in the midst of directing *The Goose Woman*, and Considine immediately started talking about a contract. Eventually, they came to terms at $5,000 a film, a major step up for Brown who only received $12,500 for all five films that he had done for Carl Laemmle at Universal.

Smouldering Fires is a very intelligent triangle: two sisters who both love the same young man. Jane Vale (Pauline Frederick), at forty, is the perfect prototype of the successful American businesswoman. She owns and manages a factory that makes children's clothes and toys. At the weekly meeting of the departmental heads, she is pleased to note that Robert Elliott (Malcolm McGregor), a young man who she has recently hired, is very sharp, and has good, fresh ideas about the promotion of certain items. She congratulates him on his progressive thinking and makes him her private assistant manager, much to the chagrin of some of the older men in her employment.

Robert and Jane see more of each other and enjoy each other's company, oblivious of the fact that all her employees are gossiping idly about how Miss Vale's appearance is changing. Her clothes are no longer off-the-rack tailored suits, and she has become neatly coiffed and is actually pretty for a woman who is "a forty-year-old spinster." Elliott is aware of some of the crude jokes that are being made among the employees, and to express his gratitude for all that she has done for him and to command respect on her behalf, he proposes marriage and is sincerely delighted when she accepts.

Before the wedding, Dorothy Vale (Laura La Plante) comes from her university studies to stay with her sister. Immediately upon meeting Robert, she suspects his motives in the relationship. He is a good fifteen years younger than Jane, and Dorothy is confident that he is only marrying her sister for money and social position. He is, she thinks, an operator, and Dorothy has nothing but contempt for him. Robert is aware of how much she dislikes him, but he tries to ignore her feelings.

Robert and Jane are married despite Dorothy's feelings, and he does everything to make Jane happy, because he holds her in great esteem. She soon becomes aware of the difference in their ages, and she tries to make herself more attractive. She brushes her hair differently, uses creams and beauty emollients, but she cannot stay the advances of time. She is, worst of all, forty years old in her thinking.

The three of them go on a holiday to Yosemite. Jane claims that the mountain climbing is too strenuous for her, so she sends Robert and Dorothy on while she settles in a hammock contentedly to read. Dorothy and Robert climb to the top overlooking the great panorama of Yosemite, and Dorothy begins to realize that she has been wrong in her judgment of Robert's character. He takes a step toward her, and she automatically steps backward without looking, nearly falling off the mountain. Robert catches hold of her and draws her slowly from the perilous edge. They look at each other and realize that they are in love. Being the type of people that they are, however, they both feel wretched about the situation.

There is a party that night, and Jane realizes that she shares no common interests with her husband's and sister's friends. Upstairs, Jane looks down on them standing together unhappily in the patio, the glass doors of which are open. Jane comes down, putting a on brave face, but then she pauses, for their images are reflected in the glass doors, and she overhears every word they say. They are both lamenting that there is nothing to be done decently. He says that it is impossible to keep pretending they are indifferent, when he knows how much Dorothy cares for him, and she must know that he loves her.

Jane draws back against the wall, trying to gain control of herself. She realizes that to go on with the marriage now would be farcical, and she stages the greatest scene of her life. She enters the room laughing almost hysterically, confessing that her marriage to Robert is a joke. Why bother to confess that she is too old for him and he is too young for her, when it is so evident? She will apply for a divorce tomorrow. She kisses them both fondly and says they have all been fools, caught in some midsummer madness, but instead of celebrating a happy marriage, why not celebrate the happy divorce that is forthcoming? Dorothy has difficulty believing her sister, but Jane is a good actress. She embraces them both, and looks offscene with tears that she tries to pretend are happy ones of relief.

This was one of the first marital dramas with real originality in its denouement. Everything is polite, everybody is well-mannered, and yet the drama is believable and holds interest. Nobody makes a scene, and yet Jane, whose heart is broken, is able to take them in her arms as if they were her children, and she tries not to think of how lonely the years ahead will be.

Perfectly cast and perfectly played, *Smouldering Fires* is a well-knit drama wherein people behave like civilized human beings. That there is so much power in this simple story is a tribute to the director. Brown avoids maudlin sentiment and turns away from melodrama. This becomes a real drama about very real people caught in emotions they cannot ignore.

DeWitt Bodeen

THE SNOB

Released: 1924
Production: Metro-Goldwyn-Mayer
Direction: Monta Bell
Screenplay: Monta Bell; based on the novel of the same name by Helen Reimensnyder Martin
Cinematography: André Barlatier
Editing: Ralph Lawson
Art direction: Cedric Gibbons
Costume design: Sophie Wachner
Length: 7 reels/6,495 feet

Principal characters:
Eugene Curry	John Gilbert
Nancy Claxton	Norma Shearer
Herrick Appleton	Conrad Nagel
Dorothy Rensheimer	Phyllis Haver
Mrs. Leiter	Hedda Hopper
Mrs. Curry	Margaret Seddon

In the early 1920's, John Gilbert frequently played the role of "the man you love to hate." When he finally signed with M-G-M, he got off to a good start with the romantic role in *He Who Gets Slapped* (1924), followed by Elinor Glyn's Russian hero in *His Hour* (1924); but he then chose to play a lead that was definitely antiheroic in *The Snob*. In that film, he played Eugene Curry, a young teacher whom most people like initially, but who has so many flaws in his character that eventually they withdraw from him. Curry is afraid that people will discover that the members of his family are very nondescript, even crudely mannered Mennonites of whom he is very ashamed. His ambition to rise in society by any means is very evident, and to this aim, he cultivates people whose acquaintance lends him distinction. He will do anything for money, and does, even at the risk of being thought insincere. He is totally amoral, and it would seem that after knowing him, no one would be his friend or lover.

He meets Nancy Claxton (Norma Shearer), who has become a teacher on the faculty of the small Pennsylvania college, where Curry also has a post. He seems to be as charmingly sincere as Nancy believes him to be, and he always makes a favorable, well-tailored appearance. He does not know that Nancy has chosen this teaching post because she welcomes obscurity at the moment, her father having been the victim of a scandalous murder. She is hiding from all close friends and hopes that a semester of teaching in so inconspicuous a college will make people forget her recent past. She is attracted to Curry and welcomes his attentions, deliberately closing her eyes to his flaws.

Soon after she meets him, however, he gets a post as a junior professor in another, more restricted, small college. He kisses Nancy good-bye and goes off to his new post, where he meets Herrick Appleton (Conrad Nagel), who once was very fond of Nancy. He does not think much of Herrick until he is told that Herrick Appleton belongs to an old Boston family. Typically impressed, he hurries at once to Herrick's studio to say, "So you are one of the Boston Appletons. Why didn't you tell me?"

Curry then meets Dorothy Rensheimer (Phyllis Haver), whose grandfather is very influential at the college. He courts Dorothy, who is not averse to being admired, and she, at his instigation, prevails upon her grandfather to give him the post of headmaster. Curry then learns that Nancy is not well and goes down to see her. She is elated to see him, and when he proposes to her, she accepts.

Curry then writes a letter to Dorothy telling her that he was tricked into the marriage. When Curry brings his bride back to the campus, Dorothy is very snobbish to her, but when he indicates that he hopes to continue his relationship with Dorothy, she is no longer angry. Meanwhile, Nancy and Appleton meet and renew their friendship. He lets her know that he has always been fond of her and regrets that Curry got to her before he was able to tell her how sorry he was for her father's death. Nancy and Appleton see each other often when she learns that she is going to have a child. One day, quite by accident, Nancy sees the letter that her husband had written to Dorothy, explaining why he had to get married, and is so shocked and hurt by his lies that she becomes ill, causing her to give birth to a stillborn child.

Suddenly apprehensive and afraid that Nancy has learned too much about him, Curry grows very contrite and asks her for forgiveness. Nancy now understands what a lying snob her husband is, however, so she tells him that she is divorcing him as soon as she can so that she can marry Appleton. Curry is then horrified to learn that Nancy is really one of the richest women in the state. All this time he was married to a real heiress and did not know it. He goes to try to get some sympathy from Dorothy, but she pays little attention to him while she powders her face before going out with a new and very handsome boyfriend. At the end of the film, Curry finds himself alone, without a friend in the world.

Later in 1924, Gilbert made *Wife of the Centaur*, again for King Vidor, playing with Aileen Pringle as the temptress and Eleanor Boardman as the understanding wife he ignores. Vidor enjoyed working with Gilbert, and he then gave the actor the best and most sympathetic role he ever had in *The Big Parade* (1925). Gilbert was fortunate because with another selfish hero, his career might have been over. As it was, he went from *The Big Parade* to another romantic film for Vidor, *La Bohème* (1926), with Lillian Gish, and then on to another adventurous one, again for Vidor, the costume swash-buckler *Bardelys the Magnificent* (1926). Gilbert, by that time, was hardly the "man you love to hate." He enjoyed nothing but adulation from 1924 until he did his first two talkies, *His Glorious Night* (1929) and *Redemption* (1930). He had just signed a new contract with the studio, but after the failure of those first two talkies, studio head Louis B. Mayer offered to settle with him so that he and the studio would be free of him. Gilbert, however, was deter-mined to hold the studio to its contract for seven more pictures. They were all second-rate except for two: *Downstairs* (1933), for which he wrote the story, and *Queen Christina* (1933), in which he supported Greta Garbo at her request. The latter film did a lot to restore him in the eyes of the public, for he was romantic, and there was obviously nothing wrong with his voice. The rumor that he had an unappealing, high-pitched voice had been a dirty trick that the sound department played on him so that he could be sabotaged by Louis B. Mayer.

Downstairs was an excellent film, but if Eugene Curry had been a thor-oughgoing snob, the hero in *Downstairs* was an untrustworthy villain, beau-tifully played with a droll sense of humor, but with absolutely no attempt at sympathy. One welcomed seeing that character get his comeuppance, just as one rejoiced when Eugene Curry eventually did. Although neither Gilbert nor Erich Von Stroheim (who hated Gilbert because he was forced to use him in *The Merry Widow*, 1925) would ever have played brothers, they were, on the screen at least, of a similar unsympathetic type in many of their prominent films.

DeWitt Bodeen

SNOW WHITE

Released: 1916
Production: Famous Players-Laskey for Paramount
Direction: J. Searle Dawley, with Winthrop Ames
Screenplay: Winthrop Ames; based on the fairy tale by the Brothers Grimm
Cinematography: H. Lyman Broening
Length: 6 reels

Principal characters:
Snow White .... Marguerite Clark
Prince Florimond .... Creighton Hale
Queen Brangomar/
Mary Jane .... Dorothy G. Cumming
Berthold, the hunstsman .... Lionel Braham
Witch Hex .... Alice Washburn

It is said in Hollywood that one young man who sat in the darkened motion-picture theaters during the era of the silent film was so affected by one particular film he saw that it influenced his later works. His name was Walt Disney, and when he did his Oscar-winning animated version of *Snow White* (1937), he admitted that he had never forgotten the seven dwarfs and the pretty little dark-haired girl, Marguerite Clark, who created the role of Snow White in the theater and for film. He patterned his characters from his memories of that picture. Clark had first done *Snow White* on the stage for two seasons in New York as a play devised and written for her by Winthrop Ames, and theatergoers, old and young, never forgot her. Her film version was also done with the assistance of Ames, who worked in association with Clark's film director, J. Searle Dawley, in presenting it as a Famous Players' screen production.

It was inevitable that Clark would do her version of *Snow White* as a film attraction, and it became her sixteenth production as a Famous Players/Paramount star. In *The Moving Picture World* review by George Blaisdell, he states that "Marguerite Clark comes into her own in *Snow White*, the Famous Players/Paramount release of Christmas Day (1916). *Snow White* may not have been made for her, but easily it may be said that she was made for *Snow White*."

It was a film done with a great deal of imagination and affection, and it represented the kind of comedy that Disney was to use in his animation, especially in the scenes depicting the dwarfs in their relation to the little princess who has sought refuge with them. Adding to the charming effects in the film, the subtitles were presented in illuminated lettering. The exteriors in the forest were all filmed in the state of Georgia, taking advantage of the Spanish moss that drips from the trees, great and small, lending a shadowy magical illusion to the scene.

The fade-in sequence is also magical and has lovely comic touches. Santa Claus climbs out of the fireplace, and from his bag he takes a beautiful selection of dolls, which he sets up on a table. A little girl runs down the stairs in her nightgown, peeks at him as he works, and then runs upstairs. The minute Santa disappears, the dolls are transformed into living miniature humans.

There is a dissolve to Babyland, where a giant stork comes bearing an appeal from the Queen. The appeal goes directly to the dispenser of heirs and heiresses, and a baby is selected and given to the stork, who loses its way in a blinding snowstorm, but safely delivers the baby, Snow White, in the nick of time.

The mother of Snow White dies, however, and the little princess is reared to maturity by Mary Jane (Dorothy G. Cumming), a lady-in-waiting, who is also the ugliest woman in the kingdom. Mary Jane aspires to be the Queen and seeks out the old witch, Hex (Alice Washburn), who promises her that if she will give her own beating heart to Hex, she will become the fairest in the land. Mary Jane gives up her heart and is transformed into a most beautiful woman, who attracts the attention of the King. He soon weds her and makes her his Queen. She takes the name of Brangomar, and, jealous of the pretty little princess, she bides her time, living on great hateful expectations. While hunting in the forest, the King falls from his horse and is killed, leaving Brangomar the complete ruler of his kingdom.

The first thing Queen Brangomar does is to take Snow White's royal garments from her and force her to work in the kitchen as a lowly scullery maid. Accidentally, away from the castle on an errand, Snow White meets a young hunter to whom she becomes attracted, while he is fascinated by her demure beauty. Neither party has any idea of who the other one really is. He is on his way to the castle, however, where he identifies himself as Prince Florimond (Creighton Hale). Queen Brangomar is furious when he asks for the hand of the Princess Snow White, whom he admits he has never seen. Brangomar had thought that the prince would surely have come to sue for her own hand, and in her disappointment, the heartless beauty plots the death of Snow White. She calls in old Berthold, the huntsman (Lionel Braham), who is also Snow White's devoted slave. She tells him that she desires the death of Snow White. He must take the girl into the forest, kill her, and bring Queen Brangomar the heart of the murdered princess.

Berthold takes Snow White into the forest, but naturally he cannot slay her. Instead, he tells her of the promise that Queen Brangomar has exacted of him. Snow White tells him to kill a young pig and take the pig's heart to the Queen. This Berthold does, and the Queen is temporarily satisfied.

Meanwhile, a saucy little bird finds Snow White in the forest and takes her to the home of the Seven Dwarfs, who welcome her. She becomes their cook and housekeeper, turning their humble dwelling into a comfortable home that is as neat as a pin. All seven of the dwarfs fall in love with Snow White, and each in his own way tries to outdo the other.

Miles away, Queen Brangomar has a magic mirror into which she gazes daily, asking the riddle, "Mirror, mirror, in my hand; who is the fairest in this land?" She is horrified when the mirror answers, "Snow White." The Queen learns where the dwarfs live, and, disguised as an old woman, she waits out of sight until all the dwarfs have gone off to their duties and then knocks on the door. She has a tray of poisoned gifts to sell. Snow White almost selects a comb, but the bird makes such a fuss about it that she chooses a beautiful red apple, which is poisoned. Brangomar exults and persuades her to taste the apple.

Snow White takes one bite and falls unconscious, with no show of life in her pretty face. Brangomar is pleased, takes off her disguise, and returns to the castle triumphantly.

When the dwarfs return from their tasks, they discover Snow White as pale and still as death. They mourn her demise and carry her in the casket to the castle for a state funeral. Everybody is shocked, except Queen Brangomar, who rejoices so tastelessly that Prince Florimond is angered and, drawing a knife, threatens to kill her.

In the ensuing excitement, the dwarfs become agitated and drop the casket. This causes the piece of apple that Snow White had eaten to be shaken loose from where it had lodged in her throat. Her eyes flutter and then open, and she sits up, very much alive. She is helped from the casket, and Prince Florimond takes her in his arms.

Queen Brangomar is wild with fury because of her thwarted efforts, but the witch Hex appears and transforms the heartless, vain woman into a screaming peacock that can only stride the grounds in its foolish pride. Thus, everyone else lives happily ever after.

It is unfortunate that *Snow White* is a "lost" film as are the rest of Clark's very popular films such as *Prunella* (1918).

DeWitt Bodeen

SO THIS IS PARIS

Released: 1926
Production: Warner Bros.
Direction: Ernst Lubitsch
Screenplay: Hans Kraly; based on the play *Le Réveillon* by Henri Meilhac and Ludovic Halévy
Cinematography: John J. Mescall
Length: 7 reels/6,029 feet

Principal characters:
Dr. Paul Giraud .... Monte Blue
Suzanne, his wife .... Patsy Ruth Miller
Maurice Lallé .... André Beranger
Georgette, his wife .... Lilyan Tashman
The detective .... Max Barwin

So This Is Paris is Parisian farce comedy as interpreted by Ernst Lubitsch, master storyteller of the amorous adventures of the upper classes. The film was released in late July, 1926, after a two-year onslaught of sophisticated romance comedies which followed the initial success of *The Marriage Circle*, directed by Lubitsch in early 1924. The number of films made about the romantic escapades of the wealthy, such as *The Marriage Circle, Open All Night* (1924), *Kiss Me Again* (1925), *Are Parents People?* (1925), and *The Grand Duchess and the Waiter*, (1926), however, did not dull the critics' reception to the latest Lubitsch offering. Richard Watts of the New York *Herald Tribune* described it as "the funniest comedy imaginable" and "adult and magnificent satirical farce," and the film was included on *The New York Times* "ten best" list for 1926.

The tremendous appeal of these Lubitsch-style or Lubitschean comedies may have been a limitation to the Berlin-born director's film career. In Germany, he acted and directed all types of films, from the slapstick "Meyer" series to historical dramas such as *Madame DuBarry* (1919, released in the United States as *Passion*) to the gypsy tale *Carmen* (1915). Once he was settled in Hollywood, however, the popularity of his sophisticated comedies kept him producing films of that genre, such as *The Love Parade* (1929), *Monte Carlo* (1930), *One Hour with You* (1932), *Trouble in Paradise* (1932), and *Heaven Can Wait* (1943), until his death in 1947.

In his book *The Lubitsch Touch*, historian Herman Weinberg chronicles Lubitsch's fascination with Charles Chaplin's romantic drama *A Woman of Paris* (1923) and its effect on the content and style of storytelling in the director's subsequent work. Weinberg writes, ". . . he learned from it how to utilize in the domain of comedy the allusive art of nuances and subtle indications." *So This Is Paris* was conceived and presented with this influence.

So This Is Paris begins with the title card "Paris—Where a good time is had by all," but the first visual images are jarring. A sheik pushes a lady of the harem onto a bed, then approaches her with knife in hand and stabs her. She lies lifeless on a bunch of pillows, as the assassin mourns over her body. The camera pans to the left, revealing a man playing a piano. The murder victim scratches her head. The sheik turns and bows. The next title explains, "M. and Mme. Lallé rehearsing the Dance of the Forbidden Fruit—Applesauce."

Next, Maurice Lallé (André Beranger) renders the Dance of Despair. This dance is done with the hands, a series of gestures alternating hands to cheeks as a stereotypical elderly Jew might be mimicked expressing "oy vay, oy vay." Maurice dances over to his wife Georgette (Lilyan Tashman) to lift her, but he does not have the strength, so Georgette lifts her sheik and announces, "If all weekends were like you—there would be no parties." She throws him onto the bed, adjusts her accoutrements, and exits. The pianist is laughing so hard that Maurice orders him out. Georgette enters with a boiled egg and milk for the weakling. As the pianist leaves, he tells Maurice, "After seeing you as a sheik—I've gained back my lost confidence."

Suzanne Giraud (Patsy Ruth Miller) loves to read "hot Arabian romances." Such was the custom for many women attracted to the amorous heathen world of *The Sheik*, particularly after the 1921 film starring Rudolph Valentino was released. Suzanne sits by the window, and across the street, Maurice Lallé sits at his window. Swooning over a hot ending, she puts down her novel and looks out the window to see Lallé in a sheik's turban. Dr. Paul Giraud (Monte Blue) arrives home at this moment to see his wife swaying by the window to follow the bobbing movements of the "sheik," who actually sits eating his boiled egg, which is out of their view. Still dazed, she greets her husband with a passionate kiss and murmurs, "my sheik!," an action and comment which he finds ridiculous.

Maurice removes his turban just before Paul looks out the window. Paul only sees a scrawny, seemingly nude man; he quickly draws the blinds and is infuriated by his neighbor's nudity. Suzanne decides he should fight a duel with the offender, so her husband leaves saying, "I'll come back with the naked truth." Then, Suzanne moves from one window to another to catch a glimpse of the nude neighbor and says, "He at least might wear a hat."

His cane in hand, Paul crosses the street to the Lallé home and finds Georgette performing a headstand; as it happens, Georgette and Paul are former lovers. They reminisce about their romantic past until Paul, looking out from the Lallé window, notes that his wife is staring into the room from across the street and remembers to tell Georgette that he is married. Maurice then enters, and Georgette introduces him to Paul. She orders her husband to put on some clothes, so he replaces the turban on his head. Paul tells Maurice he looked wonderful from the window and that he has come over to tell him as much. They decide to see more of each other, and then Paul asks Maurice to wear a shirt when standing near the window. Paul departs and Georgette shoves Maurice onto the bed.

At home, Paul tells Suzanne of the violent struggle that took place across the street, and when she inquires about his cane he tells her that it has been smashed, although he has actually left it at the Lallé's house. When Maurice comes to return the cane, Suzanne and he begin to socialize. Paul awakens from a nap and overhears Maurice's flirtation. Then Suzanne calls for help and Maurice hides behind the curtain, until Paul returns to his nap. Suzanne then tells Maurice to take back the cane and return with it when she is alone.

Next, Georgette telephones the Giraud residence and reports a sick husband when Suzanne answers, giving the name Moreau and the address of the Moreau Cafe. Paul takes the message after his nap and leaves for Moreau's. At his window, Maurice sees the doctor drive away, so he crosses the street to return the cane to Suzanne.

Paul speeds to what he thinks is a sick patient, even being stopped by a policeman along the way, but when he arrives at the address on the message, he finds Georgette waiting in front of the Moreau Cafe. They both are enjoying the joke when the same policeman arrives. An argument ensues, and the officer records the doctor's words in a notebook, insult by insult, ending with Giraud's "So's your male parent!" Inside the café, Paul says, "I wish I had my cane with me." The scene then cuts to Maurice crossing from the Giraud home back to his apartment—carrying the cane *back* with him.

The viewer then learns by the device of a newspaper headline that Dr. Giraud has received three days in prison for speeding and for insulting an officer. At breakfast, the Girauds are squabbling over the news. He says that much can happen before he is called to serve the sentence, and she says that the judgment is unfair since he was on his way to tend a sick man. She attempts to telephone the sick man, but her husband stops her.

Later, she does telephone the Moreaus and is told that M. Moreau is dead. When she tells her husband, he says that he tried to save him but his wife talked him to death. Georgette and Paul later go for a drink and decide to celebrate Moreau's death by attending that evening's Artist's Ball, but Paul receives notice that he must begin his sentence and report at eight o'clock in the evening. Not deterred, Paul dresses formally for the ball, telling Suzanne that "One meets the very best people in jail now-a-days." His wife thinks that his attitude is wonderful.

Meanwhile, at the Lallé apartment, Maurice is feigning illness, and Georgette secretly is pleased to attend the Artist's Ball without him. As soon as she has left home, however, he gets out of bed and grabs the cane to return it once more.

The Artist's Ball is one of the most acclaimed sequences in any Lubitsch film. There are black jazz musicians, Charleston dancers, people in all sorts of exotic costumes, masked men and women with exposed legs. The camera reels and becomes a kaleidoscope as a strobe light follows the wild dancers. According to historian George Pratt, two dance companies who were performing in Los Angeles at the time of the production were hired for this scene, a drunken collage of fades and double images.

While Georgette and Paul dance the Charleston, Suzanne listens to it on her radio at home. Maurice enters with the cane, but Suzanne is not pleased to see him, slaps his face (off camera), and orders him out. He throws flowers at her until the vase is empty, then throws an imaginary bloom to her. She insists that he leave, so he plops down on the sofa and cries. At ten o'clock, a detective (Max Barwin) arrives at the Giraud home to take Paul to prison. He mistakes Maurice for Paul, and, after five good-bye kisses and one attempted escape, Maurice goes with the detective. Then, the radio announces the winners of the Charleston contest are Georgette Lallé and Dr. Paul Giraud.

Suzanne is now furious, so she puts on her new gown and goes to the Artist's Ball. Meanwhile, Paul is not too drunk to remember his jail sentence. As he exits the main ballroom, Georgette is dancing on tabletops and drinking champagne with another man, so she does not notice his departure. Into the main hallway walks Suzanne wearing a mask. She finds Paul and leads him to a cab, but he is too drunk to understand what is happening. They return home, and Paul notes that the room looks familiar. When she unmasks, he notes that she also looks familiar. When he says, "You're the girl with the green garters," she slaps his face, and he sobers a bit. To illustrate the change, the camera switches from a reeling, double image to a conventional image.

Paul then asks Suzanne why she is coming in so late and having a festive time while he is in jail, which prompts her to pick up the cane to scold him until she realizes that she has divulged incriminating evidence. She explains that she has arranged for him to be pardoned and threatens, "From now on I'm the Big Boss, and you'll be the short-end of this marriage." Paul then shrinks to doll size (literally) and walks into the bedroom.

The next morning, Georgette receives a telegram from Maurice which states that he will be resting in a sanatorium for three days on doctor's orders, and immediately, Georgette telephones someone to make a date.

A title reads, "It's always fair weather when good liars get together," after which the audience sees Paul and Suzanne acting like two lovebirds at breakfast, as they read in the paper, "Dr. Giraud arrested. Heartrending love scene enacted as officer is forced to do duty." The scene then cuts to Maurice marching in a prison line, and the moral of the film is announced, "When you appear at your window put on your shirt."

So This Is Paris portrays a world of sophistication where ethics are boring and intrigue cures humdrum marriages. It is a fairy tale for the American middle class (even though the setting is Paris), a story finessed rather than recounted. The sexually symbolic cane and the street which separates the Lallé and Giraud homes take on roles in this farce. Even the moving-picture camera itself reels and sees double to contribute to interpreting the tale.

Audrey E. Kupferberg

THE SON OF THE SHEIK

Released: 1926
Production: John W. Considine, Jr., for Feature Productions/United Artists
Direction: George Fitzmaurice
Screenplay: Frances Marion and Fred De Gresac; based on the novel *The Sons of the Sheik* by Edith M. Hull
Cinematography: George Barnes
Length: 7 reels/6,685 feet

Principal characters:
Ahmed/The Sheik .... Rudolph Valentino
Yasmin .... Vilma Banky
André .... George Fawcett
Ghabab .... Montague Love
Ramadan .... Karl Dane
Ali .... Bull Montana
Diana, wife of the Sheik .... Agnes Ayres

It is always pleasant when a career ends on a high point rather than a low one, particularly when that career ends tragically. Such is the case with Rudolph Valentino, whose last film, *The Son of the Sheik*, is one of his best and was released shortly before his untimely death on August 23, 1926, at the age of thirty-one.

The Son of the Sheik may not rate as a great work of art, but it is the only Valentino film in which the star does not seem to be taking himself too seriously and appears to be having as much fun romping through this Western-style thriller set in Arabia as the audience is in watching him. Valentino's brooding, sensual face sparkles often with good humor, and he seems more manly than in some of his earlier starring vehicles such as *Blood and Sand* (1922) or *Monsieur Beaucaire* (1924). Even the rape or forced seduction of Vilma Banky is performed with a twinkle in the eye that seems to suggest that it is only play-acting and that there is no violence involved.

The sex scenes in *The Son of the Sheik* are never heavy-handed, although they positively seeth with eroticism. One of the most erotic moments in the production occurs when Valentino (as the Sheik's son, Ahmed) is captured by his enemies. With his hands strung up above his head, he is stripped to the waist and savagely whipped, while later a dwarf sadistically touches his wounds. It is a scene obviously written to allow the star to expose a pleasing amount of his flesh to the audience, and at the same time to allow a large portion of the audience to indulge its fantasies. The tortured Valentino has the same pose and the same anguished face as depicted in the paintings of the masochistic Saint Sebastian.

A more straightforward, although obviously offensive, approach to sex is presented in the scenes involving the abduction of Yasmin (Vilma Banky). As he looks at the frightened woman with vengeance in his eyes, Ahmed coldly lights a cigarette, removes his robe and begins to unbuckle his belt. Referring to her earlier betrayal of him, he says, "I may not be the first victim, but, by Allah, I'll be the one you remember." Ahmed advances on the girl as we watch her eyes show their recognition of her fate. As Ahmed savagely kisses her on the lips, he pushes her backward and the camera reveals a bed.

For *The Son of the Sheik*, Valentino returns to the environment which had brought him popular, if not artistic, success, the desert. Edith M. Hull, a purveyor of romantic trash and very popular during this period, had authored the novel on which *The Sheik* was based, and early in 1925, she provided a sequel entitled *The Sons of the Sheik*. For the film, the two sons were merged by screenwriter Frances Marion into one, and Valentino was cast to play not only the son, but also his father, the Sheik. Agnes Ayres, who had portrayed the heroine in *The Sheik*, was prevailed upon to return for a cameo role as Diana, the Sheik's wife. For his new leading lady, Valentino and his advisers selected Vilma Banky, a Hungarian-born actress, who had also appeared in Valentino's *The Eagle* (1925). Banky was the leading star of the Goldwyn Company, and her marriage to fellow actor Rod La Roque was a major Hollywood event.

In the story, Ahmed, the son of the Sheik, falls in love with Yasmin, whose father (George Fawcett), a Frenchman, is the leader of a group of thieves and cutthroats. When Ahmed is captured by the Frenchman and held for ransom, he is led to believe that it is Yasmin who tricked him. Upon his release, Ahmed abducts the girl and is in the process of raping her, when his father—who is angry over his son's disobedience—appears and orders the boy to release Yasmin.

She is led away under escort, but her father and his gang surprise the group. In the process Ahmed's friend, Ramadan (Karl Dane), who is leading the escort, learns that it was not Yasmin who had betrayed his young master, but an admirer of hers, who was a member of her father's gang. Yasmin returns to the dance hall—or the Arabic equivalent of such—where she performs, and Ahmed pursues her there. A rip-roaring, roisterous fight breaks out, at which Ahmed is joined by his father, and the two hold off Yasmin's father and his supporters. The film ends with victorious Ahmed carrying Yasmin away in his arms.

The Son of the Sheik's director, George Fitzmaurice (1895-1940), was a major figure during the silent era, although little known today because his films tended to be romantic melodramas, which have not stood the test of time very well. Aside from *The Son of the Sheik*, his best-known work was probably *Lilac Time* (1928), starring Colleen Moore and Gary Cooper. Although his work on *The Son of the Sheik* is eclipsed by the magnetic personality of the star, Fitzmaurice's direction should not be overlooked. He moves the film along at a tremendous pace. His camera setups for the abduction sequence are well considered, and his skillful editing of the climactic fight sequence cannot be faulted. So well does he intercut the shots of Valentino as Ahmed and Valentino as his father that not once is the audience aware that these two characters are not really fighting side by side.

Valentino was apparently quite pleased with his work in *The Son of the Sheik* and felt that in playing two roles he could demonstrate his acting abilities to his critics—who at this time appeared to be legion. His manager was happy to have the star play the role, because his debts were mounting. In view of the three-million-dollar profit Paramount apparently had made on *The Sheik*, there was no reason to believe that similar profits would not be forthcoming from *The Son of the Sheik*. In anticipation of such profits, Valentino spent $11,260 on his wardrobe for the film

The Son of the Sheik whose desert scenes were shot outside Yuma, Arizona, received its premiere at Grauman's Million Dollar Theater in Los Angeles in July, 1926, and Valentino attended the opening accompanied by the actress currently romantically linked with the star, Pola Negri. The critic for *Variety* (July 14, 1926) also attended the premiere and reported, "It is best described as an interesting study in psychology, showing how a son of the Desert inherited the love, passions and hate of his father. . . . Some exceptionally fine photography . . . and the excellent acting of the supporting cast help to make *The Son of the Sheik* an outstanding success." A Chicago premiere followed, as did the famous personal attack on Valentino in *The Chicago Tribune* which referred to "pink face powder and powder puffs" and accused the star of being a corrupting influence on American youth. This comment added to many rumors and personal attacks on Valentino which were circulating about his masculinity at the time.

From Chicago, Valentino went on to the New York premiere of *The Son of the Sheik* at the Mark Strand Theater on July 25, 1926. Again, the star made a personal appearance, "to see if the Sheik's offspring were as popular as his father." The anonymous critic of *The New York Times* (July 26, 1926) compared Valentino's swashbuckling style of fighting to that of Douglas Fairbanks, noting, "Be it said to those who like that sort of romantic picture, the latest Valentino effort is full of desert rough stuff and bully fights."

By the time the magazine critics came to review the film, Valentino was dead. *Photoplay* (October, 1926), commented, "He (Valentino) was the old Rudy again and his work, without question, ranked at the top of the best performances of the month. . . . And we expect every fan in the country to be saying, 'It was Rudy's best. I can never forget him.'"

Valentino probably would not have been forgotten anyway. His youthful death assured him of legend status, but even a legend must have good, solid material evidence to support his image. Most of Valentino's films today appear to be ludicrous, melodramatic exercises in tedium, particularly *Blood and Sand* and *Monsieur Beaucaire*. *The Son of the Sheik*, however, serves the legend well and continues to entertain. One may be amused by it, yet one never laughs at it, only along with it.

Anthony Slide

THE SORROWS OF SATAN

Released: 1927
Production: Adolph Zukor and Jesse L. Lasky for Famous Players-Lasky/
Paramount
Direction: D. W. Griffith
Screenplay: Forrest Halsey; based on John Russell's and George Hull's adaptation of the novel of the same name by Marie Corelli
Titles: Julian Johnson
Cinematography: Harry Fischbeck
Editing: Julian Johnson
Art direction: Charles Kirk
Miniatures: Fred Waller
Music: Hugo Reisenfeld
Length: 9 reels/8,691 feet

> *Principal characters:*
> Prince Lucio de Rimanez .... Adolphe Menjou
> Geoffrey Tempest .... Ricardo Cortez
> Princess Olga .... Lya de Putti
> Mavis Claire .... Carol Dempster
> Amiel .... Ivan Lebedeff
> The Landlady .... Marcia Harris
> Lord Elton .... Lawrence D'Orsay
> Dancing Girl .... Nellie Savage
> Mavis's Chum .... Dorothy Hughes

The decline of D. W. Griffith, the father of the American motion picture, is one of the saddest stories in the history of films. If the American cinema had a pioneer, it was Griffith, and he is frequently called the first poet of the American motion picture. This Kentuckian, the son of a Confederate officer, somewhat innocently but fortunately found himself drawn from a minor career as a touring actor and writer into the uncertain occupation of film director in an art form which was not yet an art and a business which had yet to dream of fortunes to be made, and lost.

Griffith would experience it all during his career as the first *auteur* of American films. In between the many milestones—the years at Biograph, *Judith of Bethulia* (1914), *The Birth of a Nation* (1915), *Intolerance* (1916), *Broken Blossoms* (1919), *Way Down East* (1920), and *Orphans of the Storm* (1922)—he steadfastly accepted the lean months and years in order to produce and direct those projects of his choice.

Following World War I, Griffith found himself out of step with the Hollywood film industry. His sense of sentimentality was outmoded, and he regarded the loose morality of the postwar era with disdain. The industry itself was now solidly overtaken by strong production companies run by equally strong and often meddling entrepreneurs—an atmosphere in which Griffith was unable to operate, let alone be creative.

He remained rigidly attached to his own methods of production but his precarious financial situation forced him to sign a contract with Adolph Zukor of Paramount for three films. The first was *That Royle Girl* (1925), an unsuccessful comedy with Carol Dempster and W. C. Fields. It was immediately apparent to Paramount that Griffith was not likely to provide them with any sort of moneymaker, and so the next project they offered (forced on) him was *The Sorrows of Satan*.

The Sorrows of Satan was an old-fashioned novel written by English author Marie Corelli, who also wrote *Thelma*, and who created lush, flamboyant prose and was the favorite author of Queen Victoria. The novel *The Sorrows of Satan* had been the source of two screen versions prior to Griffith's; one was a 1917 British version, and the other, a 1919 version, entitled *Leaves from Satan's Book*, was directed by Denmark's Carl Dreyer.

Paramount had owned the screen rights for some time and had planned it as a Cecil B. De Mille vehicle. De Mille, however, had been threatening to leave Paramount and organize his own independent unit and as a ploy to let him know who was boss, Zukor and Jesse L. Lasky "gave" the project to Griffith. Curiously, Griffith had admired the novel for years because of its "power of evil" theme and had even thought of filming it prior to his making *The Birth of a Nation*; that had been eleven years previous. Times had changed, the tastes of the American public had changed, and none of the changes sat well with Griffith.

There are those who say that Griffith was very much aware that the picture was assigned to him not only as a slap in the face to De Mille, but also as a project which would cause Griffith to fail and thus free Paramount of their contract with the over-the-hill director. Whether or not it was a move calculated by Zukor to hurt either or both De Mille and Griffith, Griffith still tackled the task with enthusiasm. He immediately began holding story conferences and explained how he would create the supernatural scenes in which the devil is reincarnated as a living mortal. The picture was filmed at Paramount's Long Island Astoria Studios and Griffith cast one of his favorites, Carol Dempster, as the innocent heroine.

The Sorrows of Satan is a sentimental and somewhat childish novel on the Faustian theme of the devil incarnate, a Victorian mixture of sin, sex, and religion. In 1897, George Bernard Shaw described Corelli's writing "as the cheap victories of a profuse imagination over an apparently commonplace and carelessly cultivated mind," and the novel had been variously reviewed as a good modern morality play and a cheap rework of Goethe's *Faust*.

While the book was philosophically sophomoric, however, one can see Griffith being drawn by the challenge of creating a real *machination diabolique*. One of the scenes which attracted Griffith the most was the opening one in the film, in which audiences witness the fall from grace of Lucifer by an avenging God, after which Lucifer/Satan, who wishes to regain favor in Paradise, is sent to tempt mortal man hoping to be rebuffed so he might return to Heaven.

The suave Adolphe Menjou was cast as the devil/Prince Lucio de Rimanez and Griffith opened the film with misty special effects revealing a quarrel between Lucifer and Archangel Michael over the creation of man and Lucifer's fall from grace and expulsion from Heaven. After this, Lucifer descends to Earth as a winged creature appearing in shadowy form down the hallway leading to the room of the young, impoverished poet Geoffrey Tempest (Ricardo Cortez). The film's titles describe the scene by saying "The soft wings of Satan gliding along the walls." Satan then takes on the form of the debonair Prince in white tie and tails.

The Prince entices Geoffrey with promises of riches and carnal delights if he will marry the alluring *femme fatale* Princess Olga (Lya de Putti). Geoffrey guiltily forgets about his love for the lovely Mavis Claire (Carol Dempster) and is drawn into the Bacchanalian world of sex, orgies, and vice. The film wavers between the lure of the amoral world and the lyrical love scenes with Geoffrey and Mavis, and it is beautifully photographed by Harry Fischbeck with the contrasts of light and dark depicting day versus night and faith versus sin.

Finally, Satan puts Geoffrey to the ultimate test and reveals his true identity in a startlingly realistic scene beautifully acted by Cortez. The young poet rejects the devil and all the riches he offers and returns to his demure Mavis.

The Paramount publicity department created a major campaign for the film's release hailing the return of the master Griffith. "Satan, flung from Heaven, brings Temptation to the World!" read the ads. "A strictly modern epic drama of love, temptation, thrills and regeneration stupendously conceived!" It went on to describe Lya de Putti, here in her American debut, as "the most alluring woman in the world." It was billed and promoted like a De Mille epic and in fact the plot lends itself to the kinds of excesses frequently found in De Mille's work.

Reviewers were united in their critical reaction. All praised the excellence of the supernatural effects and camera tricks and the use of low-ceilinged sets (which preceded Orson Welles' astonishing use of the same in *Citizen Kane*, 1941), but they also rebuked the story as banal. The music score by Dr. Hugo Reisenfeld was admired as was the acting, with Dempster being singled out for her sweet demeanor and Menjou highly praised for his silken, urbane portrayal of Satan. One critic made note of the minimal use of titles, stating that many of Griffith's earlier works had been marred by being "filled with narrative subtitles of a violently sententious quality."

In his 1948 memoir, *It Took Nine Tailors*, Menjou described the film as "a piece of smorgasbord." He recalled that when Paramount told him he would be starring in the film, he asked for a copy of the script and was told that Griffith did not work from a script. He said he then went and read the novel and hated it. He added that the six months that it took to finish the film were "the unhappiest I have ever experienced in this business I love."

Menjou said the cast would meet Griffith every morning in New York City at Keen's Chop House to hear him explain what they were expected to do, then they would spend "interminable hours" rehearsing. He also dismissed the special effects and trick photography as a bunch of hocus-pocus that sounded good at the story conferences but were nothing but grief to realize on the production stage. Finally, despite his own good personal reviews, he said he never saw the completed film.

There are various reasons for the failure of *The Sorrows of Satan*, not the least of which is the plot itself and also Griffith's adoring close-ups of Dempster in the romantic scenes which slowed the action a great deal. It was also apparent that Paramount had lost faith in both the project and in Griffith, and while a first cut had been executed by Griffith himself that some say was quite good, the final cut was turned over to Paramount's Julian Johnson and that is the version which was released.

It was plain to see that Griffith's career was over. His contract with Paramount was canceled and after five more films over a period of five years his career ended in 1931 with *The Struggle*, an ironic title to say the least.

Ronald Bowers

SPARROWS

Released: 1926
Production: Mary Pickford Productions for United Artists
Direction: William Beaudine
Screenplay: C. Gardner Sullivan; based on an original story by Winifred Dunn
Titles: George Marion, Jr.
Cinematography: Charles Rosher, Karl Struss, and Hal Mohr
Editing: Harald McClernan
Art direction: Harry Oliver
Length: 9 reels/7,763 feet

Principal characters:
Mama Mollie	Mary Pickford
Grimes	Gustav von Seyffertitz
Richard Wayne	Roy Stewart
Doris Wayne	Mary Louise Miller
Ambrose Grimes	Spec O'Donnell
Splutters	Monty O'Grady
The Sparrows	Muriel MacCormac
	Billy Johnson
	Camilla Johnson
	Mary McLane
	Billy Butts
	Jack Levine
	Florence Rogan
	Sylvia Bernard
	Seesel Anne Johnson

Mary Pickford was the cinema's first star, and she received the kind of first-love devotion which no other star can ever have again. No one today can sit down and watch an early Pickford film from the same viewpoint as it was originally seen. Too many good films have been made since then, and too many great stars have come and gone. Pickford, however, was the first, and that must constantly be remembered as one sees her early works. An illustration of this fact is found in the words of a contemporary reviewer who wrote of a 1915 feature of hers called *Esmeralda:* "And did Mr. Kirkwood [the director] fail to allow her to pause on the stairs or to show her in at least one close-up every hundred feet, every fondly critical standee would be able to tell at once where her director had made his vital error."

By the 1920's, film audiences had had several love affairs with actresses and actors and no longer would flock and pay only to gaze upon Pickford. Consequently, she began making spectacles such as *Rosita* (1923) and *Dorothy Vernon of Haddon Hall* (1924). When they failed to make the vast sums her previous films did, she decided it was because she was no longer portraying a child. She deliberately played a child in her next film, *Little Annie Rooney* (1925), and was pleased that the box-office take was a little better. In her following picture, *Sparrows*, she played a child-woman, but it is because of a fine screenplay and exquisite production values that it is an enjoyable film all audiences can view without any previous or special knowledge of Pickford. It is enjoyable on its own merits.

For the most part, the film takes place on a decayed farm set in the middle of a swamp. This set was built at Pickford's studio on Santa Monica Boulevard on more than four acres. Hundreds of large trees were transplanted and draped with two boxcars of Spanish moss. The decayed farmhouse and barns were made of wood, each piece of which the art director, Harry Oliver, individually aged. The finished effect gave the film a flavor like Fagin's hideout in Charles Dickens' *Oliver Twist*, slimy, rotten, and frightening in itself.

Sparrows opens with a long shot of the swamp engulfed in mist, and then close-ups of the bubbling quicksand and sliding alligators that surround the farm. A tall, sinister, hatchet-faced man named Grimes (Gustav von Seyffertitz) is introduced in a head shot buzzing with mosquitoes and flies. He owns the farm which a subtitle indicates is a baby farm, where unsuspecting parents send their children, believing it to be a nice place. He crosses the rotten boards that bridge the quicksand to his mailbox and finds a package addressed to one of the children in his care. Ripping open the box, he finds a pretty doll, and he crushes the head and throws it into the sucking quicksand.

Mama Mollie (Mary Pickford) is shown surrounded by the nine children she cares for. The youngest is an infant and the oldest is a seven-year-old boy called Splutters (Monty O'Grady). Mollie is trying to get a kite to fly. It is important because it has a message asking for help tied to its tail. When the kite does fly, she cuts the string and then watches it dart down and tangle in the skeleton fingers of a dead tree branch.

All the children are dressed in rags and live in the barn. Their food is scarce, and among their other troubles is Grimes' son Ambrose (Spec O'Donnell), an incredibly ugly boy, all freckles, squint eyes, and mean disposition. He sees Mollie steal a potato from the garden and informs his father of it. This leads to punishment of no food for a day. The infant suffers most. Mollie has made a bottle from an old whiskey bottle and the fingers of a rubber glove, but there is not enough milk, and that night, the baby dies. As Mollie sits, holding the infant, a light shines at the back of the barn, and through a beautiful orchard Christ walks. He takes the dead child from her and goes back into the orchard with it. The sequence is deeply moving and well done.

The next day a curly-haired three-year-old girl, Doris Wayne (Mary Louise Miller), is brought to Grimes' farm by two kidnapers. Grimes later becomes nervous about keeping the child when he reads in the newspaper about the all-out search for the missing daughter of the millionaire, Richard Wayne

(Roy Stewart). Mollie overhears Grimes and Ambrose planning to throw the child into the quicksand that night, so she decides they must all flee that same night. They begin to make their preparations for flight, but are caught unawares by Grimes. Mollie holds Grimes off with a pitchfork as the children cross the quicksand on boards and enter the swamp. Mollie is last and dangerously crosses with the little girl on her back. Grimes taunts them, yelling "Thanks for saving me the trouble of getting rid of them, you little fool!"

They thus begin their flight through the swamp—a nightmarish journey. The whole sequence was actually filmed at night—there are no day-for-night shots done with underexposures or filters. Pickford and the children spent many uncomfortable nights struggling through water and mud up to their waists. Six alligators were rented for the production, and they always were there on the shore, their hind legs lashed with rope.

At the edge of the swamp a pool of black water, rotten stumps, and squirming alligators block the children's exit. The only escape is over a huge rotten tree branch. Mollie starts across it on her hands and knees with little Doris strapped to her back, but midway, a slab of bark breaks away, and Mollie totters for a second before she straddles the branch. The children follow her lead in like style, but their weight causes the branch to crack and lurch down toward the pool. The alligators' snapping jaws are perilously close to the youngsters' dangling feet. Splutters is leading the children, and the little girl behind him keeps grabbing his pants for balance each time the branch jerks lower until she finally pulls his pants almost off.

The crossing on the branch is a memorable scene and came close to being very dangerous. Pickford practiced the crossing several times with a thirty-pound weight on her back. The six alligators snapped below as she crossed again and again. That night at home, she told her husband, Douglas Fairbanks, how worried she was for the little girl when they would shoot the scene for real. Fairbanks exploded. He had assumed that director William Beaudine was going to film the scene with a double exposure, and the next day he insisted that it be done as such. It was safer, but a lot more work since the effect had to be done in the camera by back-winding the film. Today an optical printer could be used, thus simplifying the process.

The two kidnapers are waiting for Mollie and the children when they come out of the swamp, but they hide from the two men in a boat, which the men later steal to escape from the police. The police finally capture the boat and find the stowaways.

Richard Wayne, the millionaire, joyfully runs to take his daughter, but Mollie refuses to let go of Doris until the police explain who Wayne is. He takes Doris away, and Mollie and her brood sit forlornly in the cold police station. At home, Doris refuses food from her nurse and cries for Mama Mollie. Mollie is sent for, and with a look of disgust throws aside the sterilized bottle with which they have tried to feed Doris and pulls out the whiskey bottle with the rubber glove nipple, and Doris is content. Wayne asks Mollie to come and be Doris' nurse, but Mollie agrees to do so only if he will adopt her nine sparrows, which he does.

Sparrows was only one of six films that United Artists released in 1926, a year when all the other studios each turned out at least fifty-two pictures. Yet, the six films that United Artists released were all classics, such as *The Black Pirate*, *The Son of the Sheik*, and *The Winning of Barbara Worth*. On the whole, United Artists pictures tended to play the downtown first-run theaters, because they had to be specially ordered, and they were expensive. All the same, *Sparrows* made a fair profit.

Larry Lee Holland

SPIES
(SPIONE)

Released: 1928
Production: Fritz Lang for Fritz Lang-Film; released by Ufa
Direction: Frtiz Lang
Screenplay: Thea von Harbou and Fritz Lang
Cinematography: Fritz Arno Wagner
Length: 15 reels/14,318 feet

Principal characters:
Sonia .... Gerda Maurus
Detective Donald Tremaine .... Willy Fritsch
Haghi .... Rudolf Klein-Rogge
Dr. Matsumoto .... Lupu Pick
Kitty .... Lien Deyers
Burton Jason .... Craighall Sherry

Fritz Lang, born in Vienna in 1890, had a distinguished directing career in the German silent film with such motion pictures as *Dr. Mabuse* (1922), and *Metropolis* (1927); in the German sound film with *M* (1931); and in the American sound film with *Fury* (1936) and *Ministry of Fear* (1944). Indeed, the above films are only some of the highlights of his nearly half a century of filmmaking. Film critics and devotees differ in their opinions of the relative quality of Lang's many films, but no one who recognizes his skill in the silent cinema can fail to appreciate the many virtues of *Spies*. In addition, a viewer who has never seen a silent film or a Lang film should be impressed with how fully developed the spy film was in Lang's hands in 1928. The modern viewer can see elements of many such popular films as the James Bond thrillers and *The Spy Who Came in from the Cold* (1965) in *Spies*—such elements as the criminal mastermind, international intrigue, and conflicts between romance and a spy's duty.

Spies begins with an exciting sequence in which a lock is opened, a document is placed in an envelope, an envelope is taken from an open automobile, newspaper headlines reveal the theft of secret papers from an embassy, and frustrated officials shout into telephones.

Detective Donald Tremaine (Willy Fritsch), who is Agent 326, is called in by Burton Jason (Craighall Sherry) to help apprehend the forces who have stolen the documents. Tremaine's identity and mission are suspected by the other side, however, for viewers see that one agent obtains a copy of a coded telegram Tremaine sends and another takes a picture of him with a miniature camera hidden in his lapel. The first agent obtains the copy by removing or breaking all but one of the pens in the telegraph office and then placing carbon paper below the blotter in the booth with the only working pen; the agent with the miniature camera works in Jason's office, and Tremaine catches him in the act of using the camera.

Jason is portrayed as the stereotypical middle-level bureaucrat who is pressured by his superiors to produce results but is rather ineffectual himself. He has to hope that his agents are more effective than he himself is.

Jason's opponent, on the other hand, is a mastermind. He has the will, the intelligence, and the determination to accomplish his ultimate goal: "Nothing can stand in my way—I'll control the world." For him, the problem is that he must, to a certain extent, depend upon underlings who lack his single-mindedness and skill. The audience is introduced to this man (Rudolf Klein-Rogge) by a title that states "The world knew and respected this man as the great Haghi, bank director and financial genius," but the audience knows he is more than that. Already seen is his rescue of a murderer on his way to be executed. By saving this man's life, Haghi has bought his complete obedience. Haghi is an imposing figure even though he is confined to a wheelchair, and Lang has said that he was made up to look like the Russian "political mastermind" Leon Trotsky.

The contest soon concentrates on the efforts of Sonia (Gerda Maurus), an agent of Haghi's, to find out what she can from Tremaine. Her method of "introducing" herself to Tremaine is effective if melodramatic. She bursts into his hotel room saying, "Save me—I've shot him." Despite the fact that he is a trained espionage agent on a mission, Tremaine protects and hides the beautiful woman. She is also unable to be professional. When the two begin to fall in love, Sonia tries to have Haghi take her off the case, but he refuses and reminds her that Tremaine's country is responsible for the fate of her father and brother. Exactly what this fate was is not specified, but the reminder seems to be enough to renew her sense of duty to the mission. As the plot progresses, however, it is seen that Sonia's chief motivations are fear of Haghi and love of Tremaine. Suspecting this, Haghi has her conversations monitored (by a microphone in a vase), and he personally follows her to the Cafe Danielle, where she is dining and dancing with Tremaine. While they are dancing, Haghi has one of his agents hand her a note which says, "Enough of this" and orders her to report to headquarters at once.

Sonia feigns illness and then deliberately drops her necklace and sends Tremaine looking for it while she leaves. Her desertion sends Tremaine to a bar to drink away his sorrow, but there he meets a Dr. Matsumoto (Lupu Pick), who tells him that he is not the first to be a victim of a beautiful spy. The reason that Matsumoto knows about Tremaine, apparently, is that he is an agent of the Japanese government and is also involved in the affair of the secret treaty. Matsumoto soon proves to be the next victim of a beautiful spy. On his way home from the bar, he discovers a young woman out on the street in the cold, rainy weather. He takes her to his home, and she begs to stay, but she is not actually a homeless waif; she is Kitty (Lien Deyers), another of Haghi's female spies. The unsuspecting Matsumoto succumbs to her charms, and it is not until sometime later when he awakes one morning to find Kitty gone and his luggage rifled that he realizes what has happened. He takes the only action his honor will allow; he commits suicide. Lang shows Matsumoto's preparation for the act and then shows his face as he kills himself with a sword. There is then a cut to Haghi throwing a string of pearls to Kitty and a cut back to the dying man.

The action then becomes brisk and complicated. Haghi, who has been holding Sonia prisoner, promises to free her and let her go to Tramaine, who is leaving the country by train. Haghi—who is now also disguising himself as a clown—has Tremaine's train wrecked. Tremaine survives, and he and Sonia are together briefly, but Sonia is soon recaptured by Haghi and held hostage in his huge bank building. Haghi promises to kill Sonia if Tremaine and the police do not leave the building, but Tremaine rescues her just in time, although Haghi escapes. Tremaine realizes that the clown must be Haghi in disguise and rushes to the theater where the clown performs. They arrive in mid-performance. Haghi, dressed as the clown, sees Tremaine and the other pursuers in the wings of the stage and shoots at them with a gun that is part of his act. When he sees that he has missed, he shoots himself, then calls for the curtain. The crowd—thinking the suicide is an act—applauds, the curtain closes, and the film ends.

Speaking about the film in 1967, Lang said that it as well as many other notable German films of the 1920's were an outgrowth of the atmosphere of postwar Germany, and atmosphere marked by "unrest and confusion . . . hysteria, despair, and unbridled vice." Some of this atmosphere is suggested in the scene in the Cafe Danielle in which a boxing match is staged in the middle of the dance floor. When it is over, the boxing ring is removed and elegantly dressed dancers replace it.

Also important in *Spies* are the many memorable images created by Lang. In one, Dr. Matsumoto, as he prepares for his suicide, sees the three couriers that he sent to death carrying fake documents. Superimposed over this image is an image of the Japanese flag. Lang also effectively used shadows, as did most of the directors of Germany's Golden Age. Perhaps the most memorable shadow imagery in *Spies* occurs near the end when Sonia, bound to a chair, is watching two men fight. The audience sees Sonia, but only the shadows of the fighting men are visible on the wall behind her.

Marilynn Wilson

THE SPOILERS

Released: 1914
Production: William N. Selig
Direction: Colin Campbell
Screenplay: Lanier Bartlett; based on the novel of the same name by Rex
  Beach
Cinematography: Harry W. Gerstad
Length: 9 reels

Principal characters:
Roy Glennister .... William Farnum
Helen Chester .... Bessie Eyton
Alex McNamara .... Tom Santschi
Cherry Malotte .... Kathlyn Williams
Broncho Kid .... Wheeler Oakman
Dextry .... Frank M. Clark
Slapjack .... Jack F. McDonald

Rex Beach's popular novel of 1906, *The Spoilers*, has been filmed five times.
The most recent version was in 1956, with Jeff Chandler and Rory Calhoun,
while the most popular was probably the 1942 adaptation with John Wayne
and Randolph Scott. *The Spoilers* was a gutsy, raw Western adventure set in
the Alaskan gold fields, and its continued interest for filmmakers is not hard
to understand. The first film version of *The Spoilers* is claimed by many to
have been the most faithful to the original work; and it certainly has a far
more earthy quality than the later glamorized Hollywood adaptations. The
film, however, has even a stronger claim to fame than that, for *The Spoilers*
was one of the American cinema's first major, feature-length productions,
preceding by some nine months *The Birth of a Nation* (1915).

The story of *The Spoilers* can be summarized in a few paragraphs. A dispute
affects the claim of Roy Glennister (William Farnum) to the Midas Mine, and
both he and Cherry Malotte (Kathlyn Williams), owner of the local gambling
saloon, are suspicious of Alex McNamara (Tom Santschi), the local gold
commissioner. Cherry is secretly in love with Glennister, but he appears to
be more interested in Helen Chester (Bessie Eyton). Meanwhile, Broncho
Kid (Wheeler Oakman), the faro-table dealer, has fallen in love with Cherry,
and he plots with Glennister to have the Midas Mine seized and its owner
arrested for the murder of the town marshal.

Glennister and his friends are able to gain control of the mine, and Broncho
Kid is killed, after telling Glennister of McNamara's plot. Glennister and
McNamara engage in a bloody fist fight, which the former wins. Cherry
Malotte discovers that Glennister was never in love with Helen, and the two
are reunited.

Recommending *The Spoilers* to viewers then, as now, was the brutal realism of the climactic fight sequence, acted out by William Farnum and Tom Santschi. Santschi was a veteran Selig player. Farnum, however, was here making an impressive film debut, and he was later to become a popular leading man with the William Fox Company; the role of Glennister fell to Farnum after Hobart Bosworth, who was originally to have played the part, left Selig to form his own company. The photography has a, perhaps unintentional, harsh documentary quality, which helps build the atmosphere of the film, but what chiefly creates an impact are the sets—unfortunately, one cannot give credit to the art director, for such a title was unknown then. The buildings and the muddy streets capture the harsh, unrelenting cruelty that must have been an integral part of the Alaskan pioneering spirit. Similarly, the characters look as though they might have stepped out of late nineteenth century photographs of the Alaskan goldfields: the costumes are drab, the women are buxom and relatively plain, and the men are shabbily dressed, with weather-beaten faces.

The direction is not particularly impressive. It seems very theatrical and encourages melodramatics from the actors. These same melodramatics are carried through into the subtitles, but presumably, the fault here is due to the fact that the script writer, Lanier Bartlett, adapted the titles directly from Rex Beach's novel. One major fault, however, which can squarely be laid at the pen of the scriptwriter, is that of having every dialogue title begin with the speaker's name; this is a style of title writing which, by 1914, had almost completely disappeared.

The Spoilers' director, Colin Campbell (circa 1866-1928), was noted as a cold, silent type—the son of a Scottish Presbyterian minister—and this frigid attitude shows in the film. Harry Carr, writing in the June, 1915, issue of *Photoplay*, called Campbell,

a keen, incisive, abrupt director. . . . He knows exactly what he wants and delivers his orders with a precision that gets action. He depends very little upon the company to supply him inspirations. He is the intellect that shoots to the mark he has selected. As a director, Mr. Campbell strikes the observer as being cold, clear and intellectual.

Campbell had joined the Selig Company around 1910 and remained with it through 1919. In 1915, *The Moving Picture World* hailed him as "among the foremost directors in the making of photoplays in America." At Selig, Campbell directed most of the company's major productions, including *The Rosary* (1915), *The Ne-er Do Well* (1915), and *The Crisis* (1916). His methods were old-fashioned, and they probably appealed to an old-fashioned company like Selig, but by the 1920's, Campbell was finding it difficult to obtain directing assignments and his career ended in 1924.

The Spoilers received its premiere at Chicago's Orchestra Hall on March

25, 1914, before an audience of some two thousand people. It was subsequently chosen as the opening night film for New York's new Strand Theater and became an immediate popular and critical success. The critic in *Variety* (April 17, 1914) commented, "To the rabid movie fan—the one who revels in action, excitement and a panoramic succession of real life adventures—this picture hands him a wallop. . . . *The Spoilers* is a red-blooded, peppery story that will catch wideawake, live Americans." *Variety* went on to applaud Beach, who had apparently kept a watchful eye on the production, particularly as far as the re-creation of the city of Nome at Selig's Los Angeles studio was concerned.

The two leading ladies of the film, Kathlyn Williams and Bessie Eyton also came in for their share of praise. Both were Selig contract players, and the previous year Williams had starred in the screen's first serial, *The Adventures of Kathlyn*. Of her performance in *The Spoilers*, *The Moving Picture World* (April 3, 1914) wrote, "She is the only character among all of them whose soul bears her above her surroundings." *Variety* thought it "doubtful if any other actress could have improved upon the part." "As for Bessie Eyton's interpretation of Helen Chester," wrote the same periodical, "she is due for all the bouquets that will come her way. Her hardest scenes were the escape from the boat and the fight in the mountain resort. She met them both and many others with consummate skill that few movie leads possess."

The Spoilers represents the high spot in the production record of the Selig Company, founded in Chicago by William N. Selig. Selig was one of the original founding members of the Motion Picture Patents Group, and he was also the first film pioneer to engage, on a regular basis, in film production in Los Angeles, setting up a studio in the city in 1909. Tom Mix began his screen career with Selig in 1910, remaining with the company through 1917. Aside from the Campbell-directed films already mentioned, the most important productions of the Selig Company were *The Two Orphans* (1911), *The Coming of Columbus* (1912), *The Count of Monte Cristo* (1913), and *The Garden of Allah* (1917). The Company was also noted for the number of its animal pictures, featuring residents of the Selig Zoo in Los Angeles. Selig continued to be involved in film production through the early 1920's and died in 1948.

When *The Spoilers* was initially released in England, reaction was favorable, but the public would not accept a film of such length—nine reels—and the British distributor was forced to reduce the film, drastically, down to four reels. The same was not the case in America, and in 1916, *The Spoilers* was reissued in an expanded twelve-reel version, which included scenes of Beach at work in his study.

Anthony Slide

THE SQUAW MAN

Released: 1914
Production: Cecil B. De Mille and Oscar Apfel for Jesse L. Lasky Feature
Play Company
Direction: Cecil B. De Mille and Oscar Apfel
Screenplay: Cecil B. De Mille and Oscar Apfel; based on Edwin Milton
Royle's adaptation of his play of the same name
Cinematography: Alfred Gandolfi
Editing: Mamie Wagner
Length: 6 reels

Principal characters:
Captain James Wynnegate	Dustin Farnum
Henry, Earl of Kerhill	Monroe Salisbury
Diana, Countess of Kerhill	Winifred Kingston
Nat-U-Rich	Red Wing
Cash Hawkins	Billy Elmer
Grouchy	Dick La Strange
Sir John	Foster Knox
Tabywana	Joe E. Singleton
Big Bill	Dick La Reno
Mr. Petrie	Fred Montague
Hal	Baby de Rue
The Dowager Lady Kerhill	Mrs. A. W. Filson
Lady Mabel Wynnegate	Haidee Fuller

The Squaw Man holds a very important place in film history but not because it ranks as an exceptional film. In the realm of filmmaking, it is noteworthy only for its action and story line, but its historical significance is that it was the first feature film of this length (6 reels) to be made in what became known as Hollywood.

In becoming so, it established the Jesse L. Lasky Feature Play Company as an important production company which would eventually grow through several transformations to become Paramount, and it was the motion-picture directorial debut (he was actually codirector) of pioneer Cecil B. De Mille, who, as a result of this achievement, would assume the title "The Father of Hollywood."

Cecil Blount De Mille was born on August 12, 1881, in Ashfield, Massachusetts. Both of his parents had been involved in playwriting. His father, Henry, collaborated with David Belasco on four plays—*The Wife*, *Lord Chumley*, *The Charity Ball*, and *Men and Women*—and his mother, Mathilda, who was also a writer, ran her own theatrical agency.

Cecil and his brother William were both educated with aspirations for careers in the theater. William became a well-known playwright and Cecil, who both acted and wrote, also managed his mother's agency where he made the acquaintance of Jesse L. Lasky, a vaudeville musician. It was Lasky with whom De Mille attended a screening of Edwin S. Porter's masterpiece, *The Great Train Robbery*, (1903), at a small film house on New York City's Sixth Avenue near 23rd Street. De Mille was so enthusiastic at the potential for storytelling in this new medium, that he convinced Lasky to join him in producing motion pictures.

They joined forces with a glove salesman named Samuel Goldfish (later Goldwyn) and an attorney named Arthur Friend and managed to collect fifteen thousand dollars to form the Jesse L. Lasky Feature Play Company with De Mille as director/general.

In announcing their venture, Lasky told *The Moving Picture World*: "We want the stories to be melodramatic, with great action and plenty of heart interest. . . . We will not engage a stock company. We will engage special casts for each play, and for a star a man or woman as the story may require."

In his memoirs, De Mille recalled that it was only natural that they turn to the stage for the choice of their first vehicle and, in doing so, purchased the rights to *The Squaw Man*, a successful play about the West set in Wyoming by Edwin Milton Royle. They hired the stage actor Dustin Farnum as the star and soon, with director Oscar Apfel and cameraman Alfred Gandolfi, were on a train headed for Flagstaff, Arizona, the site they had selected to set up production because it would be warmer there than Montana which they had originally selected for winter shooting.

When the train stopped in Arizona, however, not only was it raining, but it also simply was not the West they envisioned for their picture, and De Mille, noting that the last stop on the train was sunny Los Angeles, which had already become the production site for numerous one, two, and three reelers, suggested they try their luck there.

Their sparse budget afforded them little luxury in selecting a production site once they arrived in Los Angeles, so the first home of the Jesse L. Lasky Feature Play Company became a barn at the corner of Vine and Selma at 6284 Selma Avenue. The barn was used as a stable by citrus grower Jacob Stern and was adjacent to a pleasantly odoriferous orange grove.

Thus, in these humble beginnings was founded the forerunner of Paramount and the home of motion-picture production that would become known as Hollywood, with De Mille *accepting* credit for being the father of the Hollywood film industry.

One of De Mille's edicts of filmmaking from the beginning was an emphasis on having a good story to tell. In order to assure complete cooperation from author Royle regarding changes he was making in the script, he hired Royle as head of the company's story department.

Most of the scriptwriting was done by De Mille and Apfel on the train West. The plot of *The Squaw Man* tells of English army Captain James

Wynnegate (Dustin Farnum) who, with his cousin Henry, Earl of Kerhill (Monroe Salisbury), holds joint custody of a relief fund founded by the members of his regiment to aid war widows. Kerhill embezzles the money, but because Wynnegate loves Kerhill's wife Diana (Winifred Kingston) and wishes to save the family name, he takes the blame for the embezzlement.

He leaves England for the American West, but his ship burns at sea, and he and a few passengers are rescued and brought to safety in New York. He then travels cross country to Wyoming and changes his name to Carston. In Wyoming, he buys a ranch and falls in love with and marries an Indian girl named Nat-U-Rich (Red Wing). Wynnegate/Carston makes an enemy of cattle rustler Cash Hawkins (Billy Elmer), but Nat-U-Rich saves his life when Hawkins attempts to kill him. She bears him a child and eventually kills Hawkins.

In the meantime, the melodrama continues as Kerhill is injured in a big-game hunt but before he dies confesses to Wynnegates's innocence. Diana follows Wynnegate to Wyoming where, accused of Hawkin's murder, Nat-U-Rich commits suicide. Wynnegate returns to England with his half-breed son and Diana and becomes the new Earl of Kerhill.

Of historical note is the inclusion in the plot of an early cinematic example of Indian-white miscegenation. In this film, the Indian wife commits suicide and the father must take his son out of the country, but it is a theme that would appear in many Westerns, but most notably sound ones such as *Duel in the Sun* (1948), *Broken Arrow* (1950), and *Across the Wild Missouri* (1951).

Production of *The Squaw Man* began on December 29, 1913, and took only eighteen days. De Mille directed the actors, and Apfel and Gandolfi were in charge of the action sequences. Most of the production was shot in Los Angeles, with some location scenes done on the Green River in Wyoming and the ship-burning sequence filmed at Catalina Island.

When the film was completed and ready for previewing, the novice production company discovered that the film jumped so much during projection that it was not viewable. Fearful of faulty film stock, Goldfish urged his partners to bring the film back East to Philadelphia and duping expert Sigmund Lubin. De Mille's version of the difficulty was that the sprocket punching machine they had utilized was incompatible with current projection machines, but film historian Terry Ramsaye explained the problem of the "acute St. Vitus" as the result of their having used two different make cameras, which they indeed had. Once remedied, the film was screened for exhibitors with great success.

It was released on February 15, 1914, and eventually earned $244,700 on its modest investment. It proved an immensely popular film, and critics commended it as an exemplary adaptation of a stage play. De Mille was so confident of the universality and lasting ability of *The Squaw Man* that he remade it twice: another silent version in 1918 with Elliott Dexter and Jack

Holt and a talking version in 1931 starring Warner Baxter, with Eleanor Boardman as Diana, Lupe Velez as the Indian maiden, and Charles Bickford as Hawkins. The 1914 version survives intact as do all of De Mille's films.

The Squaw Man is a milestone in motion-picture history for its paving the way for the Jesse L. Lasky Feature Play Company's becoming Paramount and for De Mille having crossed the first hurdle in becoming one of the preeminent motion-picture pioneers.

Ronald Bowers

SQUIBS WINS THE CALCUTTA SWEEP

Released: 1922
Production: Welsh-Pearson
Direction: George Pearson
Screenplay: George Pearson and Hugh E. Wright
Cinematography: Emile Lauste
Length: 6 reels

Principal characters:

Squibs Hopkins	Betty Balfour
Sam Hopkins	Hugh E. Wright
P. C. Lee	Fred Groves
Ivy	Annette Benson
The Weasel	Bertram Burleigh
Detective	Hal Martin
Reporter	Donald Searle
Nosey	Sam Lewis
Bob	Tom Morris
Mrs. Lee	Mary Brough
Mr. Lee	Ambrose Manning

Squibs Wins the Calcutta Sweep was never released in the United States as far as can be ascertained, and there are many who would question its importance in the history and development of the cinema, as it applies not only to Great Britain but also to the world. The film is, admittedly, a minor one, but it is one of the few extant—and accessible—films of a major British silent director, George Pearson, and also, the only surviving example of the popular series of Squibs films that the director made in the early 1920's.

George Pearson (1875-1973) was the foremost thinker and innovator among British silent-film directors. Unlike most of his contemporaries, he was an intelligent man, having been educated at Oxford, and he pursued the career of a schoolmaster before entering the film industry in 1912, at a time when most middle-aged, well-educated men would have considered a more respectable occupation. In the teens, he directed many important films, notably a version of the Sherlock Holmes classic *A Study in Scarlet* (1914); a series of "Ultus" mystery thrillers along the lines of the popular, contemporary French "Fantomas" serials; and *The Better 'Ole* (1918), a brilliant example of World War I humor (remade in Hollywood in 1926 with Syd Chaplin). In 1920, Pearson directed *Nothing Else Matters*, featuring a young British stage actress named Betty Balfour, whom the director selected as the star for the Squibs series, *Squibs* (1921), *Squibs Wins the Calcutta Sweep* (1922), and *Squibs M.P.* (1923). The heroine was nicknamed Squibs because it hinted at fireworks and suggested the vibrant humor which Balfour represented in the British cinema of the 1920's.

Squibs Wins the Calcutta Sweep is an unusual film in that it begins and ends on a tragic note. This mixture of tragedy and comedy, unusual in British films, was suggested to Pearson by a remark of Rupert Brooks, "Tragedy and comedy will not leave the world while two things stay in it . . . Death and Fools." Squibs Hopkins (Betty Balfour), a cockney flower seller (similar to Eliza Dolittle, the heroine of George Bernard Shaw's *Pygmalion*), has a sister, Ivy (Annette Benson), who is married to a cat burglar named the Weasel (Bertram Burleigh), who, being caught by the owner of a house he is robbing, murders the unfortunate householder. The Weasel escapes to Paris, where he is later joined by his wife.

In the meantime, Squibs must cope with a policeman named P. C. Lee (Fred Groves) as a fiancé and a drunkard—albeit a likable one—for a father. The father, brilliantly played by the British character actor Hugh E. Wright (who also coauthored the screenplay), has been stealing money from Squibs to pay for his beer, and to compensate her and to try and make amends, he purchases for Squibs a sweepstake ticket. Of course, Squibs wins the sweepstake. Her father receives the news in the local bar, where he promptly passes out, while Squibs is told of her windfall while selling flowers beneath the statue of Eros in Piccadilly Circus. In a delightful scene, Squibs learns of her win and rushes across the street, kissing a policeman who is directing traffic. This entire sequence was filmed using a camera hidden inside a parked van and has an obvious freshness and unplanned, carefree feel to it. It is *cinéma vérité* before the phrase was invented.

Squibs uses her new-found wealth to purchase gifts for her friends and needy neighbors. In a scene, which obviously has its origins in *Intolerance* (1916)—Pearson was an unqualified admirer of D. W. Griffith—charity workers visit Squibs and advise her against spending her money, unwisely, on the poor and suggesting it would be better to channel her funds through their organization. Squibs puts on phoney airs, arriving at the cottage of her policeman-fiancé's parents (Mary Brough and Ambrose Manning) in a limousine, and pretending to be a "lady," first upsetting and then amusing the elderly couple. In these scenes, Balfour's acting talents really shine, as she enters the couple's humble abode with all the austerity and coldness of a dowager addressing pathetic members of the working classes. Later, witnessing the parents' distress, she kicks up her legs and loses all signs of decorum. It is a sequence that Mary Pickford would have been proud to handle as well.

Ultimately, Squibs decides to spend part of her money on a trip to Paris to find her sister and husband. Again, Pearson goes out on the streets, filming the boulevards and back alleys of Paris. The London police follow Squibs's trail, and when she finds the Weasel, he kills himself rather than be taken by the police. There is a touch of symbolism here as the Weasel thinks of the gallows awaiting him and there is a shot of the cord on the blinds at his window resembling the hangman's noose. The film ends with Squibs comforting her bereaved sister, an unusual and poignant ending for a film which might be dismissed as little more than a slight British comedy.

The acting for the most part is fairly restrained, although one might wish that the scenes of the celebrations of Squib's good fortune were not quite so prolonged and that the extras were a little less exuberant. The only other criticism might be directed toward the casting of Fred Groves as Balfour's policeman-boyfriend. He is really much too old and stolid to be attractive to a young flower seller.

After *Squibs Wins the Calcutta Sweep*, Pearson went on to direct several major silent films starring Balfour, the most notable of which was *Reveille* (1924), a study of a group of slum-dwelling Londoners coping with the aftermath of World War I. In 1930, Pearson came to Hollywood to supervise production of *Journey's End*, the first film to be directed by James Whale. Sadly, Pearson ended his days in the commercial film industry directing so-called "quota quickies," the British equivalents of poverty row productions. With the outbreak of World War II, the director became involved with the GPO Film Unit and the Colonial Film Unit. He finished his working days teaching young would-be filmmakers from the British colonies the techniques of direction. Pearson's autobiography, *Flashback*, was published in 1957.

Betty Balfour (born 1903) was the only major star to emerge from the British silent cinema. She became immensely popular in Great Britain and throughout Europe and was dubbed the British Mary Pickford. A number of her late silent films were screened in the United States, but she made little impact. Thanks to a stage career in the teens, the actress was able to make an easy transition to talkies, and she is best known to American audiences for her supporting role in the 1934 Jessie Matthews vehicle, *Evergreen*. In 1935, Balfour remade *Squibs Wins the Calcutta Sweep* as a musical under the title of *Squibs*, with Stanley Holloway portraying her policeman-boyfriend and Gordon Harker her father.

Squibs Wins the Calcutta Sweep was produced by Pearson's own company, which he had formed in association with T. A. Welsh, and which had a small, one-stage studio in the Craven Park district of London. The film cost ten thousand pounds to produce—considerably more than Pearson was to spend on some of his 1930's films—and grossed approximately twice that amount. Pearson saw the film at a 1952 tribute at the Cinémathèque Française, and wrote a colleague,

It was a most surprising experience for me . . . an evening I shall remember while life lasts. I was really scared before the film began . . . I felt that it would be a miracle if 1922 could stand up to the intelligence and probable cynicism of 1952. That the test was there I knew, and had to be faced. Well, the old film has done its job, and can go back into the quiet retirement of the archives without disgrace. I know all its faults, and smile at them now, in the same kindly way that the audience did.

Anthony Slide

STARK LOVE

Released: 1927
Production: Karl Brown for Paramount
Direction: Karl Brown
Screenplay: Karl Brown
Cinematography: James Murray
Length: 7 reels/6,203 feet

Principal characters:
Barbara Allen	Helen Mundy
Rob Warwick	Forrest James
Jason Warwick (Rob's father)	Silas Miracle
Quill Allen	Reb Grogan

Stark Love is a remarkable film, shot entirely on location in the Appalachian mountains of North Carolina. It is a documentary, and, at the same time, it is a fictionalized drama, but unlike, for example, the documentaries of Robert Flaherty, it has an honesty in its storytelling. Unlike Flaherty, who would re-create incidents or life-styles to simulate current reality, *Stark Love*'s director and creator, Karl Brown, set out to make a fictional feature which, through its story, would capture on film the lives of Americans who still adhered to the primitive moral standards and ways of life of an earlier age. As Kevin Brownlow wrote in *The War, the West and the Wilderness*,

> Apart from the two leads, every member of the cast is an authentic mountaineer. There is no make-up; the quality of the faces, the texture of the rough skin, is carefully and affectionately captured by the camera, and the effect is reminiscent (in original prints) of seventeenth-century Dutch painting. The compositions crystallize the atmosphere but are never obtrusive.

Karl Brown (born 1895) first came to prominence in the film industry as an assistant cameraman to G. W. Bitzer, working on *Intolerance* (1916) and other D. W. Griffith productions. He became a director of photography in the 1920's, filming many major productions, notably *The Covered Wagon* (1923), *Beggar on Horseback* (1925), and *The Pony Express* (1925), all directed by James Cruze. He became a director and scriptwriter with *Stark Love*, but this was Brown's only production to make any impact—and its impact was purely aesthetic—and in the 1930's and the 1940's, Brown was reduced to writing or directing (or both) "B"-grade pictures such as *A Woman Is a Judge* (1939), *Before I Hang* (1940), and *Hitler Dead or Alive* (1942).

The idea for *Stark Love* originated with earlier films on which Brown had worked, in particular *The Covered Wagon* and *The Pony Express*. Brown was fascinated with the pioneer spirit and believed that no actor or actress could ever entirely duplicate what a true pioneer had taken for granted as a way of life. Paramount gave the go-ahead for the production chiefly because its budget was so low; there were no studio overheads, a minimal crew, and virtually all the performers were nonactors. The leading lady, sixteen-year-old Helen Mundy, was a Knoxville, Tennessee, high-school girl. Playing opposite Mundy was Forrest James, another Knoxville High School student, whom Brown spotted one evening in a restaurant.

The theme of *Stark Love* is expressed by the title, "Man is the absolute ruler—Woman is the working slave." The women in the film are not only subservient, but they look it, in their eyes and the way in which they carry themselves. The focal point of these people's lives is not a person or persons, but the log cabin in which they live. In fact, Karl Brown wanted to title the film *The Log Cabin*, but Paramount went with *Stark Love*, suggested by Walter Woods.

"In their inaccessible mountains," explains the opening title, "these people remain undeveloped by culture." One inhabitant, who has higher ambitions, is Rob Warwick (Forrest James), who has taught himself to read. Rob's dreams for a better life are impressed on his girl, Barbara Allen (Helen Mundy), who also yearns for an escape from her current existence. As portrayed by Mundy, the character of Barbara Allen has something of an ethereal quality. In the scene in which she is chopping wood, there is more than a hint of Lillian Gish in her mannerisms, and at times—such as in this sequence—Mundy's acting seems at odds with the stark, realistic quality of the rest of the film.

Once a year, the mountain people gather for a "funeral feast," at which they honor the past dead, and at which all "wild marriages" are legalized by the circuit preacher. Rob decides to go to the city with the preacher, and there he will sell his horse to pay for an education for Barbara. When Rob returns from the city to collect Barbara, however, he finds much has changed. In his absence, Rob's mother has died, and his father, Jason (Silas Miracle), feels the need for a woman to take care of his log cabin. At the death of his wife, the farmer speaks an epitaph which summarizes perfectly the woman's place in this society: "She hoed the field—she did the wash—she chopped the firewood—she put the children to bed—and she died." Barbara proves a more than adequate substitute for Rob's mother, and in time, Jason decides to marry her. Barbara's feelings on the subject are not considered in this society, and the matter is concluded between Jason and Barbara's father, Quill Allen (Reb Grogan).

When Rob returns to claim Barbara, he is introduced to his new "maw." A fight develops between Rob and his father. The boy is beaten, but Barbara picks up an axe and threatens the old man. Then she and Rob escape by floating down the swollen river to the valley below. The final river sequence was not in the film as Brown planned it, but Paramount insisted on a climactic

finale for the production, and so Brown and his crew returned to the mountains, creating the sequence by building a dam upstream, and then blowing
it up.

One major sequence which the studio insisted be cut from the production
was Barbara's violent rape by Rob's father. Other short sequences also appear
to have been cut, such as the scene where the preacher asks a young child,
"Have you ever heard of God, my boy?" and the youngster scratches his head
and responds, "Um. . . . I think so, isn't his last name Damn?"

In a lengthy interview with Kevin Brownlow, Brown noted, "The real cause
for genuine regret is that I made the picture at a time when the screen was
heavily censored and that some of the more powerful scenes were banned by
the censors. I regard the picture as a pallid ghost." Despite Brown's personal
misgivings, the critics found much to admire in the production. *Photoplay*
(May, 1927) called it

> A mighty fine picture, in some ways as noteworthy as Robert Flaherty's *Nanook* and
> *Moana*. . . . *Stark Love*, despite its garish boxoffice title, is a picture of genuine merit.
> It is astonishing how well the mountaineers act. Helen Mundy . . . is excellent as the
> heroine, while a hill boy, Forrest James, gives an amazingly good performance. An old
> timer, Silas Miracle, plays the boy's father in a way to outshine Wally Beery's best work.
> Don't miss this film.

In *The New York Times* (February 28, 1927), Mordaunt Hall wrote,

> An engrossing and trenchant pictorial transcript of the daily life of those slothful moun-
> taineers of North Carolina and Tennessee has been brought to the screen by Karl
> Brown. . . . By adhering closely to his subject and scorning to permit any stereotyped
> movie spasms to interfere with its natural trend, Mr. Brown reveals a feeling akin to that
> of Robert Flaherty. . . . The chronicle . . . is merely a thread on which to unfold the
> details in the lives of these mountaineers."

Long considered a "lost" film, *Stark Love* was recovered in the early 1970's
and is now preserved in the National Film Collection at the Library of Congress. It stands today not only as a work of film art, but also as a unique
record of the daily lives of a group of true American pioneers. Everything
from how they wash their clothes to cleaning their shoes and baking their
bread is captured here on film, which successfully combines art and entertainment.

Anthony Slide

STEAMBOAT BILL, JR.

Released: 1928
Production: Buster Keaton Productions; released by United Artists
Direction: Charles F. Reisner
Screenplay: Carl Harbaugh
Cinematography: Dev Jennings and Bert Haines
Editing: Sherman Kell
Technical direction: Fred Gabourie
Length: 7 reels/6,400 feet

Principal characters:
William Canfield, Jr.	Buster Keaton
William Canfield, Sr. ("Steamboat Bill")	Ernest Torrence
John J. King	Tom McGuire
Kitty King	Marion Byron
Tom Carter (Canfield's first mate)	Tom Lewis
Barber	Joe Keaton

Steamboat Bill, Jr., the last of Buster Keaton's independent productions, ranks as one of his unqualified masterpieces. Although often overshadowed by the stunning originality and epic scale of *The General* (1926), *Steamboat Bill, Jr.*, is in many ways a deeper, more personal work. It is a graceful, aesthetically satisfying film, representing Keaton at the height of his creative powers. In addition, it is virtually a catalog of his favorite themes, and in retrospect seems a kind of summing-up of a brilliant career that was about to be cut tragically short.

In 1920, following a three-year "apprenticeship" in support of comic Roscoe "Fatty" Arbuckle, Keaton had inherited Arbuckle's Comique Film Corporation when the latter moved on to star in feature films for Paramount. With one exception—*The Saphead* (1920), which is not considered a major work—all of Keaton's films through *Steamboat Bill, Jr.*, were produced under the auspices of this company which within a few years became Buster Keaton Productions, Inc. The head of the company since its inception in 1917 was Joseph M. Schenck, a shrewd businessman whose principal enterprise prior to that time had been the production of films starring his wife, Norma Talmadge. Schenck came to serve Keaton not only as a producer but also as a father figure—a paternal relationship enhanced by Keaton's 1921 marriage to Norma's younger sister Natalie.

Schenck's careful management of Buster Keaton Productions freed Keaton from monetary concerns and allowed him to direct his energies into his work. He was able to maintain a more or less permanent production staff, a truly collaborative filmmaking team whose members were not only thoroughly professional, but also (and just as importantly) personally compatible with Keaton. His biographers have often remarked on the relaxed atmosphere that surrounded the creation of Keaton's films and have concluded that his comic genius functioned best under such circumstances. For an intuitive artist working in such an economically demanding art form, this was perhaps the nearest thing possible to an ideal creative environment; in retrospect, however, this insular arrangement seems a curse as well as a blessing. It undoubtedly exacerbated Keaton's almost legendary lack of business acumen, ultimately a major factor in this tragic decline. On the other hand, however, without it, his comic potential might have remained largely untapped. In any case, Keaton's output during this period (nineteen two-reel films and ten features) represents a concentrated outburst of brilliance—one of the finest bodies of work in the American cinema.

By the time of *Steamboat Bill, Jr.*, however, the protective umbrella of Buster Keaton Productions was leaking badly. Beginning in 1924, when Schenck was named a full partner in United Artists, he had progressively become more involved in the affairs of that troubled company. He was named its president in 1926, and he decided at that time to bring Keaton into the United Artists fold. Before that time, the Keaton features had been released through the Metro Company and later Metro-Goldwyn-Mayer. This was a step up in prestige for Keaton, and Schenck felt obliged to finance Keaton's biggest production to date, on a scale commensurate with the other members of United Artists, Mary Pickford, Douglas Fairbanks, and Charles Chaplin. The happy result was *The General*, considered by many to be Keaton's greatest achievement.

Despite its deserved status as a comic masterpiece, however, *The General* was a box-office failure and a financial disaster for United Artists. Schenck, determined to prevent the recurrence of such a fiasco, began to make inroads into Keaton's creative freedom. In addition to his insistence on a smaller, more "sure-fire" film—this was to be *College* (1927)—he also authorized the enlargement of Keaton's staff. Some of these added personnel were "supervisors," financial watchdogs who were instructed to apprise Schenck of any unnecessary delays or cost overruns during production, while others were "creative" people who proved to be little more than dead weight.

Keaton had always received at least a shared credit for the direction of his films, but his last two United Artists releases bear the names of others— James W. Horne for *College* and Charles F. (Chuck) Reisner for *Steamboat Bill, Jr.* Although *College*, definitely a lesser Keaton work, seems to have suffered somewhat from these restrictions, *Steamboat Bill, Jr.*, reveals emphatically that the comedian was still in control. Much of the film's homogeneity with Keaton's earlier work can be attributed to the continuing presence of such key collaborators as cameramen Bert Haines and Dev Jennings (who had both shot Keaton's three previous films, including *The General*) and technical director Fred Gabourie, indispensible when it came to mechanical matters, who had been with Keaton since his short-subject days. For all the importance of his technical team, however, the guiding intelligence was still Keaton's and *Steamboat Bill, Jr.*, both thematically and stylistically, is clearly allied to his other works.

Steamboat Bill, Jr., set in the town of River Junction, centers around the rivalry between "Steamboat Bill" Canfield (Ernest Torrence), a grizzled old-timer with a ramshackle boat called the *Stonewall Jackson*, and John J. King (Tom McGuire), a wealthy businessman who virtually owns the town. The bank, the hotel, and numerous local businesses all bear King's name, as does his steamboat, a "floating palace" that he hopes will send Canfield's operation into bankruptcy. Canfield, stubbornly holding out, is cheered by a telegram from his son, William Canfield, Jr., whom he has not seen since the boy was a child. The telegram announces that Junior has graduated from college and is coming to River Junction for a visit because it was "his mother's wish." (The absence of Mrs. Canfield is not explained.) Enthusiastic at the prospect of a "chip off the old block" to help him in his fight against King, Bill is severely disappointed when he finally meets his son (Buster Keaton). Mustachioed, foppily dressed, carrying a ukelele and wearing a beret, "Willie" is the exact opposite of his father's idealized image. Disgusted at this mockery of a man, Bill sets out to make his son over. The first stop is the barber shop, where the mustache is removed in two deft swipes of the razor, and where Willie also encounters King's daughter, Kitty (Marion Byron), whom he knows from school. Eventually, with Kitty's "help"—and despite Bill's efforts—Willie's ensemble is transformed from collegiate to that of a natty yachtsman, equally inappropriate for work on the *Stonewall Jackson*. Ultimately, Willie ends up in his father's outsized work clothes.

Willie soon proves himself totally incompetent in steamboatsmanship, and his budding romance with Kitty is discouraged by both their fathers. When Willie sneaks out at night to visit Kitty, his disobedience is discovered by his father, who the next morning hands him a return ticket to Boston. Later that morning, Bill discovers that the town's "Public Safety Committee" has had his boat condemned. Presuming King to be responsible, Bill assaults him and lands in jail. Willie, packed and prepared to leave, tears up his ticket when he learns of his father's predicament. That night, he trudges to the jail through a rainstorm to bring Bill a loaf of bread. Bill refuses the bread until Willie pantomimes that the loaf contains the tools necessary for a jailbreak; the sheriff's suspicions are aroused, however, and the ruse is discovered when the bread breaks apart, spilling the tools onto the floor. Willie manages to overpower the sheriff, allowing his father to flee, but while locking the unconscious lawman in the cell, he also catches his pants in the door. By the time he frees himself, he is cornered by two deputies, then knocked unconscious by a vicious blow from the revived sheriff. Bill, indignant at this brutal mistreatment of his son, emerges from his nearby hiding place, slugs the sheriff, and surrenders himself. Willie, meanwhile, is taken away to a hospital.

By the next day, the previous night's storm has gathered tremendous force and begins to wreak havoc on River Junction. The town's inhabitants take shelter, as the wind destroys many buildings and the raging river collapses the pier, freeing both steamboats from their moorings. Willie, exposed to the elements when the walls of the hospital are blown away, wages a long battle with the storm. He triumphs in the end, rescuing Kitty and both their fathers from the river, resolving the rivalry between the two men, and clearing the way for his marriage to Kitty.

In many ways, *Steamboat Bill, Jr.*, is a typical Keaton film. Its theme is common to his work—the transformation under duress of an effete or incompetent youth into an athletic, divinely graceful hero—and many of its individual elements were also Keaton staples. As in *Our Hospitality* (1923) and *The General*, the setting is of high visual interest, and Keaton, as usual, spared no expense in the pursuit of authenticity (important as a counterpoint to the near-surreal comedy). Once again, the "love interest" here exists as a sort of necessary narrative evil, with the unfortunate actress, like so many before her, treated somewhat like an animated prop.

Familiar as much of *Steamboat Bill, Jr.*, was for Keaton, however, several aspects were more fully developed than in his earlier work, contributing to the film's exceptional quality. In particular, the film's central relationship, between the junior and senior Canfields, is one of genuine warmth—in contrast to Keaton's often mechanical handling of such matters. Willie himself is one of Keaton's most charming and guileless characters, and the brawny Ernest Torrence enhances the amusing visual contrast between himself and the diminutive Keaton with an excellent performance as "Steamboat Bill." Torrence, in fact, is more of a true co-star to Keaton than any of his leading ladies had ever been. Carefully constructed on this solid foundation, the film's narrative effortlessly accommodates some of Keaton's most inspired comedy, most notably the justly famous cyclone sequence that climaxes the film. One of the most remarkable passages in Keaton's work, it is perhaps the most concentrated example of the surrealistic, dreamlike side of his comic world, achieving a sense of the nightmarish that is all the more effective for its "realistic" context.

The cyclone sequence begins when the narrative has reached a dual crisis point: Canfield, Sr., is in jail and on the verge of losing his beloved steamboat; Willie is in the hospital, with his romance with Kitty apparently doomed. A brief establishing sequence depicts the enormous force of the storm, as the townspeople scramble for shelter. Suddenly, the wind lifts away the walls of the hospital, revealing the startled Willie sitting up in bed. He takes flight, but the abrupt collapse of the building immediately in front of him sends him scrambling back to his bed, which is then whisked away by the wind. It scoots eerily along through the deserted streets, pausing briefly in a stable, where Willie is momentarily the object of curious regard by the resident horses. On the move again, the bed makes another stop, in front of a two-story house. Willie cowers underneath his bed, having been blown out of it. Meanwhile, the front wall of the house begins to break off, and from the upstairs window, a man leaps to safety, using the bed—and thus Willie—to break his fall. The man runs off; the bed is blown away; and Willie stands dazed, rubbing his neck—oblivious to the wall of the house, poised to topple toward him. In a moment, it comes crashing down—but the opening of the upstairs window passes miraculously around Willie's body. Startled, he takes off running, tumbling through the streets partly under his own power, partly tossed about by the storm. He runs, leaps, and crawls in a futile attempt to make his way against the wind, eventually taking refuge in a deserted theater.

Temporarily sheltered, he has a freakish encounter with a series of theatrical devices and props, including a painted backdrop of a lake (which, in a daze after being struck by a falling sandbag, he mistakes as real, diving into the canvas), an eerily grinning ventriloquist's dummy that for a chilling moment seems possessed with a malevolent life of its own, and a magician's disappearing chamber. Fleeing from this strange interlude, he continues his perilous odyssey through the devastated town. He finally clings in desperation to a small but sturdy-looking tree, which is promptly uprooted by the cyclone and deposited in the swollen river. Clambering onto the deck of the drifting *Stonewall Jackson*, Willie then engineers a series of spectacular rescues: first of Kitty, as she floats by on a house; then of his father, in danger of drowning in the jail (which has been swept into the torrent); then of King, from the wreckage of his steamboat. Finally, having thus heroically resolved the various parental conflicts, Willie dives into the water one last time, emerging with a preacher in tow—the film's final shot.

Like the retelling of a dream the following morning, no words can do justice to the qualities of this sequence. Even a fairly detailed description omits dozens of details, all of which are orchestrated into a rousing, apocalyptic, fully satisfying climax, which takes up nearly the last quarter of the film's running time. The cyclone itself is played straight and is an awesomely believable event, a *tour de force* for Keaton's technicians; the comedy arises largely from the bizarre physical results of Keaton's attempts to function normally amidst the havoc. Simply to move from place to place in the wind, his body assumes seemingly gravity-defying angles; like walking in a dream, his efforts to go in one direction are often counter-productive. Huge buildings fill the screen, forming a solid backdrop to Keaton's tiny figure—then abruptly collapse in a heap. This scene is aided by composition and camera placement throughout the sequence which are superbly calculated for maximum effect.

The most famous and often-noted gag—the falling wall—was a dangerous and precisely calculated bit of business that involved no photographic trickery.

The wall weighed several tons, and the clearance of the window above Keaton's head was approximately three inches. His crew nearly rebelled because of the danger of the stunt, but Keaton insisted, and the result is one of the silent cinema's most memorable—and breathtaking—moments. ("First time I ever saw cameramen look the other way," Keaton recalled dryly.)

Underscoring the dreamlike qualities of the sequence is the feeling one gets that Keaton is not really *going* anywhere. He appears to be simply buffeted about, until the malevolent natural forces see fit to deposit him in a position where he must watch the characters of his personal drama float by on the river and must take decisive action. The resulting rescues, as Willie athletically transcends his natural incompetence, mastering the steamboat and triumphing over the elements, are a neat wrapup of the film's narrative and thematic concerns—yet Keaton also provides a typically unsettling ending with the apprehensive expression on his face as he hauls the preacher out of the water. The entire sequence is in perfect harmony with the central conception of Keaton's comedy, that of his body in a constant struggle to come to grips with the physical universe. Maintaining this image frequently pits him against the mechanical world of man and often against the forces of nature itself— nowhere more explicitly and spectacularly than in *Steamboat Bill, Jr.*

In addition, the cyclone sequence (and the entire film, for that matter) has an even deeper level of personal resonance with Keaton's life and career. The sequence itself, in fact, seems inspired by one of the key Keaton legends: as a small boy, he was allegedly picked up by just such a cyclone and deposited unhurt several blocks away. He was also known to have often declared in later years that the tiny Kansas town in which he was born was literally blown away by a storm, thus leaving him with "no birthplace." More specifically, the bizarre interlude in the abandoned theater is clearly a reference—and an unsettling one—to Keaton's early career in vaudeville, when he was billed as "The Human Mop" and was hurled about the stage by his father—who was an alcoholic and apparently abused him offstage as well, which is an interesting contrast to the father-son relationship in *Steamboat Bill, Jr.*

As brilliant as the cyclone sequence is, however, it shares the spotlight with many other equally inspired, although less spectacular, comic moments. One of the most delightful is the long sequence in which Canfield, Sr., attempts to rid his son of the noxious "collegiate" look. The gigolo mustache poses no problem, but it is Willie's beret that becomes the focal point of his father's disgust. In a beautifully executed scene, Willie tries on, at his father's request, a series of hats, each of which looks more ridiculous on his head than the last. In one brief, magical moment, the familiar Keaton porkpie hat is placed on his head, then he quickly snatches it off, with a furtive, reproachful glance to the side. Among other things, the hat shop scene is a superb example of Keaton's pantomimic skills, as is the scene of Willie's visit to his imprisoned father. In the latter, he employs an elaborate and hilarious pantomime in an attempt to convey to his uncomprehending father the somewhat complex message that the loaf of bread which he has brought contains all the tools necessary for a jailbreak. These are only a few of the film's comic gems, all of which flow beautifully within the narrative framework.

Willie Canfield, Jr., may have come through the cyclone unscathed and triumphant, but Keaton was not to fare as well in real life. Keaton's precipitous creative decline has been attributed to many factors, but the chronicle of his personal problems—including alcoholism—has tended to overshadow the basic economic reality. Keaton's films, unlike those of his contemporaries Harold Lloyd and Charles Chaplin, were never immensely profitable—and all of his United Artists releases had in fact lost money (at least in part because of the company's inadequate marketing). By the time of the production of *Steamboat Bill, Jr.*, in late 1927, Schenck, his personal resources strained by the box-office failure of his recent productions (including, but not exclusively, *The General* and *College*), had decided to abandon his independent production interests and devote his time exclusively to running United Artists. One of the major casualties of his decision was Buster Keaton Productions, Inc.— and by extension, Keaton himself. Schenck's brother, Nicholas, was then president of Metro-Goldwyn-Mayer's parent company, Loew's Inc., and Keaton was persuaded that his fortunes would be in good hands if he signed with M-G-M; in fact, he had very little choice, given his lack of box-office appeal. In January, 1928, before the release of *Steamboat Bill, Jr.*—which was to prove the least profitable of Keaton's films—he signed a two-year contract. He was later to call this "the worst mistake of my career."

With the dissolution of Buster Keaton Productions, Keaton's decline was inevitable, although not immediate. Nicholas Schenck was disinclined to serve as a protective figure in the manner of his brother, and Keaton was ill-prepared to fend for himself under the stewardship of the M-G-M studio heads, Irving Thalberg and Louis B. Mayer. Although Keaton was unhappy at M-G-M, he did manage to make one excellent film, *The Cameraman* (1928), and another good one, *Spite Marriage* (1929). He found his creative freedom increasingly circumscribed, however, by the studio's highly structured operations. There has been some speculation that Keaton could have made a successful transition to sound pictures, but he was never given a decent chance. His unstable personal life, combined with misunderstanding and mismanagement of his unique talents by M-G-M, brought an untimely end to his days of comic brilliance. He continued to work, in films and television, until his death in 1966—but during this long period he was merely a living shadow of his own greatness.

Howard H. Prouty

STELLA DALLAS

Released: 1925
Production: Samuel Goldwyn for United Artists
Direction: Henry King
Screenplay: Frances Marion; based on the novel of the same name by Olive Higgins Prouty
Cinematography: Arthur Edeson
Editing: Stuart Heisler
Length: 11 reels/10,157 feet

Principal characters:

Stella Dallas	Belle Bennett
Stephen Dallas	Ronald Colman
Laurel Dallas	Lois Moran
Helen Morrison	Alice Joyce
Ed Munn	Jean Hersholt
Mrs. Grosvenor	Beatrix Pryor
Richard Grosvenor	Douglas Fairbanks, Jr.

In the unfortunately anachronistic "women's-pictures" genre, a classification of picture making which is now relegated to television films and soap operas if tolerated at all by the modern women's movement, *Stella Dallas* was one of the most popular.

It began as a best-selling novel by Olive Higgins Prouty in 1923, and predictably went on to become a stage success in 1924 starring Mrs. Leslie Carter. There is no equivocating, *Stella Dallas* was a tearjerker *extraordinaire* and many colleagues thought that Samuel Goldwyn was a bit foolish in not only purchasing the property for the screen but also in investing $500,000 in its production—not a small sum at that time. Yet, it grossed more than two million dollars between 1925 and 1930, an exceptional return on Goldwyn's original investment, proving that the semiliterate Goldwyn always seemed to have the knack for putting his fingers on the pulse of the American filmgoing public and recognizing what it wanted. He had complete—if blind—faith in *Stella Dallas* as a screen vehicle and his success in making it a viable production makes him one of the best examples of the creative Hollywood producer. He cast the film with an eye toward believable characterizations rather than superstar appeal hiring the expert Frances Marion to write the script and the talented Henry King to direct. The rest was simply a matter of relying upon the moving and sentimental plot.

Stephen Dallas (Ronald Colman) is a young man from Massachusetts of good family background, but when his father's suicide leaves him penniless, he is unable to marry the patrician Helen Morrison (Alice Joyce), to whom he had been engaged. Thus, he takes up with the recalcitrant, lower-class

Stella Dallas (Belle Bennett) by whom he has a daughter Laurel (Lois Moran). Yet, when Stephen pursues a better job in New York City, Stella refuses to go along with him, choosing to remain with her local cronies, particularly Ed Munn (Jean Hersholt). Munn is likable but crude and wants to marry Stella but feels that their life together would be encumbered by Laurel's presence. Munn's drunken conduct on a train on which he is accompanied by Stella leads the town gossips to misjudge Stella's behavior as a mother, and in retaliation, the town parents refuse to allow their children to attend Laurel's birthday party. This was one of the most moving scenes in the film, with mother and daughter all alone with the party preparations and refreshments.

Laurel visits her father in New York City to find that he has renewed his friendship with Helen Morrison, now a widow. Stephen Dallas wants a divorce from Stella, but she refuses and takes Laurel on a holiday—at Stephen's expense—to a fashionable resort. Here, she suddenly realizes that her lack of polish is inhibiting her daughter's chances for a happy life and marriage to the eligible Richard Grosvenor (Douglas Fairbanks, Jr.).

The crude but clever Stella realizes she is hurting her daughter's future, and she visits Helen Morrison and tells her that she will grant Stephen a divorce if Helen will take Laurel and rear her as her own. Helen agrees, but Laurel objects, whereupon Stella, shrewdly throws a vulgar scene in which she purports to want to spend her life with the drunken Munn. She leaves Laurel with Helen and later writes to Laurel saying that she has gone to South America with Munn, thereby putting her daughter out of her life for good in order to provide her with a chance at happiness that she herself has never had.

Finally, Laurel marries Richard in a ceremony which takes place in the drawing room of Helen Morrison's townhouse and is visible from the street through large windows. The day of the wedding is a rainy one and standing on the sidewalk in the rain, shabbily dressed, is Stella Dallas, watching her beautiful daughter receive her wedding kiss. It is a scene in which the full impact of the story of mother-love and sacrifice merge quintessentially—with not a dry eye in the audience.

Despite plot contrivances which strain logic and credulity, *Stella Dallas* is a remarkably believable film and a great deal of the credit for this goes to King's direction. King is a director who made audiences believe in romantic love and honest sentiment. Prior to *Stella Dallas*, King's most noted film was *Tol'able David* (1921) starring Richard Barthelmess, but his post-*Stella Dallas* credits include *State Fair* (1933), *The Song of Bernadette* (1943), *Love Is a Many-Splendored Thing* (1955), and *Carousel* (1956). King had a facility for intercutting long, medium, and close-up shots to register action, emotion, and reaction, and in *Stella Dallas* there are at least three noteworthy examples of this ability to draw the audience into the action of the film.

The first half of the film contains the memorable birthday party sequence in which young Laurel is able to control her utter disappointment until the moment she takes a bite of her birthday ice cream and then her tears flow. As a matter of fact, when Ernst Lubitsch, who had refused to direct this "overly sentimental" film, saw this scene, he wondered how King could top himself. Then he saw the famous wedding scene at the end and realized that King had indeed topped himself.

The third memorable "drawing in" scene was the resort where viewers see Laurel enjoying the company of her rich young friends, when she spies her ill-bred, tackily dressed mother lumbering into their midst. The shots of Stella coming closer, interspliced with the reaction of Laurel, then of Laurel reacting to the reactions of her friends, is filmmaking of a high order.

The ultimate success of this kind of film, however, is acting, and Belle Bennett (1891-1932) was a perfect Stella. Bennett was a popular leading lady of silents who had retired from acting in 1918, but begged Goldwyn for the chance to do this part, even going as far as to pull a pre-Shelley Winters weight-gaining act. She gives an outstanding performance, creating a character that critic Richard Griffith described as a cousin to Dorothy Parker's "Big Blonde." It is the kind of performance that would have been nominated for an Academy Award had the Academy existed at that time. Lois Moran, a comely young brunette, is still remembered affectionately for her portrayal of Laurel as both a child and a young lady.

Stella Dallas is not a man's film, but Ronald Colman was not completely wasted as the somewhat caddish, hard-to-like Stephen Dallas. Goldwyn had been impressed with Colman after seeing him with Lillian Gish in *The White Sister* (1923) and *Romola* (1924) and signed him to a contract which made him a major Goldwyn star from 1924 to 1933.

Another major factor contributing to the success of *Stella Dallas* was Marion's intelligent screenplay. Marion was one of Hollywood's outstanding screenwriters, and by 1925, her extensive list of credits included several Mary Pickford vehicles and several Goldwyn productions: *Cytherea* (1924), *A Thief in Paradise* (1925), *The Dark Angel* (1925), and *His Supreme Moment* (1925). Goldwyn had great admiration for Marion: "The work accomplished from Miss Marion's scenarios is so directly to the point. . . ," and she returned that admiration in kind: "Sam has taste and integrity. There is never any pretense with him." Goldwyn so valued Marion's screenwriting talent that he put her under exclusive contract in 1926. She ended her career at M-G-M where her impressive credits included *Anna Christie* (1930), *Dinner at Eight* (1933), and *Camille* (1937).

Stella Dallas appeared as number nine on *The New York Times* Ten-Best List for 1925, an impressive list which included, in order of choice: *The Big Parade*, *The Last Laugh*, *The Unholy Three*, *The Gold Rush*, *The Merry Widow*, *The Dark Angel*, *Don Q, Son of Zorro*, *Ben-Hur*, *Stella Dallas*, and *A Kiss for Cinderella*.

Stella Dallas went on to become a long-running radio soap opera debuting October 25, 1937, with Anne Elstner playing Stella and a young MacDonald Carey as one of the several actors who played Richard. Goldwyn went on to exceed even himself by remaking the film in 1937. This version starred Barbara Stanwyck (an Oscar nomination) and Anne Shirley and was directed by King Vidor and was even more popular than the first version.

Ronald Bowers

STELLA MARIS

Released: 1918
Production: Paramount/Artcraft Films
Direction: Marshall Neilan
Screenplay: Frances Marion; based on the novel of the same name by William J. Locke
Cinematography: Walter Stradling
Length: 6 reels

> *Principal characters:*
> Stella Maris/Unity Blake .... Mary Pickford
> John Risca .... Conway Tearle
> Louisa Risca ...... Camille Ankewich (Marcia Manon)
> Lord Blount .... Herbert Standing
> Lady Blount .... Ida Waterman

Mary Pickford was not merely a star; she was—and is—a legend. For twenty-three years, in fifty-two features, and more than 125 shorts, she was the most popular actress on America's film screens, playing child and adolescent roles into her twenties and even thirties. She may not have been the best actress of her era—she was no Lillian Gish or Mae Marsh—but she was adept at playing both comedy and drama in contemporary and period settings, usually acting the tomboy who still managed to retain her femininity.

Pickford was in her prime between 1914 and 1919, when she was in her mid-twenties; in appearance, she was indescribably lovely, no longer a child but not quite a woman. *Stella Maris*—not to be confused with *Stella Dallas* (1925)—is not the most famous Pickford heroine and is not as fondly recalled as Tess (of the Storm Country), Rebecca (of Sunnybrook Farm), Pollyanna, or Little Annie Rooney. The film features, however, *two* of Pickford's most impressive performances, and may very well be her best film.

Stella Maris parallels the lives of two young girls, one rich and pretty, the other unattractive and miserable. Garbed in her well-known curls and beautiful dresses, "America's Sweetheart" stars first as the title character, a wealthy, sensitive, beautiful, but crippled and bedridden girl. Stella is brought up by her devoted uncle and aunt, Lord and Lady Blount (Herbert Standing and Ida Waterman), in a happy little dream world. She lives in a castle amidst gardens and rustic walkways, protected from all the sadness and evil in the world by her enforced isolation. Stella thinks that everyone else is exactly like her; a sign above the room in which she is confined reads: "The court of Stella Maris / All unhappiness and world wisdom leave outside / Those without smiles need not enter."

Pickford's other role is Unity Blake, a poor, homely, unloved waif who was the first "ugly" character Pickford portrayed. The film begins with Unity in a dreary orphan asylum beating a carpet. These shots are crosscut with ones of Stella, in her mansion, lying on a large bed, and petting a white rabbit. Stella's best friend is John Risca (Conway Tearle), a journalist who pampers her, protecting her from the harsh realities that exist beyond her immediate environment. Risca is Stella's idol, but she does not know that he is married.

Risca's wife, Louisa (Camille Ankewich), is semi-insane and a drunkard. She goes to the orphanage to select a servant, and she picks Unity, believing that an ugly girl will work harder than others. Unity tries to say good-bye to her fellow orphans, but they are indifferent or jealous of her supposed good luck. One day, Unity's shopping bag is stolen at the market, and, as a result, Louisa beats her with a hot poker. For this act, Louisa is sentenced to three years in prison. Unity is at first placed in Stella's mansion, but because her family feels that Unity may expose Stella to "real life," the orphan then goes to live with Risca and his aunt. When she accidently breaks a vase, Unity cowers and lies. She thinks she will be beaten, but is surprised to realize that she will be forgiven. Unity is hungry for love and affection, and she grows to care for Risca with slavish devotion.

Three years pass, and Stella undergoes an operation for her paralysis. Miraculously, she is cured, but, now, she will be forced to enter the real world—to her shock and consternation. She meets a poor woman and her starving children and reads crime stories in the newspaper. By now, she and Risca are in love—but John is still a married man, and his wife is released from jail. Stella visits Unity and tells the girl of her feelings, but Unity too has fallen for Risca. She holds a photo of Stella, peers into a mirror, and covers her face in disappointment. As this occurs, shots of Risca kissing Stella are crosscut in. Stella goes to the journalist's official address and finds the drunken, insanely jealous Louisa, who tells her that he is not free. Stella realizes that Risca does not live in a castle, that he is not really a Prince Charming, and that he had previously lied to protect her. She becomes disillusioned.

Meanwhile, Unity is still hopelessly in love. She speaks to an image of Risca—his jacket on a hanger, with his hat hanging on a hook above—and proposes marriage. Risca, depressed because Stella's faith in human nature has been destroyed, makes out his will and seems ready to kill himself. His aunt tells Unity that he will never be free as long as Louisa lives, so the girl sneaks into Louisa's house and shoots her with a pistol. Later, Unity is found dead next to Louisa's body. Superficially, her motive is revenge; but she leaves Risca a note, telling him that no one else had ever been kind to her, and that she wishes Stella and Risca happiness. They are married, and they both remember the little Cockney orphan who sacrificed her life for them.

Stella Maris is by far the most unusual film in Pickford's career, not so much for her dual role but for her performance as the homely Unity. As the title character, she has her golden curls, pouts, smiles, and cute mannerisms which are typical of the sweet and radiant Pickford America adored. Stella is indeed a typical Pickford role. Audiences, however, were shocked by her casting as Unity. Production of the film began when Adolph Zukor, Paramount's chairman of the board, was away for several weeks. Pickford instigated the making of the film. Zukor would probably never have approved *Stella Maris* and was aghast at seeing her made up as Unity, but the actress had the foresight to play Stella as well.

While Pickford is fine as the title character, she gives a brilliant character performance as Unity. The orphan is the key character in the film, the driving force in the scenario; a weak performance would have added emphasis to the sentimental, melodramatic nature of the plot. Pickford's curls are combed out and slicked down with vaseline; in their place are two braids that hang down her back. She acts with her shoulders hunched, her eyes squinted, her lips tightened, her face dirty and vacant. By means of the effect of twice exposing the film, in several scenes, both Unity and Stella appear together, and it is difficult at times to believe that both characters are being portrayed by the same actress.

As it is, *Stella Maris* is a mawkish film, but not cloyingly so because of Pickford's superior acting. Also, it has beautiful lighting; cinematographer Walter Stradling emphasizes the actress' already luminous face with just the right amount of backlighting. The scenes with Stella and Risca in her garden are particularly lovely. (The film's photography is sometimes erroneously attributed to Charles Rosher, who with Stradling shot Pickford's features during this period.)

The year 1917 was the greatest in Pickford's distinguished career, with one feature released practically every other month. Although released in January, 1918, *Stella Maris* was produced during the previous year. In 1917, Pickford worked with Maurice Tourneur in *The Pride of the Clan* (released in January) and *Poor Little Rich Girl* (March), for Cecil B. De Mille in *A Romance of the Redwoods* (May) and *The Little American* (July), and for Marshall Neilan in *Rebecca of Sunnybrook Farm* (September) and *A Little Princess* (November). There is not a weak film in the group.

Marshall "Mickey" Neilan, who directed *Stella Maris*, is one of the forgotten pioneers of the American cinema. In addition to his 1917 films with Pickford, he also worked with her in *Amarilly of Clothes-line Alley* (1918), *M'liss* (1918), *Daddy Long Legs* (1919), and *Dorothy Vernon of Haddon Hall* (1924); they acted together in *Rags* (1915), *A Girl of Yesterday* (1915), *Madame Butterfly* (1915), and *Daddy Long Legs*. Neilan was a talented, innovative director with a special ability to create and sustain mood, but he was also a playboy, with a fondness for alcohol, and he never seriously applied himself to his work. He could have become one of the great directors; instead, he developed a reputation for unreliability. By the end of the silent era, he was already a has-been. The last two films he directed, *Sing While You're Able* (1937) and

Swing It, Professor (1937), were "D"-grade musicals for Ambassador Pictures. Years later, Elia Kazan cast him in a character role as a senator in *A Face in the Crowd* (1957). He died a year later in a charity ward.

Pickford is ably supported in *Stella Maris* by Conway Tearle, who is poised and sympathetic as Risca, and Camille Ankewich, appropriately nasty as Louisa. Tearle, half-brother of Godfrey Tearle, was a leading actor in dozens of silents whose career lasted into the 1930's. Ankewich, an obscure silent-film actress, changed her name to Marcia Manon just after the release of *Stella Maris* and appeared in about a dozen features through the 1920's.

The film was written by Frances Marion, Hollywood's most in-demand writer of the silent and early talking eras. Marion also wrote the scenarios for many of Pickford's other films, including *Rebecca of Sunnybrook Farm*, *A Little Princess*, *Amarilly of Clothes-line Alley*, *M'liss*, *Poor Little Rich Girl*, *How Could You, Jean?* (1918), *Johanna Enlists* (1918), *Captain Kidd* (1919), *Pollyanna*, and *The Love Light* (1921).

Stella Maris received excellent reviews, with critics predictably highlighting Pickford's performance as Unity. Some writers had previously contended that she could not act, and that her only asset was her personality and inherent cuteness. These barbs were impressively refuted by her work in the film. In *Stella Maris*, Pickford proves herself a more than capable actress. The film, however, was a moderate box-office success.

The property was remade in 1925 with Mary Philbin as Stella/Unity, Elliot Dexter as Risca, and Gladys Brockwell as Louisa. Here, however, Stella also has another beau, Walter Herold (Jason Robards, Sr.); at the finale, Risca realizes that Stella really loves Herold and blesses their marriage. The director of the 1925 *Stella Maris* was Charles J. Brabin, and this film was paled by the original.

Rob Edelman

STORM OVER ASIA
(PATOMAK CHINGIS-KHAN)

Released: 1928
Production: Mezhrabpomfilm
Direction: Vsevolod Pudovkin
Screenplay: O. Brik; based on an original screen story by I. Novokshenov
Cinematography: Anatoli Golovnya
Length: 11 reels/10,114 feet

Principal characters:
Bair, a Mongol huntsman .... Valery Inkishinov
Bair's father .... I. Inkishinov
Mr. Smith .... V. Tsoppi
British Colonel .... A. Dedintsev
Colonel's daughter .... A. Sudakevich
Partisan leader .... A. P. Chistiakov

Vsevolod Pudovkin's *Storm over Asia* is, like many of the major Soviet films of the 1920's, a story of revolution and of political rites of passage in which an innocent (in this case a young Mongol hunter) progresses from a state of naïveté to an awareness of the oppressed condition of his compatriots and finally leads them in an uprising that drives the opportunistic imperialists from their land. Yet, *Storm over Asia* has achieved a heightened significance because it is revolutionary in form as well as in theme, since it employs some interesting uses of cinematic montage. It was, in fact, a product of a director educated in the tradition of the radical and innovative film-making style of the "Kuleshov Workshop" founded by Len Kuleshov, one of the true pioneers of the Soviet cinema.

In 1917, Kuleshov found that he was unable to work within the formal structure of the V.G.I.K. (All Union State Institute of Cinematography), the state film school, but he was deemed to be so talented that he was permitted to form his own group outside the orthodox curriculum. Pudovkin and other young aspiring directors, including Sergei Eisenstein, flocked to the radical director and were profoundly stimulated by his ideas, although they were hampered by a shortage of film stock and other equipment that caused them to concern themselves, initially, with theoretical experiments in film editing. They would, for example, write screenplays (or more properly scenarios) and would subsequently direct and perform them as if they were actually shooting them with cameras. Later, they would arrange these imaginary shots on paper into completed films.

In 1919, however, D. W. Griffith's *Intolerance* (1916) somehow made its way into the Soviet Union and exerted a powerful influence upon the group and, indeed, upon the entire fledgling film industry. According to Jay Leyda, in his book *Kino*, the major history of the Soviet cinema, Griffith's film was the first significant critical and popular success in the brief history of the country's cinema. Lenin was apparently so impressed with what he judged to be the proletarian sympathies of its modern story, that he ordered it to be shown repeatedly throughout the nation. Subsequently, an entire sub-industry evolved just to make prints of the picture and all available film stock was gobbled up in the process. It ran continuously for ten years and as Leyda points out, no Soviet film of any importance made during the 1920's was free of the American production's influence. According to some unsubstantiated reports, Lenin actually offered Griffith a position as head of the entire Soviet film program—a position that the American supposedly refused only because of the imminent opening of his new studio at Mamaroneck, New York.

Intolerance and later *The Birth of a Nation* (1915) were screened repeatedly at the Kuleshov Workshop until they practically disintegrated. The primary interest in both works, on the part of the students, was the manner in which Griffith constructed his elaborate, detailed narrative from thousands of individual shots. After mastering the fundamental principles, they fragmented his works and then reassembled the sequences in a multiplicity of combinations to test the relationship of shot arrangement to thematic meaning and narrative form.

The most famous experiment to evolve from the explorations of Griffith's method was an episode later recounted by Pudovkin in which Kuleshov took a segment of unedited footage featuring the completely expressionless face of actor Ivan Mozhukhin and interspersed it with shots of three emotion-evoking subjects—a bowl of hot soup, a dead woman, and a child playing with a teddy bear. Random showings to varied audiences indicated a uniform tendency on the part of viewers to equate the emotional significance of the intercut images with the quality of the actor's performance. In essence, the audiences reacted as if the actor's expressionless face was somehow conveying the emotions inspired by the images. Since the actor's face never changed, Kuleshov concluded that each shot in a filmed sequence possessed not one but two intrinsic values. The first one obviously consisted of whatever value the shot possessed in and of itself as a photographic representation of reality. The second, as Kuleshov discovered, was the quality it acquired when placed in various juxtapositions with other shots in a series. Through this latter effect, it became possible to manipulate the meaning of a sequence through the placement of individual images and to convey variable or opposing values merely by altering the order of the relationship of specific images to the actors. This power, in Kuleshov's mind, made it the more important vehicle for conveying cinematic meaning.

Although the fundamental properties of the shot and the variety of uses to which they might be put had been demonstrated on an instinctual basis in the Griffith films studied by the workshop, it was Kuleshov who actually codified the principles involved and established the theory of sequential arrangement as a cinematic tool for the process of articulating meaning through image symbolism. Thus, the concept which would have a profound effect upon the development of the motion picture through the works of Eisenstein and Pudovkin first became known as the "Kuleshov effect."

The process as structured in Pudovkin and Eisenstein was in reality the beginning of what is referred to today as montage (from the French verb *monter*, meaning to mount), a concept that holds that on the screen actual time and space become subordinate to the editing process. An adroitly edited strip of film finds its power not in itself but in its effect upon the audience's powers of perception. Kuleshov's pupils viewed montage as a figurative or suggestive process whereby dissimilar images could be artificially linked to produce a metaphorical meaning and to alter time and space. Eisenstein and Pudovkin, however, had individual differences of interpretation and went on to redefine Kuleshov's theories of montage in highly stylized ways.

Eisenstein viewed montage in terms of a collision of shocks in which various autonomous, capricious, and emotionally tinged ingredients were assembled in juxtaposition to produce an emotional effect that differed radically from what one would logically expect from a collection of the individual units. In effect, in terms of meaning, the whole was fundamentally superior to the sum of its parts. Pudovkin, on the other hand, believed more in a linkage of images rather than in a collision. Thus, his montages even in their most figurative phases always fulfill some narrative purpose. While Eisenstein theorized that cinematic meaning is signified through a random interaction of not necessarily related frames (and all of the units of meaning therein) within the viewer's mind, Pudovkin felt that meaning was instead dependent upon a viewer's perception of some kind of visual linkage.

Such a montage of linked images was magnificently constructed in *Storm over Asia* (*Patomak Chingis-Khan*) to produce a brilliantly symbolic conclusion in which shots of a blowing wind and a sandstorm are interspersed with views of horde upon horde of Mongol horsemen riding against their oppressors until the image gradually resolves itself into a metaphorical gale sweeping tyranny from the land. This allegory, which resolves the film in scenes of epic visual poetry, is based upon the tension between movement in the frame and the alternation of conceptually related shots, and it thus provides an integrated optical and emotional peak that is, in fact, a trademark of Pudovkin's best work, particularly *Mother* (1926) and *The End of St. Petersburg* (1927). The montage ending of *Storm over Asia* is also impressive in a purely statistical sense because of the fact that almost twenty-five percent of the approximately two thousand shots that comprise the film went into the final gallop of the horsemen over the Mongolian landscape.

The film concerns the 1920 adventures of Bair (Valery Inkishinov), the son of a Mongolian fur trapper, who, because his father (I. Inkishinov) has been taken ill, goes to the annual fur market with the family's most valuable possession, the pelt of a silver fox. The successful sale of the fur would keep the young man and his family quite comfortable for at least a year. At the market, however, he is swindled by a Mr. Smith (V. Tsoppi), an agent of a British fur company, who pays the lad only a fraction of the true value of the pelt. Bair, realizing that he has been defrauded, attempts to regain the pelt but runs afoul of soldiers of the White Army (foreign soldiers intervening in the Russian civil war to fight against the Bolshevik Red Army in Asia) who support the English fur traders. He escapes into the mountains where he is given shelter by a band of rebels.

Pudovkin very subtly, up to this point, delineates Bair's rising consciousness of the political currents surging around him. Much is made of the fox pelt by the various characters, and its value is established by comments concerning its rich fur and the scarcity of the animal. Up until he sells the skin, Bair is portrayed as a good-natured, passive peasant. After the sale, however, Inkishinov, under Pudovkin's direction, allows his character to become increasingly sullen as he seemingly becomes more and more aware of the exploitive nature of the foreigners occupying his homeland.

Bair is soon captured by soldiers of the White Army, and because he has been discovered in the uniform worn by the rebels, he is sent out to be shot. In a touching sequence, the boy, with no knowledge of what is to come, strides along before his executioner. Although his arms are bound, he has faith in his captor, a young corporal whom he senses to be a friend. The soldier is, in fact, against such barbaric rites but is bound to obey his commander and carry out his orders. He reluctantly orders Bair to turn his back to him in a manner not unlike that of a boy about to put his aging cocker spaniel to sleep. It is a poignant scene which ends with a rifle shot.

In the interim, a British Colonel (A. Dedintsev) has discovered an amulet among the prisoner's belongings that indicates that Bair is a direct descendant of Genghis Khan. No sooner does his executioner return than he is ordered to set forth again and bring back his victim. The soldiers find Bair, who is fortunately still alive, although gravely injured. He is returned to the camp and given the best medical care until he begins to recover. The Colonel has the idea of utilizing Bair's lineage to establish him as a puppet ruler of Buryat Mongolia. Although the young man grows accustomed to his new position as a prized hostage ruling the country for the British, a change has come over him. He is now more suspicious where formerly he was trusting.

Valery Inkishinov, at this point, applies still more subtle nuances to the trapper's character, gradually darkening and deepening it as his political education continues. Pudovkin helps this development along through a series of minor but finely tuned episodes. One of these, an instance in which the Colonel's daughter (A. Sudakevich) gives him a drink of water, shows how far he has come from the stolid peasant boy who first went to the fur market.

Bair takes the glass and holds it until the daughter and the other visitors leave the room. Then, although he is dying of thirst, he pours the water on the floor and his innocence and trust flow away with it.

Afterward, Bair notices that the girl is wearing his silver fox fur (which the devious dealer had given her for a present) as a stole around her neck. This incident starts Bair on the road to active revolution. When the British attempt to execute a young Mongolian boy, the final spark is struck and Bair explodes, almost literally pulling the British headquarters to pieces and knocking it down upon the heads of his captors. Finally, he steals a horse and gathers the rebel band under the leadership of a partisan (A. P. Chistiakov) and leads them against the British. The horsemen seem to increase in number as they race across the screen in wave upon wave against their oppressors. Ultimately, they evolve into an abstraction—a raging windstorm that savages the foreigners and blows them off the land.

Storm over Asia, with its symbolic conclusion, opened to a decidedly mixed reception. The Communist Party and those critics laboring under its ideological influence found it lacking in its presentation and interpretation of Soviet philosophy as well as being highly unrealistic in a thematic sense, particularly in its reliance upon symbolic devices, such as the windstorm. They also found the excellent photographic values to represent a needless self-indulgence that was not altogether appropriate. Western critics, however, particularly *The New York Times*, singled out the excellent cinematography and the performances by what it termed as "the eminently suitable cast." Yet, the American paper, like its Soviet counterparts, was critical of the realism embodied in the film's climax. "In the closing episodes," the paper stated, "it becomes hysterical and absurd incidents occur, including a man, who through injuries is hardly able to move around, suddenly becoming a veritable Samson." As for the narrative theme, these critics termed it "the same old theme which the Bolsheviks delight in presenting with prejudice."

Today, although the film as a whole seems slow in building to the final crescendo, *Storm over Asia* is still a dynamic narrative that is at all times fluid and well controlled. Also notable for its appearance of superb restraint is the acting of the Mongolian principals, particularly Valery Inkishinov, who very deliberately and subtly paces Bair's growing political awareness so that it occurs in a realistic manner. A. P. Chistiakov, too, gives an interesting performance as a leader of the rebellious partisans that is particularly memorable for the use of extraordinary facial expressions.

Storm over Asia was Pudovkin's last great film. As an epic poet utilizing the medium of cinema, he was at his best when using purely visual means of expression. The advent of talking pictures pretty much ended his effectiveness as a director since the demands of spoken dialogue conflicted with the sweep of his visual narrative forms. It was not until his final film, *The Return of Vasili Bortnikov* (1953) that he was able to restore his visual concerns to a semblance of the predominance that they enjoyed in his silent films. Current critical opinion regards him (perhaps unfairly) as of more importance to film history as a theoretician than as a filmmaker. Yet, the unfolding of cinema owes a great debt to Pudovkin and his masterpieces, *Mother*, *The End of St. Petersburg*, and the most exciting Soviet silent film of all—*Storm over Asia*.

Stephen L. Hanson

STRAIGHT SHOOTING

Released: 1917
Production: Butterfly-Universal
Direction: John Ford
Screenplay: George Hively
Cinematography: George Scott
Length: 5 reels

Principal characters:
Cheyenne Harry	Harry Carey
Joan Sims	Molly Malone
"Thunder" Flint	Duke Lee
"Placer" Fremont	Vester Pegg
Danny Morgan	Hoot Gibson
Sweetwater Sims	George Berrell
Ted Sims	Ted Brooks
Black-Eyed Pete	Milt Brown

John Ford made *Straight Shooting*, his first full-length film, in 1917, the same year that Maurice Tourneur directed *Pride of the Clan* and *Poor Little Rich Girl*, and Charles Chaplin filmed *Easy Street* and *The Immigrant*. It followed by a year D. W. Griffith's *Intolerance* and Cecil B. De Mille's *The Trail of the Lonesome Pine*. Thus, although films were still in their infancy, they were not as unsophisticated as the crudities of *Straight Shooting* would seem to indicate. So many early Ford films have been lost, that it is difficult to ascertain where this one stands in his overall opus. He directed nine films in 1917; half were two and three reelers and half were features. This five-reel film, however, more or less complete in its original form, was supposed to be cut to two reels. According to Peter Bogdanovich's interview with Ford:

. . . Mr. Laemmle [Carl Laemmle, head of Universal] happened to run it. When it was over and they told him it was going to be cut down to two reels, he said, "Why?" "Well," they said, "it was only *supposed* to be a two reeler." And Laemmle said, "If I order a suit of clothes and the fellow gives me an extra pair of pants free, what am I going to do— throw them back in his face?"

Ford was born Sean Aloysius O'Feeney in 1895. His older brother, Francis, had taken the name Ford and was a contract director-writer-actor at Universal Studios, so when Sean followed in his brother's footsteps (Ford rode with the Klan in *The Birth of a Nation*, 1915, and played other bits as well), he took the name "Jack Ford." It was not until *Cameo Kirby* (1923) that "Jack" became "John Ford."

Straight Shooting is one of many films that Ford made with Harry Carey playing Cheyenne Harry as the perpetually reforming outlaw. Carey, who began his career with Biograph before the teens, made about two dozen films before his long and successful association with Ford began. Carey was not only the star of these films, but he would also work with Ford on various other aspects of the production, such as direction or scenario. The Carey *persona*, whether manifested in Cheyenne Harry or another character, was that of a plain, hard-working cowboy more in the William S. Hart mold than in that of Tom Mix. Ford deliberately chose to make his star this way so that the depth of his character could be revealed in film after film instead of his abilities in riding or roping. Cheyenne Harry is the precursor to many an outcast type of hero that intrigued Ford and which reached its most significant manifestation in Ethan Edwards, the protagonist of *The Searchers* (1956). As the 1956 film closes with Ethan silhouetted against the horizon and then walking away from the closing door, so Cheyenne Harry, in this film, remains in social limbo, renouncing the girl he loves in favor of someone whom he feels is more suitable for her. The Cheyenne Harry figure is seen figuratively silhouetted against the sky, leaving the hearth for the range. Notes on the film state that Harry renounces Joan Sims for something "just over yonder" in the original version and heads into the setting sun alone. The present ending may have been added in 1925 when it was reissued. The fade out of the print available today suggests that Harry will stay with Joan and it ends with their embrace. Yet, this ending hardly makes sense as Cheyenne Harry continued as a character in fifteen more films, all directed by Ford (there had already been two), each with a different girl, although many of the heroines were actually played by Molly Malone.

Straight Shooting is the oft-repeated story about the ranchers versus the farmers, with Harry squarely in the middle. He is an outlaw who starts as a friend to the cattlemen but takes the farmers' side when he learns of the ranchers' foul play. His friends are the members of the Sims family: Sweetwater (George Berrell), Joan (Molly Malone), and Ted (Ted Brooks). After Ted is ambushed by the ranchers, Harry immediately comes to the aid of the dirt farmers. Joan gathers the neighbors to help repel an assault by the cattlemen and their hired hands against her father's farm. With Harry's help, they fend off the seige. After the battle, Harry realizes that Danny Morgan (Hoot Gibson) is in love with Joan, but is also pleased to discover that she is falling in love with him instead. He toys briefly with the idea of settling down as a farmer, but ultimately concludes that "the open range is for me." Joan finds him meditating on his predicament, and they kiss as the film ends.

The film is primitive by any standard. It is mechanical; fading in and out with clockwork regularity; using a static camera indoors and a slightly freer one outside; and allowing the wind to blow without restraint both indoors and out. One can almost imagine a piano playing out of camera range to get the actors in the mood. Yet, considering that Ford was twenty-two when he made *Straight Shooting*, it is quite sophisticated in some respects and anticipates the preoccupations of his later films: the family as a unit of society; true love; and renunciation and reformation, which was a theme Ford would explore many times, as in *Marked Men* (1919), *Three Bad Men* (1926, yet another Cheyenne Harry motion picture), and *Three Godfathers* (1948, with Harry Carey, Jr., as one of the three). They were all essentially the same film with different casts.

The shifting nature of friendships in the West is encapsulated in the idea of Carey's midfilm switch. The man that he intends to kill one day becomes his would-be father-in-law the next; his drinking buddy—in the archetypal neutral zone, the saloon—becomes his enemy; and the girl is unattainable, beloved, and lost within a day's time (depending on which ending one subscribes to). Like all of Ford's films, *Straight Shooting* is about transition, the pattern of the old giving way to the new, the present to the future. Ford favors change over immutable continuity, stressing kinesis over stasis.

Ford's camera work was still crude in 1917, but within certain limitations, he manages some fine moments. Among these are scenes of Harry and a rancher friend bellying up to the bar with a fat, beady-eyed barkeep watching their every move; and another of Harry popping out of a hole in a tree upon which a marshal has just tacked a wanted notice for him. There is a shot over Harry's shoulder down toward Joan's face when she learns that Harry is leaving, and also one of her sad expression when she puts away her brother's dinner plate after his death. The look of terror on the face of "Placer" Fremont (Vester Pegg) as he squares off against Harry for the shootout is also a memorable shot.

The entire film has a look of verisimilitude. For example, the town sits on a dusty plain; the jail is a one-room blockhouse with other, equally unprepossessing buildings scattered around it, and the Sims's homestead is a one-room shack. Harry always looks dusty and worn with his shirt full of holes. Joan's hair is a rat's nest of tangled curls, albeit with a ribbon, that matches her dress, twined in her locks. Sweetwater looks like a precursor of Gabby Hayes, white-bearded and stoop-shouldered.

There are a few moments of pictorial loveliness, such as a shot of cattle clambering down a ravine with the riders on the hill above as the steers move into open space seemingly as if from the sky. The gnarled branches and the leafy trees around them suggest mutability—birth, death, and rebirth and is a fitting setting for their brief romance. Most of *Straight Shooting*, however, is resolutely simple, deliberately unadorned as though gussying up the West would be a betrayal of its traditions. Those traditions, of course, had been established by motion pictures themselves, and, at that, only a few years before; but Ford never tampered with a sure thing. He embellished the Western, made it finer and purer, but he never changed what he saw as its immutable, honorable character.

Judith M. Kass

THE STRONG MAN

Released: 1926
Production: The Harry Langdon Corporation for Associated First National
Direction: Frank Capra
Screenplay: Arthur Ripley, Hal Conklin (adaptation), and Robert Eddy (adaptation)
Titles: Reed Heustis
Cinematography: Elgin Lessley and Glenn Kershner
Editing: Harold Young
Length: 7 reels/6,882 feet

Principal characters:
Paul Bergot	Harry Langdon
Mary Brown	Priscilla Bonner
"Lily of Broadway"	Gertrude Astor
Parson "Holy" Brown	William V. Mong
Roy McDevitt	Robert McKim
"Zandow the Great"	Arthur Thalasso

During the height of his career, baby-faced Harry Langdon vied with Charles Chaplin for the position of the era's most popular screen clown. In fact, any serious discussion of the great silent clowns finds Langdon's name tied with Chaplin, Buster Keaton, and Harold Lloyd. Among modern audiences, however, Langdon is a nearly forgotten figure—certainly the most obscure of the four names.

The reason for this obscurity can be attributed to his rapid rise and fall within the industry. If Langdon's career as a leading actor was all too brief, however—peaking in 1926 and almost ended by 1928—it was also marked by superlative comic crescendos. In 1926 alone, a year in which Chaplin did not star in any film, Langdon starred in *Tramp, Tramp, Tramp*, *The Strong Man*, and *Long Pants*. These films represent Langdon at his zenith, and *The Strong Man* ranks as one of the period's great comedies.

A film that veers effectively from pathos to ribald slapstick, *The Strong Man* is the consummate showcase for Langdon's comic character: a pasty, powdered face with painted-on eyebrows, and a hesitant smile, combined with a costume of baggy pants, overcoat, cloth hat, and flat shoes. The resulting look suggested an overgrown baby, as if Langdon were a child, indulging in a strange game of "dress-up."

In keeping with his physical presence, Langdon's screen character was eternally optimistic, invariably passive, and incredibly naïve. He also possessed a wistful, engaging quality—as did Langdon's best work. His character did not suggest a wide range of comic expectations, but when Langdon was at his best, the effect could enthrall.

In discussing the performer, James Agee once noted, "It seemed as if Chaplin could do literally anything, on any instrument in the orchestra. Langdon had one queerly toned, unique little reed. But out of it he could get incredible melodies." Artistically speaking, those melodies became out of tune when Langdon parted company with the co-workers who had been behind his most successful efforts. Among them was director Frank Capra, who, early in his career, had worked as a gag writer for Langdon. Langdon's comedy-star status was also hampered by the inevitable reality brought about by encroaching years. Signed for his first film at the age of thirty-nine, he was well into his forties when his character enjoyed notoriety. Unfortunately, his peculiar man-child screen *persona* could not go on forever and, in fact, faded with Langdon's advance to middle age.

A great deal has been written about Langdon and his brief period of stardom. Of his one-time performer, Mack Sennett wrote, "He was hurt and bewildered at the end and he never understood what had happened to him." Capra has said, "He was the most tragic figure I ever came across in show business." Yet, the film vaults attest to a durable career—one that was peppered by disappointments and drawbacks, but also marked by the apparent will to survive. Simply put, Langdon kept bouncing back. Not to the stardom he once had—but to work within the industry.

Bankrupt in 1928, Langdon made a comeback a year later, with two-reel talkies for the Hal Roach studio. Following several barren years he returned again, this time with a string of short subjects, and he worked on short subjects off and on through the 1940's. He also went to work at Hal Roach as a writer for Stan Laurel and Oliver Hardy, working on scripts for films such as *Block-Heads* (1938), *The Flying Deuces* (1939), *Saps at Sea* (1940), and *A Chump at Oxford* (1940). He even drew the caricatures that accompany the titles for *Block-Heads*.

In all, Langdon appeared in some seventy silent and sound shorts, and in addition to starring in six features, he appeared in seventeen others as a supporting actor. At the time of his death, in 1944, he was at work on the Republic musical, *Swingin' on a Rainbow*.

Throughout the years, personal revelations about Langdon have varied drastically. For example, Capra has said that he died broke. Mabel Langdon, the comic's widow (and third wife), however, has disputed that notion. If anything is certain, it is that Langdon—for a brief period a truly great performer—remained hard at work in his film career for three decades. He was never merely a has-been.

Born in Council Bluffs, Iowa, in 1884, he was the son of Salvation Army officers. At the age of twelve he ran away and reportedly joined either a circus or a traveling medicine show (historically, the point is not clear). His background definitely included some time spent with the Kickapoo Indian Medicine Show (Langdon hawked medicine). He later performed as a song and dance man, and did a chair-balancing act, for a minstrel show before making his way to vaudeville, where he performed as a clown.

Perhaps Langdon's background contributed to his curiously touching screen *persona*. As film historian William K. Everson has noted, "In some ways, his was the most complex screen character of all the clowns, with roots in both vaudeville and non-comedic films, and later echoes in unrelated fields." Indeed, the complexities of his character are heightened by *The Strong Man*, which underlines a pensive quest for love, as well as uproarious hilarity.

As the film opens, Paul Bergot (Harry Langdon), a young Belgian soldier, is stationed at the front during World War I. An inadequate warrior, he cannot master the machine gun. Instead, he uses a bean shooter against the enemy. He also makes appropriate use of the army's hardened biscuits—catapulting them. These very funny moments contrast with the fact that Bergot is corresponding with Mary Brown (Priscilla Bonner), an American "pen pal." Although he has never seen this girl, Bergot seems to be in love with her. Unaware that Bergot is inept, the girl envisions him as a hero.

Climaxing the wartime scene is Bergot's capture by a hulking German (Arthur Thalasso). Following the Armistice, it is learned that the German is actually "Zandow the Great," a strong man. With Bergot as his pathetic manservant, Zandow journeys to America.

Once in Mary Brown's homeland, Bergot tries vainly to find the girl he has never seen. His search begins, inappropriately, on Broadway in New York City. There he encounters a floozie on the run from police. Anxious to stash some money, she tucks it into Bergot's pocket—and runs. "Lily of Broadway" (played by the gifted comedienne Gertrude Astor) later returns and lures a perplexed (and completely naïve) Bergot to her room. Pretending to be his sweetheart, Mary Brown, she attempts to retrieve the money by riffling through his clothes. He thinks she is trying to seduce him, to make "cave woman love" to him (a result of her rough treatment). He also tries to reconcile his thoughts about the Mary of his dreams and this brazen street hustler. The sequence is an excellent blend of hilarity and pathos.

The case of mistaken identity eventually is discovered, and Bergot later finds himself on yet another adventure, this time aboard a bus heading West, to a rough town where Zandow is supposed to perform. Suffering from a cold, Bergot doctors himself by making a mustard plaster with Limburger cheese—not linament. The predictable reactions of his fellow passengers makes the bus trip hilarious.

Once in the rough and tumble town, Bergot chances to find the beguiling Mary Brown herself. As fate would have it, the heroine of the film is blind. She cannot see her pasty little admirer, but she can gently hold his hand. Bergot is so shy that during an encounter on a park bench, he haltingly places his hat so that their intertwined hands are not in view.

As it happens, the frontier town is torn with dissent between churchgoers—

led by Mary's father, Parson "Holy" Brown (William V. Mong)—and evil-doers, who gather in the town's saloon. When Zandow is unable to make his scheduled appearance before the rabble-rousers, he sends Bergot in his place. A most unlikely strong man, Bergot is also an unlikely hero. Yet, the film climaxes with a wild melee erupting in the saloon, in which Bergot swings from the trapeze, bombing those beneath him with whiskey bottles. Brimming with slapstick, this sequence finds Bergot cleaning out the saloon—thanks to the use of a cannon, and at film's end, he is reunited with his Mary Brown.

In reviewing *The Strong Man*, *Photoplay* wrote, "It's a grand and glorious laugh from the start to the finish. It begins with one laugh overlapping the other. Chuckles are swept into howls. Howls creep into tears—and by that time you're ready to be carried out." Even today, *The Strong Man* remains an excellent comedy and, as such, garners frequent showings at silent-film retrospectives.

Often wistful, frequently brilliant, and infused with hilarity, *The Strong Man* offers Langdon at his best. It also marks the directorial debut of Capra, who went on to pursue other tales of innocents caught in a decaying world in his classic films such as *Mr. Deeds Goes to Town* (1936), and *Mr. Smith Goes to Washington* (1939).

Following the success of his trio of 1926 films which prompted *Photoplay* to note, "Ask Harold Lloyd who gives him his biggest celluloid laugh. Ask any star. They will all say Langdon. In a year, he has taken up his comedy post right behind Keaton and Lloyd." Langdon wanted control of his films—including the directorial reins. The films that followed, notably *Three's a Crowd*, were infused with too much pathos, however, and this time, the blend of laughter and tears did not work. As a result, the once-revered Langdon found his career on the wane.

Despite his rapid fall from stardom, however, Langdon left a legacy of three exceptional features and a string of hilarious silent shorts. Also, the Langdon name still survives in Hollywood through the celebrated glamour photographs by his son, Harry Langdon, Jr.

Pat H. Broeske

THE STUDENT OF PRAGUE
(DER STUDENT VON PRAG)

Released: 1913
Production: Bioscop
Direction: Stellan Rye
Screenplay: Hanns Heinz Ewers
Cinematography: Guido Seeber
Art direction: Robert A. Dietrich and K. Richter
Length: no listing

Principal characters:
Baldwin .... Paul Wegener
Scapinelli .... John Gottowt
The girl .... Lyda Salmonova
The girl's father ....Lothor Korner

Although frequently dismissed by film scholars and many historians, the horror genre has quietly (perhaps even sinisterly) wrought a significant impact upon the development of an unsuspecting cinema. While viewed by adherents of various critical schools as little more than a cathartic for the nightmares of the struggling masses, these grim films of suspense have instead emerged as highly ritualized myths of a violent age—modern counterparts of society's primitive legends which have become embellished by cinematic treatments after centuries of lavish reworking and thematic elaboration.

These early horror themes, in the hands of skilled interpreters such as Paul Wegener, Robert Wiene, and F. W. Murnau, were instrumental in freeing film from its early stagebound conventions of theatricality and also in the development of cinematic expressionism as a viable method of thematic narrative form. The principal objective of this mode of locution was the external manifestation of man's inner psychological or spiritual world; consequently, the outward symbolic representation of such fundamental human feelings as hatred, love, and fear constituted the usual concerns of the genre.

The formal introduction of the expressionistic school into filmmaking is generally recognized to have been effected in Robert Wiene's *Das Cabinet Des Dr. Caligari* (*The Cabinet of Dr. Caligari*, 1920), in which he employed a form of the school that had existed in visual arts, particularly painting, since 1903. Although his presentation somewhat mimicked that of the stage, with its hand-painted sets and poor lighting (the result of power shortages while shooting), the sheer abstraction of these cubist-inspired sets effectively portrayed the duality of man's nature and communicated a certain morbidity inherent in the human psyche.

Another type of expressionism, however, emanated from the writings of German poets around 1910 and was hinted at in the film works of actor-producer Paul Wegener and director Stellan Rye as early as their 1913 collaborative version of *Der Student von Prag* (*The Student of Prague*). Wegener's and Rye's approach to literary expressionism followed lines of morbidity and gloom similar to that embodied in the German romantic tradition, but they avoided the characteristic visual style later introduced by Wiene. Like the poets, the two filmmakers utilized the world of nature as a vehicle for reflecting their exploratory efforts at symbolism.

Much of the filming was done outdoors on location in the old section of Prague, whenever possible, and the actual settings were exaggerated and shaped along particular lines through imaginative use of light and shadow. The end result of this combination of natural settings and manipulative portrayal was a representation that was more subtle than that later effected by Wiene, in its expression of the duality, elemental emotions, and psychological states inhabiting the soul of man. The projection of this theme would be treated in a more sophisticated manner in Wegener's 1920 version of *The Golem* which makes as strong a case for its literary derived expressionism as *The Cabinet of Dr. Caligari* does for the films which evolved from the visual arts.

The Student of Prague (if one overlooks a lost 1910 version of *Frankenstein* listed in the Edison catalog) is probably the first legitimate example of the flowering of the horror genre. Its screenplay, written by Hanns Heinz Ewers and principal actor Wegener, was concerned with an interpretation of the *Doppelgänger* theme—that of the supernatural double. This subject in various forms had become something of an obsession in German literature. Ewers' immediate inspiration, however, was Adelbert Von Chamisso's *Peter Schlemihl*, which concerned a young man's sale of his own shadow, and E. T. A. Hoffmann's *Das Abenteuer der Sylvester-Nacht*, about a man who lost his reflection. Other motifs were less directly derived from Johann Wolfgang von Goethe's *Faust* and from Edgar Allen Poe's "William Wilson."

Wegener, who had played classical stage roles in Max Reinhardt's Deutsches Theater, had the idea that the cinema, unlike the stage, could become the definitive medium for realistically depicting dream states, realms of the imagination, and about any type of spiritual or psychological phenomenon that transcends the normal boundaries of time and space. From the stage, Wegener adapted a number of techniques developed by Reinhardt, particularly *chiaroscuro* lighting, to establish certain moods and tones that took on a new meaning in the medium of film. He was assisted in *The Student of Prague* by Danish director Stellan Rye, who also had a well-developed feeling for *chiaroscuro* and an affinity for naturalistic settings which merged well with Wegener's own delvings into expressionism (although he never applied that term to his experimentations) in which nature played a significant role.

This amalgamation of talents and interests produced a film in which a student, Baldwin (Paul Wegener), in the tradition of the Faust legends, trades his mirror reflection to the sorcerer Scapinelli (John Gottowt), for riches, social position, and an advantageous marriage to a beautiful countess. Baldwin, with the impetuosity of youth, enters into this written compact only dimly aware that Scapinelli is the devil incarnate, that the mirror image will eventually assume his soul, and that it too will eventually belong to the Devil. Baldwin is young, though, and wants the advantages that Scapinelli offers him. Thus, under the sorcerer's direction, the image is lured out of the mirror (in a scene of unusual visual complexity) to become a flesh-and-blood twin to the student but with a psyche of its own.

The student achieves his riches and meets and woos a beautiful, wealthy countess (Lyda Salmonova), which causes some consternation on the part of her family-approved suitor, who immediately challenges the young interloper to a duel. This is an unfortunate development, since Baldwin has the reputation of being an excellent fencer. At the behest of the young woman's father (Lothor Korner), however, the student agrees to spare the "official" suitor's life, a deal which should virtually cinch Baldwin's marriage aspirations.

Baldwin rushes to the agreed-upon dueling area to call off the fight but is blocked and delayed by the devices of Scapinelli. He does not reach it in time to be a factor in the contest, and, unknown to him, his double, who has also been following him around at night attempting to thwart his plans, supplants him in the duel and slays the suitor to breach the agreement with the girl's father. Baldwin's hopes are dashed. He is unable to convince the countess of his innocence or of the existence of the double who frustrates all his plans.

At last, desperate, Baldwin lures his look alike back to the old garret where the contract with Scapinelli was signed. The student takes a gun and futilely tries to shoot the other personage but succeeds only in smashing the mirror and killing himself. Scapinelli then enters and tears up the contract, whose pieces drift down through the air to cover the corpse.

Scapinelli thus obtains Baldwin's soul, because the double, as only a projection of one of the two sides of the student's personality, has pushed the other side into the temptation of achieving unearned wealth and love. In assuming an existence of its own—independent of Baldwin—it betrays and ultimately destroys the other, positive side of the student's psyche which causes the subversion of the entire entity.

The thematic expressionism depicted in *The Student of Prague*, as opposed to the visual kind of abstractionism that so jarred film critics viewing *The Cabinet of Dr. Caligari*, with its cubist designed sets, involved a much subtler manifestation of Baldwin's internal states within the psychical environment. The incarnation of his soul as a participant in the drama initiates a cycle of physical projection of various aspects of his spiritual duality. A parallel projection also occurs later on the part of Scapinelli when, as Baldwin and the countess meet secretly on a castle rampart amidst the shadows of columns, another more sinister shadow, that of the sorcerer, separates itself from the other shades and intrudes itself upon the viewer's consciousness as its owner spies upon the lovers.

Stellan Rye expertly used the winding streets, alleys, and moody architecture of the old town of Prague to maintain his theme in a naturalistic manner representative of his characters' states of mind. The Jewish cemetery, the only major external set to be artificially constructed, was re-created in a forest adjoining the city. Although there was some manipulation of atmosphere with the placement of large tombstones amidst the trees with a concern for natural lighting, the effect is one of reality. Other constructions of interior sets including certain modifications of the student's living quarters through creative lighting and furnishings (stark and light before he sells his reflection; heavy and gloomy after he has become wealthy) work equally well. The physical expression of Baldwin's psychological and spiritual state is thus developed naturally. As a point of contrast, in *The Cabinet of Dr. Caligari*, the setting appeared as if in some kind of disjointed dream, with highly visual sets, logical in a psychological sense but looking artificial, not arising naturally from the story's thematic concerns.

The Student of Prague, however, foreshadows the more sophisticated expressionistic atmosphere employed by actor-director Wegener in his 1920 film, *The Golem*, which owes very little to abstractionist conceits. In both films, the imagery forms a chain between the character and the setting. Not only does a particular edifice, such as a roof or a tombstone, reveal an individual's psychological state, but the image also reverts back to the character or to his neighbors through costume or appearance. A beard (particularly in *The Golem*) may mimic a tombstone, or a roof gable may be revealed in a windblown goatee or in a physical gesture such as the wave of a hand. The image is expressionistic but also ultimately reflexive in returning to the person whose psychological or spiritual state it represents. This reflexiveness is most vividly demonstrated when Baldwin, in attempting to destroy his mirror image, destroys himself.

The Student of Prague, in addition to being the first legitimate horror film, thus also foreshadowed the concerns and attributes exhibited by many of the major films of Germany's great period in the early 1920's, expressionism: a concern for lighting, atmospheric interiors and exteriors, and a preoccupation with setting that would become increasingly peculiar to German filmmakers.

The acting in *The Student of Prague* was not particularly noteworthy as a precursor of the expressionistic school but was not totally without interest. A remarkable contrast was established between the dramatic, stagelike acting of Wegener in the part of Baldwin and the more subtle, restrained performance of John Gottowt in the role of Scapinelli. As Lotte Eisner points out in *The Haunted Screen*, the standard work on German expressionism, Wegener adapted his acting style more completely to the screen in *The Golem*, in which he exhibited great restraint and control in portraying the enigmatic

The Student of Prague

figure who became the protector of the Prague ghetto.

Yet, Wegener, both as an actor and writer, introduced to the screen in *The Student of Prague* a theme that would not only form the basis for most of the major horror films to be developed in succeeding years, but it also started an examination of the "self" that would occupy German directors in the 1920's. This theme, an exploration of the roots of identity and the concept of the duality of the soul, was conducted through a drama of man pitted against himself—a search that would culminate in the films of the golden age of the German cinema and would be more fully and completely defined in sophisticated styles and techniques by directors such as Fritz Lang, F. W. Murnau, and, indeed, Wegener himself.

Stephen L. Hanson

THE STUDENT PRINCE IN OLD HEIDELBERG

Released: 1927
Production: Irving Thalberg for Metro-Goldwyn-Mayer
Direction: Ernst Lubitsch
Screenplay: Hans Kraly; based on the book *Alt Heidelberg Schauspiel in funf Aufzugen* by Wilhelm Meyer-Forster and the play *The Student Prince* by Dorothy Donnelly and Sigmund Romberg
Titles: Marian Ainslee and Ruth Cummings
Cinematography: John J. Mescall
Editing: Andrew Marton
Art direction: Cedric Gibbons and Richard Day
Length: 10 reels/9,435 feet

> *Principal characters:*
> Prince Karl Heinrich .... Ramon Novarro
> Kathi .... Norma Shearer
> Dr. Juttner .... Jean Hersholt
> King Karl VII .... Gustav von Seyffertitz
> Heir Apparent .... Philippe De Lacey

The Student Prince in Old Heidelberg is a retelling of an unabashedly sentimental story of true love thwarted by royal duty. Under famed director Ernst Lubitsch, however, it became something else entirely. Well known for his films of boudoir frolics and sly sexual innuendo, Lubitsch brought another dimension to this romance. In *The Student Prince in Old Heidelberg*, a darker side of Lubitsch can be viewed, for the film is tinged with bitterness. What Lubitsch did was to take the plot of the play and operetta and manipulate it so that a simple love story took on a tone of loss and despair. The contrast between the court life of Prince Karl (Ramon Novarro), stiff, regimental, and with his ever present duties to fulfill, and his carefree days at the University of Heidelberg is marked.

The journey to Heidelberg is, for the Prince, a journey from darkness to light, from duty to freedom. Lubitsch cleverly contrasts the ceremonies at court, which are lifeless and routine, to the student rituals of the cadets at the University, which are joyous and spontaneous. A motif running through the Heidelberg life that Karl learns to love and share is the lifting of the beer steins by the students in a gesture of abandon. This is very different from the movements of Prince Karl's future subjects who lift their top hats when he passes by in a manner that is formal and mechanical. The film even seems to be photographed in two different styles. In the Kingdom of Karlsberg, the crowds move like puppets, and the city seems grey and lifeless. In Heidelberg, light seems to be everywhere and a sense of lyric beauty abounds.

The love story is tender, without being cloying, and even contains some traces of the sly Lubitsch, as when Kathi (Norma Shearer) shows Karl his large, comfortable bed for the first time and bounces on it unself-consciously, and the Prince's reaction shows him to be quite aware of her innocent sexuality. Lubitsch manages to get beyond the histrionics of the essential plot by imposing his own fastidious style upon the idea. The result is a film that is complex, moving, and full of contrast: love versus duty, childhood versus manliness, and protocol versus spontaneous feeling.

As usual, Lubitsch's casting is flawless. Novarro plays Prince Karl as a genuine romantic. His life has been a dull one with most emotions suppressed. When he first sees the beautiful barmaid Kathi, he is thunderstruck and knows for the first time what it feels like to be young and in love. Norma Shearer as Kathi is the very stuff of adolescent fantasy and is photographed throughout as a Pre-Raphaelite damsel. Jean Hersholt's character acts as a bridge between the two lives of Prince Karl. He plays Dr. Juttner, Karl's tutor, whose duty it is to instruct the Prince "in etiquette, obligation, demeanor and formality," but who is more concerned with teaching him to be human as he teaches the youth wrestling, pillow fighting, and even how to sneak a smoke.

The film opens in the small kingdom of Karlsburg where Crown Prince Karl Heinrich, nephew of the reigning King, Karl VII (Gustav von Seyffertitz), lives a joyless existence. Trained in the art of learning to be a king, the younger Karl is dutiful and obedient, but melancholy. His only joyful moments are spent in the company of his tutor, Dr. Juttner, who realizes that youth must be served and tries to give Karl some lighter moments both in the sports field and in the classroom. After several years, Juttner takes Karl off to study at the renowned University of Heidelberg where a new world opens up to the repressed Prince. Here he is treated by his fellow students as one of their own kind: he is expected to down his stein of beer with one gulp, to sing their songs with them, and to share their irreverent sense of community. In the student beer hall, Karl meets Kathi, the beautiful barmaid who greets him with flowers. She feels no discomfort in the presence of royalty and treats him as an equal.

Karl Heinrich falls deeply in love with Kathi, love that she returns, and together they enjoy an idyllic spring with frequent romps amidst fields of flowers. This interlude soon ends, however, when the King dies and the Prince is called back to Karlsburg to take the throne. In time, Karl's beloved Dr. Juttner dies as well. The Prince feels alone and emotionally sterile. He cannot shake the memory of his life as a student and of his beautiful Kathi, and although he is now betrothed to an unattractive Princess, Karl decides to return to Heidelberg for a visit. He finds everything changed: the comrades that were once his classmates greet him stiffly; he does not fit into their lives as the King and only Kathi welcomes him as before. After a brief reunion, Karl and Kathi part again, this time for good, and he returns to his kingdom to celebrate his marriage. The last scene shows Karl riding joylessly in his marriage procession through the streets of Karlsberg.

The Student Prince in Old Heidelberg, although treated in an unsentimental fashion, is filled with sentiment. More than that, however, it is a ruthless social comment about the emptiness of life that exists only for duty and without love. With a less talented director, the film would have been merely a romantic potboiler, but in Lubitsch's capable hands, the story becomes a complex film full of deep human emotion and a telling tale of duty versus desire.

Joan L. Cohen

SUDS

Released: 1920
Production: Mary Pickford for United Artists
Direction: John Francis Dillon
Screenplay: Based on the play *'Op 'o Me Thumb* by Frederick Fenn and Richard Bryce
Cinematography: Charles Rosher
Length: 5 reels

Principal characters:
Amanda Afflick .... Mary Pickford
Horace Greensmith .... Albert Austin
Benjamin Pillsbury Jones .... Harold Goodwin
Madame Jeanne Gallifilet Didier .... Rose Dione

'Op 'o Me Thumb was a one act play, introduced as a curtain raiser to James M. Barrie's *The Little Minister* at New York's Empire Theater on February 6, 1905. Like *The Little Minister*, it starred Maude Adams, and its chief *raison d'être* was to demonstrate the histrionic abilities of its star.

Why Mary Pickford should have chosen such a subject for her second United Artists release is unclear. Perhaps she wanted an entirely different characterization to follow the sunny sweet *Pollyanna* (1920), or perhaps the actress, like Adams, felt in need of a subject that could illustrate her performing talents. *Suds*, which was the release title for *'Op 'o Me Thumb*, was certainly not the first occasion on which Pickford had portrayed an ugly little girl. She had done it to perfection in *Stella Maris* (1918), and her role of Amanda Afflick in *Suds* cannot hope to equal her part as Unity Blake in the former film. The major difference between the two characters is that Unity Blake is a completely scarred human being, unloved and basically humorless, whereas Amanda Afflick has humor; her existence is not totally tragic. Most critics, however, felt that Amanda Afflick was a poor substitute for Unity Blake. With *Suds*, Pickford seemed to be taking a look back to an earlier period in filmmaking, the era of Keystone comedies. The comedy is broad, but the production is short and ends abruptly.

The introductory title warns the audience not to expect a story, but rather to be entertained by the "tale of a shirt." The shirt in question was brought to the London laundry where Amanda works by Horace Greensmith (Albert Austin) eight months previous. Amanda tells her fellow workers that the shirt belongs to her fiancé, Sir Horace (or 'Orace as she calls him). Her father, a duke, objected to Sir Horace, but before the fiancé was thrown out of her family castle, the well-known saying, "He'd give her the shirt off his back," became a reality. Amanda was sent out into the world by her father so that she may be "loved for herself and not for her jewels."

When Lavender, the old laundry horse, is considered too old to work and about to be sent to the glue factory, Amanda uses her savings to purchase the animal. When she takes the horse to her lodgings, however, he is thrown out the following morning by the indignant tenants below. When Lady Burke, one of those philanthropic individuals who forever people film slums, visits Amanda, she arranges to have Lavender sent to her country estate.

Amanda is loved by Ben Jones (Harold Goodwin), a driver for the laundry, but the girl's thoughts are only for the coming of Sir 'Orace. When Horace Greensmith eventually arrives to claim his shirt, Amanda tries to persuade him to pretend to her fellow workers that he is her lover. He agrees to do it and then decides to take Amanda to the races at Hampstead Heath, until he suddenly realizes how shabby and unattractive she is. Horace departs, and Amanda is left alone in the laundry. Realizing her own ugliness, she sobs, "How could anyone love me?," while outside the faithful Ben Jones stands alone, looking at some flowers he had bought for Amanda. For its initial screening at New York's Strand Theater, this was the ending, but, perhaps because of widespread criticism of the production's harsh conclusion, a happy ending was also filmed in which Amanda is seen at Lady Burke's country estate, living in happiness with Lavender and Ben Jones.

In her autobiography, *Sunshine and Shadow* (1955), Pickford remembers the film best for its leading character, Lavender. She recalls finding the horse working on a sand pile in Los Angeles, "more dead than alive." Unfortunately, during the weeks he was at the studio the horse became healthier and heavier (by sixty pounds). In order to disguise the white animal's sudden change in health, gray streaks had to be painted on the horse's stomach to make it appear that its ribs were standing out. Her comment that Lavender's performance represents the most outstanding supporting role in the production does not speak very well for the acting of the two male leads, Albert Austin and Harold Goodwin. The scenes with Pickford and Lavender, particularly when the latter sends the ceiling down on the tenants below, are the comedy highspots of *Suds*.

Critical reaction to *Suds* was extremely mixed. Laurence Reid in *Motion Picture News* (July 10, 1920) wrote,

> It is problematical how Mary Pickford's latest production, *Suds*, will be received by her vast host of admirers. . . . That she can play other than glad roles was testified to when she appeared as Unity Blake. . . . Her role of the little laundry apprentice is a vest pocket edition of Unity, without one-half the color and vitality. *Suds* lacks the story interest of the aforementioned picture since it is, at best, a simple character study without shading or contrast or moving moments.

Exhibitor's Trade Review (July 10, 1920), however, hailed the production as "an unique specimen of comedy-drama, a bit of real drab tragedy lightened by flashes of humor, laughter, struggling with tears, the net result, an intensely happy one."

Variety (July 2, 1920) commented,

> No sane person can possibly have the temerity to allege that any picture made by Mary Pickford will fail to draw. There is but one other thing to have misgivings about, namely, will the audiences be satisfied with the vehicle. . . . *Suds* is very pleasing entertainment while it lasts, but it is safe to assert that had the little English laundry girl consummated a romantic marriage after passing through a series of pathetic vicissitudes the paying auditors would have been "satisfied."

Wid's Daily (July 4, 1920) wrote,

> There was an audible murmur of dissatisfaction at the final fade-out. However, the fact that it's Mary Pickford will get them in and notwithstanding the slight material contained in *Suds*, the star's own personal charm and some really good comedy bits that she puts over alone and others with an old white nag, will help to compensate for other shortcomings. They take a whack at some slap-stick which doesn't add to the production's attractiveness.

Burns Mantle in *Photoplay* (September, 1920) called *Suds* "an effort to compromise between the real and the unreal, and to me such compromises are never entirely satisfactory." In *Motion Picture Classic* (September, 1920), Frederick James Smith wrote,

> Personally, we do not believe *Suds* will make the broad appeal of the more popular Mary Pickford vehicles. It runs too strongly in the single key of drab farce. Not that Miss Pickford does not give a very carefully drawn portrayal of the slavey. No other feminine star would hide herself beneath the fearful make-up of Amanda. And only one does she discard the dirt and grime of the laundry drudge, in the brief flashes of the slavey's imaginary romance built around the shirt. Nowhere, however, does she achieve the poignancy of her Pollyanna.

Suds is a curious, minor Pickford film, which seems to be trying to put across a message that those gifted with imagination can give color to the world, a message surely aimed at millions of Pickford's working-class followers. The pathos of the production's conclusion, however, with Amanda sobbing an answer to her question "How could anyone love me?" with "Nobody could love me—Nobody every wont," spoils the film's earlier sentiment. Pickford followed *Suds* with two other minor films—*The Love Light* (1921) and *Through the Back Door* (1921)—neither of which could remotely hope to provide the appeal of *Suds*, and it was not until *Little Lord Fauntleroy* in 1921 that Pickford seemed to hit her stride again.

Anthony Slide

SUNRISE

Released: 1927
Production: William Fox for Fox Film Corporation
Direction: F. W. Murnau
Screenplay: Carl Mayer; based on a short story by Hermann Sudermann
Titles: Katherine Hilliker and H. H. Caldwell
Cinematography: Charles Rosher and Karl Struss (AA)
Editing: Katherine Hilliker and H. H. Caldwell
Length: 9 reels/8,729 feet

> *Principal characters:*
> The Man .... George O'Brien
> The Wife .... Janet Gaynor (AA)
> The Woman from the City .... Margaret Livingston

Director F. W. Murnau's *Sunrise* has been described by film critic Molly Haskell as "surely one of the most beautiful and influential films of all time" and in 1957 was selected by the critics of the French film journal *Cahiers du Cinema* as the best film ever made. In addition, in the first year that Academy Awards were given, it won three, including one for "artistic achievement." The quality of this exceptional film can be attributed to two important factors that came together at that particular point in film history: the highly developed state of silent-film art and the veneration in Hollywood of German filmmakers that brought about the remarkable combination of German and American talent and resources for the film.

During the early and middle 1920's, German films and German film directors were highly regarded in Hollywood. Indeed, the situation led humorist Will Rogers to remark bitterly in 1922 about one of his own pictures that if he had said it was made in Germany everyone would have called it art. The high regard for German films was based on more than a snobbish belief that foreign goods were better, however, for some of the greatest talents of the cinema of that time were German, and the decade after World War I is still known as the Golden Age of German cinema. Such directors as Ernst Lubitsch, Fritz Lang, and Robert Weine as well as Murnau were part of this period of excellence.

When William Fox, head of the Fox Film studio, saw Murnau's films, particularly *Nosferatu* (1922) and *The Last Laugh* (1925), he invited the director to come to the United States to make a film for his studio. Murnau said he would accept the offer only if he could have complete control of the film, with no interference from the studio. It was a request that has seldom been granted before or since in Hollywood, but Fox agreed. The script (based upon a short story by Hermann Sudermann) was written by Carl Mayer, who had also written *The Last Laugh*, and the design of the film was largely planned by Murnau and his German staff before he left for the United States.

In Hollywood, Murnau ordered the construction of enormous and intricate sets, and having received *carte blanche* from the studio, spared no expense to achieve the look and the effects he desired. A major help to him was the fact that he was able to use two talented cinematographers, Charles Rosher and Karl Struss. Their work was recognized when they received the first Academy Award for cinematography for their work on *Sunrise*.

The story Murnau had chosen to tell is a simple and elemental one. Indeed, the three main characters are simply designated as The Man, The Wife, and The Woman from the City, and the beginning title states that it is "a story of two humans . . . of no place and of every place." The plot can be described briefly, although the artistry of its presentation and its aesthetic effect cannot.

The Man (George O'Brien), a simple farmer with a wife (Janet Gaynor) and a small child, is seduced by The Woman from the City (Margaret Livingston). She persuades him that he should kill his wife, sell his farm, and go to the city with her. The man takes his wife out on a boat intending to drown her, but at the last moment he cannot. When they reach shore she runs from him; they take a trolley car to the city and are reconciled there and happy together again. On the trip back from the city to the farm, the boat is capsized in a storm, and the wife is lost and feared dead. She is finally found alive and the other woman then goes back to the city, leaving the radiantly happy couple together.

The plot is essentially that of a man's progression from darkness to light, both literally and figuratively. The first significant sequence takes place at night with the man under the influence of the dark-haired vamp; the film ends with the shot of the man with his blond wife, a shot that dissolves into a shot of a sunrise. Besides the contrast between dark and light, the film also focuses upon the contrast between the city and the country.

These contrasts and other themes and motifs are brought out by various cinematic devices, among the most notable being the presentation of mental images on the screen. When the vamp begins to describe the attractions of the city to the man, viewers see a montage of flashy, jazzy images of the city. When she suggests the drowning of his wife, a quick image of a body falling into the water is seen. As the man considers his situation after he has left the city woman, his image dissolves into that of rushing water, and soon after, multiple images of the city woman superimposed over the image of the man are seen. In the most elaborate subjective sequence, which occurs shortly after the man and wife have been reconciled, the two walk magically through city traffic directly into the country. When they stop and kiss, they are suddenly brought back to reality as they find they are in the center of a busy street and have caused a traffic jam by blocking traffic.

It is not, however, only through such cinematic devices that the themes and emotions of *Sunrise* are conveyed. There are several poignant scenes that are presented aesthetically but straightforwardly, and it is the situation and the acting that affects the audience. For example, after the trolley ride to the city, the man goes with his wife through the streets trying to persuade her not to be afraid of him, but she is unable to discard her fear easily. Then they see a wedding and go into the church and sit in a back pew. The man is moved nearly to tears by hearing the wedding vows, and his wife turns and comforts him. Later, during their celebration of their reunion in an amusement park, a band plays a peasant dance. When the wife begins to dance, the man holds back because he is ashamed to display their rustic ways before the sophisticated city people watching. Soon, however, he removes his coat and the two dance in a joyous celebration, even overcoming the initial derision of the onlookers.

Janet Gaynor won the 1927-1928 Academy Award for Best Actress for her acting in *Sunrise* and two other films, *7th Heaven* and *Street Angel*. In the first part of the film she is given a limited range of expression, chiefly looking forlorn but not bitter when her husband responds to the vamp's whistle and leaves the house just as she is bringing him his supper. Later, however, she conveys her terror as her husband moves toward her in the boat and then her ambivalance as she tries to forget the horror and accept the renewal of her husband's love for her. Margaret Livingston is appropriately sophisticated and seductive in the role of the city woman, and George O'Brien depicts a man bewitched but burdened by the spell. (In fact, Murnau had him wear lead-weighted shoes in some scenes to help him give his walk the proper look.) O'Brien also conveys well the torment of the husband after the storm when he thinks he has lost his wife just when he had again found his love for her.

Sunrise was, of course, a great triumph for Murnau, the director, but it was to be his last major work. He died in an automobile accident in 1931, just after completion of his last film, *Tabu*.

Timothy W. Johnson

SURRENDER

Released: 1927
Production: Universal
Direction: Edward Sloman
Screenplay: Charles Kenyon and Edward J. Montagne; based on the play *Lea Lyon* by Alexander Brody
Titles: Albert De Mond
Cinematography: Gilbert Warrenton
Length: 8 reels/8,249 feet

Principal characters:
Lea Lyon .... Mary Philbin
Constantine .... Ivan Mosjukine
Joshua .... Otto Matiesen
Rabbi Mendel .... Nigel De Brulier
Tarras .... Otto Fries
Russian General .... Daniel Makarenko

Edward Sloman and Ivan Mosjukine are only vaguely familiar names to even the most ardent film buffs. Sloman was a director and Mosjukine (spelled Mosjoukine in France, Moskine in Germany, and Mozhukhin in his native Russia) was an actor. Practically all of Sloman's films have been lost, while Mosjukine only made one American feature—*Surrender*, directed by Sloman. While far from a masterpiece—in particular, the narrative is rather stiff and predictable—it features unusually strong direction and above-average cinematography.

Surrender is based on Alexander Brody's play *Lea Lyon*, written around 1915. The setting is a year earlier, in a small Galician town near the Russian border. Lea (Mary Philbin), the only child of Rabbi Mendel (Nigel De Brulier) the spiritual adviser of the community, enjoys spending her time wading in a quiet brook. While there, she meets Constantine (Ivan Mosjukine), an aristrocratic Cossack prince garbed as a peasant, who is out hunting. He is at once enchanted by her: "Pardon me, Little Cinderella, did you lose your slipper?" he asks her. Lea's father, however, objects to Constantine's interest in his daughter. He insults the prince, admonishing him for taking the girl's hand and orders him to leave.

War is declared, and the Russians—under Constantine, who is Colonel of the Cossacks—invade and occupy the town. Lea and the Rabbi are both shocked to discover Constantine's real identity, and they must now address him as "Royal Highness." Constantine lusts for Lea and invites himself to the Rabbi's house, where he is sarcastically polite to the girl, offering to help, and then forcing his attentions on her. She is engaged to Joshua (Otto Matiesen), a young village boy, and resists the Cossack. Constantine orders the Rabbi to remove a holy scroll from a cabinet, then stays for dinner, partaking with Lea and her father in the drinking of the sacramental wine, and watching as the girl lights the holiday candles and says a prayer.

Constantine threatens to burn down the town unless Lea agrees to "surrender" herself to him. Lea courageously decides to sacrifice herself in order to save her father and her neighbors; she visits the prince and is prepared to follow his will. Suddenly, however, he falls in love with her, thinking her to be an "angel from heaven," and he cannot seduce her. He treats her gently and with respect; he gives her a ring, which she treasures, and tells her he cares for her too much to harm her. Constantine looks at the sky and complains that the same stars that look down on lovers also look down on armies.

Lea may have been willing to risk her honor to save the lives of the townspeople, but they jeer and throw stones at her when she leaves Constantine, and when she arrives home, her father orders her to leave. She tells him that the Cossack is really a gentleman and that she is still pure. Constantine, in his kindness, has won her heart. Eventually, Rabbi Mendel dies. Years pass and, at the finale, the war has ended. The Jews have triumphed, as their town is no longer occupied, and they have survived. Constantine returns to Lea.

The plot of *Surrender* is melodramatic and unbelievable, particularly Constantine's sudden realization that he cares for Lea. The film, though, is beautifully directed by Sloman. The opening sequence is particularly lovely. Constantine is first pictured hunting in the forest. As film historian Kevin Brownlow writes in *The Parade's Gone By. . .* ,

> He catches sight of game, and raises his gun. Dissolve to close-up of his eyes as they squint down the barrel . . . dissolve to a closeshot of his dog, straining at the alert . . . dissolve to Mosjoukine's viewpoint, as he sights down the barrel, and settles on a close-up of a squirrel sitting in a tree. Cut back to Mosjoukine, who grins and lowers his gun. The squirrel darts away. The dog rushes off, but ignores the squirrel, and returns with a shoe. Intrigued, Mosjoukine finds Mary Philbin paddling in a stream nearby.

Brownlow aptly describes the camerawork as "inventive"; the cinematographer, Gilbert Warrenton, shot dozens of features during the 1920's, including *The Plastic Age* (1925), *The Cat and the Canary* (1927), *Lonesome* (1928), and *Showboat* (1929). Warrenton also worked with Sloman on *Butterflies in the Rain* (1926) and *Alias the Deacon* (1928).

Originally a stage and vaudeville actor and director, the London-born Sloman first appeared in and wrote scenarios for silent films. His earliest directorial credits date back to 1915. He made several dozen shorts and features from that year through the late 1930's; Sloman's favorite film, and one of his greatest popular and critical successes, was *His People* (1925), focusing on Rabbi David Cominsky (the great Yiddish stage actor Rudolph Schildkraut, father of Joseph), a pushcart peddler on New York's lower east side, and his relationship with his two sons. Sloman was Jewish, and a number of his other films featured Jewish and/or Russian themes or characters. Some even acknowledge and explore the issue of anti-Semitism. According to Brownlow, however, the director had informed him that "I really haven't a penchant for Jewish pictures. I've only done three, and these were forced on me by the powers that be because of the success of *His People*."

This is not quite accurate. In *The Woman He Loved*, released three years before *His People*, William V. Mong and Marcia Manon play Nathan and Esther Levinsky, who leave Russia for the United States because of a pogrom; their son David (Eddie Sutherland) is adopted by a wealthy gentile family, and the father of the girl he loves is vocally anti-Semitic. Among Sloman's other films are *The Beautiful Cheat* (1926), starring Laura La Plante as shopgirl Mary Callahan, who is transformed by press agent Harry Myers into Maritza Callahansky, a Russian actress; *We Americans* (1928), with George Sidney and Beryl Mercer as the Levines, Russian-Jewish immigrants whose son (George Lewis) dies in World War I while saving the life of one Hugh Bradleigh (John Boles), who in turn cares for their daughter, played by Patsy Ruth Miller; *The Kibitzer* (1930), whose main character is Ike Lazarus (Harry Green), a tobacconist who earns a fortune in the stock market.

Mosjukine is yet another actor who tragically faded from the spotlight after a career as one of the most popular screen stars of his time. He began his career in a theater troupe which toured his native country (he was born in Penza, Russia, in 1889). Then, he concentrated on both stage and screen roles and was the most acclaimed leading man and matinee idol in the pre-Revolutionary cinema. He fled Russia at the outset of the Bolshevik Revolution, eventually settling in Paris, and became a star of French films. Mosjukine remained one of the top cinematic attractions in his adopted country throughout the 1920's, making several films in Germany and only *Surrender* in the United States. He supposedly spoke no English, so Sloman had to direct him through an interpreter. His career was destroyed when talkies became the rage and he could no longer claim top-quality parts. The actor appeared on screen into the mid-1930's, but only in smaller roles in lesser films. He died in 1939, impoverished and ignored.

Mosjukine's co-star in *Surrender* is pretty Mary Philbin, whose best-recalled performance is opposite Lon Chaney in *The Phantom of the Opera* (1925). She also worked with Sloman in *Love Me and the World is Mine* (1928) and retired at the advent of sound. Nigel De Brulier, who played Rabbi Mendel, was a prolific character actor whose career spanned from the early teens to the mid-1940's. He was prominently featured in some of the most popular films of the 1920's: *The Four Horsemen of the Apocalypse* (1921), *The Hunchback of Notre Dame* (1923), *Ben-Hur* (1925), *Don Juan* (1926), *The Beloved Rogue* (1927), and *Wings* (1927). His best role was Cardinal Richelieu in *The Three Musketeers* (both the 1921 and 1935 versions) and *The Iron Mask* (1929).

Surrender opened to fair reviews, with some of the more positive comments centering around the glimpses of Jewish custom that might be of interest to audiences. The film has been almost completely obscured by time, but certainly, like the careers of its director and star, it is worthy of rediscovery.

Rob Edelman

A TALE OF TWO CITIES

Released: 1917
Production: William Fox
Direction: Frank Lloyd
Screenplay: Clara Beranger; based on the novel of the same name by Charles Dickens
Cinematography: Billy Foster
Length: 7 reels

Principal characters:
Charles Darnay/Sydney Carton .... William Farnum
Lucie Manette .... Jewel Carmen
Marquis St. Evremonde .... Charles Clary
Jacques DeFarge .... Herschel Mayall
Madame DeFarge .... Rosita Marstini
Dr. Manette .... Josef Swickard
Roger Cly .... Ralph Lewis
Gabelle .... William Clifford
Jarvis Lorry .... Marc Robbins
Miss Pross .... Olive White

Charles Dickens has always been popular with filmmakers. Not only do his novels and stories offer excellent cinematic possibilities, but also, as with William Shakespeare, his work is in the public domain and available to any would-be producer without charge. *A Tale of Two Cities*, along with *A Christmas Carol* or *Scrooge*, is surely the writer's most-filmed work. It was first produced in the United States as a three-reel drama by Vitagraph in 1911, then William Fox filmed it in 1917. Ronald Colman was the star of a 1935 version for Metro-Goldwyn-Mayer. In Great Britain, it was filmed in 1925 by Herbert Wilcox under the title of *The Only Way*, starring John Martin Harvey who had long been the leading man of a stage version of the novel under that title. The most recent feature film version of the classic was made in England by J. Arthur Rank in 1958, featuring Dirk Bogarde.

When Vitagraph first filmed *A Tale of Two Cities* in 1916, it used two actors, Maurice Costello and Leo Delaney, to play the look-alikes, Charles Darnay and Sydney Carton. In 1917, however, with the established use of double exposure cinematography, Fox was able to have the same actor play both roles. For the dual role, the company selected one of its contract stars, William Farnum, who had been active on the stage since childhood and who had entered films in the William N. Selig production of *The Spoilers* (1914). Not particularly handsome by present-day standards, Farnum was a good, solid actor who was also muscular and virile. He brought to the roles a strong masculinity, which compares more than favorably with the somewhat effete performances later offered by Colman and Bogarde. Of Farnum's work, Edward Weitzel wrote in *The Moving Picture World* (March 31, 1917),

> His performance of the first character [Charley Darnay] is thoroughly adequate. He has the polish, charm of manner and fineness of nature required of the young Frenchman. His Sydney Carton is well contrasted with Darnay. Mr. Farnum brings out the man of good instincts, chained to an overmastering passion, clearly and effectively. . . . But the soul of Sydney Carton, when put to the final test, eludes the actor. Technically he is beyond criticism. The art of acting is strongly influenced by personality, however, and the spiritual exaltation which Martin Harvey, the English actor, gives to the part is lacking in Mr. Farnum's portrayal.

Playing opposite Farnum, in the role of Lucie Manette, is Jewel Carmen, an actress with an elusive quality of beauty, who commenced her career under D. W. Griffith's guidance at the Fine Arts Company. She was a major Fox star of the late teens, but disappeared from motion pictures after her marriage to director Roland West.

When Julian Johnson reviewed the film in *Photoplay* (June, 1917), he wrote,

> I wish the program gave us the name of that fair victim of "Citizen" wrath who, enroute in a tumbril with Carton to the guillotine, looks into his eyes with the sunrise of eternity in her own, and asks only that he hold her hand to the foot of the scaffold.

The actress in question was Florence Vidor, who was destined to make a name for herself as a major dramatic star of the 1920's. It is interesting to note that in the earlier Vitagraph production of *A Tale of Two Cities*, another unknown actress in the tumbril with Carton was singled out for attention by critics and fans; her name was Norma Talmadge, and she also gained fame as one of the cinema's best-known dramatic stars. There can be few other examples in the history of the cinema of history repeating itself so completely.

The Fox film follows Dickens' novel fairly closely, taking a few liberties with the characterizations of some of the protagonists but fewer liberties with the plot. The film concerns Charles Darnay (William Farnum), an heir to the Evremonde fortune in prerevolutionary France, who feels a sympathy with the peasants of his native land, and who has come to England to live. There he falls in love with and marries Lucie Manette (Jewel Carmen), whose father Dr. Manette (Josef Swickard) has long been imprisoned in the Bastille by Darnay's father. A barrister named Sydney Carton (also William Farnum) is also in love with Lucie, and it is he who saves Darnay from a false accusation of treason by showing how closely the two resemble each other, thus proving that a witness's identification of Darnay has no validity.

Following upon the revolution in France, Darnay goes there on an errand of mercy, but is arrested by the Republican guards. Darnay is placed on trial, but thanks to the efforts of Dr. Manette, he is acquitted. At a second trial, however, Jacques DeFarge (Herschel Mayall), a former servant of Manette, produces a document written in prison by the doctor which curses all of the Evremonde family, and Darnay is sentenced to the guillotine. Out of devotion to Lucie, Sydney Carton decides upon a plan of action to save Darnay. On the morning of the execution, he visits Darnay in his cell and persuades him to change clothes with him. He chloroforms Darnay and has him removed to a waiting carriage, which will take him, Lucie, her daughter, and Dr. Manette to the coast, en route to England and safety. Carton answers to the name of Darnay and is driven to the guillotine and his death, thus making the supreme sacrifice for the woman he loves.

A Tale of Two Cities was generally well received by contemporary critics. Peter Milne in *Motion Picture News* wrote, "More pictures like *A Tale of Two Cities* and the millennium of the picture business would be near at hand." In *The Moving Picture World*, Edward Weitzel commented, "As a picture of the French Revolution, told in fictional form, it is unrivaled." Both critics praised director Frank Lloyd and the handling of the mob scenes, for which, of course, Lloyd should take full credit.

Frank Lloyd (1888-1960) was a major figure in Hollywood film production for almost three decades, being responsible for such features as *Oliver Twist* (1922), *Cavalcade* (1932), and *Mutiny on the Bounty* (1935). He also directed another major Fox production from the same period as *A Tale of Two Cities*, *Les Miserables* (1918). Lloyd was a reliable, trustworthy director, who could always turn in a good, if uninspired, production. Such is the case with *A Tale of Two Cities*, which is a strong, solid film, but lacks any real emotion and any major visual techniques. Its sets are particularly impressive; in fact, the French streets built for the film at the Fox Western Avenue studios in Hollywood were used in countless other Fox and Twentieth Century-Fox productions until the company closed the studios in the 1960's.

Typical of the reaction to Lloyd's direction is this comment from Peter Milne:

Mr. Lloyd in the handling of the scenario and in the production of it has truly earned himself a place in the hall of fame of directors. Better than his masterly handling of the mob scenes, his delightful reproduction of the atmosphere of the period; better than his remarkable double exposure scenes and the selection of proper types, is the manner in which he has handled the plot itself. In so doing he has shown himself a master of picture craft.

A Tale of Two Cities is preserved at the Museum of Modern Art.

Lennox Sanderson, Jr.

TARZAN OF THE APES

Released: 1918
Production: National Film Corporation for Associated First National
Direction: Scott Sidney
Screenplay: Lois Weber and Fred Miller; based on the novel of the same
 name by Edgar Rice Burroughs
Cinematography: Enrique Juan Vallejo
Editing: Isidor Bernstein
Length: 8 reels

> *Principal characters:*
> Tarzan .... Elmo Lincoln
> Tarzan (younger) .... Gordon Griffith
> Jane Porter .... Enid Markey
> Tarzan's father, Lord Greystoke ...... True Boardman
> Tarzan's mother,
> Lady Greystoke .... Kathleen Kirkham
> Professor Porter .... Thomas Jefferson
> Binns, the sailor .... George French

Edgar Rice Burroughs' 1912 novel, *Tarzan of the Apes*, has been filmed
three times, but faithfully only once, in 1918. The 1932 film starring Johnny
Weissmuller and the 1981 version with Miles O'Keefe and Bo Derek had only
a character named Tarzan in common with the novel. When Burroughs had
Tarzan of the Apes published in *All Story Magazine* in 1912, no one would
have guessed that the character would become a godlike figure in the twentieth
century cinematic and literary pantheon, along with Superman, Sherlock
Holmes, and James Bond. *Tarzan of the Apes*, in fact, has been one of the
most sought-after motion-picture properties in the last sixty-five years.

Burroughs' novel really took off after it was published in book form in
1914, and he immediately began looking for the best offer from a motion-
picture producer. William N. Selig had made wild-animal films with great
success since he bought his first lion in 1909 to fake a jungle scene in his
Chicago studio. The scene he faked was one of Theodore Roosevelt shooting
a lion on a jungle safari, which the public was closely following in the newspapers. Selig's faked newsreel was a great success, and he quickly assembled
the largest private zoo in the United States. Burroughs sold two stories to
Selig, *The Lad and the Lion* and *Ben, King of the Jungle*, in 1915, for eight
hundred dollars. Selig was also seriously considering purchasing *Tarzan of the
Apes* and conducted several feasibility studies, but would not offer Burroughs
enough money. Burroughs' dissatisfaction with Selig grew when, in May of
1917, Selig announced without warning that *The Lad and the Lion* was to be
released immediately. Burroughs had an understanding with Selig that they

would time the film's release with a simultaneous magazine publication. One month later *All Story Magazine* came out with *The Lad and the Lion*. Burroughs was upset more by Selig's changes with his story than by the hasty release, though, and he vowed to make sure *Tarzan of the Apes* would be more faithfully adapted to the screen.

By early 1917, Burroughs entered into an arrangement with an independent film producer named William Parsons to film *Tarzan of the Apes*. Parsons offered the writer five percent of the picture's gross, fifty thousand dollars in stock, and five thousand dollars cash. The first snag occurred in the writing of the scenario. The writers they hired all wanted to take liberties with the story, with the foremost problem being the novel's ending. Burroughs himself called it "the rather unpopular ending of the first Tarzan story. . . ." Anyone reading the novel will be struck by the perfect incongruity of the ending, set in Wisconsin with Tarzan swinging through the forest dressed in a suit, with the beautiful and brilliant first nine-tenths of the story set in Africa. Wisely, Burroughs agreed to drop the American scenes and leave Tarzan in the jungle.

Lois Weber, a brilliant director, under contract to Universal and responsible for the successful careers of silent stars Mary MacLaren, Mildred Harris, Claire Windsor, and Billie Dove, wrote a lovely and somewhat faithful script of which Burroughs half approved. One item in particular bothered him and that was the removal of D'Arnot, the Frenchman who teaches Tarzan to speak, with the substitution of a shipwrecked sailor named Binns. Actually, the substitution was an improvement on the novel since the Frenchman taught Tarzan French and created confusion—something a silent film did not need.

Burroughs grew more and more disenchanted with William Parsons and foolishly sold his fifty thousand dollars of stock before the film's premiere for five thousand dollars. That was most unfortunate for him because the film was one of the very first to make one million dollars in profit.

During preproduction, as locations were scouted, animals rented, and props assembled, a group of creative costume makers was given the task of making ape costumes. In the novel, the apes that rear Tarzan are described as weighing between two and three hundred pounds—too small for gorillas, too large for baboons, and are thus mythological creatures. In order to solve the problem, body suits were made with goat skins sewn together, and the ape faces worn by the extras playing the apes were created in sponge covered with latex. This allowed the "apes" to move their faces realistically and was a great step forward in film special effects.

Elmo Lincoln, a handsome and muscular young man with an immense chest, was hired to play Tarzan. He was fitted with a long wig to resemble more closely the character Burroughs described in his novel. It was decided that the swamps in Louisiana would best suit the film's need of an African locale, and the company was sent to New Orleans by train. There, a number of gymnasts were hired to fill the ape costumes, and filming began.

The story begins in 1892 as Lord and Lady Greystoke (True Boardman and Kathleen Kirkham) are sailing along the African coast when a mutiny breaks out among the ship's crew. After killing the captain and officers, they turn on the Greystokes, but are induced to spare them by one of the crew, Binns (George French), to whom they had shown kindness previously. They are marooned instead on a stretch of uncharted African coastline with their luggage and a gun. Terrible animals roam about them, and they must constantly guard themselves with the gun. Lord Greystoke immediately builds a strong one-room cabin to keep out the wild intruders, but they are particularly bothered by a group of large apes that seem intent on destroying them, so Greystoke makes his cabin strong with bars on the window and a thick door with a latch. Lady Greystoke gives birth to a son, but she dies after a year of their hard life. Lord Greystoke is so grief stricken after his wife's death that he forgets to close the door.

Out in the jungle, the leader of the apes has killed the baby of a young female ape named Kala. The apes make for the little cabin as usual, with Kala tagging along behind carrying her dead baby. The ape leader is surprised to find the door open and catches Greystoke weeping unaware. As the leader kills the man, Kala snatches Greystoke's baby son from the rustic cradle and drops in her dead child. The apes close the door behind them, locking it and preserving the scene with the three dead bodies.

Kala defends her new child from the leader's cruelty and nurses the baby. She carefully holds her child, whom the apes name "Tarzan," as the ape group swings through the trees in search of food. Tarzan learns to swing from the branches and vines even before he walks and is soon keeping up with his young ape friends.

One day at play with a friend by a pond, Tarzan (Gordon Griffith) looks into the water and sees his reflection next to his playmate's. He is ashamed of his puny size, little nose, and tiny teeth. He wishes he were as handsome as his friend when suddenly he sees the reflection of a lion behind them. He dives into the pond, the lesser of two evils, thus saving himself while his not-so-intelligent friend becomes the lion's meal.

One day Tarzan finds the little locked cabin, which has successfully kept out the animals through the years, and he uses his innate intelligence to lift the latch. The skeletons do not bother the young man, who eats raw flesh with the apes, so he does not disturb the scene. He spends much time there, looking through the books; and photographs of the Greystokes convince him that he is not the only white and hairless ape. He learns to read slowly, but, even more importantly, he finds a knife, and soon learns that he has an advantage over the animals.

As a grown man, Tarzan (Elmo Lincoln) is a strong and fearless fighter. His enemies are the ape leader and Numa, the lion. When the cruel ape leader kills Kala, Tarzan's adopted mother, he fights the three-hundred-pound beast and sinks his knife into its heart, thus becoming the new leader of the apes.

Binns finds the cabin one day while fleeing slave traders, and he befriends Tarzan and teaches him to speak. He reads Greystoke's diary, and then notices the infant skeleton is that of an ape. Convinced that Tarzan is the Greystoke heir, he leaves the young man and makes his way to England. When he tells old Lady Greystoke about her grandson, Tarzan, she has him thrown into an insane asylum. Binns' story, however, is believed by young Greystoke, Tarzan's cousin. He takes a search party to Africa with his fiancée, Jane Porter (Enid Markey), and her father, Professor Porter (Thomas Jefferson).

The search party finds the cabin, and all are surprised by the muscular physique of Tarzan. Jane, in particular, is attracted to Tarzan, but fights the impulse, believing young Greystoke more civilized. When the young lord makes a lustful advance upon her and is stopped by Tarzan, however, she changes her mind about the jungle man.

The climactic scene finds Jane alone in the cabin, with a lion sniffing outside. The beast paws at the window bars until one breaks, and it then jumps up and puts its head through the grill. It is pushing the bars dangerously far apart when Tarzan swings down from the trees at the sound of Jane's screams. Running up behind the lion, he stabs the beast in the back.

Originally, the director wanted Lincoln to pull the lion out of the window by its tail, as in the book—but common sense prevailed, and it was not tried. The lion, old and heavily drugged, gave Lincoln little resistance, but his tough hide broke the knife blade. A bayonet was then substituted with success. Then, as directed, Tarzan placed one foot on the dead lion, beat his chest, and gave his victory cry. Lincoln's weight caused the lion's lungs to expel, making a roar which thoroughly unnerved the actor. His startled reaction was cut out of the finished film.

Jane then rushes to his arms, saying "I love you"—and the film ends, thus paving the way for countless sequels, remakes, and spin-offs, prevalent to the present day. Lincoln himself starred in several, including the serials *The Romance of Tarzan* (1918) and *The Return of Tarzan* (1920).

Larry Lee Holland

TELL IT TO THE MARINES

Released: 1927
Production: Metro-Goldwyn-Mayer
Direction: George Hill
Screenplay: E. Richard Schayer
Titles: Joe Farnham
Cinematography: Ira Morgan
Editing: Blanche Sewell
Length: 9 reels/8,800 feet

Principal characters:
Sergeant O'Hara .... Lon Chaney
Private "Skeet" Burns .... William Haines
Norma Dale .... Eleanor Boardman
Corporal Madden .... Eddie Gribbon
Zaya .... Carmel Myers
Chinese Bandit Leader .... Warner Oland

Lon Chaney, who was called the man of a thousand faces, wore one or more masks in most of his features. In his two most famous, *The Hunchback of Notre Dame* (1923) and *The Phantom of the Opera* (1925), he was the deformed Quasimodo and Erik, the Phantom, respectively. He starred as a crazed wax museum worker in *While Paris Sleeps* (1923); a lunatic scientist in *The Monster* (1925); a ventriloquist who masquerades as a lady in *The Unholy Three* (1925, remade as a talkie in 1930); and a Scotland Yard inspector and human vampire in *London After Midnight* (1927), among others.

Chaney, however, occasionally played "normal" characters. Despite his success in offbeat roles, it was in a straight adventure film that he scored one of his biggest triumphs—*Tell It to the Marines*. He stars as the virile Sergeant O'Hara and acts without a bit of makeup. Throughout film history, only a handful of actors have created a military *persona* that transcended the films in which they appeared—most memorably Victor McLaglen's Captain Flagg in *What Price Glory?* (1926) and John Wayne's Sergeant Stryker in *Sands of Iwo Jima* (1949). On a par with them is Chaney's Sergeant O'Hara. He was so effective in his portrayal of this archetypal marine sergeant that the Marine Corps made him an honorary member for life.

The film centers on Skeet Burns (William Haines), a wise-cracking, self-confident young man from Kansas who travels to San Diego allegedly to join the Marines. Quite simply, Burns is a bum, a useless wise guy who simply wants a trip to the West Coast at the government's expense and who goes immediately to Tijuana upon his arrival. He soon returns, starved and broke. He now joins the service and is under the care of Sergeant O'Hara (Lon Chaney), a tough, iron-jawed disciplinarian. The sergeant's favorite question to the volunteers is, "Anybody here want to drive the general's car?" Burns is eager for what he thinks will be an easy task—only to discover the "car" is a barrow filled with stones that has to be wheeled.

Burns is as raw a recruit as there ever was, so the sergeant sets out to break him in and to teach him how to become a marine. This occurs at their barracks in San Diego and, later, aboard a battleship where they are assigned. In one sequence, the irrepressible Burns knocks down a sailor carrying a pot of paint. Just as they are about to fight, however, O'Hara announces that their differences shall be settled in the ring. Burns is introduced first. He looks confident—until the referee announces that his opponent is the Navy's champion pugilist. The sailor easily defeats the marine, who has been humbled. The lesson is that no nonsense will be tolerated in the Marines; a recruit who shirks his responsibility will pay the price; a recruit must earn the right to feel he is a trained combatant.

Tell It to the Marines does not feature an all-male cast. Burns is attracted to the charming Norma Dale (Eleanor Boardman), a commissioned Navy nurse. Coincidentally, O'Hara is in love with her, too, and it seems that she is the only person who has ever made the crusty old sergeant smile. O'Hara talks to himself about his feelings for Norma as he gazes into a mirror and studies the lines on his face. He looks at his bulldog and decides that at least he has an edge on his pet for the nurse's affections. There are a number of comic moments in the film, elicited via the subtitles and the characters' facial expressions, but this is one of the most memorable.

Burns then becomes smitten with Zaya (Carmel Myers), a South Sea siren, while on a tour of the Philippines, and when Norma hears of the affair, she becomes jealous and angry and blames the sergeant. Just after this she is ordered to Hangchow. Her party, endangered by Chinese bandits, is rescued by O'Hara, Burns, and a company of marines in a bloody encounter. O'Hara is wounded, and when Burns extends his hand to the sergeant, he belts his protégé for being too "sentimental." He is really pleased, though, that Burns has become a *real* fighter and a man, that he has become a hardened marine and learned to love the service. After his hitch, Burns and Norma are married. The exmarine visits his old sergeant, who is as ornery as ever—suckering a new recruit into "driving the general's car."

Tell It to the Marines, made with the assistance of the Marine Corps, is a romanticized recruiting poster for that branch of the armed forces. The soldiers are not really depicted in battle, unlike *The Big Parade* (1925) or *Wings* (1927). They do not kill, and they do not die: the conflict in the scenario is between noncommissioned officer and recruit, not between armies. Still, the men of the Marines are presented as tough and worldly, with a warm camaraderie existing between them. Boys—and bums like Skeet Burns—become men in the Marines. The service is as much their home as their career. According to the film's philosophy, women only mean trouble for career soldiers like Sergeant O'Hara: they are vain, jealous, and seductive coquettes who cannot be trusted. The Marine Corps, though, will always be there. *Tell It to the Marines* is badly dated today, mostly because its basic story line has been endlessly revised and imitated over the decades, but it is still entertaining. Fifty-five years ago when it was a fresh idea, it received stunning reviews and was a box-office hit.

The square-jawed Chaney offers a wonderfully subtle performance as O'Hara. He is not simply a one-dimensionally gutsy, hard-boiled soldier with a tender heart underneath; he is still appropriately caring and sympathetic, yet his concern for Burns is real. His acting ranks on the same level as Burt Lancaster's Sergeant Warden in *From Here to Eternity* (1953), one of the best performances in that actor's career. Chaney makes O'Hara such a likable character that perhaps he is more deserving of Eleanor Boardman's affections than Burns. This is no small compliment, as Burns is the film's younger and handsomer romantic lead. Essentially, O'Hara has been conceived as a character role.

William Haines is fine as Burns. Handsome, energetic, and optimistic, his characters were consistently similar to those played by Harold Lloyd—but without the comedy. He portrayed the bold, brash all-American kid who would honestly like to succeed but who is nevertheless a wiseacre and must be humiliated somewhat before attaining his goals. Skeet Burns is the best role of Haines's career; among his other films are *Brown of Harvard* (1926); *Slide, Kelly, Slide* (1927); *The Adventures of Get-Rich-Quick Wallingford* (1931); and, in the spirit of *Tell It to the Marines*, *The Marines Are Coming* (1935). He retired from films during the 1930's and became a successful interior decorator.

Boardman is excellent as Norma Dale. A solid but forgotten performer of the 1920's, she appeared in *Souls for Sale* (1923), *Three Wise Fools* (1924), *Bardelys the Magnificent* (1926), and many others, but her best performance was in King Vidor's classic *The Crowd* (1928). Carmel Myers vamped through films for two decades in *Beau Brummell* (1924), *Ben-Hur* (1925), *Sorrell and Son* (1927), and *Svengali* (1931). Appearing near the end of *Tell It to the Marines*, as the leader of the Chinese bandits, is Warner Oland, who later became the best of all Charlie Chans.

George Hill—not to be confused with George Roy Hill—was a director of great promise whose work on *Tell It to the Marines* is commendable. Among his silent film credits are *Through the Dark* (1924), *Zander the Great* (1925), and *The Callahans and the Murphys* (1927). His top credits came at the advent of sound: *The Big House* (1930), the original prison drama, with Wallace Beery outstanding as Butch, a killer; *Min and Bill* (1930), with Beery and Marie Dressler, which earned the latter an Academy Award; and the less successful *The Secret Six* (1931), a gangster saga with a great cast including Beery, Clark Gable, Jean Harlow, Lewis Stone, Ralph Bellamy, Johnny Mack

Brown, and Marjorie Rambeau. Unfortunately Hill's potential was to remain for the most part unfulfilled as he died in 1934, an apparent suicide.

Rob Edelman

THE TEN COMMANDMENTS

Released: 1923
Production: Cecil B. De Mille for Famous Players-Lasky Corporation;
   released by Paramount
Direction: Cecil B. De Mille
Screenplay: Jeanie Macpherson; based on the Book of Exodus
Cinematography: Bert Glennon
Color cinematography: Ray Rennahan
Editing: Anne Bauchens
Special effects: Roy Pomeroy
Length: 10 reels/9,946 feet

Principal characters:
The Biblical story
Moses, the Lawgiver .... Theodore Roberts
Rameses, the Magnificent .... Charles De Roche
Miriam, sister of Moses .... Estelle Taylor
Aaron, brother of Moses .... James Neill
The wife of the Pharaoh .... Julia Faye
The Modern story
Mrs. Martha McTavish .... Edythe Chapman
John McTavish .... Richard Dix
Dan McTavish .... Rod La Rocque
Mary Leigh McTavish .... Leatrice Joy
Sally Lung .... Nita Naldi
Redding, an Inspector .... Robert Edeson

The silent version of *The Ten Commandments* is a classic and highly successful example of pure Hollywood melodrama, mixing sex, piety, and preachiness in almost equal measure. Cecil B. De Mille, the director whose name had been synonymous with glamorous sex comedies in the late teens and early 1920's, was now, with *The Ten Commandments*, giving his mass audience short Biblical stories followed by an object lesson on breaking the Ten Commandments set in modern times.

That this first version of the Exodus story should appear in 1923 was no accident. The American film industry was reeling under the censorious aftereffects of the Fatty Arbuckle rape case and other recent scandals, and producers were desperately hunting for material that was both sexy and moral. They knew what their audiences wanted, but they also knew what the Hays Office, which was responsible for censoring objectionable material, was demanding. De Mille's approach was to satisfy both factions at once with showy, simple-minded melodrama mitigated by corny, heavy-handed sermonizing.

An example of De Mille's combining both the lascivious and the moral aspects of a story was the Golden Calf sequence of *The Ten Commandments*. The orgy scene is explicit to the extent that it shows a number of female extras in various revealing costumes, but it got past the censors because it was a literal depiction of a scene from the Bible. In fact, the four-reel prologue of *The Ten Commandments*—originally shown in two-strip Technicolor—is the best part of the film and the most honest with its straightforward depiction of Moses (Theodore Roberts), with God's help, intimidating Rameses, the Pharaoh (Charles De Roche), into releasing the children of Israel from bondage. Theodore Roberts steals the film with his virtuoso performance as the fiery, self-righteous Moses, putting Charlton Heston's stolid piety in the 1956 De Mille remake of the story to shame. Roberts looks like the image of God's stuttering, reluctant leader as depicted in Renaissance art: a white-haired patriarch charged with indignation. Roberts is unfamiliar to modern audiences in other roles (although he made dozens of other silent films, few of them are ever shown), thus making his performance all the more convincing.

The same could not be said of the "modern story," however, which makes up the bulk of the film. In that segment, San Francisco businessmen John and Dan McTavish (Richard Dix and Rod La Rocque) love the same woman, an orphan named Mary Leigh (Leatrice Joy), whom their religious mother, Martha (Edythe Chapman), has taken under her wing and into their home. Mary marries Dan, a building contractor who is rising in the world of construction through graft and the help of a crooked building inspector named Redding (Robert Edeson). Dan's biggest contract—and his eventual undoing—is a cathedral built with one part cement to twelve parts sand.

His brother, John, is his carpentry foreman, and the one who discovers the weak foundation, but not in time to save their mother, who was visiting the cathedral when a wall collapsed, burying her alive. Dan, meanwhile, has other problems. Discovering that his Eurasian mistress, Sally Lung (Nita Naldi), has given him leprosy, he throttles her to death and flees to Mexico in his motorboat, symbolically named *Defiance*. Just as Dan is on his way to the Mexican border, however, a storm dashes his boat against a lighthouse, killing him instantly. In the final reel, Mary tries to kill herself, believing that she has contracted leprosy from Dan, but she is saved by John, who convinces her that she can regain purity of mind and body through prayer and faith in God.

There is absolutely no restraint in the script or in De Mille's direction of it. He illustrates every commission of "sin" and its resulting side effect for all it is worth, so that the audience will feel both edified and superior. Some critics have felt, however, that the characters are so wooden that the audience cannot help but feel superior in relation to them. Richard Dix as the "good" brother, John, is so holier-than-thou that he is almost completely unsympathetic as the hero; and Rod La Rocque as the "bad" brother, Dan, is incredibly callous and materialistic; Leatrice Joy is so good and pure as Mary, that her attraction to the transparently insensitive Dan seems unbelievable; the other principals are equally unrealistic.

Audiences, however, endured long lines in 1923 to enjoy the film, and it was De Mille's biggest commercial success up to that time. In modern audiences, however, such ludicrous contrivances are often greeted with enthusiastic laughter. Yet, the four-reel prologue, with all its cinematic flair, is a splendid example of Biblical storytelling, and modern audiences are much more receptive to it.

In comparison to the Biblical portion of *The Ten Commandments*, the 1956 remake is technically more polished, but stolid and much too long. The dialogue is generally stilted with performances to match, but the cast members are enjoying themselves, and De Mille keeps the whole overblown epic moving at an entertaining pace, so that it becomes three hours and forty minutes of campy, if somewhat stiff, fun. Audiences seemingly should not enjoy it, but they do, which is why ABC television shows it in its entirety every Easter, getting a top ten rating every time. On the whole, it is far less exciting than the silent original, and the Golden Calf sequence especially is disappointingly tame; the extras are more modestly dressed than in the 1923 film, and they look as though their fun is forced.

It is worth noting that some of the technicians who worked on the silent version also worked on the remake, including assistant cameraman J. Peverell Marley and De Mille's principal film editor, Anne Bauchens, whose editing of the Parting of the Red Sea sequence in both versions contributes as much to its cinematic power as the labors of the special effects department.

Much has been made of the seemingly mysterious means by which the Red Sea was parted in both versions, but its creation was relatively simple. In the silent version, the "parting" is a film of wiggling red gelatin matted into the frame. In the remake, for greater realism, the parting is a film of ocean tides running backward with the Israelites and Egyptian charioteers matted in. Although the explanation is simple, the special effects for the 1956 version won an Academy Award.

On the whole, both versions of *The Ten Commandments* have their merits, although neither as a whole could be considered a great, or even very good, film. Cecil B. De Mille was not a great director, but he was an accomplished showman who knew what audiences wanted to see and what the moralists demanded, so he contrived to make films that would please both.

Whether or not either version of *The Ten Commandments* is an aesthetic success is a moot point. What is more to the point is that both in the 1920's and the 1950's, De Mille accurately judged his marketplace and made a fortune doing so. His biggest silent success became his biggest talking success and, therefore, fittingly his last film. In that sense, and perhaps in that sense only, he was a great filmmaker.

Sam Frank

TESS OF THE STORM COUNTRY

Released: 1914
Production: Adolph Zukor for Famous Players; released by Paramount
Direction: Edwin S. Porter
Screenplay: Based on the novel of the same name by Grace Miller White
Cinematography: Edwin S. Porter
Length: 5 reels

> *Principal characters:*
> Tessibel Skinner .... Mary Pickford
> Frederick Graves .... Harold Lockwood
> Teola Graves ...... Olive Fuller Golden (Olive Carey)
> Daddy Skinner .... David Hartford
> Elder Graves .... W. R. Walters

In her autobiography, *Sunshine and Shadow*, Mary Pickford wrote,

> While *Hearts Adrift* was the most successful picture I had made up to that time, it was
> completely overshadowed by the next one, *Tess of the Storm Country*. Mr. Zukor told me
> some years later that *Tess* saved him from bankruptcy; that in order to meet the pay roll
> he had borrowed on his life insurance and pawned his wife's diamond necklace. All I
> know is that after the release of *Tess* I was Mr. Zukor's fair-haired child.

Adolph Zukor backed up Pickford's statements in his own autobiography,
The Public Is Never Wrong.

Tess of the Storm Country was Pickford's fifth film for Zukor's Famous
Players Company and the fifth and last of her features to be directed by Edwin
S. Porter. In 1903, Porter had revolutionized the film industry with his production of *The Great Train Robbery* and had done nothing since to indicate
that he was keeping abreast of developments in motion-picture technique.
Like all of his other features, *Tess of the Storm Country* shows absolutely no
directorial imagination, utilizes a static camera, and scrupulously avoids close-
ups. Porter quite obviously was of the decided opinion that a film audience
is no different from a theater audience and should observe a motion picture
as if sitting in the first or second rows of the orchestra.

It was Porter, however, who brought the book to Pickford's attention and
persuaded her to overcome her natural antagonism toward an unglamorous,
unromantic part. Like *Hearts Adrift*, *Tess of the Storm Country* was shot in
Los Angeles, where the Pickford company had moved—at the insistence of
her mother, Charlotte—to avoid Pickford's drunken husband, Owen Moore.
In her autobiography, Pickford remembered,

> The studio, in the back of a dilapidated mansion outside Los Angeles, consisted of a
> platform with adjustable cotton screens that were run on wires above. The sun did not

come over the roof until ten in the morning and it sank behind the back-yard fence at four, which meant that we could not work on "interiors" before or after that six-hour period. Mother and I used all our personal belongings as "props."

The exterior scenes of the fishing village were shot on the ocean front in Santa Monica. Porter acted not only as director but also cameraman, a position for which he was perhaps better qualified than the former. Because Famous Players had no processing laboratory on the West Coast, the film was shipped East for developing and no members of the company saw the results of their labors until the film was completed. The entire production, including Pickford's salary, cost a mere ten thousand dollars.

"Tess" is Tessibel Skinner (Mary Pickford), a wild, motherless creature, who lives with her father (David Hartford) on the shore of Lake Cayuga, which, because of its sudden and regular squalls, is known as the "storm country." Tess's father makes a living through poaching and illegally netting fish. One day, he is discovered near the body of a murdered gamekeeper and accused and convicted of the murder on circumstantial evidence. Frantic with grief, Tess is befriended by Frederick Graves (Harold Lockwood), a handsome theological student, and by his sister, Teola (Olive Fuller Golden). Frederick tells Tess of the Bible and urges her to pray and have faith in God. The girl steals a Bible from the Mission Church and carefully spells out its lesson, gaining strength and hope from her newfound Christianity. Frederick grows fond of Tess, while she places him on a pedestal, worshiping him as the symbol of the God she had never known until this moment.

Meanwhile, Frederick's father, Elder Graves (W. R. Walters), a bigoted and narrow-minded individual, is seeking the conviction of Tess's father, because he is a "squatter" and a representative of all that Elder Graves despises. Also, Teola has become engaged to Dan Jordan and the two make love shortly before Jordan is killed in a fire and thus unable to make Teola an honest woman. Teola does not dare tell her father that she is pregnant, but she does confide in Tess, who takes her to her own hut, where the child is born.

Tess takes and cares for the child, even stealing milk with which to feed it. When Frederick calls on her, he finds the child there and supposes it is Tess's. Rather than expose Teola, who has become ill, Tess claims the baby as hers and is denounced by Frederick as a worthless woman. He takes her Bible away, but Tess declares that even with her Bible gone, there is no one who can take away her faith. She is denounced and humiliated by everyone, including the fellow squatters, but through her faith in God, Tess remains strong.

Eventually, Elder Graves publicly denounces Tess inside the church as she comes forward to baptize the infant. Teola can stand it no longer and comes forward to take the baby in her arms and proclaim it as her own. Elder Graves is stricken with remorse, while both Teola and her baby die. Frederick comes to ask Tess for forgiveness, bringing with him a letter from his father seeking forgiveness as well. Tess and Frederick are reunited, and another fisherman is discovered to have been guilty of the gamekeeper's murder. Thus, "Tess finds the reward of her faith in a great love and happiness," and the film ends.

From the synopsis, it is obvious that *Tess of the Storm Country* was the type of melodrama which is all too often associated with the silent motion picture. What raises the film above the sordid and maudlin nature of its plot, however, is Pickford's performance, an extraordinary mixture of humbleness and strength. She is no broken, weak-willed heroine, but a woman of fire and anger—the one solid point in a morass of sentimentality and bigotry. The Christianity which the Pickford character preaches by word and deed is the Christianity created by Christ, and Pickford's performance contains as much truth and meaning for today's generation as it did two generations ago.

From its release, by Paramount, on March 30, 1914, *Tess of the Storm Country* proved to be a tremendous success. It was rightfully described as the film which built Paramount. It enabled Zukor to consolidate his control over the new organization and to establish an executive production career which was to continue for the next sixty years. *Tess of the Storm Country* also gained for Pickford a doubling in her salary—to two thousand dollars a week—and firmly established in her mind the point that her films were successful only because they starred her. Whatever Pickford wanted from that time on, the film industry was going to have to supply.

Tess of the Storm Country was a mixed blessing for the supporting players in the drama—both in front of and behind the camera. After *Tess of the Storm Country*, Edwin S. Porter was to begin his slow fade to obscurity, having only two more years left as a director. Harold Lockwood, Pickford's leading man here and in *Hearts Adrift*, became a popular matinee idol of the late teens, usually playing opposite May Allison, until falling a victim to the Spanish influenza epidemic which took his life in 1918. Olive Fuller Golden never became a major screen star, but she did marry cowboy actor Harry Carey and was to become a crusty character actress in many sound features, notably those of John Ford.

The film obviously held a special place in Pickford's heart, for it was the only one of her features that she decided to remake—in 1922, under the direction of John S. Robertson. *Tess of the Storm Country* was subsequently remade by Fox, with Janet Gaynor, in 1932, and by Twentieth Century-Fox, with Diane Baker, in 1960.

Lennox Sanderson, Jr.

THAÏS

Released: 1917
Production: Goldwyn Pictures
Direction: Frank Crane
Screenplay: Margaret Mayo; based on the novel of the same name by Anatole France
Cinematography: Arthur Edeson
Length: 6 reels

Principal characters:
Thais	Mary Garden
Paphnutius	Hamilton Revelle
Nicias	Charles Trowbridge
Mother Superior	Alice Chapin
Nun	Margaret Townsend
Lollius	Crauford Kent
Cynius	Lionel Adams

After Samuel Goldfish was pushed and bought out of the Lasky Company, he decided to use his millions to start another film company. He joined forces with a theatrical producer, Edgar Selwyn, who had the film rights to a large number of popular plays, and by combining their surnames, they devised the name Goldwyn Pictures, and thereafter Goldfish used the name Goldwyn as well. The first picture the new company released was *Polly of the Circus* starring Mae Marsh, released in September, 1917, but the first picture they began work upon was the spectacle, *Thaïs*. *Thaïs* was released three months after *Polly of the Circus* because of production problems, the most serious of which was a storm that destroyed the huge outdoor set representing the city of Alexandria. It was built in New Jersey and had sixty-foot columns in front of the massive temple set.

Thaïs is based on a novel by the famous French writer Anatole France. The novel was one of the most internationally acclaimed masterpieces of the 1890's, and it was turned into an opera in 1894, which quickly became a fixture in the American opera repertoire. Mary Garden, a Scottish singer, made the lead role of *Thaïs* practically her own so that when the new Goldwyn company approached her to do film parts, they had the production of *Thaïs* in mind. She was won, however, only after she was promised the extravagant sum of $150,000 for her services.

Goldwyn was extremely confident of the box-office potential of *Thaïs*, for another historical spectacle, set in the same city, Alexandria, had been a moneymaking hit that same year, *Cleopatra* with Theda Bara. Goldwyn magnanimously gave France ten thousand dollars for the screen rights to his novel, even though it had never been copyrighted in the United States.

The opera *Thaïs* varied somewhat in plot from France's novel. Goldwyn's scenario writer, Margaret Mayo, was free to follow the opera or the novel. Unfortunately, Garden pressured Mayo into following the opera's plot, which is compressed and distorted into seven scenes in three acts.

The story concerns Thais (Mary Garden), the abused daughter of a poor innkeeper in Alexandria. Her only friend is the family's black slave, who tells her stories about Jesus. She is secretly baptized, but must hide the fact from her brutal pagan father. One day an angry mob crucifies the black Christian, and so he becomes a martyr. Later, after Thais has been more severely beaten than usual and sits crying in the street, an old woman approaches her. She tells Thais lies and coerces her into leaving home and coming to live with her. She grooms the girl, teaches her to dance, and generally shows her how to please men. Soon the old woman is selling Thais to old men at orgies.

One day, a handsome, rich young man named Lollius (Crauford Kent) sees Thais, and they are mutually attracted to each other. He pays off the old woman, and Thais and he live together in love for six months. When their love dies, however, Thais wanders, lost again.

She then joins a pantomime troop and learns their craft. She soon becomes a great success and has all Alexandria at her feet. Now she meets a rich young philosopher named Nicias (Charles Trowbridge). He is a cynic and believes in nothing, while Thais believes in everything, for not only has she retained her Christianity, but she has added a belief in all the gods of Egypt and Rome as well. She lives with Nicias until one day, when she says: "I hate and despise all the Happy and the Rich. There is no goodness except in the Unfortunate," and she leaves him.

She decides to give up everything and live in poverty, but the next day, she returns to the pleasures of her wealth and fame and builds herself a beautiful palace. She even had a grotto in her garden, where she would often go and check her body for signs of aging. Meanwhile, off in the desert, an ascetic monk named Paphnutius (Hamilton Revelle) lives in a twig hut. He is young, but he has lived ten years in solitude and has not seen a single woman. As he meditates one day, he remembers an actress he had seen in an Alexandrian theater before he left the world. Suddenly, she, Thais, appears to him in startling clearness, and he takes it as a sign that he should save her soul.

He walks out of the desert to find her, with twigs in his long beard and wearing a tattered robe. When Paphnutius gets to Alexandria, he meets his old friend Nicias, who asks what has brought him to the city. When Nicias finds out, he laughs, but then promises to invite Thais to supper that night. Nicias has his friend bathed and combed and gives him a new, richly embroidered robe to wear. Thais comes that evening and is strangely attracted to the severe-looking Paphnutius. Soon, she is under his spell, and they go back to her house. He convinces her to give up worldly possessions, and she sets fire to her home.

An angry mob gathers as Thais sets fire to the last of her belongings in the front of her burning home, and they decide to kill Paphnutius for bewitching her. Nicias saves them by throwing gold coins into the mob, thus giving them time to escape. They travel through the burning desert for weeks before they reach their destination, a nunnery. Paphnutius takes Thais to the Mother Superior (Alice Chapin) and asks her to take in the reformed woman. They place Thais in a cell, but before Paphnutius leaves, he makes her promise not to leave her room. He pastes one of his hairs over the door to make sure she does not deceive him.

He then goes to an ancient ruined temple and climbs to the top of a lone standing column, where he sits for a year, gathering fame in the surrounding countryside. When he returns to the nunnery, the Mother Superior informs him that Thais is near death. He rushes into her cell, sees that the seal is unbroken and finds her dying on her cot. Suddenly, he sees his mistake in never having loved her physically, for now it is too late. With her last breath she tells him that she sees God.

Garden's acting was not liked by the critics or the public, so Goldwyn used her quickly in one more film, *The Splendid Sinner* (1917). Her film career, however, was not as great a fiasco as that of Enrico Caruso, for his two films in 1918 were withdrawn from release and shelved. Of all of the opera singers in the teens and 1920's, only Geraldine Farrar was really successful in films, especially in the six films she made for Cecil B. De Mille.

Unfortunately, *Thaïs* has never been remade by an American company. W. Somerset Maugham, however, was influenced by *Thaïs* when he wrote his famous short story, "Miss Thompson," which was dramatized as *Rain* and filmed several times.

Larry Lee Holland

THE THIEF OF BAGDAD

Released: 1924
Production: Douglas Fairbanks Pictures for United Artists
Direction: Raoul Walsh
Screenplay: Lotta Woods; based on a story by Elton Thomas (Douglas Fairbanks)
Cinematography: Arthur Edeson
Editing: William Nolan
Art direction: William Cameron Menzies
Costume design: Mitchell Leisen
Length: 12 reels/11,230 feet

Principal characters:
The Thief of Bagdad	Douglas Fairbanks
His Evil Associate	Snitz Edwards
The Holy Man	Charles Belcher
The Princess	Julanne Johnston
The Mongol Slave	Anna May Wong
The Slave of the Lute	Winter-Blossom
The Slave of the Sand Board	Etta Lee
The Caliph	Brandon Hurst
The Indian Prince	Noble Johnson
The Mongol Prince	So-Jin

During the 1920's, when he scored his biggest hits, Douglas Fairbanks was the epitome of the film star. He was the athletic, swashbuckling, high-spirited, larger-than-life hero with a lock on the imaginations of filmgoers who packed the motion-picture houses to be mesmerized by his make-believe world of magic carpets, pirate ships, and castles. He was the first great adventure star; along with Mary Pickford, Charles Chaplin, Lillian Gish, and a handful of others, he was the most beloved of silent-film actors, as popular as any performer ever.

Fairbanks entered films in 1915. In 1919, with Chaplin, D. W. Griffith, and Pickford—who a year later became his second wife—he founded United Artists. His most impressive and popular films were yet to come, however: *The Mark of Zorro* (1920), *The Three Musketeers* (1921), *Robin Hood* (1922), *Don Q, Son of Zorro* (1925), and *The Black Pirate* (1926). In all these films, he wore period costume. Although in his forties, he insisted on doing his own stunts and thoroughly and accurately researched the eras in which the stories were set. He is at his peak climbing walls and leaping balconies in *The Thief of Bagdad*, a delightful fantasy-adventure based on several Arabian Nights tales.

Fairbanks stars as the title character, an attractive, self-confident, cynical scoundrel who ignores the teachings of the Holy Man (Charles Belcher) and gallivants through the streets of Bagdad bare chested, tanned, and garbed in pantaloons. His assistant (or "sidekick," more appropriately) is known as, simply, the Evil Associate (played by the seemingly rubber-faced Snitz Edwards); with the help of a magic rope he has stolen, the Thief scales the walls of the palace of the Caliph (Brandon Hurst) so that he can steal some pearls from a treasure chest. Instead, he sees and promptly falls in love with a Princess (Julanne Johnston), the Caliph's daughter, who is sleeping while surrounded by her handmaidens. The Thief lies to the Princess, telling her that he is a prince who has come to the city with other suitors to win her affection. He subsequently is actually selected to wed his beloved when he is thrown into a rosebush that must be touched by the suitor who will be awarded the honor of marrying the fair lady.

The Thief, however, must first prove that he is worthy of the Princess. The Caliph learns his true identity, and has him beaten and thrown to the palace ape. The Princess, however, who has become captivated by the Thief's charm and good looks, secretly has him freed so that he may participate in another contest the Caliph has devised for the suitors: they must travel to faraway lands on a Journey of Seven Moons and return with the most unusual treasure. The Thief has been transformed by his love for the Princess, and the Holy Man counsels him that he must humble himself if he hopes to change his life.

One of the suitors, the Mongol Prince (So-Jin, a Siamese actor imported to play the role, and one of the few real Orientals in the cast) plots to raise an army and capture Bagdad, with the Princess' Mongol Slave (Anna May Wong) as his cohort. The Thief and his rivals then leave the city to find the booty. He experiences innumerable adventures and overcomes terrifying obstacles: he journeys to the Mountains of Dread Adventure, the Valley of Fire, the Cavern of Enchanted Trees, the Midnight Sea, the Citadel of the Moon; he rides a winged horse, and fights a dragon and sea spider. Predictably, he wins the contest when he finds the Magic Chest of Nazir, which holds his Birthright of True Manhood. He is now deserving of the Princess.

The Mongol Prince has by now overthrown the Caliph, however, so with the chest, the Thief creates an army of his own and saves Bagdad and the Princess from the Mongol invaders. At the finale, the lovers fly away on a magic carpet, out through a palace window and over the rooftops of the city, headed for the Land o' Love. Shining stars spell out the film's moral: "Happiness Must Be Earned."

The Thief of Bagdad is truly an epic, one of the most ornate spectacle films of its time. In Fairbanks' previous film, *Robin Hood*, he and art director William Cameron Menzies constructed a full-scale Norman castle. For *The Thief of Bagdad*, they wanted to surpass this, so they designed and built a whimsically imaginative fantasy land, a palace and city complete with shiny cupolas and towers, surreal bridges and staircases. The floors were glazed, and the buildings were reflected on them. Walls were painted silver, to make the city seem to float like a balloon, literally to drift off the ground among the clouds.

Props—windows, vases, and flowers—were designed out of proportion to reality. The film was tinted green in sequences with monsters, tinted rose when the Thief romances the Princess, sepia in shots of Bagdad, and Maxfield Parrish blue throughout the rest of the film. Trick photography was effectively used to add to the film's illusion, most notably when the Thief and the Princess speed through the air on the magic carpet. The "carpet" had a steel frame and was hoisted by a large crane offcamera, the cables of which were painted white to make them appear invisible. With a wave of his hand, thousands of soldiers magically appear as the Thief stands alone and unarmed outside the gates of the city. He also becomes invisible, donning a Cloak of Invisibility, and rescues the Princess from the clutches of the dastardly Mongol Prince.

Lost in the artistry of Menzies and Fairbanks' wizardry is the solid contribution of Raoul Walsh, director of *The Thief of Bagdad*. The film was Walsh's first major directorial effort; he had made his initial film in 1912 (*Life of Villa*, codirected with Christy Cabanne), and played John Wilkes Booth in D. W. Griffith's *The Birth of a Nation* (1915). He went on to do his best work with Victor McLaglen and Edmund Lowe in *What Price Glory?* (1926) and *The Cock-Eyed World* (1929), and James Cagney and/or Humphrey Bogart in *The Roaring Twenties* (1939), *They Drive By Night* (1940), *High Sierra* (1941), and *White Heat* (1949). In addition, the stunningly exotic costumes were designed by Mitchell Leisen, who later directed *Death Takes a Holiday* (1934), *Easy Living* (1937), *Midnight* (1939), and *Hold Back the Dawn* (1941), among others.

The Thief of Bagdad was more costly to produce than *Robin Hood*, which itself was twice as expensive as Griffith's lavish *Intolerance* (1916). At more than one million dollars—perhaps even close to two million dollars—*The Thief of Bagdad* had the largest budget of any film to date. It received rave reviews: *The New York Times* named it to its "Ten Best" list, and it was universally hailed as Fairbanks' best film. The film was described by critics as "the greatest picture we have ever seen or ever expect to see," "the world's greatest 'movie,'" "an entrancing picture, wholesome and beautiful, deliberate but compelling, a feat of motion picture art which has never been equalled," "a picture so fine and so full of incident that it demands several visits for its full enjoyment." Publicists could not have written better copy. If Academy Awards had existed in 1924 (the initial ceremony took place in May, 1929, with all eligible films released between August 1, 1927, and July 31, 1928) *The Thief of Bagdad* certainly would have had many nominations and been a logical choice for the Best Picture Award.

Oddly, though, the film was not as popular at the box office as Fairbanks' *Robin Hood*. The property was remade in 1940 by Ludwig Berger, Tim Whelan, and Michael Powell. The special effects in this British-made film were in Technicolor and are wonderful; however, the star, Sabu, is no Fairbanks. A dreary version, starring Steve Reeves, directed by Arthur Lubin, and produced in Italy, also came out in 1961. The original remains today a magical entertainment, one of the most creative and imaginative of all silent films.

Rob Edelman

THE THIRD DEGREE

Released: 1926
Production: Warner Bros.
Direction: Michael Curtiz
Screenplay: Graham Baker; based on the play of the same name by Charles
  Klein
Cinematography: Hal Mohr
Length: 8 reels/7,647 feet

> *Principal characters:*
> Alicia Daley .... Louise Dresser
> Annie Daley .... Dolores Costello
> Daredevil Daley .... Tom Santschi
> Underwood .... Rockliffe Fellowes
> Howard Jeffries, Jr. .... Jason Robards, Sr.
> Howard Jeffries, Sr. .... David Torrence

The importation of European film directors to Hollywood in the 1920's was a move to revitalize the semistagnant American film industry. The industry was in need of new blood, and the European filmmakers had a well-founded reputation for innovation in the cinematic arts. Among these expatriates were such well established directors as Austria's Josef von Sternberg, Germany's Ernst Lubitsch, and Sweden's Mauritz Siller. Many of these filmmakers were placed under contract in such a manner as to make them almost literally members of the directorial stables maintained by the major studios. This type of director has thus come to be known by the almost derisive term, "studio director."

A studio director of the 1920's supposedly operated at the opposite end of the creative spectrum from the *auteur*, although this view has been largely refuted in recent years. It was a studio director's responsibility to complete up to five or six films per year, regardless of the quality or the difficulty of the scripts given to him. He was charged with producing a cinematic commodity that was at least minimally sound and possessed sufficient audience appeal to be economically successful. Some films made in this hurried manner were masterpieces made by directors who were able to imprint them with their own personal stamp. Other films were not great, and others (the majority) were terrible. In order to maintain the difficult production schedules, a considerable amount of agitating and whipcracking was, of necessity, done by the directors. As a result, European directors have acquired the stereotyped slave driver and insensitive ogre image.

One of the most workmanlike of these studio directors was Michael Curtiz, who was staunchly loyal to Warner Bros., at a time when the studio was a virtual assembly line for films. Like other directors at the studio, Curtiz was under contract to make so many films in a year that he virtually had no time to prepare for each succeeding project. In fact, Warner Bros. directors had such little foreknowledge of the nature of the scripts that filmmaking became a matter of walking onto the set and making rapid decisions on a daily basis. Curtiz had to carry this practice through the 1940's, and, in fact, developed it into an art on the production of the Oscar-winning *Casablanca* (1943). Curtiz was continually under intense pressure to deliver his finished products quickly and that pressure was, in turn, keenly felt by his casts and crews, since he drove them furiously in an effort to meet the deadlines. As a result, Curtiz was considered by many members of the film industry to be one of the most thoroughly distasteful directors with whom to work.

An interesting film from 1926 which typifies the Curtiz high-pressure method was *The Third Degree*, the first American effort by the Hungarian-born director. Curtiz came to the United States in the early 1920's after achieving a reputation as a major pioneer in the Hungarian film industry. He was quickly added to the directorial pool at Warner Bros. and given the script of *The Third Degree*. This film revealed Curtiz's already ripening stylistic virtuosity that manifested itself in a startling use of severe camera angles and almost dreamlike lighting. Curtiz also adapted and made heavy use of a shooting style featuring an almost continuously moving camera, a technique developed originally by D. W. Griffith. As with most of Curtiz's work, stylistic considerations had a far more prominent place in *The Third Degree* than did the story line. Although, in substance, it fell short of being a horror film in the strict sense of the genre, the film contained a heavy dose of strong emotional tension between the actors that presaged his later film *The Mystery of the Wax Museum* (1933).

In *The Third Degree*, Alicia Daley (Louise Dresser), a former circus performer, is unhappily married to Daredevil Daley (Tom Santschi), who performs diving, tightrope-walking, and knife-throwing acts for the circus which are very popular. Alicia is planning to run away with Underwood (Rockliffe Fellowes), the ringmaster of the circus, to escape her soured marriage to Daredevil. On the night of the planned departure, Daredevil is trying out a new stunt—riding a motorcycle in a slatted bowl with their baby daughter Annie hanging around his neck—when he catches a glimpse of Alicia and Underwood in an earnest conversation. He has a sudden premonition of what will take place later that evening, and the thought throws him off balance. The motorcycle then lurches and tips, hurling Daredevil and baby Annie over the side of the bowl. Although the fall fractures his skull, Daredevil draws enough strength to prevent Alicia from running away with their child. Alicia, however, who imagines life with the ringmaster to be more desirable than life with her own family, leaves without Annie. The combination of the fractured skull, the fight over the child, and his wife's desertion become too much for Daredevil, and he finally collapses and dies.

The sympathetic circus owners take Annie under their wing, and, over the years, she develops into the star attraction at a Coney Island sideshow. The grown Annie (Dolores Costello) is like her father, walking a tightrope and diving from a tiny platform into a minuscule tank, plunging one hundred feet. While Annie's death-defying acts show that she truly has her father's nerve and daring, she also reflects her mother's beauty. While many men find her attractive, she becomes interested in Howard Jeffries, Jr. (Jason Robards, Sr.) and they fall in love and marry. Jeffries is the son of a millionaire, and when he takes Annie to meet his father, Howard Jeffries, Sr. (David Torrance), the father is so appalled that his son would marry a circus performer that he throws them both out.

At this point, the audience learns that the elder Jeffries should not be so repelled by his son's involvement with a circus performer because Annie is actually the daughter of his second wife, Alicia, Annie's long-lost mother. Jeffries, Sr., is not aware of the relationship, however, and he tries to break up the marriage. He hires a private detective to help him, and the detective turns out to be Underwood. Underwood develops a plan wherein Howard, Jr., will become jealous and suspicious, thinking that Annie is illicitly involved with the detective. Howard, believing the worst, goes to the detective's home and a violent brawl ensues, resulting in Howard's being knocked unconscious.

Complicating matters even further, Alicia bursts into the detective's home a moment after the fight and shoots her former lover when he threatens to reveal her past to her current husband, Jeffries, Sr. She quickly leaves and allows her son-in-law to be arrested for the murder. At first, Annie tries to take the blame and confess that it was she, not her husband, who shot the detective, but Alicia's conscience eventually gets the best of her, and she confesses to the crime—perhaps the first unselfish act of Alicia's life.

The Third Degree is a direct predecessor to a series of films labeled "speaking shadow stories" that derived their characters through settings of the underworld. These melodramas utilized an abundance of murder, intrigue, and illegal activities. *The Third Degree* is typical of this type of Warner Bros. film of the late 1920's and early 1930's in that it deals with shady characters, ramshackle settings, and the lower strata of society. The underworld film was one of the most popular genres of the period.

Curtiz's obsession with the harshness of life's realities may have been somewhat overdone in this film, however, as the too frequent trick and freak shots tend to overpower the viewer at times. Throughout his career, Curtiz never seemed to acquire the crucial ability to avoid the plot entanglements that an overly lengthy script presented. In addition to his favorite camera trick shots, many of the bloated scripts were responsible for the addition of an extra reel or two to the length of many of his films. *The Third Degree* required a good deal of additional footage because of extraneous subplots and dramatic complications that could not be resolved in shorter fashion. Had Curtiz been able to recognize some of the unnecessary plot elements in this film, it may have been far more popular over the years. *The Third Degree* is an immensely interesting, if overly lengthy film, and it deserves to be included in any consideration of the more memorable films of the 1920's.

Thomas A. Hanson

THREE BAD MEN

Released: 1926
Production: Fox Film Corporation
Direction: John Ford
Screenplay: John Stone and John Ford; based on the novel *Over the Border* by Herman Whitaker
Titles: Ralph Spence and Malcolm Stuart Boylan
Cinematography: George Schneiderman
Length: 9 reels/8,710 feet

> *Principal characters:*
> Dan O'Malley .... George O'Brien
> Lee Carlton .... Olive Borden
> Layne Hunter .... Lou Tellegen
> Mike Costigan .... J. Farrell MacDonald
> Bull Stanley .... Tom Santschi
> Spade Allen .... Frank Campeau
> Joe Minsk .... George Harris
> Millie Stanley .... Priscilla Bonner
> Old Prospector .... Jay Hunt

John Ford, director of *Young Mr. Lincoln* (1939), *The Grapes of Wrath* (1940), and *The Sun Shines Bright* (1954), is arguably the greatest American filmmaker and filmmaker of Americana. He is best recalled as a director of Westerns, from *Straight Shooting* (1917), his first feature, to *Cheyenne Autumn* (1964), one of his last. Ford did not simply make "shoot-'em-ups," with the hero outwitting the heavy in the final reel and riding off into the sunset with the heroine. His films were complex if romanticized sagas visually depicting either the settlement of the American West and the fulfillment of Manifest Destiny, or the protagonist's personal turmoil set against a Western backdrop. *Three Bad Men* (1926) is not the director's most famous early Western—*The Iron Horse* (1924), his first cinematic success, is one of the classic silent films. Still, on its own merits, *Three Bad Men* is an enjoyable work that very clearly bears the stamp of its maker.

Like *Tumbleweeds* (1925), with William S. Hart, and Wesley Ruggles' Oscar-winning *Cimarron* (1931), *Three Bad Men* is set during a land rush. It is 1876, and the Sioux tribes have been defeated: the lands of the Dakotas have been made available for settlement in a proclamation issued by President Grant. Immigrants and farmers travel across the country to begin new lives in the virgin territory as a title card proclaims, "Westward the course of empire takes its way." Among the settlers are also prospectors, for there is the promise of gold and instant riches in the newly available territory.

Colonel Carlton of Kentucky and his daughter, Lee (Olive Borden), have traveled to the Dakotas with their thoroughbreds. There, they meet Dan O'Malley (George O'Brien), a harmonica-playing young Irishman, who flirts with Lee and almost kisses her. He repairs their broken wagon wheel and then departs. The trio of the title are Mike Costigan (J. Farrell MacDonald), a bank robber who wears a stovepipe hat; Spade Allen (Frank Campeau), a card sharp; and Bull Stanley (Tom Santschi), a horse thief and the gang's leader. They are wanted by the law from Mexico to Canada and want the colonel's animals. The horses are pilfered instead by Layne Hunter (Lou Tellegen), the sheriff of Custer, a small but wild little mining town.

Hunter's henchmen make off with the thoroughbreds, killing the colonel in the process. The "three bad men" who have arrived with the intention of taking the horses for themselves, rescue Lee instead. They are really gentlemen, more comical and sentimental than cynical and insensitive, as outlaws are supposed to be. They take a liking to the girl and decide to stick with and protect her, without promise of any monetary compensation. A contemporary reviewer appropriately stressed that the film be referred to as "Three Bad *Men*," and not "Three *Bad* Men."

Sheriff Hunter is the real villain here. He had promised to marry Bull's sister, Millie (Priscilla Bonner), and she went off with him, but when she informs him that a preacher is in town, he rebuffs her and even decides to give her as a "present" to another man. Millie sees her brother in the town saloon but is too ashamed to make contact with him. Lee, meanwhile, looks to Bull for comfort now that her father is dead. Bull becomes uneasy and decides Lee should have a husband. Playing cupid, he finds Dan, who also "hires" on with Lee.

Bull decides to lead a revolt against the crooked lawman, whose cohorts eventually burn down a church filled with women and children. As the ladies panic and their babies cry, Dan, Bull, and other townspeople successfully come to the rescue. In the melee, though, Millie is shot, and she dies in her brother's arms.

Dan is in possession of a map showing where gold may be found, obtained from an old prospector (Jay Hunt) later killed by Hunter's gang. Hunter and his men pursue Lee and her men once the land rush to the Black Hills commences. One by one, Mike, Spade, and Bull are all killed, but they are gladly willing to die for Lee. Bull is the last one to lose his life—but not before killing Sheriff Hunter. Dan and Lee later marry and name their baby after their three friends, whose ghosts ride off into the sunset. In essence, they have become "Three Godfathers," the title of a 1948 Ford Western, which was in itself a remake of his *Marked Men*, released in 1919. In fact, *Three Bad Men* has often been confused with *Three Godfathers*.

Although the story line is sentimental and melodramatic, *Three Bad Men* is refreshing in that it does not feature a one-dimensional hero who is beyond reproach and who triumphs, against all odds, over the slimy outlaw-villain.

The characterizations are ambiguous. The "three bad men" may be lawbreakers, but they are still inherently good. They rescue a helpless young woman and do not exploit her vulnerability; instead, they take responsibility for her safety. The sheriff, supposed to represent law and civilization, is really a despicable thief and killer. Even honest farmers and settlers are more concerned with gold, with wealth and materialism, than with sweating, tilling the land, and building the American empire.

The title trio may be alienated from society, loners who have acted antisocially and cut themselves off from life, but Bull, after all, rejects Lee's advances after her father's death, instead choosing to defer to Dan. Like similar characters in Ford Westerns, from Cheyenne Harry in *Straight Shooting* through the Ringo Kid in *Stagecoach* (1939), the trio of bank robbers in *Three Godfathers* and Tom Doniphon in *The Man Who Shot Liberty Valance* (1962), they are the true heroes of the story. They live by their own strict moral code that is in a certain sense higher and more admirable than the rules of the society from which they are estranged. The settlers are not dishonest, but still see pots of gold waiting to be taken from the earth. Mike, Spade, and Bull choose instead to go with their feelings for Lee and Dan when the land rush begins and sacrifice their lives for the happiness of the young people.

Three Bad Men, filmed on location in Jackson Hole, Wyoming, and in the Mojave Desert, is not as visually striking as Ford's later masterpieces. Still, there are hints of the director's style. More memorably, he frames characters and settings throughout: at the beginning of the film, Dan and Lee are framed by a wagon wheel; Millie and Hunter are framed by a window as the sheriff laughingly reneges on his marriage promise, and then closes the window, symbolic of his rejection; Millie is again framed by a window when she first sees her brother (the two will only be united when she dies); a wagon train of pioneers heading for the land rush is shot through the arch of a wagon, with a mother, clutching her child in the foreground, watching the wagons roll by. The latter shot is particularly evocative of vintage Ford, as are panoramic shots of the scenery. The land-rush sequence is also superbly staged, on a par with those in *Tumbleweeds* and *Cimarron*. It is beautifully detailed. For example, viewers see such things as a newspaper being printed on board a wagon; a baby is forgotten and rescued just in time from under a rolling wagon wheel; and a bicycle is broken and dragged by a horse. More than two hundred vehicles and hundreds of men on horseback were used in the staging; the film was advertised as having "25,000 in the cast," and actual land-rush veterans offered Ford their input during the filming.

With the exception of Tom Santschi's, Frank Campeau's, and J. Farrell MacDonald's picture-stealing performances, the acting in *Three Bad Men* is secondary to the story line and directorial touches. George O'Brien, a popular leading man of the 1920's who reached stardom in *The Iron Horse*, is serviceable as Dan O'Malley; in a more conventionally structured film, he would have handled more of the heroics. During the 1930's, he became a star of "B"-grade Westerns and later worked in Ford's *Fort Apache* (1948), *She Wore a Yellow Ribbon* (1949), and *Cheyenne Autumn*. Olive Borden, who played Lee, is a now-forgotten silent star. She could not adjust to talkies, and she eventually ended up on Los Angeles' skid row, dying at age forty-one in a hotel for destitute women. Lou Tellegen, who played Hunter, was Sarah Bernhardt's leading man on the Paris stage and played sophisticated leading men in many silents. He committed suicide at age fifty-three. The actors who played the title roles were each character performers with lengthy filmographies, with Santschi best recalled as one of the stars of the first version of the early Western classic, *The Spoilers* (1914). Their roles were originally intended for stars: Tom Mix, Buck Jones, and O'Brien. When the first two dropped out of the project, O'Brien was given the Dan O'Malley part and Santschi, Campeau, and MacDonald were hired as the title characters.

Three Bad Men received uniformly excellent reviews, with some critics claiming it superior to *The Iron Horse* and James Cruze's *The Covered Wagon* (1923). It was not, however, the box-office success of its predecessor. Epic Westerns, it seemed, no longer interested audiences in 1926.

Rob Edelman

THE THREE MUSKETEERS

Released: 1921
Production: Douglas Fairbanks for United Artists
Direction: Fred Niblo
Screenplay: Lotta Woods; based on Edward Knoblock's adaptation of *Les Trois Mousquetaires* by Alexandre Dumas, *père*
Cinematography: Arthur Edeson
Editing: Nellie Mason
Art direction: Edward M. Langley
Technical direction: Frank England
Costume design: Paul Burns
Music: Louis F. Gottschalk
Length: 12 reels/11,700 feet

Principal characters:
D'Artagnan .... Douglas Fairbanks
Athos .... Leon Barry
Porthos .... George Siegmann
Aramis .... Eugene Pallette
Comte de Rochefort .... Boyd Irwin
Louis XIII .... Adolphe Menjou
Cardinal Richelieu .... Nigel De Brulier
Constance Bonacieux .... Marguerite De La Motte
Milady de Winter .... Barbara La Marr
Duke of Buckingham .... Thomas Holding
Monsieur Bonacieux .... Sidney Franklin
Planchet .... Charles Stevens
Captain de Treville .... Willis Robards
Queen Anne of Austria .... Mary MacLaren
Bernajoux .... Charles Belcher
D'Artagnan, père .... Walt Whitman
Father Joseph .... Lon Poff

In 1920, Douglas Fairbanks virtually invented the screen swashbuckler with *The Mark of Zorro*. His previous twenty-nine films had all been two- to five-reel contemporary comedies, and Fairbanks was so uncertain of the reception of his first costume adventure that he followed it with another contemporary comedy, *The Nut* (1921). When *The Nut* flopped while *The Mark of Zorro* turned out to be his biggest success to date, Fairbanks decided to commit himself to historical swashbucklers. His next project was not hard to find, for his favorite literary character, from boyhood on, had been D'Artagnan. *The Mark of Zorro* was derived from a pulp magazine serial, but for its successor, Fairbanks turned to the classic swashbuckling novel *The Three Musketeers* (1844), by Alexandre Dumas, *père*. In 1918, Fairbanks had made *A Modern*

Musketeer, about a contemporary young man who rescues people in danger, but now he prepared to play the real D'Artagnan.

Determined to make a prestige film, Fairbanks did not follow his usual practice of writing his own screenplay under the pen name Elton Thomas, but hired an established English playwright, Edward Knoblock, to do the adaptation. He had his art director, Edward M. Langley, make elaborate and well-researched sets and had sculptor Willie Hopkins create statuary for the palaces. To train the cast in swordplay, he hired Professor H. J. Uyttenhove, a former world championship fencer; and to compose a special music score to accompany the film, he selected Louis F. Gottschalk, a descendant of the American composer and pianist Louis Moreau Gottschalk (1829-1869).

Knoblock's adaptation covers only the first third of Dumas' lengthy novel— the episode of the Queen's diamond studs. In the story, Queen Anne of Austria (Mary MacLaren), wife of Louis XIII of France (Adolphe Menjou) has been conducting a surreptitious romance with the Duke of Buckingham (Thomas Holding). If she is detected, she is vulnerable not only to a charge of adultery but also to one of treason for consorting with her country's enemy, the commander of the English army. Cardinal Richelieu (Nigel De Brulier), the gray eminence and power behind the throne, is perpetually maneuvering to increase his influence, and, aware of the Queen's infatuation, he seeks a way to drive a wedge between her and the King.

Meanwhile, a penniless young man from Gascon named D'Artagnan (Douglas Fairbanks) sets out for Paris with his father's sword and blessing, a yellow plowhorse, and a letter of recommendation to Captain de Treville of the King's Musketeers. As proud as he is poor, D'Artagnan brooks no insults to his honor; and when at Meung, the Comte de Rochefort (Boyd Irwin), an arrogant agent of the Cardinal, ridicules his horse, D'Artagnan draws his sword and challenges de Rochefort, whose lackeys smash him over the head, break his sword, and knock him senseless while their master drives off in his coach.

Finally arriving in Paris, D'Artagnan, while in an interview with Captain de Treville (Willis Robards), looks out the window and spots de Rochefort passing by. In a rage, he dashes out and down the stairs, only to collide with Athos (Leon Barry), a musketeer recently wounded in a fight with the Cardinal's guards. D'Artagnan apologizes, but Athos chides him for his clumsiness, and the two of them agree to settle the dispute by a duel at noon. Resuming his pursuit, D'Artagnan entangles himself in the cloak of Porthos (George Siegmann), another musketeer, and another duel is scheduled—for one o'clock. By now, D'Artagnan has lost so much time that when he emerges onto the street, his adversary has vanished. Instead, he finds a third musketeer, Aramis (Eugene Pallette), engaged in a dispute over a lady's handkerchief, which Aramis claims he did not drop. Trying to be helpful, D'Artagnan picks up the handkerchief and returns it to Aramis, who thanks him by arranging for a third duel—at two o'clock. Thus, within a few hours after arriving in Paris, D'Artagnan has managed to arrange to fight three of the best swordsmen in France. His only consolation is that if he is killed, it will be by a King's musketeer.

Knowing no one who can act as his second, he arrives alone at the dueling ground. Athos, however, is seconded by Porthos and Aramis, and when all three realize that they are to fight the same person, they are amused and impressed by D'Artagnan's rash courage. As dueling has been outlawed, just as D'Artagnan and Athos cross blades, a detachment of the Cardinal's guards appear and order the musketeers to place themselves under arrest. Instead, the musketeers issue defiance and prepare to fight, although outnumbered five to three. Five to four, says D'Artagnan, who insists on fighting beside his erstwhile adversaries. In the melee that follows, D'Artagnan amazes everyone by his spectacular swordplay. He wounds Jussac, the most dangerous of the guards, and rescues the wounded Athos, when the latter is hard-pressed. He and the musketeers win the field, and instead of having three enemies, D'Artagnan finds that he has three blood brothers. They adopt the motto "All for one, and one for all."

Shortly thereafter, D'Artagnan is challenged in a tavern by Bernajoux (Charles Belcher) another of the Cardinal's guards, and once more he is victorious. When he and the three musketeers are summoned before the King, supposedly to be punished, Louis XIII is so jubilant at his men's triumph over the Cardinal's that he rewards them.

D'Artagnan engages a lackey named Planchet (Charles Stevens) and takes lodgings at the home of M. Bonacieux (Sidney Franklin), whose niece Constance (Marguerite De La Motte) is lady-in-waiting to the Queen. Not long afterward, a band of the Cardinal's guards break into the downstairs and attempt to abduct Constance. Overhearing the fracas, D'Artagnan dashes down from his upstairs apartment and single-handedly routs the entire band. He finds himself enamored of Constance, who asks him to walk some distance behind her as a bodyguard that night when she goes to the palace. As D'Artagnan does so, he observes her meeting a gentleman. Assuming that it is a lovers' tryst, he jealously overtakes them and challenges the man to fight. To his embarrassment, though, the gentleman turns out to be the Duke of Buckingham, whose tryst is not with Constance but with the Queen.

As a token of her love, Queen Anne gives Buckingham a necklace of diamond studs that was a gift from her husband. Cardinal Richelieu, learning of the token through his spy, orders the beautiful but deadly Milady de Winter (Barbara La Marr) to steal two of the studs so that even if the Queen reclaims the necklace, it will not be as the King gave it to her. Richelieu then persuades Louis to schedule a ball and to request that the Queen attend it wearing the diamond necklace. Anne is panic stricken, but Constance volunteers D'Artagnan to go to England and bring it back in time. He in turn recruits the three musketeers to accompany him. En route, they are repeatedly ambushed by the Cardinal's men, who put all three musketeers out of commission. D'Artagnan and Planchet alone succeed in getting through to Buckingham. When the Duke is ready to return the necklace, he is dismayed to discover that two studs are missing. Racing against time, he has them replaced, and D'Artagnan arrives back in Paris in the nick of time. The ball is already in progress, and the King registers his displeasure when the Queen appears without the necklace. He sends her to get it, and, during her absence, Richelieu hands the King the two stolen studs and bids him ask the Queen to explain them. When she reappears, joyfully wearing the necklace that D'Artagnan has just returned to her, the embarrassed and chagrined Cardinal explains that he had intended the two additional studs as a present.

Here the film ends, omitting the remaining two-thirds of the novel, in which Milady works considerable evil and is finally captured and executed by D'Artagnan and the three musketeers. Knoblock made a few other changes from the book such as having Constance be the niece rather than the wife of Bonacieux, so that her love scenes with D'Artagnan would not be adulterous and offend the lingering Puritanism of contemporary American sensibilities.

Fred Niblo, who had directed *The Mark of Zorro* and was to direct the silent *Ben-Hur* (1925), directed competently, although the opening sequences between the King and the Cardinal are so stately that they drag. Whenever Fairbanks is on screen, things are brisk enough, although his role has very few of the acrobatics and stunts that are his hallmark. The only memorable bit of acrobatics takes place during the first swordfight, when Fairbanks, dagger in hand, does a somersault during which he impales an opponent's hand to the ground. Despite coaching by a champion fencer, Fairbanks' swordplay is more vigorous than skillful and seems crude by comparison to that of later stars such as Basil Rathbone, Errol Flynn, Tyrone Power, and Cornel Wilde. Fairbanks tends to overact, with extravagant gestures, but he has an engaging panache, contagious high spirits, and his stylized performance is immensely enjoyable, if not very realistic.

The rest of the cast provided good support. Marguerite De La Motte, who had been the heroine of *The Mark of Zorro* and several other Fairbanks films, was a charming Constance, and Barbara La Marr, Black Michael's tormented mistress in *The Prisoner of Zenda* (1922), was equally effective as the *femme fatale*. Adolphe Menjou, in his first major role, was a suave monarch, and Nigel De Brulier a sinister Cardinal. Among the musketeers, it is worth mentioning the casting of Eugene Pallette as Aramis. Pallette was then considered one of the handsomest men in films, but a change in body chemistry transformed him into the paunchy, jowly, gravel-voiced character actor more familiar to filmgoers, who remember him as Friar Tuck in *The Adventures of Robin Hood* (1938) and as the padre in *The Mark of Zorro* (1940).

The Three Musketeers met with enthusiastic acclaim. *The New York Times* critic called its debut (attended by Fairbanks, Mary Pickford, Charles Chaplin, and Jack Dempsey) the "fullest and most satisfying night of the year" and hailed Fairbanks' D'Artagnan as "the personification of all the dashing and slashing men of Gascony that ever fought their way through French novels."

His second immense success as a swashbuckler confirmed Fairbanks in the genre, and he followed *The Three Musketeers* with *Robin Hood* (1922), *The Thief of Bagdad* (1924), *Don Q, Son of Zorro* (1925), *The Black Pirate* (1926), *The Gaucho* (1928), and *The Iron Mask* (1929).

The Iron Mask is based upon the fourth volume of *Le Vicomte de Brage-lonne*, which follows *Twenty Years After* as sequels to *The Three Musketeers*. Fairbanks' film, however, opens with a sequence from the end of Dumas' *The Three Musketeers*, in which Milady de Winter murders Constance Bonacieux; young D'Artagnan arrives too late to prevent the tragedy. For the rest of the film, Fairbanks played the aging D'Artagnan, with more dignity but no less panache. Also returning were De La Motte as Constance, De Brulier as Richelieu, Leon Barry as Athos, Charles Stevens as Planchet, and Lon Poff as Father Joseph. La Marr could not repeat Milady de Winter. A troubled woman who had been twice raped and was deceived by a bigamist, she committed suicide in 1926 at the age of twenty-eight.

The Iron Mask was the last of Fairbank's silent films and his last great success. Subsequently, there were four more Hollywood films and two French films of *The Three Musketeers* and one version made for American television, plus two more films and one television production of *The Man in the Iron Mask*. In 1935, Walter Abel was badly miscast as an undashing D'Artagnan. In 1939, Allan Dwan, who had directed Fairbanks' *The Iron Mask*, made a musical comedy version of *The Three Musketeers* with Don Ameche as a singing D'Artagnan and the three Ritz Brothers as sissified impersonators masquerading in place of the real musketeers. Like Fairbanks' version, these two dealt only with the adventure of the Queen's diamond studs. In 1948, M-G-M filmed the entire novel, with Gene Kelly (whose favorite film had been Fairbanks' *The Three Musketeers*) playing an acrobatic D'Artagnan; and Richard Lester directed the entire book in two installments, *The Three Musketeers* (1974) and *The Four Musketeers* (1975). Filmed on location in Europe, Lester's pictures had the best production values by far, with much inventive use of details of seventeenth century life. None of the film versions, however, is altogether satisfactory. Fairbanks, at thirty-eight, was clearly not the eighteen-year-old D'Artagnan, and his florid performance was more operatic than realistic. Ideally, the young Errol Flynn should have played the role, but since he did not, Fairbanks, for all of his extravagant overacting, comes closest to the dashing bravado of Dumas' Gascon swashbuckler, and audiences still find his film a rousing entertainment.

Robert E. Morsberger

THE THREE MUST-GET-THERES
(L'ÉTROIT MOUSQUETAIRE)

Released: 1922
Production: Max Linder
Direction: Max Linder
Assistant direction: Fred Cavens
Screenplay: Max Linder; suggested by the novel *The Three Musketeers* by
   Alexandre Dumas, *père*
Cinematography: Max Dupont and Harry Vallejo
Length: 5 reels/4,900 feet

Principal characters:
Dart-In-Again ....Max Linder
Louis XIII .... A. J. Cooks
Bunkumin .... Hank Mann
Octopus ....Clarence Wertz
Walrus ....John J. Richardson
Porpoise .... Charles Mezzetti
Rich-Lou .... Bull Montana
Connie ....Jobyna Ralston

There is a famous photograph among Max Linder's personal possessions. Dated May 12, 1917, it shows a very young Charlie Chaplin in a slightly ill-fitting suit from which his hands protrude like those of a child posing during a dressing-up escapade. Across the top is written "To the one and only Max, 'The Professor,' from his Disciple, Charlie Chaplin." Linder, once the world's highest paid actor, an international celebrity between 1910 and 1920 and the only French silent comedian to make a significant impact on Hollywood, has all but vanished from the public memory. When Chaplin wrote his autobiography in 1964, the need to be the complete original, the father of sophisticated screen comedy, led him (that is the generous interpretation) to omit all mention of Linder. Yet, he need not have worried: the styles of the two comedians are very different. Linder's elegant bachelor, as opposed to Chaplin's Little Tramp, is neither sentimental nor particularly likable. He also tends to operate in a much purer world of basic comedy stereotypes—those of the suitor or the married man, for example. What Linder did share with Chaplin, however, and with other great silent comedians such as Buster Keaton and Harold Lloyd, was a basic understanding of the medium of cinema and a determination to control his work within it.

Born Gabriel Leuvielle near Bordeaux, France, in 1883, Linder's first ambition was to become a serious actor. He had some success in Bordeaux, but his move to Paris at the turn of the century relegated him to a succession of walk-on roles in melodramas. Financial need took him to the Vincennes studios in 1905: pay there was twenty francs a day for an extra, as against the 150 francs a month he got in the theater. By 1910, he was an international star, receiving three thousand francs a day for personal appearances. He rapidly became producer and director of his own films, possibly the first cinema comedian to realize the importance of controlling the means of recording the performance as well as the performance itself. Between 1909 and the outbreak of World War I, Linder was the star of considerably more than one hundred films, turned out at the rate of about one every two weeks, and, more often than not, incorporating his own name into the title: *Max et son chien Dick (1912-1914)*, *Max professeur de Tango* (1911), *Max Toréador* (1911), *Max et son chien Dick* (1912-1914), and many others. When he was ill in 1910, he produced a documentary, *Max et sa Famille*, to explain the circumstances, and this was as much of a box-office success as his other films.

Linder was released from the French Army in 1915 with pneumonia; he had made a few more films in France when he was approached by George K. Spoor, the "S" in Essanay, an American company which had recently lost the services of Chaplin and was seeking a successor. Spoor gambled on Linder. His first three American films—*Max Comes Across, Max Wants a Divorce*, and *Max and His Taxi* (all made in 1917)—were not especially successful and failed to rescue Essanay; but they did teach Linder two important lessons: that the American film industry was better organized than its European counterpart and thus offered better facilities for his work; and that control of that work was just as important on either side of the Atlantic. In 1920, he returned to America, this time to Hollywood (Essanay had been based in Chicago), to make his three best films: *Be My Wife* (1920), *Seven Years' Bad Luck* (1921), and *The Three Must-Get-Theres* (1922). The films did well, but Linder's health was failing. He returned to France, where he made two more films, one of which, *Au Secours!* (1923), he merely wrote in collaboration with his friend Abel Gance. On October 31, 1925, in a Paris hotel room where they were staying until their apartment was ready, Linder killed his wife and committed suicide. The circumstances surrounding the deaths are still not known.

The Three Must-Get-Theres (also known by its French title, *L'Étroit Mousquetaire*, which involves a similar play on words) is, like most of Linder's work, not concerned with social reality or modern social problems. This may be one reason for his obscurity: comedians like Charlie Chase and Linder, who do not give audiences a sense of moral justification to bolster their laughter, have never really caught the critical attention, particularly since, in the case of film criticism, content has, until very recently, always received more attention than style.

Linder's film is all style, since it belongs to that most artistically incestuous of genres, parody. *The Three Must-Get-Theres* is a parody, both of Alexandre Dumas' novel and, especially, of the previous year's Douglas Fairbanks swashbuckler, *The Three Musketeers*. Dart-In-Again (Max Linder; D'Artagnan), a hapless country youth with a quite unjustified belief in his own prowess, arrives in Paris. Through a bizarre combination of circumstances, he falls in with Octopus (Clarence Wertz; Athos), Porpoise (Charles Mezzetti; Porthos), and Walrus (John J. Richardson; Aramis), and he sets off for England on the famous quest for the Queen's diamonds, in the possession of Bunkumin (Hank Mann; Duke of Buckingham). He succeeds, thanks mainly to chance and to his unscrupulous willingness to resort to the kinds of tricks which, in earlier films, had helped Linder rid himself of an unwanted rival in love.

It is not, of course, the plot which is the important element in *The Three Must-Get-Theres*: even those contemporary audience members who had never heard of Dumas would have been likely to remember the story from the Fairbanks film. Like all parodies, Linder's film plays on—and with—the viewers expectations. A dramatic leap from a bedroom window onto the back of a waiting steed is a staple of the Fairbanks repertoire; Linder misses. Neither courageous nor particularly athletic, Dart-In-Again escapes from an encounter which leaves him surrounded by the rapiers of his attackers (in a perfect geometric shape, like something from a Busby Berkeley dance routine of the 1930's) through the simple device of dropping out of the line of fire so that the swordsmen impale one another.

Much of the film shows Linder's admiration for the achievements of American slapstick, especially the films of Mack Sennett. The shenanigans around the necklace involving the musketeers, the Cardinal's guards, the Queen, and Connie (Jobyna Ralston; Constance Bonacieux) have all the verve of a Keystone Kops film. Linder adds a few good gags which are very much his own, though. Arriving at the English Channel and finding no ship available to take him across, Dart-In-Again hoists a sail on the back of his horse and launches happily out to sea. His most striking innovation in the film—and also the riskiest—is his widespread use of anachronism. Jazz musicians suddenly burst into view at the court of Louis XIII (A. J. Cooks). Rich-Lou (Bull Montana; Cardinal Richelieu) gives instructions to his guards over the telephone. Messages are written on typewriters. Almost caught by his pursuers, Dart-In-Again pulls out a motorcycle combination and speeds off into the distance. Like Rich-Lou, he uses the telephone: an *ad hoc* booth in the back of a tree bordering a rural French lane. The use of anachronisms seems as much as anything else a recognition of the fact that film versions of romantic novels themselves based on distant historical events already have a strong element of inauthenticity built into them. In *The Three Must-Get-Theres*, the anachronisms accord well with Linder's D'Artagnan, an amiable dandy who, presented with the point of a rapier, is less likely to leap *en garde* than to take its blade gingerly between two fingers and inspect it, with apprehension but also with polite interest. This D'Artagnan is more a camp follower than a campaign leader.

The culmination of his career and Linder's biggest film in almost every respect, *The Three Must-Get-Theres* deserves to be better known by modern audiences. Its most recent appearance was in *En compagnie de Max Linder*, a compilation put together in 1963 by his daughter Maud. In that film, René Clair, one of the great directors of the French cinema, claims to have learned from Linder what film comedy could be. With tributes like that and the one from Chaplin, it seems that modern audiences might also have something to learn from Linder. His films, and above all *The Three Must-Get-Theres*, are ripe for revival.

Nick Roddick

THREE WEEKS

Released: 1924
Production: Goldwyn/Cosmopolitan
Direction: Alan Crosland
Screenplay: Carey Wilson and June Mathis; based on the novel of the same
name by Elinor Glyn
Cinematography: John J. Mescall
Editing: June Mathis
Length: 8 reels/7,468 feet

Principal characters:

The Lady/The Queen	Aileen Pringle
Paul Verdayne	Conrad Nagel
Dimitri	Nigel De Brulier
Lady Henrietta Verdayne	Helen Dunbar
Lord Charles Verdayne	H. Reeves-Smith
Isabella	Joan Standing
Anna	Dale Fuller
Curate	William Haines
The King	John Sainpolis

British novelist Elinor Glyn spent the 1920's in Hollywood and was treated the whole time like visiting royalty. Her pronouncements were eagerly printed in the fan magazines, and motion-picture studios paid her vast sums for the rights to the romantic novels and original stories which she wrote.

She first became famous in 1907 with the publication of *Three Weeks*, a romantic bit of fluff which seemingly every schoolgirl and housewife in the world read. In the years that followed, she turned out a novel annually. Each novel sold extremely well, but *Three Weeks* kept selling more and more and eventually became one of the best-selling books ever printed. With the growth of the film industry and the start of large sums being paid for film rights, *Three Weeks* became a much sought-after property. Goldwyn Pictures secured the rights, and Glyn was invited to Hollywood to advise on the production. She arrived in Hollywood as if she were its dowager queen. She was nearly sixty and typified British dignity, despite her shocking red hair, gleaming false teeth, false eyelashes, and intense perfume. She immediately turned her suite at the Hollywood Hotel into an Arabian tent with Persian carpets, incense burners, and a giant tiger-skin rug.

Before any work was done on *Three Weeks*, she sold two properties to Paramount to be made into Gloria Swanson features: *The Great Moment* (1921) and *Beyond the Rocks* (1922). In 1923, work got under way at the Goldwyn studios on *Three Weeks*. It was the story of a runaway queen and her commoner lover, so a regal actress and a handsome young man were required for the principal roles. Glyn looked at almost every actress in Hollywood before she approved Aileen Pringle. They were posed together in photographs for industry magazines to show that they looked like mother and daughter, and Pringle was also posed on tiger-skin rugs since they were known to be a personal fetish of Glyn.

Still, the search for the hero continued. Glyn was particularly fond of young blond men and demanded that the fairness of her book's hero be faithfully depicted in the screen version. Rudolph Valentino and Ramon Novarro were the leading idols of the time, and there were not that many blond leading men from which to choose. Goldwyn Pictures decided to surprise Glyn and buy the contract of a young blond actor from Paramount. Unfortunately, they had to give Richard Dix to Paramount in exchange.

When Glyn was first presented to the newly acquired actor as the hero of her book, she screamed. The studio insisted and she desisted. The actor, Conrad Nagel, felt terrible. Each time she passed him on the lot, she would dramatically raise one arm to her forehead in anguish and sob.

Nagel did a fine job as the Queen's lover, despite Glyn's reservations, and went on to become a star. Pringle got excellent notices in her role as the Queen, and subsequently played in two more Glyn stories: *His Hour* (1924) and *Soul Mates* (1925).

The film *Three Weeks* opens in a mythical European principality called Sardalia. The people are protesting in the streets against the tyranny of the King. Only one thing keeps them from breaking down the doors of the palace: the love they have for the Queen (Aileen Pringle).

Meanwhile, inside the palace, the King (John Sainpolis) fondles a servant girl when he is surprised by the sudden entrance of the Queen. The King is a nasty little man, and as the Queen turns to leave, he yells at her, "Woman, get me an heir!" The Queen leaves that day with her bags, her maid, Anna (Dale Fuller), and her servant, Dimitri (Nigel De Brulier). She tells the King she has to be alone for awhile, and he happily allows her to go. Soon, she is in Switzerland among the beautiful mountains that surround Lucerne.

Meanwhile, in England, Lady Henrietta and Lord Charles Verdayne (Helen Dunbar and H. Reeves-Smith) are upset because their son Paul (Conrad Nagel) has fallen in love with Isabella (Joan Standing), the daughter of a poor vicar, so they decide to send him abroad for a month to see if he will forget Isabella. Paul arrives in Lucerne distracted by love. He seems totally uninterested in anything, not in the beautiful country or in the meals the waiters place before him.

Then one night, after Paul has been at the hotel more than a week, he suddenly feels conscious of the presence of a lady. He looks about the dining room, and off in a corner, he sees the mysterious beauty. She rolls her wine about her glass with languor; then without warning, she suddenly looks at Paul and smiles faintly. She looks back down into her glass, but Paul cannot tear his eyes away. He orders wine too, and for an hour they sit and slowly drink—separately but together.

After dinner, Paul walks in the moonlight on the terrace, longing to see the lady, but she does not appear. The next morning, Paul asks about the lady at the hotel front desk, but they can give him little information. For three days, he does not see her and then, on the third night, as he leans over the rail of the terrace, he feels her presence nearby. Expecting and fearing disappointment, he looks to his right and sees her standing there, looking at the stars.

They become friends and then lovers. They travel to Venice and spend three weeks in a glorious romance before she returns to her country alone. Paul returns to England in the same lovesick condition, but the object of his affection has changed. He breaks his engagement, to his parents' joy, and lives quietly.

The Queen gives birth to a son eight months after she returns from Venice, and the King kills her. He, in turn, is slain in an uprising. When the love child is six years old, he is crowned King in the cathedral, and Paul is one of the spectators in the crowd.

Three Weeks did quite well upon its release and assured Glyn of the highest prices for her stories. Paramount put her under contract in 1925 to write, develop, and supervise production. Her most famous venture there was *It* (1927), which made Clara Bow a star. "It" then became a word synonymous with sex-appeal. Another of her Paramount concoctions was *Three Week Ends* (1928), again with Clara Bow.

Glyn went back to England at the changeover to sound and began making films there. She chose a number of handsome young blond men and starred them in the films she wrote and produced. None of them became famous, nor did the films do well, and she lost forty thousand pounds of her own money in those ventures. Despite these failures, Glyn had already left her mark on the world when she died in London in 1943.

Larry Lee Holland

THREE WOMEN

Released: 1924
Production: Warner Bros.
Direction: Ernst Lubitsch
Screenplay: Hans Kraly; based on an original screen story by Hans Kraly and
    Ernst Lubitsch and the novel *The Lilie* by Yolande Maree
Cinematography: Charles Van Enger
Art direction: Svend Gade
Length: 8 reels/7,400-8,200 feet

> *Principal characters:*
> Mrs. Mabel Wilton .... Pauline Frederick
> Jeanne Wilton .... May McAvoy
> Harriet .... Marie Prevost
> Edmund Lamont .... Lew Cody
> Harvey Craig .... Willard Louis
> Fred Armstrong .... Pierre Gendron
> His mother .... Mary Carr
> Fred's friend .... Raymond McKee

The German-born director Ernst Lubitsch's third film made in Hollywood had its premiere on August 18, 1924, at the Mark Strand Theater. The film, *Three Women*, is a serio-comic society drama billed as a satire of "female psychology." Lubitsch, famous for a dazzling stylistic unity displayed throughout his career which transcended his varied material, was highly praised for his direction of this early American effort. Critic Mordaunt Hall, after attending the initial showing, recognized Lubitsch's genius, heralding the director as ". . . a talented stylist . . . who makes the most of every detail and whose work scintillates with original ideas." In his *New York Times* review of the film, he also suggested that *Three Women* was "an exposition of as pretty a piece of direction as has been seen on the screen in some time." Film historian Charles Higham, in his book *The Art of the American Film*, assesses *Three Women* as one of Lubitsch's masterpieces, a superb example of his skill in directing actors.

The screenplay by Hans Kraly, based on a story by himself and Lubitsch and a novel by Yolande Maree, was supposed to be inspired by the infamous William Desmond Taylor murder case of 1922. The story, built upon a popular, yet to this day unproven, theory about the case, suggested that Taylor had been shot and killed by Mrs. Shelby, the mother of popular young star Mary Miles Minter. The apparent motive was (or could have been) jealousy, as Taylor was known to have had affairs with both mother and daughter, among others.

Despite a strong basis on a well-publicized case, however, the story concentrated more on visuals than on plot. For this reason, several critics pointed out the weakness of the story in comparison to the direction. Many imitators were to try and master the famous "Lubitsch touch," but none could match his ingenious visual mannerisms. In *Three Women*, for example, Lubitsch uses only one written title in the entire sequence about the young daughter's downfall, instead choosing to suggest every indiscretion subtly by gestures and facial expressions. In an earlier film, *The Marriage Circle* (1924), Lubitsch opened the story with a scene showing a man discovering a hole in his sock, thus cleverly establishing the man's character without written explanations.

Referred to as a "comedy of manners," as well as a "merciless dissection of three silly women," *Three Women* opens with a shot of the registering needle on a weighing machine. The audience next sees the leading character, Mrs. Mabel Wilton (Pauline Frederick) eating a lemon as she gazes unhappily at the upward movement of the needle. Mrs. Wilton is the mother of an eighteen-year-old girl, Jeanne (May McAvoy), who has the slim, youthful appearance that the slightly overweight, wrinkling mother wishes she still had. Lubitsch emphasizes the difference between the two with lights and gestures that illustrate the joyless importance which Americans place on youth and beauty.

Mrs. Wilton meets an unscrupulous Casanova named Edmund Lamont (Lew Cody), who attempts to woo her. Besieged by creditors, Lamont sees Mrs. Wilton's obvious wealth as a means of helping him out of his financial problems. Lubitsch employs close-ups of various diamonds and other jewels worn by different women as seen from Lamont's point of view to indicate the mental calculations which the fortune hunter uses to assess the value of his wealthy preys' possessions before asking one of them to dance at a party. Mrs. Wilton's jewels seem to appeal to him most.

Lamont manages to win Mrs. Wilton's heart and swindles her out of $100,000 of her three-million-dollar fortune before preparing for the big kill, marriage. At this point, however, Jeanne returns from school and interrupts her mother's romance. When Lamont realizes that the daughter is to receive half of the family fortune on the day of her own marriage, he rapidly transfers his affections to the younger heiress. He compromises her, making marriage a necessity, but as soon as the marriage is secured, he starts philandering again and establishes a liaison with a hedonistic flapper named Harriet (Marie Prevost). To complicate matters further, Fred Armstrong (Pierre Gendron), the young doctor with whom Jeanne is really in love, comes to New York from California and surprises Mrs. Wilton. When Jeanne begs Lamont for a divorce, he refuses her. To save her daughter's happiness and get revenge on the villain, Mrs. Wilton demands her daughter's freedom; and when Lamont refuses and attacks her, she shoots and kills him. Mrs. Wilton is acquitted by a sympathetic jury after her pitiful disclosure of events in a rather feeble courtroom scene, and Jeanne is free to revive her romance with Fred.

Audiences were somewhat puzzled by Lubitsch's mixing of moods (tragedy, melodrama, and comedy) in this decidedly European-flavored story, which was filmed principally in New York but with a few earlier scenes taking place in Berkeley, California. Lubitsch specialized in films about sophisticated, promiscuous, and realistic sex relationships which, veiled in innuendo and good manners, were very popular in Europe. Not until *Design for Living* (1933) did he make a truly "American" comedy of the sexes. Of his early successes in the United States, *The Marriage Circle* was set in Vienna, *Kiss Me Again* (1925) and *So This Is Paris* (1926) in Paris, and *Lady Windermere's Fan* (1925) in London. All of these films are very European, capitalizing on glances, gestures, and tone. Lubitsch described his technique and his confidence in the audiences' intelligence when he said, "I'll let the audience figure out for themselves what happened behind the closed door, and only show the result." Critics were so preoccupied with what Lubitsch naughtily deleted from the screen that his incredible wit, simplicity, and imagery were often overlooked. He rendered subtitles unnecessary for long periods of screen time, his sets and lighting were perfect, and his pacing was excellent, carrying his stories along like melodies.

The performances in *Three Women* were very much admired, particularly that of Pauline Frederick as the aging mother. Marie Prevost, remembered principally as Charles Chaplin's leading lady in countless shorts and a few features, was also very good as the fiery flapper. Lew Cody cleverly makes Lamont a manipulating scoundrel and May McAvoy is sympathetic as Jeanne.

In his next film, Lubitsch was to combine this sophisticated comedy with the costume-drama genre for which he had been identified in Europe. *Forbidden Paradise* (1924) dealt with the amorous adventures of Russia's Empress Catherine the Great. Later successes included *Trouble in Paradise* (1932), *Ninotchka* (1939), and *Heaven Can Wait* (1943). His last film before his death in 1947 was *That Lady in Ermine* (1948), released posthumously after being completed by Lubitsch's friend Otto Preminger.

The last of the genuine "continentals," Lubitsch deftly interspersed witticisms (first visual and after sound, verbal) on sex, court etiquette, and political diplomacy in all his films. He also sensed the American penchant for lavishness and spectacle, evoking a feeling of spaciousness with tall columns, ornate draperies, towering staircases, and elaborate decoration. His keen sense of atmosphere complemented his titillating comedies of manners. He was able to convey words or thoughts without dialogue (or even titles to a large extent) by his evocation of a period or style. Such was the case particularly in *Lady Windermere's Fan* in which Lubitsch did not use any of playwright Oscar Wilde's original words, but wrote his own titles, presenting the spirit of the play instead of the well-known epigrams.

Lubitsch's sound films were brilliant and he was easily the most versatile of the early sound directors. He gave mobility to the camera, once again, and moved the heretofore static microphone in accompaniment. His *The Love Parade* (1929) became the model musical, just as *Forbidden Paradise* had been the model for the silent sophisticated comedy, full to the brim with double entendres, suggestive pantomime, and scintillating deletions.

Tanita C. Kelly

TILLIE'S PUNCTURED ROMANCE

Released: 1914
Production: Mack Sennett for Keystone/Alco
Direction: Mack Sennett
Screenplay: Hampton Del Ruth; based on the musical comedy *Tillie's Nightmare* by Edgar Smith and A. Baldwin Sloane
Cinematography: no listing
Length: 6 reels/4,796 feet

Principal characters:
Tillie Banks	Marie Dressler
Charlie, the city slicker	Charles Chaplin
Mabel, his partner	Mabel Normand
Tillie's father	Mack Swain
Douglas Banks, the rich uncle	Charles Bennett
A Detective	Charles Murray
A Guest	Chester Conklin
A Guest	Alice Davenport
A Guest	Alice Howell
A Maid	Minta Durfee
A small child	Milton Berle

Commenting upon a fairly early reissue of *Tillie's Punctured Romance*, Epes W. Sargent wrote in the January 24, 1920, issue of *The Moving Picture World*, "Probably no comedy production has ever made more money than *Tillie's Punctured Romance*." Today, more than sixty years later, that statement is still relatively true, and, in addition, one might add that no comedy production has been more revived or is as well known. Unfortunately, *Tillie's Punctured Romance*—despite its fame—is a fairly weak production, far from totally amusing and, more certainly, far removed from any artistic integrity. Were Charles Chaplin not one of its leading players, it would long ago have been relegated to the obscurity which it deserves; this commentary is true despite the presence of two other fine talents, Marie Dressler and Mabel Normand.

Charles Spencer Chaplin (1889-1977) had made his screen debut in a Mack Sennett produced Keystone comedy entitled *Making a Living*, released in February, 1914. It was not until his second Keystone film, a half-reeler entitled *Kid Auto Races at Venice*, released only a few days after *Making a Living*, however, that Chaplin adopted his familiar tramp costume. Two half-reelers, twenty-two one-reelers, and six two-reel comedies followed before the release of *Tillie's Punctured Romance* in November, 1914. Of those, the best two were probably *His Musical Career* and *His Trysting Place*, released immediately prior to *Tillie's Punctured Romance*, and both directed by Chaplin.

In these early Keystone comedies, Chaplin can be seen to grow in stature and to take more care in the working out of his routines. As early as *His Trysting Place*, Chaplin demonstrates a flow, a tempo, almost a ballet-like precision in the restaurant scene where the comedian's eating habits annoy his neighbor.

Unfortunately, those around Chaplin do not appear to be developing with him. Normand's style of acting is still crude, vulgar, and at times offensive. Only much later, under the direction of F. Richard Jones in *Mickey* (1918), can one begin to discern an original comedy talent under the crude Normand veneer. Similarly, Sennett never really developed into a good director. He was a genuine pioneer of the cinema and a good spotter of talent, but as a director he was scarcely a success once the days of the one-reel comedies were over, and many of the problems with *Tillie's Punctured Romance* can be linked to his direction.

Tillie's Punctured Romance first came to life as a musical comedy entitled *Tillie's Nightmare*, which opened at New York's Herald Square Theater on May 5, 1910, under the supervision of Lew Fields and Ned Wayburn. Edgar Smith contributed the book, A. Baldwin Sloane the music, and the star was portly Marie Dressler.

Since Dressler had starred in the original stage production and because she was a major figure in the entertainment world, it was she who was starred in *Tillie's Punctured Romance*, with Chaplin and Normand supposedly in supporting roles. Dressler portrays Tillie Banks, "a country maiden," who first meets Chaplin's character, Charlie, when a piece of wood she is throwing for her dog to fetch strikes him in the face. Chaplin plays the stereotypical city slicker, who, upon seeing that Tillie's father is financially stable, persuades her to get the money and come with him to the city. Charlie takes Tillie to a cabaret and introduces her to the joys of alcohol. Also at the cabaret, Charlie meets his girl friend Mabel (Mabel Normand), and leaves with her after first relieving Tillie of her bankroll.

A drunken Tillie is thrown out on the street and then thrown into jail. When the jailers learn she is Tillie Banks, they telephone her millionaire uncle, Douglas Banks (Charles Bennett), whom Tillie has never seen. Tillie makes such a nuisance of herself while at her uncle's mansion, however, that she is again thrown out on the street, and, having nowhere to go, Tillie finds work as a waitress. In the meantime, Tillie's uncle has gone mountain climbing, had a fall, and is assumed dead. As a result, a search is immediately started for his sole heir, Tillie.

Charlie and Mabel happen to visit the restaurant where Tillie is working, and the sight of Charlie causes Tillie to faint. Leaving the restaurant, Charlie and Mabel read a newspaper story of the search for the missing heiress; Chaplin promptly sneaks away from Mabel, renews his acquaintance with Tillie, and drags her to a minister, who marries the pair. At this point, the uncle's secretary appears and tells Tillie of her inheritance.

Charlie and Tillie return to the uncle's mansion, which is now Tillie's, and throw a tremendous ball, which is disrupted by Mabel in the guise of a maid. Thereupon the uncle reappears and throws everyone again out onto the street. Charlie and Mabel again sneak off, pursued by a vengeful Tillie, her uncle, and the Keystone Kops (including Al St. John, Slim Summerville, Eddie Sutherland, and Hank Mann). The entire company arrives at the water's edge, where Tillie is struck by a carload of Kops and both she and the Kops are thrown into the water. Tillie is saved by Mabel. Charlie begs Tillie's forgiveness, but both Mabel and Tillie renounce Charlie, and he is taken away by the Keystone Kops. It is a riotous finish to a film which has few sophisticated moments of comedy and which relies too heavily on pie-throwing, drunkenness, and comic policemen, all of which seem a little passé even for 1914, a year during which D. W. Griffith completed *The Birth of a Nation* (released in 1915), Mary Pickford had shown an extraordinary emotional range in *Tess of the Storm Country*, and Colin Campbell had brought Rex Beach's classic novel *The Spoilers* to the screen.

Of course, *Tillie's Punctured Romance* was enthusiastically received on its initial release. The critic in *The Moving Picture World* (November 14, 1914) commented,

> It is six thousand feet of undiluted joy. There is a "laugh in every flicker," not to mention a scream in every third one. If laughing really does put fat on the population of the United States, it will take on several tons in weight when this picture goes the rounds. At the private showing case hardened reviewers, trained to sigh at ordinary humor, laughed until the tears streamed down their careworn faces.

The reviewer went on to praise the dull, static direction of Sennett, noting

> Not content with humor alone he filled the picture with excellent scenes, and saw to it that the photography was of the best. Briefly, he has produced the longest and at the same time one of the best comedies yet seen on the screen.

Variety's critic was likewise enthusiastic, writing in the issue of January 1, 1915, "Mack Sennett directed the picture and right well has he done the job." *Motography* (November 14, 1914) was even more hysterical, with its critic describing *Tillie's Punctured Romance* as "the *Cabiria* of comedy."

The Moving Picture World announced that Dressler would never again appear in films, but, in fact, the actress starred as Tillie in two further features, *Tillie's Tomato Surprise* (1915, produced by Lubin) and *Tillie Wakes Up* (1917, a World production).

At least Chaplin seems to have been unimpressed by the feature. In his autobiography, published in 1964, he does not refer to *Tillie's Punctured Romance* by name, but does state, "It was pleasant working with Marie, but

I did not think the picture had much merit. I was more than happy to get back to directing myself again." Certainly, history has proven Chaplin's view correct. He wrote, directed, starred in two further comedies for Sennett and then moved on to Essanay, where *The Champion*, *The Tramp*, and *A Woman* (all released in 1915) show still burgeoning talents, which were to climax as far as Chaplin's career in the early to mid teens is concerned with the Mutual two-reel comedies of *The Cure* and *The Immigrant*, 1917 shorts which co-starred the diminutive Edna Purviance in place of the boisterous Normand.

Anthony Slide

TOL'ABLE DAVID

Released: 1921
Production: Charles Duell, Henry King, and Richard Barthelmess for Associated First National
Direction: Henry King
Screenplay: Edmund Goulding; based on a short story of the same name by Joseph Hergesheimer
Cinematography: Henry Cronjager
Length: 7 reels/7,118 feet

Principal characters:
David Kinemon .... Richard Barthelmess
Esther Hatburn .... Gladys Hulette
Luke Hatburn .... Ernest Torrence
Allen Kinemon .... Warner Richmond
Mrs. Kinemon, David's mother .... Marion Abbott
Mr. Kinemon, David's father .... Edmund Gurney
Rose Kinemon, Allen's wife .... Patterson Dial
John Gault .... Lawrence Eddinger

Director Henry King (1892–   ) had one of the longest careers in film history, from a few minor films in 1916 to the 1962 production, *Tender Is the Night*. In the era of sound films, he became a director at Twentieth Century-Fox, where he turned out innumerable Tyrone Power films and made many well-crafted pictures, such as *The Song of Bernadette* (1943). King's career was so long and he made so many films, a large number of which were routine commercial fare, that his reputation has not received all the credit it deserves. King has excelled at the vivid re-creation of old-fashioned and rural Americana in such films as *Stella Dallas* (1925), *The Winning of Barbara Worth* (1926), *State Fair* (1933), *Ramona* (1936), *Jesse James* (1939), *Margie* (1946), *The Gunfighter* (1950), *Wait 'Till the Sun Shines, Nellie* (1952), and *Carousel* (1956). The best regarded of King's pictures of Americana is the very first of the genre, *Tol'able David*, made in 1921.

Based on a short story by Joseph Hergesheimer, *Tol'able David* takes place during the horse-and-buggy era in the town of Greenfield, a tranquil West Virginia mountain community. The valley in which Greenfield lies is an idyllic place, both geographically and socially, for the town is a closely knit community in which people treat one another with respect and dignity. Young David Kinemon (Richard Barthelmess), however, is only "tol'able," for he is too small, too young, and too inexperienced to be given the respect due a proven man. David is an idealistic dreamer for whom the mountain and valley landscape is poetically beautiful. He is in love with Esther Hatburn (Gladys Hulette), who returns his affection.

The idyll is shattered by the arrival of three Hatburn cousins, degenerate criminals fleeing from the law in another state, who are relatives of Gladys and who take refuge at her father's farm. There, they terrorize the family and neighbors who cross their path. David is outraged at the way they order Esther and her father around, but she urges him to leave matters alone and not interfere lest the situation become even worse. When the brothers kill the Kinemons' dog Rocket for casual sport, however, David's older brother Allen (Warner Richmond) goes to challenge them. While Allen is denouncing their viciousness and threatening to go for the law, the oldest Hatburn brother, Luke (Ernest Torrence), strikes him from behind with a boulder and then steps savagely on his head. As a result, Allen is crippled for life. Only a few weeks earlier, the family had been celebrating the birth of a child to Allen and his wife Rose (Patterson Dial), but now Allen is a helpless invalid, and his wife is embittered.

Nevertheless, the sheriff is afraid to do anything, and the posse that had been pursuing the brothers cannot cross the state line. When Allen's and David's father (Edmund Gurney) takes down his rifle and prepares to fight the Hatburns, he is stricken with a fatal heart attack. David swears to avenge his father and brother, but his mother (Marion Abbot) begs him not to risk his own life too, and he reluctantly gives in to her pleas. With the father dead and Allen no longer able to keep his job as a driver of the mail, the family has to give up their farm and move into poor lodgings in town. David is now head of the family, but the townspeople consider him too young and untested to hold a position of responsibility.

He does get a job helping out in the store of John Gault (Lawrence Eddinger), the richest man in town. Gault is also the postmaster, and one day when the mail driver is too drunk to make his rounds, Gault entrusts the mail route to David. During the run, the Hatburn brothers waylay him and try to steal the mail. The monstrous brothers try to terrify David, but although he is small and little more than a boy, he defends himself, shoots two of the sadistic Hatburns, and has a desperate hand-to-hand fight with the oldest and most brutal brother. Although Hatburn is much larger and a vicious veteran of dirty fighting, David stands up to him. The fight is one of the most savage on film. David is shot and brutally beaten, but he desperately fights on and succeeds in killing Luke Hatburn. It has been a case of little David overcoming Goliath. Then, despite his injuries, David drives the mail hack the rest of the route and returns to town. He collapses, but he has proven himself worthy of the trust given him and has shown the townspeople that he is considerably more than "tol'able."

A synopsis of the film sounds melodramatic, but *Tol'able David* transcends its plot, thanks largely to a sensitive performance by Richard Barthelmess and outstanding direction by King. King was from the Shenandoah Valley of Virginia, and instead of filming the picture on a Hollywood back lot, he went on location to the scenes of his boyhood and provided a remarkably authentic picture of rural American life and folkways in the homespun days. The screenplay is attributed to Edmund Goulding, an Englishman who later became a distinguished director himself with such films as *The Dawn Patrol* (1938), but Goulding was unfamiliar with the details of Appalachian life, and so King rewrote a good deal of the story, putting in considerable detail from his own early experience, such as having the family kneel around the chairs each night for prayers. Goulding was worried that King had ruined the story, but Hergesheimer was delighted and told the director, "You put into this all the things that I left out."

Instead of playing up the melodrama of the narrative, King gave the film a leisurely pace and dwelt lovingly on details of valley and village life, family and community relationships, and the Appalachian countryside and culture, all beautifully photographed in a way that provides a vivid record of a part of Americana that was already passing. The Russian film directors greatly admired *Tol'able David* for its *mise-en-scène* and use of montage, and Vsevolod Pudovkin discussed it at length as a superb example of the use of plastic cinematic material. The reviewer for *The New York Times* observed that the story follows the formula for homespun melodrama but that this time the drama and the people seem real. "*Tol'able David* is sentimental in places, but not sloppy. It is bucolic, but its rusticity is not rubbed in."

The cast members were uniformly fine, with Barthelmess outdoing himself. A year before, he had played a similar role in D. W. Griffiths' *Way Down East*, as an honest farm boy who loves Lillian Gish, but in *Tol'able David*, he abandoned some annoying mannerisms, exaggerated stances, and a foolish yokelish grin. Instead, he imparted to David a combination of gentle sensitivity and grace under pressure that made him embody some of the best qualities of youthful idealism. Although he was twenty-six years old at the time, Barthelmess was entirely convincing as a teenage boy. He gave the finest performance of his career, and David is the role for which he is best remembered. Although he made five more films with King, none of them was nearly as good. With the coming of sound, Barthelmess' career declined (although his performance in the 1930 *The Dawn Patrol* is outstanding), and he retired from films in 1942.

In 1930, *Tol'able David* was remade as a sound film, directed by John G. Blystone, with Richard Cromwell in the title role, but this version lacks the authenticity of its predecessor and has fallen into well-deserved obscurity. The 1921 version remains one of the great silent films and the masterpiece of both Barthelmess and King.

Robert E. Morsberger

THE TOLL OF THE SEA

Released: 1922
Production: Dr. Herbert T. Kalmus and Joseph M. Schenck for Technicolor/ Metro
Direction: Chester M. Franklin
Screenplay: Frances Marion
Cinematography: J. A. Ball
Length: 5 reels/4,600 feet

> *Principal characters:*
> Lotus Flower .... Anna May Wong
> Allen Carver .... Kenneth Harlan
> Barbara Carver .... Beatrice Bentley
> Little Allen .... Baby Marion
> Gossip .... Etta Lee
> Gossip .... Ming Young

The Toll of the Sea has no great artistic importance in the history of the cinema. Certainly, it is competently directed, fairly well acted, and the plot, a retelling of the *Madame Butterfly* story, is moving, but what makes *The Toll of the Sea* a major turning point in the history of the motion picture is that it was the first full-length feature to be shot using the two-color Technicolor process.

Technicolor had filmed its first feature, *The Gulf Between*, in Florida in 1917, utilizing the two-color additive process. *The Toll of the Sea* was photographed by the subtractive process, which used a beam splitter prism camera, making red and green exposures on two frames of film simultaneously, with one frame being inverted. The film moved through the camera, two frames at a time, using twice as much film as would be needed for a regular black-and-white feature. Two prints were made from the negative—one for each color—utilizing stock of half-normal thickness. These two pieces of film were then cemented together and dyed complementary colors.

Because this process used two strips of film cemented together, the image did not project as sharply as it should on the screen, and, in addition, the film was more likely to scratch than regular black-and-white film. Further, the process used only two colors, red and green, meaning that certain colors—in particular blue—could not be filmed satisfactorily. The dye-transfer process, introduced in 1929 with *Redskin*, did away with the need for two strips of film, and, in 1932—with *Flowers and Trees*—Technicolor brought in its three-color dye transfer (or imbibition) process, using the three colors of magenta, cyan, and yellow. This was to be the industry standard through the 1950's, when Eastman color negative/positive film stock was introduced.

The Toll of the Sea was filmed mainly on location in Santa Monica, California, using a local schoolgirl, Anna May Wong, for the leading role. Anna May Wong (1907-1961) had worked as an extra in films from the late teens, and, as a result of her performance in *The Toll of the Sea*, was signed by Douglas Fairbanks for the major part of the Mongol Slave in *The Thief of Bagdad* (1924). Eventually she became more of a European star than an American one, being expected to play little more than Oriental villainesses in domestic features. The film which brought her to stardom was originally supposed to be only a short subject, but cinematographer Ray Rennahan realized there was enough footage for a five-reel feature and persuaded the Technicolor Corporation to release it as such. It is worth noting that the first two all-Technicolor features were actually produced by Technicolor, not by a major Hollywood studio, none of whom had much faith in the color process. Technicolor, however, did hire producer Joseph M. Schenck to oversee the filming.

Although screenwriter Frances Marion does not acknowledge it, the plot of *The Toll of the Sea* bears more than a slight resemblance to that of *Madame Butterfly*. Anna May Wong is Lotus Flower, who discovers an American, Allen Carver (Kenneth Harlan), washed up on the rocks of her native China. She rescues him, despite the warning of an old man that Chinese legend has it that the sea takes in pain twice as much as it gives in joy. Lotus Flower and Carver fall in love and are married, but the latter returns to the United States without his wife. In time, Lotus Flower gives birth to a son, but when Carver does return, it is with his American wife Barbara (Beatrice Bentley). A grief-stricken Lotus Flower persuades the couple to take the child back with them and then commits suicide by throwing herself into the sea.

The Toll of the Sea is shot almost entirely outdoors, with only one or two interior scenes—probably because of the need for excessive light with the Technicolor camera. It is a beautiful film to view, even today, with the acting unstilted and natural. There is no question, however, that its appeal today, to contemporary critics and audiences, is due to its well-considered use of color. *The New York Times* (November 27, 1922) reported,

> The scenes of *The Toll of the Sea* are nearly all satisfying to the eye and many of them are distinctly pleasing. For the most part they are clear, true and bright without being harsh. There are delicate, as well as strong, shades in them, and they are nicely, sometimes exquisitely, detailed. They are enjoyable in themselves and promise the further and furthering development of chromatic cinematography.

Sime Silverman, the editor of *Variety*, was harsh in his appraisal of *The Toll of the Sea*. Writing in the December 1, 1922, issue of his newspaper, he commented,

> Nothing in a moving picture story can rise superior to the story. Coloring never will, never has, and doesn't here. The coloring runs without streaks, the camera catching the natural

colors . . . the coloring in this Technicolor product is attractive, as it brings out the foliage or strikes the colorful dress of the Chinese, but as with all devices tried for in pictures as something new, other than story, direction or settings, the newness becomes part of the picture almost immediately, and thereafter is accepted, with the story remaining as the main thread or holding power, if there is a story such as here, and not a display of flowers or some particular objects to accentuate the colors. . . . But *The Toll of the Sea* will do on the regular programs if too much is not looked for from it.

The New York Times particularly liked the performance of Anna May Wong, whom *Variety* thought cried too much. *The New York Times* critic wrote,

Miss Wong stirs in the spectator all the sympathy her part calls for, and she never repels one by an excess of theatrical "feeling." She has a difficult role, a role that is botched nine times out of ten, but hers is the tenth performance. Completely unconscious of the camera, with a fine sense of proportion and remarkably pantomimic accuracy, she makes the deserted little Lotus Flower a genuinely appealing, understandable figure. She should be seen again and often on the screen.

Variety, which was still referring to Chinese as "chinks," expressed concern that the film might arouse racial hatred against Americans. Robert E. Sherwood thought the film "extraordinarily beautiful throughout" and included it in his volume *The Best Moving Pictures of 1922-1923*.

The Toll of the Sea was not the first color film or even one of the first color subjects. As early as 1896, audiences had seen films colored by hand. Stencil coloring was particularly utilized by the Pathé Company for many of its pre-teens subjects. Kinemacolor was introduced in 1908 and reached its peak around 1913. Prizma Color first came to New York in 1919, and one of *The Toll of the Sea*'s major competitors in 1922 was *The Glorious Adventure*, produced in Prizma Color in England by J. Stuart Blackton, and starring the British beauty Lady Diana Manners.

The first screening of *The Toll of the Sea* took place at the Rialto Theater in New York City on November 26, 1922. Many noted artists of the day, including Maxfield Parrish and Charles Dana Gibson, praised the film, and it was purchased for release by Metro. Unfortunately, Technicolor's laboratory capacity was such that it could not turn out prints fast enough for an immediate general release, and *The Toll of the Sea* was not seen by the rest of America until 1923. The film grossed $250,000, of which Technicolor's share was $165,000.

More important than the critical response to *The Toll of the Sea* was the industry response, and that was immediate and positive. Rex Ingram requested permission to scrap the footage already shot for *The Prisoner of Zenda* and to refilm it in Technicolor, while D. W. Griffith announced plans for a Technicolored production of *Faust*. Neither of these schemes came to fruition, but Technicolor sequences were added to a number of upcoming black-and-white features, in particular *The Ten Commandments* (1923), and two all-Technicolor features were filmed by major studios: *The Wanderer of the Wasteland* (1924) and *The Black Pirate* (1926). The age of color had commenced for the film industry, although it was to be another twenty-five years before the color film supplanted black-and-white.

Anthony Slide

TRACKED BY THE POLICE

Released: 1927
Production: Warner Bros.
Direction: Ray Enright
Assistant direction: Eddie Sowders
Screenplay: John Grey; based on an original screen story by Edward D. Meagher and Gregory Rogers (Darryl F. Zanuck)
Titles: Jack Jarmuth
Art titles: Victor Vance
Cinematography: Edwin B. DuPar
Art direction: Lewis Geib and Esdras Hartley
Electrical effects: F. N. Murphy
Costume design: Alpharetta
Length: 6 reels/5,813 feet

> *Principal characters:*
> Satan .... Rin Tin Tin
> Dan Owen .... Jason Robards, Sr.
> Michael Sturgeon .... Tom Santschi
> Marcella Bradley .... Virginia Browne Faire
> John Bradley .... Wilfred North
> Wyoming Willie .... Dave Morris
> Bull Storm .... Theodore Lorch
> Crook .... Ben Walker
> Princess Beth .... Nanette

Rin Tin Tin, the most famous animal performer of his time, was found in a deserted German trench by Air Force Captain Lee Duncan during World War I. The officer brought the German shepherd puppy back to Los Angeles and trained him for films, with the talented canine achieving stardom in his second film, *Where the North Begins* (1923). He made promotional appearances with his films much like his two-legged co-workers at Warner Bros., and, in his prime, he was accorded many of the luxuries associated with stardom—in the dog's case, a small orchestra to play mood music, a diamond studded collar, and Chateaubriand steak. "Rinty," as he was nicknamed, not only made Duncan rich, but he also was known as "the mortgage lifter" because his films's earnings helped the studio out of more than one financial difficulty.

As insurance against his demise, Warners trained several German shepherds to stand in for their star. Darryl F. Zanuck, who wrote some of the scripts for Rin Tin Tin's films, both pseudonymously as Gregory Rogers and under his own name, said that there was "one for long shots, one for close-ups, one to play the gentle parts, one to fight. Another could jump and do terrific stunts. Another had marvelous eyes." The original Rinty made at least twenty-one features (and one serial) before his death in 1932 (he was born in 1916), and five successors carried on the name in serials and features. A pallid half-hour television series during the 1950's capitalized on the fame of the early films, but demonstrated little of the excitement or expertise of its forerunners. *Won Ton Ton, the Dog Who Saved Hollywood*, a witless pastiche inspired by the surprise success of Rin Tin Tin in the 1920's, was released in 1976.

Tracked by the Police is cobbled together from the most rudimentary of melodramatic ingredients. Its greatest distinction (aside from the superb *chiaroscuro* of the cinematography) is that the hero is not the good-looking young man played by Jason Robards, Sr., but the German shepherd who rescues the heroine and foils the villains' plot.

The banal story concerns a construction crew in the employ of the mysterious "E. and J. people" and their mission to sabotage a recently built dam. The putative hero, Dan Owen (Jason Robards, Sr.) spends most of his time running around futilely, stuck down a mine shaft, and nursing an injured shoulder. Satan (Rin Tin Tin) receives an identical wound from the same thug, but perseveres courageously on his three good legs. He woos a canine co-star, Princess Beth (Nanette), turns off the locks which the malefactors have opened to flood the valley, and saves Marcella Bradley (Virginia Browne Faire) who is suspended over the raging waters.

Satan's final effort, saving Marcella, required him to make an interesting moral decision—shall he save *his* lady love or Owen's? The criminals have weighted Princess Beth with chains and tossed her in the water; Marcella, blinded by the pepper she threw at the head crook Sturgeon (Tom Santschi) in an attempt to avoid his lecherous clutches, staggers against a beam which swings her out over the flood. Here, one senses a scenarist desperate for a device which puts the heroine in sufficient danger to give Satan a difficult task in extricating her. Needless to say, he does the right thing and maneuvers the lock closed with his teeth, then leads Marcella to safety. As the human lovers are reunited and the thugs vanquished, the dog mourns his lost sweetheart, staring gloomily at the embracing couple as he lies by the water which claimed Princess. She, however, evidently a canine Harry Houdini, emerges chainless from the river so that the four protagonists can pose for a happy fade-out.

Rin Tin Tin is indeed a wonder. There is limit to what an animal can accomplish using only his jaws and paws—since the film is silent he cannot even bark to attract attention—but within these restrictions Rinty performs miracles: undoing pin and hole locks, turning handles, pushing levers, and scrambling from a shaft. He looks awkward and even embarrassed when his frantic actions leave him stranded with his head and feet straddled over the edge and oblige him to make three tries. He runs enormous distances, goes directly to the location of the trouble, and even indulges in some reasoning (according to the titles) which is hard to believe is within a dog's capabilities. At different points, the script claims that Satan experiences guilt, a feeling of failure, and senses that Dan is making a mistake when he leaves him locked in a shack. He also knows enough not to confront an armed opponent.

The scriptwriter goes to great lengths to place Satan in danger so that he can extract himself cleverly. In the course of the action, Sturgeon uses Princess to track her boyfriend (in itself a cute bit of canine treason) to Marcella's house. She hides Satan in a clock case, Sturgeon shoots the case full of holes, discovering that the dog has escaped through a rear panel and climbed a hidden staircase to the attic. There Sturgeon is prevented from killing Satan because of the time-honored device of running out of bullets.

Satan, "the sentinel of the desert," has "the heart of a lion and the soul of a child," according to the titles, and, indeed, when he believes his friend is dead, one can see tears in his eyes. He is silhouetted against the natural backgrounds of the area, looking alert and noble, and behaves with consummate loyalty, bravery, and cunning. The "area" itself is a geological improbability: the desert appears to abut a scrubby mountainous zone alongside the river. Since the film was shot at both the Iverson Ranch location in Chatsworth, California, and at preliminary sites for the Hoover Dam in Arizona/Nevada, and the two kinds of terrain are never shown in the same shot, it seems likely that the company simply took Rinty to Yuma, or a similar region, for a day's filming and spliced the footage together regardless of topographical reality.

Beside the problematical geography, there are illogical elements in the plot that are swept aside by the rapid development of the story—the film spans only one day—and the necessity of keeping Rin Tin Tin occupied screen center. The "E. and J. people" are never identified, nor is the reason for Sturgeon's all-purpose villainy. He is equally determined to blow up the dam and kill both Satan and Princess, but not Dan, who is presumably less of a threat than his furry companions. Caviling aside, however, *Tracked by the Police* is an enjoyable motion picture with production values far exceeding what one expects from a low-budget adventure.

Since there are no police in the film and the only tracking is done by Princess, the title deserves some explanation. According to film historian William K. Everson, in the 1920's, films were block booked in advance, sometimes before they were made, and, if a distributor did not deliver the title for which it was contracted, the exhibitor could cancel or refuse a substitute. To forestall any quibbling, Warners added a title card at the end showing Rin Tin Tin in a policeman's cap, standing before jailhouse bars with a truncheon. The end title states that, "as a reward for his valor Satan was made a first grade detective. When the criminals were caught, the citation read TRACKED BY THE POLICE."

Judith M. Kass

TRAFFIC IN SOULS

Released: 1913
Production: George Loane Tucker for the IMP Company; released by Universal
Direction: George Loane Tucker
Screenplay: Walter Macnamara
Cinematography: no listing
Editing: Jack Cohn
Length: 6 reels

Principal characters:
Mary Barton ....Jane Gail
Lorna Barton .... Ethel Grandin
Isaac Barton .... Fred Turner
Larry Burke, Officer 4434 .... Matt Moore
William Trubus .... William Welsh
Mrs. Trubus ....Mrs. Hudson Lyston
Bill Bradshaw .... William Cavanaugh

Traffic in Souls has gained a legendary reputation, thanks largely to Terry Ramsaye's comments in his monumental history of the cinema, *A Million and One Nights.* Ramsaye hailed *Traffic in Souls* as the film by which the American cinema discovered sex, a ridiculous and completely erroneous statement, for sex (in whatever form that word may imply) had been a part of the cinema since its creation, and, further, *Traffic in Souls* contains absolutely no scenes of an explicit sexual nature. Certainly, however, the production did herald the era of the exploitation film. It was advertised as being inspired by the Rockefeller White Slavery Report and the New York District Attorney investigation into vice: highly exploitive promotion and enough surely to gain the film an immediate and enthusiastic audience.

The film was supposedly made at Carl Laemmle's IMP studios in New York without the studio president's knowledge or approval. The idea originated with director George Loane Tucker, who would later direct *The Miracle Man* (1919), the film which made Lon Chaney a star. Yet, Tucker died in 1921 at the height of his career and without ever seeing *Traffic in Souls* in a theater. (Immediately following the production's completion, Tucker left to direct films in England.) The director discussed the scheme with editor Jack Cohn (who was later to be one of the founders of Columbia), and the two shot the film in four weeks while the studio manager was out of the country, borrowing the money for the production from their friends and using whatever film stock they could acquire. It is a fanciful story, though, and one that is a little hard to believe. Surely, Carl Laemmle would have realized the commercial value of such a subject, and surely someone at the studio would have wondered what so many actors—and there are a considerable number of players in *Traffic in Souls*—were being paid for.

The production is not a particularly impressive one. It is poorly constructed, trying unsuccessfully to develop different themes simultaneously, and is difficult to follow at times. What praise it deserves is due to its obviously unintentional documentary approach to the subject. There are a number of pleasing scenes on New York and New Jersey streets, and the acting is fairly restrained for such an early film. The two leading ladies, Jane Gail and Ethel Grandin, are particularly delightful, and, on the whole, avoid the melodramatics which might very well have been considered necessary in view of the lurid nature of the plot.

Gail and Grandin play sisters, Mary and Lorna Barton, respectively, who both work at a candy store. Mary's sweetheart is a policeman, Officer 4434 (Matt Moore), who is attached to what would be currently described as the vice squad. He sees two poor immigrant girls (from Sweden) being lured into a house, becomes suspicious, and checks out the situation. After fighting off a few thugs, he is able to secure the girls' release and have the gang arrested.

In the meantime, a well-dressed scoundrel, Bill Bradshaw (William Cavanaugh), has persuaded Lorna to have dinner with him. He takes her to a fashionable restaurant and then on to a dance hall. While Lorna is dancing with one of his accomplices, the villain puts a sleeping potion in her lemonade, and, when she begins to feel drowsy, he has her whisked away in the taxi of another accomplice to the headquarters of the white slavers. She is imprisoned and threatened with a beating by a buxom "madame" who runs the establishment.

The scene now changes to the office of a wealthy social reformer, William Trubus (William Welsh), who is secretly the head of the white slave ring. Using a dictaphone device in his office, Trubus is able to control the white slave operations taking place in the office below. One day, however, Mrs. Trubus (Mrs. Hudson Lyston) visits her husband's legitimate office, discharges the switchboard operator, and gets the job for Mary, whom she had met at the candy store. Alone in the office one day, Mary picks up the dictaphone and realizes what is happening. She traces the wire from the dictaphone through the window, down the fire escape, and to the office below. Mary, who is distraught over the disappearance of her sister, tells Officer 4434 of her suspicions. He arranges for her to record Trubus' conversations over the dictaphone, using a device invented by the two girls' father, Isaac (Fred Turner), "for intensifying sound waves and recording dictagraph sounds on a phonograph record." The use of this pre-Watergate bugging device is amusing and gives the film additional contemporary interest.

Trubus is arrested while giving a party to announce his daughter's engagement to a wealthy young socialite, who is described as "the catch of the season." The shock of Trubus' arrest forces cancellation of his daughter's engagement, and the trauma also kills his wife. In the final scenes, Trubus and the rest of the gang are seen behind bars.

There can be little question that *Traffic in Souls* is basically a bad film, entertaining and reasonably well made for the period, but nevertheless trash. To attempt to claim it as art is tantamount to maintaining that today's cycle of horror exploitation films are works of art. Yet, on its initial release, *Traffic in Souls* stirred a storm of controversy concerning censorship and the ethics of filmmaking.

Only the critic for *Variety* (November 28, 1913) seemed to have a clear sense of the production and its impact. He wrote,

> Professedly based on data gathered by the Rockefeller white slave researches, there's a laugh on the Rockefeller investigators in the play in the personality of one of the white slavers, a physical counterpart of John D., himself so striking as to make the observer sit up and wonder whether the granger of Pocantico Hills really came down to pose for the Universal. . . . Offered frankly as a melodrama, the production fairly meets the expectations its title arouses. It shows in moving picture reproduction approximations of what newspapers print from day to day of the barter of women.

Motography (November 15, 1913) was forced to editorialize at great length on the question of censorship of such subjects as *Traffic in Souls*, noting,

> Censorship is primarily intended for the good of the children. It is a recognized principle that adults choose their own paths of morality. If they did not, all the police power of a civilization could not hold them to the way of rectitude.

"It is with no light heart that a reviewer of motion pictures with an ordinary sense of responsibility can approach this production," opined George Blaisdell in *The Moving Picture World* (November 22, 1913).

> Its theme is indicated in the title. It is a big subject—one that has been given grave consideration by many thoughtful men and women. . . . The picture is bound to arouse bitter antagonism. Surely its friends, and among these are the members of the National Board of Censorship, are entitled to ask that the production be seen before it is condemned.

It is truly amazing that a film such as *Traffic in Souls* could arouse such rhetoric, but it obviously appeared at precisely the right moment in film history. Less amazing is that the film should have created immediate imitators, the most lurid of which was undoubtedly *The Inside of the White Slave Traffic*, which appeared on the scene a month after the premiere of *Traffic in Souls*; what the latter had only suggested, the former revealed. Motion-picture makers were quick to learn what the public wanted and then give it to them.

Anthony Slide

TRAMP, TRAMP, TRAMP

Released: 1926
Production: Harry Langdon Corporation; released by Associated First National
Direction: Harry Edwards
Screenplay: Frank Capra, Tim Whelan, Hal Conklin, J. Frank Holliday, Gerald Duffy, and Murray Roth
Cinematography: Elgin Lessley
Length: 6 reels/5,831 feet

Principal characters:
Harry Logan	Harry Langdon
Betty Burton	Joan Crawford
Nick Kargas	Tom Murray
Amos Logan	Alec B. Francis
John Burton	Edwards Davis

Harry Langdon came to the motion-picture industry late in 1923, at the age of thirty-nine, following a lengthy but unremarkable career in various areas of show business, most recent the vaudeville stage. Langdon's first films were rather ordinary two-reel comedies; his potential was not fully tapped until his employer, Mack Sennett, put him under the charge of director Harry Edwards and writers Frank Capra and Arthur Ripley. This creative team was largely responsible for the development of Langdon's unique child-adult screen character, and under their guidance, his extraordinary talent for pantomime was fully utilized. Within a few years, he had become one of the most popular film comedians of his time. When Langdon left Sennett to produce his own feature films for Associated First National, he took the trio along.

After the first of the three films for which Langdon was orginally contracted, *Tramp, Tramp, Tramp* (1926), Edwards left the team, so Capra assumed the directorial reins for *The Strong Man* (1926) and *Long Pants* (1927). These three features, generally regarded as Langdon's best work, represented the peak of his critical and popular acclaim, and Associated First National exercised their contractual option for three additional films. Capra and Langdon had a falling out, however, and Langdon himself took over the direction of his subsequent productions. His next three features—*Three's a Crowd* (1927), *The Chaser* (1928), and *Heart Trouble* (1928)—were box-office and critical failures, and his contract was not renewed. This sudden career downturn coincided with the end of the silent era, and Langdon never regained his former stature. He continued to appear in films, however, as the star of inferior two-reel comedies and in occasional supporting roles in features, until his death in 1944.

Many elements of Langdon's career were not uncommon among silent-film comedians—the vaudeville or music-hall background, the extensive work in short films, and the difficult transition to talking pictures—but in the sum of its parts, his career, like his comedy, was unique. While the other great silent-film clowns—Charles Chaplin, Buster Keaton, Harold Lloyd—enjoyed a decade or more of success, barely four years elapsed between the release of Langdon's first film for Sennett (1924) and his last feature for Associated First National (1928). During that brief period, he rose to a critical and popular position that rivaled that of Chaplin, only to plunge even more rapidly back to the obscurity from which he had emerged.

This simple outline tends to mask the unresolved critical and historical issues which remain suspended from the parabola of Langdon's career. The critical orthodoxy on Langdon stems largely from the interpretation offered by James Agee (who quotes Capra uncritically on the subject) in his famous 1949 *Life* magazine essay, "Comedy's Greatest Era." This view, later reinforced by the respective autobiographies of Capra and Sennett, holds that Langdon never fully understood the nature of the character created for him by others, and he let success go to his head, ultimately ruining his own career through a combination of arrogance and ineptitude. There is undoubtedly more than a little truth in this commonly accepted story, yet it seems an inadequate explanation for such an abrupt downturn in both critical and popular favor—especially in the light of recent reevaluation of *Three's a Crowd* and *The Chaser*, neither of which is nearly as poor as has long been assumed. (Unfortunately, *Heart Trouble* is apparently no longer extant.)

The influence of Agee's essay, one of the indispensable pieces of writing on silent-film comedy central to the rescuing of Langdon from the critical disfavor into which he had fallen, cannot be overestimated. Although Agee's Capra-influenced opinions of the comedian's rise and fall may be suspect, his eloquent descriptions of Langdon as "an elderly baby" and "a baby dope fiend" cannot be bettered, nor can his succinct observation that Langdon "could do more with less than any other comedian." Most critics and historians at least pay lip service to Langdon as a significant talent, but Agee went so far as to rank him with Chaplin, Keaton, and Lloyd. The common perception of Langdon as a performer rather than a creator, however, has mitigated against his full-fledged admission to this critical pantheon.

Much of the continuing debate on Langdon's ultimate importance focuses on the relative contributions of Capra, Edwards, and Arthur Ripley to the patterns of Langdon's career, especially concerning the development and maintenance of his screen *persona*, and on the question of whether Langdon himself "understood" it. Because of Capra's later prominence and Agee's promulgation of his opinions, most discussions of Langdon are filtered through Capra's point of view, exacerbating an already thorny problem. In his autobiography, Capra immodestly claims the lion's share of the credit for Langdon's success, but his factual imprecision raises some lingering doubts. The coincidence of Capra's departure and Langdon's subsequent decline has generally been seized upon as "proof" of Langdon's dependence on Capra, although it is more akin to circumstantial evidence. The commercial failure of the post-Capra films is a matter of record, but *Three's a Crowd* and *The Chaser* refute the assertion that Langdon had no understanding of his character and was a "bad" director. At this point, the contradictions may be too firmly entrenched to be dispelled, although a detailed study of Langdon's work (most of which still exists) would be a helpful tool.

A major focal point of such a study would be the passage from *Tramp, Tramp, Tramp* to *The Strong Man*, both of which have their advocates as Langdon's "best" film. Although such preferences—particularly when it comes to comedy—are largely matters of personal taste, the differences between the two films are indicative of the relative contributions of Capra and Edwards to Langdon's films. By the time of the later Sennett shorts, Capra states that he had become "very close" (collaboratively speaking) to Edwards, and on *Tramp, Tramp, Tramp*, he claims to have functioned as "co-everything"—co-producer, co-director, co-writer. Whatever the literal truth of this claim, *Tramp, Tramp, Tramp* nevertheless seems more closely allied visually with the earlier, Edwards-directed films than with *The Strong Man*; thematically, both features contain "Capraesque" elements, which are (not surprisingly) given much greater emphasis in the latter film. While one might argue the superiority of some of the individual gag sequences in *The Strong Man*, its structure is overly episodic; *Tramp, Tramp, Tramp* is more carefully constructed and seems more fully articulated as a feature film.

Generally speaking, a self-effacing director with a restrained, consistent style would seem best equipped to serve Langdon's peculiar brand of deliberate, reactive comedy; judging from the comparative evidence of these two films, Edwards filled that bill better than Capra. *The Strong Man* is the work of a novice director attempting to assert his identity; while the film's direction may be more "stylish" (and one cannot deny that Capra had a natural cinematic talent), it is also flashy, uneven, and occasionally misjudged in terms of comic effectiveness. In all discussions of Langdon's creative team, Ripley—who remained with Langdon through his final Associated First National film—is a somewhat shadowy figure. Capra describes him as "a talker" and generally portrays his contributions as limited to matters of overall dramatic construction.

In any case, *Tramp, Tramp, Tramp* marked an important milestone in Langdon's career, not only as his first feature film but also as the final work of the complete collaborative team of Edwards, Capra, and Ripley. In the course of a very well-paced six reels, it demonstrates an effortless control of the Langdon character and incorporates virtually all the basic principles of his comedy. A brief outline of the film's plot can serve as the basis for examining these principles through a detailed look at several of the film's best sequences.

Tramp, Tramp, Tramp is structured around a coast-to-coast walking race, from Massachusetts to California, sponsored as a publicity stunt by the giant Burton Shoe Company. Harry Logan (Harry Langdon) enters the race, determined to win the twenty-five thousand-dollar prize money so that his crippled father, Amos Logan (Alec B. Francis), can save his small shoemaking business from failure. Harry has another goal—to win the love of Betty Burton (Joan Crawford), the daughter of shoe magnate John Burton (Edwards Davis), with whom he has become infatuated as the result of seeing her picture on the company's ubiquitous billboards. Harry's chief opponent in the race is the Argentine champion, Nick Kargas (Tom Murray); Kargas also happens to be the landlord of the Logan shoemaking business and is threatening to foreclose.

During the race, Harry must cope with a constant stream of obstacles and delays, including a term of imprisonment on a chain gang. Finally nearing the finish line, Harry and Kargas, the last remaining walkers, are delayed in a desert town by a cyclone, which wreaks havoc until Harry chases it away by throwing bricks at it. The race is then completed, with Harry defeating Kargas in a final sprint. He gets the girl, and a brief coda to the film presents their offspring—a baby Harry (also played by Langdon).

Whatever the differences between such diverse comic types as Chaplin, Keaton, Lloyd, and Roscoe "Fatty" Arbuckle, their bodies were all solid and amazingly agile. Langdon's body, on the other hand, was as substantial as a bowl of jelly and as athletic as a pillow. This has led some critics to dismiss his body as "insignificant," which indicates a complete lack of appreciation for his bodily movements as an organic extension of his mental processes, which are in turn at the heart of his comedy. Harry's utter inability to cope with a decisionmaking situation, for instance, manifests itself in the hesitant, back-and-forth skittering which is one of his comic trademarks. Near the beginning of *Tramp, Tramp, Tramp*, following his confident declaration that he will get the money to save his father's business "in three months if it takes a year," Harry steps outside to begin his quest and is immediately struck by indecision. He takes a step, hesitates, starts in the opposite direction, has a thought, turns again, and so forth, waffling back and forth until he comes to a dead stop, totally bewildered. His course of action is ultimately determined not by himself but by Nick Kargas, standing nearby, who engages Harry to carry his bags—which in turn leads to Harry's entry in the walking race.

The manner in which Harry is thus provided with the means to save his father's business and win his girl illustrates the basic rule of Langdon's comedy. This rule was articulated by Capra as "the principle of the brick" and is essentially the idea that Harry's life is in the hands of a benevolent force that is completely beyond his comprehension. "Langdon might be saved by the brick falling on the cop," as Capra wrote, "but it was *verboten* that he in any way motivate the brick's fall." This principle receives a more extended expression in the lengthy sequence of Harry's escape from the chain gang, where he has landed as the result of an inept attempt at pilfering a chicken and a watermelon (both of which he tries to conceal beneath his bulging sweater).

In this sequence, Harry first demonstrates his inimitable approach to problem solving: unable to wield a full-sized sledge hammer, he selects a tiny hammer and sets off to begin work—a typical Langdon "reduction" gag. A guard insists that he use a bigger hammer, but when he tries, the head drops off; as he and the guard rummage through the pile of tools looking for a better hammer, Harry somehow manages to come up with the guard's rifle. He is, of course, oblivious to the advantage to be gained, and when the guard panics, so does Harry, and he tosses the gun away. As it strikes the ground, it discharges, and another guard runs up as the first guard recovers his weapon, thus negating Harry's own initiative to escape. Another plot is being hatched, however; as Harry sits contentedly breaking up little rocks with his little hammer—having exasperated the guard in his attempts to change his mind—he is surreptitiously handed a pistol by another convict. Harry, completely failing to grasp the implications, considers it as simply an alternative tool. Weighing the gun against the hammer, Harry tosses the hammer away and continues his work using the handle of the gun. When he gets a little more ambitious and tries to crack a bigger rock, the gun goes off; Harry is startled and totally bewildered, but the other convicts take advantage of the resulting confusion to overpower the guards. They all manage to free themselves from their ball-and-chain encumbrances, but Harry lacks similar wherewithal and can only gather his ball up in his arms and dash after them as they make a break for a passing train. He succeeds in throwing the ball up into a gondola car, but is unable to get aboard the car himself and is forced to run behind the train for forty miles.

When the train finally comes to a halt, his shoes are completely worn through. As he sits and soothes his feet in a puddle of water, he fails to notice that his chain, lying across the tracks, is severed when the train pulls away. He spots Kargas on the road and, thinking he is still bound to the ball, picks it up and charges after him. Harry tries excitedly to explain what has happened to him and does not notice when Kargas takes the ball away from him. At the moment that Harry turns his head away, Kargas flings the ball down the hill next to the road—but the loose end of the chain has caught in his legging, and he is dragged down the hillside by the ball. Harry, still intent on his story, turns his head back to discover to his astonishment that Kargas has vanished. Then he notices that his ball has disappeared as well, shrugs, smiles, and continues jauntily down the road—neither caring about nor knowing what, exactly, has happened. He has been freed from the chain gang, from the ball and chain, and from his chief competitor (temporarily), entirely by provident accident—a perfect illustration of the "principle of the brick." Surely, as Capra stated, "his only ally was God."

The "brick" principle is violated, however, in the climactic moments of *Tramp, Tramp, Tramp*. In this sequence, Harry routs the cyclone, ironically, with bricks. Certainly it is an amusing idea for Harry to believe that he can shoo the twister away (and a typical Langdon "boomerang" gag when the first brick is hurled back at him), but for him actually to accomplish this feat strains credibility. Harry's victory over Kargas in the final sprint of the race is equally unlikely—the notion that Harry's cream-puff body could best anything in a contest of speed is ludicrous. Perhaps in recognition of this fact, the staging of the race's finish is anticlimactic, almost a throwaway. Harry's dual triumphs in *Tramp, Tramp, Tramp* are his most aggressive actions in the film; they do not play particularly well because they run counter to the essentially passive nature of his character. It should be noted, however, that the climax of *The Strong Man*—directed by Capra, who articulated the principle and claims primary credit for its conception—violates this rule also, as Harry single-handedly brings order to a saloon full of rowdies (a very "Capraesque" finale). In general, the mantle of heroism does not sit well on Harry; in both films it seems as though his writers were acknowledging the limits of his character. Langdon's talents were considerable, but he was hardly an ideal figure around which to build a feature-film narrative.

Harry's childlike character usually seemed slightly ridiculous in the stock comedy roles required in his short films for Sennett—henpecked husband, nervous bridegroom, man-about-town, World War I soldier, in fact any sort of "adult" role. This did not necessarily work against his comedy—since his contrast with an otherwise-sophisticated world was one of its tenets—but once free of Sennett's dictates, his writers (six are credited on *Tramp, Tramp, Tramp*) evidently decided that Harry should be, as nearly as possible, an actual child. *Tramp, Tramp, Tramp* in fact contains the most literal manifestation of Langdon's childishness in any of his films: the absolutely delightful final scene, with Harry in a crib playing his own infant son, who exhibits the entire catalog of Langdon gestures, expressions, and reactions.

In his first scene, Harry reacts to his father's financial plight by plaintively wondering if he will still get his new bicycle. This is an unnecessary overstatement, but it serves the important purpose of establishing Harry as a character with no knowledge of the realities of the adult world. This points to another key aspect of Langdon's comedy—the manner in which he assimilates new information (in fact, all information seems to be new to Harry).

One critic aptly described his rate of comprehension as "glacial"; new data are absorbed slowly, one bit at a time, and Harry's subsequent (delayed) course of action is usually predicated on his raw emotional response. When confronted with a situation requiring reason rather than reflex, Harry seems to go on "hold." His initial reaction is minimal—merely an uncomprehending, wide-eyed stare. He blinks; the stare continues; he blinks again. The tortuous path from observation to comprehension, as his tiny mind struggles to assess the situation, is fully visible on his face and in his eyes, and is externalized via his limited yet highly expressive catalog of tentative, agonizingly hesitant gestures. Harry is capable of logical thought, on a rudimentary level, but it takes a very long time and his conclusions are usually wrong. His response, once formulated, is usually (and often inappropriately) friendly. He flashes an infantile grin, accompanied by one or the other (or both) of his two basic gestures of greeting—one a spasmodic upward flip of his arm, hand splayed palm-up (a silly-looking action which seems to send a jolt through his whole body, threatening to upset him), the other a hesitantly offered handshake, seldom accepted by its intended recipient.

Perhaps the best example in any Langdon film of the peculiar manner in which he externalizes his incomprehension is the famous scene in *Tramp, Tramp, Tramp* in which he comes face to face with the girl whom he adores, even though he has known only her image of the Burton Shoes billboard. Joan Crawford as Betty stands in the left foreground of the shot, back to camera (a position reportedly necessitated by her inability to keep from laughing at Langdon's antics, although it seems aesthetically a perfect choice), with the billboard itself in the right background. Harry, sitting on a bench between them, turns away from his adulation of the image to discover the girl in the flesh. He leaps up from the bench, then his knees begin to buckle; he starts to greet her, hesitates, then looks back and forth from the billboard to the girl. He finally starts to tip his hat, and immediately—as though frightened by his own boldness—starts to run away; he goes a few feet, stops, comes back, sits again on the bench, stands up, looks again at the billboard, finally musters the courage to greet her, then retreats behind the bench in embarrassment. He recovers himself for a moment, feigning nonchalance by leaning casually on the bench, but then scoots farther away and sits on a more distant bench. He is soon up again, dashing back toward the girl (and running into the bench on the way). Once he arrives in her vicinity, he proceeds to look her over closely and curiously. Finally, convinced she is real, he is very happy, but he still does not know what to do and sits stunned on the bench. When she sits next to him, he leaps up instantly and begins another retreat; she coaxes him back, but he sits nervously on the far end of the bench. At this point, the scene finally proceeds with its narrative function—she has come to give him the materials to enter the walking race.

There is very little cutting in this sequence, and the camera remains in one spot throughout its major portion. This device clearly illustrates one of the visual principles of the Langdon style—the necessity of the long take. There are moments when the camera must simply watch, patiently, while Harry does what he does at his own pace. There is one other excellent example in *Tramp, Tramp, Tramp*—the scene in which Harry is unable to sleep the night before the big race. Kargas, with whom Harry is sharing a hotel room, gives him a handful of sleeping tablets and a healthy shot of whiskey with which to swallow them. Harry accepts these unquestioningly, and in a medium close-up which lasts nearly two minutes, he hilariously struggles with the alternate realities of being both drunk and drugged. This shot, interrupted only by a brief cutaway to a pitcher of water, ends as Harry starts across the room to get a drink. He never makes it; his walk becomes a stagger, and he slowly curls up into a huddled ball on the floor, where he remains fast asleep until race time the following day. Interestingly, such judicious use of the extended take is not only evident in the Edwards-directed *Tramp, Tramp, Tramp* but also in the features directed by Langdon himself, although in the latter case this method may be due more to Langdon's own lack of filmmaking ability.

The manner in which Langdon could take familiar material and infuse it with his own peculiar comic style can be seen in the film's most spectacular gag. As Harry clambers over a fence marked "KEEP OUT" to escape a herd of sheep (only Harry would be frightened by sheep), the camera switches to a reverse-angle, extreme long shot to reveal that the fence is situated at the edge of a straight drop of hundreds of feet. Harry, however, gets his belt caught on a nail in the fence, and, struggling to release himself, he tosses a casual glance over his shoulder, but totally fails to recognize the danger, so preoccupied is he with freeing himself from the nail. He glances again, goes back to his task, and very nearly succeeds in freeing himself before the realization of his predicament arrives at his brain. At that point he panics.

As Agee points out, the "double-take" was standard in the repertoire of most silent comedians, but Langdon's variation would be described as a "triple-take" because Harry always needs an extra look. Until this point, the sequence (aside from Harry's manner of realization) is not markedly different from the way it might have been done by, say, Harold Lloyd. What follows, however, is uniquely Langdon. Most comedians would take the logical step of climbing back over the fence, but not Harry. So intently focused has he been on unhooking himself from the nail, he can now think only of securing himself to it again. He rebuckles his belt and wraps his sweater over the nail, desperately trying to keep himself in one place—a reflex action rather than a logical response. Harry even attempts to reinforce this tenuous hold by extracting more nails from the corner of the fence and hammering them through his sweater, which soon loosens the entire fence, and it becomes a sort of toboggan on which he slides safely down the hill. The film cheats somewhat at this point, since what was formerly a steep drop now appears to be a relatively gentle incline. At the bottom, the fence blocks the road, and the other walkers, rounding a bend on the opposite side from Harry, see the "KEEP OUT" sign and take a detour; Harry, oblivious to their presence, picks himself up and continues the race. The conclusion of this sequence is the "brick" principle at its most sublime.

A type of innocence which is completely alien to modern audiences was central to Langdon's comedy, yet it is not only the passage of time but also the increased sophistication of film audiences that makes contemporary appreciation of Langdon difficult. Langdon was unique, and therein lies much of the problem. His style, at its purest, runs counter to most people's expectations of silent-film "slapstick." He does not take charge of the screen as did most comedians; he lacks Chaplin's cunning, Keaton's ingenuity, Lloyd's ambition, and the physical abilities of all three. Even in the wake of increased critical attention in recent years, Langdon remains a shadowy figure among silent-film comedians, because his work is rarely shown. Like Chaplin, Keaton and Lloyd, Langdon established and refined his basic character and style in short films. Unlike them, however, his feature-film output was relatively small. Six feature-length silents may at first glance seem like a substantial body of work (compared, for instance, to Chaplin's five), but the physical and critical attrition noted above has reduced the number of "worthwhile" Langdon features to three—*Tramp, Tramp, Tramp*, *The Strong Man*, and *Long Pants*— hardly the stuff of which festivals are made.

Langdon has also been affected by a certain retrospective bias favoring feature films over short subjects, which has also harmed the critical reputations of Arbuckle and Charley Chase, to name only two. Furthermore, the vagaries of silent-film print quality and presentation tend to transform Langdon's greatest strength—his pantomimic skill—into a disadvantage. The effectiveness of any film—comedy or drama, silent or sound—is dulled considerably by an inferior print, but Langdon's art was so delicate that its effect is virtually nullified by anything less than the ideal conditions of a clear and sharp 35mm print, projected at the proper speed, with appropriate musical accompaniment. Modern audiences, if robbed of the rhythm and nuance of Langdon's comedy, can hardly be blamed for losing patience with this unhealthy looking little man, or for failing to appreciate what they literally cannot see. The sad truth is that, one way or another, Langdon remains largely unseen.

Howard H. Prouty

TRUE HEART SUSIE

Released: 1919
Production: Paramount/Artcraft Films
Direction: D. W. Griffith
Screenplay: Marian Fremont
Cinematography: G. W. Bitzer
Editing: James Smith
Length: 6 reels/5,542 feet

Principal characters:
Susie May Trueheart ....Lillian Gish
William Jenkins .... Robert Harron
Bettina Hopkins .... Clarine Seymour
Susie's aunt ....Loyola O'Connor
Sporty Malone ....Robert Cannon
Bettina's girl friend .... Carol Dempster
Bettina's aunt .... Kate Bruce

Cinemagoers tend to remember D. W. Griffith's spectacles, such as *The Birth of a Nation* (1915), *Intolerance* (1916), *Hearts of the World* (1918), *Orphans of the Storm* (1922), and *America* (1924) and forget how marvelously he could handle intimate stories with low production costs. *Broken Blossoms* (1919) is a prime example of Griffith's genius with a small cast and simple settings, and so is *True Heart Susie*.

The story unfolds in a small Indiana village. Susie May Trueheart (Lillian Gish) lives with her maiden aunt (Loyola O'Connor) in the little house left to Susie by her mother. Susie, at sixteen, is untrained in the art of flirtation, but she loves the neighbor boy, William Jenkins (Robert Harron). At school, she competes in a spelling bee with William, and it almost breaks her heart when William misspells "anonymous," and she then spells it correctly. After school, they walk home together and stop by a tree where she tells him that she is sorry he failed in the spelling contest. He is too shy to kiss her, but he carves their names in the oak tree's trunk.

William wants to go to college and become a preacher, but his father tells him that they do not have enough money. One day, while Susie and William are walking through the village, a stranger makes their acquaintance and boastfully tells of how many great men he has started off in life. When William tells of his desire to go to college, the stranger takes William's name and assures the boy that he will see to it. When the man leaves, they are ecstatic and sure William will be going to college. Months pass, however, and there is no letter from the stranger. William grows used to the idea of being simply a farmer the rest of his life, but Susie is determined that William will go to college and then marry her.

Over the objections of her aunt, she sells her cow, Mary, and some other necessities. Then Susie goes to another town and anonymously mails the money to William, telling him to use it for college. William naturally assumes that it came from the stranger, and he goes to college, where he works part-time as a waiter. His letters home are few and far between, but Susie takes heart with little things like "So far I haven't met anybody I like better than the people at home." He finally returns as a minister, sporting a moustache. He and Susie walk in the woods as he practices his first sermon for her, a wild fire-and-brimstone speech. Shortly after they see two girls at the village store, William tells her, "You see those two painted and powdered girls. Men flirt with that sort, but they marry the plain kind," and later, Susie writes in her diary that they will eventually marry.

At the party for the departing minister, whose place William is taking, William meets a young flapper type, Bettina Hopkins (Clarine Seymour), who has come to the village to visit her aunt (Kate Bruce). Susie's aunt tells her to separate them, but Susie recalls William's remark at the store and replies, "He doesn't like that type." She is not so sure, however, when he escorts the new girl to her aunt's home.

Bettina is a milliner, but does not care for the work, so she sets out to win William as a husband. One day, Susie is walking along, hears the familiar voice of William, and stops behind a bush to listen to him and Bettina. Bettina is throwing herself at William, and it breaks Susie's heart. Soon William announces to his congregation that he will marry Bettina, and Susie finds herself helping the bride dress before the ceremony.

After the wedding, William finds that Bettina cannot cook, nor is her hair naturally curly, nor her cheeks rosy. When he complains about her housework, she explodes by saying she hates the place. Susie sees their domestic unhappiness and feels sorry for William's sake. He, too, realizes that he has made a mistake after having dinner at her house one night.

One day, some of Bettina's friends from before her marriage come to visit her. Sporty Malone (Robert Cannon) has an open car, with his name painted on the door and is accompanied by two flapper types. Soon they have the record player on and are dancing cheek to cheek. William walks in and finds his wife in Sporty's arms and he is furious, but Bettina finally convinces William that nothing is wrong.

A few days later, Sporty convinces Bettina to come to a party. She sneaks from the house that night and has a wild time. On the way home, however, a sudden rainstorm soaks them. Bettina then finds that she has lost her key and is locked out of the house. Her only hope is Susie, so she goes to her and begs her to lie to William and say that she spent the whole night at Susie's house. Susie reluctantly agrees and then has the torture of having Bettina sleep in her bed next to her.

William believes Bettina's story, with Susie's help; but Bettina's soaking leads to pneumonia, and she dies. William vows never to marry again, so Susie's aunt goes to him and tells him that Susie supplied his college money. Then one of Bettina's girl friends (Carol Dempster) tells him about the wild party. The last scene shows William coming to Susie's house, where she stands in an open window, waiting for him.

Even if *True Heart Susie* was not a masterpiece, it would be notable for the presence of three of Griffith's most famous leading ladies: Lillian Gish, Clarine Seymour and Carol Dempster. Gish will always be identified as Griffith's greatest star; her successes were his successes: *The Birth of a Nation, Hearts of the World, Broken Blossoms, Way Down East* (1920), and *Orphans of the Storm*.

Seymour was just rising to full stardom at the time *True Heart Susie* was made. She co-starred with Dempster in Griffith's *The Girl Who Stayed at Home* (1919) and *Scarlet Days* (1919), one made shortly before and the other immediately after *True Heart Susie*. Her first starring role was in *The Idol Dancer* (1920), a South Seas drama which is hardly one of Griffith's better pictures. Seymour's performance, however, was singled out by the critics and public alike for praise, and she found herself one of the hottest new stars in film. Griffith then cast her in the role of Kate Brewster, the neighbor girl betrothed to the character played by Richard Barthelmess in *Way Down East*. The climax of the film was shot in a snowstorm and Seymour caught pneumonia and died only days afterward. Mary Hay took over the role of Kate Brewster and married Richard Barthelmess shortly thereafter. It is ironic that Seymour died of exposure to the cold in *True Heart Susie* and died less than one year later in reality of the same.

Dempster appeared as one of Bettina's "fast" friends in *True Heart Susie*. She quickly rose to starring status for Griffith with *The Love Flower* in 1920. She is as closely identified with Griffith's decline as Gish is with his rise. Dempster appeared in *Dream Street* (1921), *One Exciting Night* (1922), *Sally of the Sawdust* (1925), and *That Royale Girl* (1925), all films that lowered Griffith's prestige. To her credit, however, she also appeared in *America, Isn't Life Wonderful* (1924), and *The Sorrows of Satan* (1927).

Robert Harron was probably Griffith's most tragic star. Like Gish, he is identified almost totally as a Griffith player. He was a prop and errand boy at Biograph before Griffith arrived in 1908 and had even appeared in a few child roles. Born in 1896, he literally grew up with Griffith at Biograph. His first success was as "Weak Hands," the inventor of the stone axe in *Man's Genesis* (1912). That film also teamed him with Mae Marsh for the first time; they would later become a team which was very popular with the public in such films as *Hoodoo Ann* (1916), *Intolerance, Sunshine Alley* (1917), and *Home Sweet Home* (1926). In *Intolerance*, he gave one of the cinema's greatest performances as the boy who stands with a noose about his neck as his wife races to the prison with the governor's pardon. He played a World War I soldier in *Hearts of the World*, the first of six films he would make with Gish for Griffith. All were masterpieces. They are *The Great Love* (1918), *The Greatest Thing in Life* (1918), *A Romance of Happy Valley* (1918), *True Heart Susie*, and *The Greatest Question* (1919). *A Romance of Happy Valley* is very similar to *True Heart Susie*. He plays a country boy loved by the Gish character who leaves her and goes to the city, vowing not to return until he is rich. He starves in New York for several years as he works to perfect a mechanical swimming frog, and at the end, he returns a success just in time to save his childhood love from becoming an old maid.

Griffith had a habit of casting aside his players just when they had reached stardom. It was an expensive habit for him and is possibly responsible for his failure in the 1920's. He let Marsh go to Goldwyn in 1917; Blanche Sweet to Cecil B. De Mille in 1915; Barthelmess to Inspiration/Associated First National in 1921; and Gish to Metro in 1922.

In 1920, Griffith helped Harron set up a production company which would release through Metro. Griffith had been using another young leading man who resembled Harron somewhat, Richard Barthelmess, but who was handsomer, and had a better physique (Harron weighed about 120 pounds). Barthelmess got the male lead in *Way Down East*, and did a superb job. Harron went to New York for the premiere of *Way Down East* and saw the fine work of his successor. He shot himself and died a few days later, with Gish and Griffith at his side. Griffith never used Barthelmess as a leading man again.

Larry Lee Holland

TUMBLEWEEDS

Released: 1925
Production: William S. Hart Company; released by United Artists
Direction: King Baggot
Screenplay: C. Gardner Sullivan; based on an original screen story by Hal G. Evarts
Cinematography: Joseph H. August
Length: 7 reels/7,254 feet

> *Principal characters:*
> Don Carver .... William S. Hart
> Molly Lassiter .... Barbara Bedford
> Kentucky Rose .... Lucien Littlefield
> Noll Lassiter .... Gordon Russell
> Bill Freel .... Richard R. Neill

William S. Hart was a stage actor in his forties when he entered the film business in 1914. In his autobiography, *My Life—East and West*, he states that his chief motivation for turning from stage to screen was the deplorably inaccurate and glamorized Western films that were being made at the time. He had some knowledge of the real West from his youth and hoped to make films that reflected his knowledge and love of the time and place known as the Old West.

Hart very quickly advanced from a few roles in short melodramas to featured roles in full-length films. Within a year, he was recognized by the public as a Western star, and for a time before his popularity faded, he was—in the opinion of many film historians—as famous as Charlie Chaplin or Mary Pickford. In addition, he directed or co-directed many films and virtually always had a major role in shaping the films in which he appeared. Since all of his films were made during the silent era, they are seldom seen today, but they have had a tremendous effect on the development of the Western film.

In 1925, Hart made what turned out to be his last film, *Tumbleweeds*. Ironically, the theme he chose was the end of the Old West, the story of the land rush in 1889 when the United States government opened to settlers twelve thousand square miles of prairie that had previously been used for the raising of cattle. The title refers to the old-time cowboys—like the tumbleweed, they did not establish firm roots or a settled way of life.

The film focuses on two "tumbleweeds," Don Carver (William S. Hart) and his companion, who is called Kentucky Rose (Lucien Littlefield), and the effect of the land rush upon them. It is developed in three parts. The first and longest part establishes the character of Carver and the changes that occur in the anticipation of the land rush. The second part is short but visually and emotionally powerful; it is the actual land rush. The third part brings about a happy ending for Carver.

At the beginning of the film, Carver is the range boss of the Box K ranch, "the most fertile spot in a fertile land." He sees a rattlesnake but does not kill it because he feels it has just as much right to be there as he himself does. Soon, however, word comes that this area of land, called the Cherokee Strip, will be opened to homesteaders, and the small town of Caldwell, Kansas, is introduced.

When a government order calls for the removal of the cattle from Cherokee Strip, large herds of cattle are seen being driven across the landscape as the men and animals from each ranch vacate the land. Carver looks over this scene, takes off his hat, and says, "Boys—it's the last of the West."

Now the action switches to the town of Caldwell, which is growing larger every day as more and more settlers arrive. Carver at first refuses to be caught up in the fever for land. He will not, he says, settle down until he is under a tombstone, but he soon falls under the influence of Molly Lassiter (Barbara Bedford). Although he is awkward and ill at ease around women, he plans to stake out the Box K ranch house for himself and Molly. "I'm getting real house broke," he remarks.

Interfering with Carver's plans, however, are two villains—Noll Lassiter (Gordon Russell), Molly's half-brother, and Bill Freel (Richard R. Neill). They conspire to have him arrested as a "sooner," a person who goes into the Cherokee Strip to claim land before the official opening of the territory. Then a title announces that "The Day" finally has come, that the signal will be given at high noon and the rush to establish land claims may begin. It is a well-edited and effective series of shots that conveys the excitement and anticipation of the people in Caldwell (as well as the frustration of Carver, who is in the stockade). The series is composed of more than two dozen separate shots, some of which last less than one second. Following the firing of a cannon to begin the land rush is the depiction of the scramble and dash of the settlers into the Strip. This sequence is no less artistic than the preceding one as it portrays the release of the action and excitement that was built up in the previous sequence. It combines long shots, which show the mass of settlers, with shorter and closer shots, which show details of the land rush. When Carver escapes from the stockade and mounts his horse, the most visually and emotionally thrilling element of the sequence begins. He gallops across the landscape outdistancing all the other settlers in a brilliantly photographed dash to reach the Box K ranch before anyone else. The whole land rush sequence is done so well that film historian Kevin Brownlow calls it "among the finest sequences of pure action in film history." Nineteen cameras were used, and in some shots the horses seem to run right over the camera.

Although Carver reaches the Box K ranch, he finds that Noll and Freel have beat him there. When he checks their horses, however, he finds that they are rested and the two villains have obviously violated the deadline.

Although he drives off the interlopers and stakes his claim, he finds when he gets back to town that Molly believes that he is a "sooner" and a thief. In disgust, he says, "Women ain't reliable—cows are," and plans to go to South America.

Before that can happen, he catches Noll and Freel red-handed terrorizing an old settler couple and ties them up and marches them off to the law. He is then reunited with Molly, and the film concludes with two telling shots. First, some actual tumbleweeds are blown by the wind and roll until they are stopped by a barbed wire fence. Then, Carver and Molly are standing in silhouette against a Western landscape, with Carver's horse off to the side.

Tumbleweeds was well received by both the public and the reviewers, but the studio, United Artists, deliberately mishandled the film's distribution, causing it to be less successful than it could have been. Hart proved in court the fault of United Artists and won a judgment of $278,000, but by then his film career was over. *Tumbleweeds* was re-released in 1939 with a spoken prologue by Hart in which he reveals his deep feelings for the art of making motion pictures, and his regret that his age and the injuries he had sustained during his career "preclude my again doing these things that I so gloried in doing."

Timothy W. Johnson

UNDER TWO FLAGS

Released: 1922
Production: Universal-Jewel
Direction: Tod Browning
Screenplay: Edward T. Lowe, Jr., and Elliott Clawson; based on Tod Browning's and Edward T. Lowe, Jr.'s adaptation of the novel of the same name by Ouida (Marie Louise de la Ramée)
Cinematography: William Fildew
Length: 8 reels/7,407 feet

Principal characters:

Cigarette	Priscilla Dean
Corporal Victor	James Kirkwood
Sheik Ben Ali Hammed	John Davidson
Marquis de Chateauroy	Stuart Holmes
Princess Corona	Ethel Grey Terry

The role of Cigarette, the darling of the French Legion, had become instantly popular when Blanche Bates first introduced it to theatergoers in 1901 in the play *Under Two Flags*. Cigarette first came to films in 1916 at Fox, when Theda Bara created the half French, half Arabian heroine for cinema audiences. Six years later, in 1922, Cigarette became popular with film audiences again when Priscilla Dean presented her as a lovable hoyden. Thus, in films, Cigarette went from vamp to tomboy, and when Twentieth Century-Fox subsequently presented her in a talking version in 1936, she was played by Claudette Colbert as a gamine. Colbert, however, did not have much time to prepare the part on loan-out, because Simone Simon, who had originally been cast as Cigarette, suddenly decided that she was not right for such an antiquated heroine and refused to play the part. They were lucky to get Colbert to fill in, but Simon was probably right. The soubrette was old-fashioned by the late 1930's, a leftover from French farce and musicals.

In 1922, however, when Dean played Cigarette, the girl was a lovable, gutsy heroine, and the time was right for such an interpretation. It quickly fitted into the scheme of the program calendar as set up by Universal on her behalf. Her performance was exemplary. Universal must have been in the middle of one of its routine financial crises, however, which was reflected in the set designs. It was only a paper moon that shone over the Sahara, and the walls of the mosque were like cut-outs in a Maxfield Parrish drawing. Economy waves always give a five-and-dime store appearance to what should be luxurious sets; it would have been better to move the action out into an oasis with real palm trees instead of making do with *papier-mâché*.

Cigarette became one of Dean's best roles. Originally playing bits and pieces for Biograph and Pathé, Dean got her first legitimate billing in 1913 at Edison Studios in *The Man Who Wouldn't Marry*. She played nearly fifty one-reel comedies, most of them as leading lady to Eddie Lyons and Lee Moran, and finally she graduated to leads in Universal Specials and a sixteen-chapter serial, *The Gray Ghost*, in 1917. The next year she was playing leads in Bluebird features, always provocatively titled, such as *The Two-Soul Woman*, *The Brazen Beauty*, and *Wildcat of Paris* (all 1918).

Under Tod Browning's very capable direction, she played a series of crook heroines in such films as *The Wicked Darling* and *The Exquisite Thief* (both 1919). As the lead in a series of Universal-Jewel specials, which Browning also directed, such as *The Virgin of Stamboul* (1920), *Outside the Law* (1921, with Lon Chaney), *Under Two Flags* (1922), *Drifting* (1923), and *White Tiger* (1923), Dean took her place as the foremost heroine of action thrillers at Universal. She was one of the best natural actresses ever signed by that studio, one who rose to stardom because her public demanded that she get starring roles. Her best feature was a dual role, mother and daughter, in a backstage mystery drama entitled *Reputation* (1921).

When she left Universal, Dean made another series of action thrillers for PDC/Metropolitan release. When talkies came, she starred in several for independent studios, but after becoming the wife of Leslie P. Arnold, one of the four "Around the World Flyers," she eventually retired permanently from films. Her husband, who was vice-president of Eastern Airlines, was promoted to a colonelcy, and he and his wife traveled by air everywhere in the world. He died in 1961, but she still lives in Leonia, New Jersey, where she is a driver for the Leonia Ambulance Corp. Time has not stopped this indefatigable woman.

Under Two Flags opens when an English nobleman (James Kirkwood) arrives in Algiers to join the French Foreign Legion. He is known only by the name Victor, and he does not reveal his true identity. He enrolls as a private, and he stays to himself, obviously preferring to be alone.

A gay-hearted, impulsive, French-Arabian girl named Cigarette (Priscilla Dean) is the mascot of the regiment. Victor immediately arouses her interest, but, he not only pays her no attention, he flatly ignores her. She is shocked, hurt, and then furious. Learning something of his past, she discovers that his great love had been the Princess Corona (Ethel Grey Terry), and she steals into Algeria with the intention of killing the Princess. She is able to talk to her, however, and the Princess draws her respect and admiration.

Cigarette also learns that the Sheik Ben Ali Hammed (John Davidson) is determined to destroy Victor as well as the city of Algiers. She goes to the military authorities with the evidence that she has gathered, thereby clearing Victor of the treason that the Sheik has falsely accused him of having committed. Unfortunately, knowledge of Victor's innocence cannot be gotten to the fort in time, for in Cigarette's absence, he has been convicted and will be executed at sundown. Mounting her horse and riding like the wind back to the fort, she is followed by the Sheik and his Arabs, who are, in turn, pursued by the French cavalry. It is a wild, stirring ride, and the lone girl, driven by a passion that she cannot deny, is determined to win.

Victor, condemned to die before the firing squad, is led to his execution, and Cigarette, nearing the fort, prays grimly that she will not be too late. As she gets to the fort, she sees the sun sinking below the horizon, and she enters the fort just in time to see the executing squad raise their guns and aim. She dismounts and rushes to Victor, as the order, "Fire!" is given, throwing herself in front of Victor and taking the bullets intended for him. The Sheik and his Arabs are caught and held by the cavalry. Victor holds Cigarette tenderly, and she dies with his kiss upon her lips.

Reviewers noted that *Under Two Flags* had all the dynamics, color, and romance of the star's previous big success, *The Virgin of Stamboul* plus an electric performance by Dean, climaxing with her wild and gallant ride to save her lover from a death that was determined wrongly to be his fate.

DeWitt Bodeen

UNDERWORLD

Released: 1927
Production: Hector Turnbull for Famous Players-Lasky/Paramount
Direction: Josef von Sternberg
Screenplay: Charles Furthman and Robert N. Lee; based on an original story
by Ben Hecht (AA)
Titles: George Marion, Jr.
Cinematography: Bert Glennon
Art direction: Hans Dreier
Length: 8 reels/7,453 feet

Principal characters:
"Bull" Weed .... George Bancroft
"Rolls Royce" .... Clive Brook
"Feathers" McCoy .... Evelyn Brent
"Slippy" Lewis .... Larry Semon
"Buck" Mulligan .... Fred Kohler
Mulligan's Girl .... Helen Lynch
Paloma .... Jerry Mandy
"High Collar" Sam .... Karl Morse

Little Caesar (1931), starring Edward G. Robinson as Cesare "Rico" Bandello; *The Public Enemy* (1931), with James Cagney as Tom Powers, the "Public Enemy"; and *Scarface* (1932), featuring Paul Muni as Scarface Tony Camonte were all classic prohibition-era melodramas, and all were regarded as revolutionary in their presentation of organized crime and the American gangster.

They, however, were not the first of their genre. This auspicious distinction belongs to *Underworld*, based on an original story by Ben Hecht, who later adapted *Scarface* for the screen. The film made a star of its principal player, George Bancroft, and was the initial popular success for its director, Josef von Sternberg—who did not work only with Marlene Dietrich, as is commonly believed.

Bancroft is "Bull" Weed, a Chicago hood who is king of the city's underworld. He is a thief and murderer, who is also temperamental, vicious, vain, and sarcastic. Yet, he has been romanticized by Sternberg in that he has a big heart and a sense of humor: in one scene, for example, he is shown feeding a starving kitten. This aspect of Weed's character separates him from the Scarfaces and Little Caesars, who are all thoroughly repugnant.

At the beginning of the film, Weed (George Bancroft) has just pulled off another bank heist. While escaping, he is observed by a gentle, sophisticated bum on a streetcorner, and the mobster takes an immediate liking to the fellow, an alcoholic former attorney (Clive Brook). Weed literally throws money at the man, nicknaming him "Rolls Royce" and adopting him as a gang member and confidant. Rolls is steadfast in his loyalty to Weed, his savior. He is entrusted with the keys to the gang's hideout and quickly becomes an integral member of Weed's criminal organization.

Weed has a moll, Feathers McCoy (Evelyn Brent), who is attracted to Rolls. Bull leaves them together while he goes to steal some jewels, and Rolls and Feathers fall in love, although they hide their feelings out of respect for their leader. Bull's underworld rival, "Buck" Mulligan (Fred Kohler), flirts with Feathers at a gangland party, a lavish sequence highlighted by balloting for the "Queen of the Ball" election. Bull is paranoically jealous; a smile at his girl is enough for him to fly into a rage, so he murders Buck by putting a bullet in him while in his flower shop. (The film was derived from Hecht's experiences while a newspaper reporter in Chicago. Buck's death is a re-creation of the actual murder of mobster Dion O'Bannion in 1922.)

Bull is arrested, however, found guilty of the crime, and sentenced to be hanged. Rolls and Feathers scheme to free Bull, but the police are prepared, and the plans fall through. Bull, though, thinks Rolls has stolen his girl, so he escapes on his own to get revenge. The film has a rousing climax: Bull is barricaded in his stronghold, determined to die fighting, and in a furious machine gun battle with the police, Rolls is fatally wounded. Bull now understands and acknowledges his friend's loyalty and surrenders quietly to the authorities.

Underworld is a tense, compact drama with a keen feeling for characterization and a strong sense of realism. The film put its director on the Hollywood map. Sternberg was the opinionated, egocentric, arrogant *enfant terrible* whose first feature was *The Salvation Hunters* (1925), a depiction of slum life in a large city that Charles Chaplin called "a masterpiece of human realism." He glutted *Underworld* with close-ups, dissolves, and unusual camera angles, all of which heighten the film's tension. For example, when Bull robs a jewelry store, the face of a clock is ripped apart by a bullet. The clerk backs off, and the baubles are grabbed, while a flower—symbolizing the innocent Buck Mulligan—is dropped to the floor.

The film is the highlight of the career of its star, George Bancroft, who is appropriately menacing yet lovable as Weed. In particular, his confrontation scenes with Buck, as played by Fred Kohler, a capable supporting performer as equally lost in the annals of Hollywood history, are memorable and gripping. The burly actor made his film debut in *The Journey's End* (1921) after a career in Broadway musicals and dramas. One of his best roles before *Underworld* was in James Cruze's *The Pony Express* (1925) as the heavy, Jack Slade, his first important role. In that film, he stole the picture from Wallace Beery, Betty Compson, Ernest Torrence, and Ricardo Cortez, all billed above him (Cortez, in fact, was originally scheduled to play Bull Weed). Another of his best roles was in *Old Ironsides* (1926) as the seaman Gunner, also directed by Cruze.

Bancroft received a Best Actor Academy Award nomination in 1928-1929 for his role as yet another gang boss in *Thunderbolt* (1929), also directed by Sternberg, but he lost to Warner Baxter's Cisco Kid in *In Old Arizona* (1929). He again starred for the director in *The Drag Net* (1928, also with Kohler and Evelyn Brent, who played another gangster's moll, "The Magpie") and *The Docks of New York* (1928). Bancroft was then earning between five thousand and six thousand dollars a week. Quickly, though, fame allegedly went to his head, his star faded, and he wound up a supporting performer. His best later films are *Angels with Dirty Faces* (1938), *Stagecoach* (1939), and *Each Dawn I Die* (1939). He retired from films in 1942.

Clive Brook and Brent lend solid support to Bancroft. The suave Brook appeared in films from the 1920's to the 1960's, most memorably in Sternberg's *Shanghai Express* (1932) and the Academy Award-winning *Cavalcade* (1933). Brent also did her best work for Sternberg and was in his *Last Command* (1928) in addition to *Underworld*. Her career ended in the 1940's with such exotically titled programmers as *Daughter of Shanghai* (1937), *Tip-Off Girls* (1938), and *The Mad Empress* (1940).

In addition to predating *Little Caesar*, *The Public Enemy*, and *Scarface*, *Underworld* is significant for many other firsts. It was Hecht's first story written for the screen, and he received the first-ever Best Original Story Academy Award for it at the 1927-1928 ceremony; he gladly accepted, even though he had been displeased with Sternberg's reworking and romanticizing his outline (the director later claimed to have written the film's scenario; the adaptation was credited to Charles Furthman, the screenplay to Robert N. Lee) and unsuccessfully requested that his name be removed from the credits. Paramount executives were allegedly wary of how the film would be received and opened it in New York cold, with no advance notice. Yet, it was an enormous box-office success, one of the biggest of the silent era: New York's Paramount Theater even had to schedule all-night showings because of the clamor for seats—still another first. The Temple Players, a Syracuse, New York, stock company, even presented a dramatic adaptation of the story, written by Walton Butterfield, a comedian with the troupe. This was among the first instances of a screen story produced later for the stage.

The reviews for *Underworld* were good, although some critics were shocked by the film's sympathetic depiction of criminals. *The New York Times* cited the film as one of the "Ten Best" features of 1927, and Jesse L. Lasky awarded Sternberg a ten-thousand-dollar bonus and a gold medal in appreciation of the film's success. It was also popular abroad, particularly in France, where it was released as *Les Nuits de Chicago*, and England, under the editorialized title of *Paying the Penalty*.

Rob Edelman

THE VANISHING AMERICAN

Released: 1925
Production: Famous Players-Lasky; released by Paramount
Direction: George B. Seitz
Screenplay: Ethel Doherty; based on Lucien Hubbard's adaptation of the novel of the same name by Zane Grey
Cinematography: C. Edgar Schoenbaum and Harry Perry
Length: 10 reels/9,916 feet

Principal characters:
Nophaie	Richard Dix
Marion Warner	Lois Wilson
Booker	Noah Beery
Earl Ramsdale	Malcolm McGregor
Amos Halliday	Charles Crockett
Indian Boy	Nocki
Gekin Yashi	Shannon Day

Throughout film history, the American Indian has been depicted mostly as a stock heavy, a savage who speaks in monosyllabic baby talk and murders, rapes, and scalps the white pioneers who innocently seek their manifest destiny. Yet, the Indian is the only true American native, and the idea that the settlers were, in fact, no more than imperialists has rarely been dealt with by Hollywood. A few notable exceptions are, *I Will Fight No More Forever* (1975), a made-for-television film about Chief Joseph of the Nez Percé (Chopunnish) tribe; *Little Big Man* (1970), with Dustin Hoffman as 121-year-old Jack Crabb, an adopted Indian and survivor of Custer's Last Stand; *Cheyenne Autumn* (1964), the saga of the tribe's government-forced march from Oklahoma to Wyoming, directed by John Ford; *Broken Arrow* (1950), with Jeff Chandler as Cochise, chief of the Apaches; *Massacre* (1933), with Richard Barthelmess as an Indian rodeo star fighting corrupt government officials; and *Redskin* (1929), with Richard Dix as a rebellious Navajo who discovers oil on his reservation and outwits crooked white agents from pilfering the mineral rights.

One of the earliest and best films in this regrettably small genre has the most appropriate title of all: *The Vanishing American*, which also stars Dix. The film is based on a novel by Zane Grey, who published eighty-nine books in his lifetime, fifty-six of which were set in the West. It opens with a quotation from Herbert Spencer's "First Principles" about the survival of the fittest, and a shot of majestic Monument Valley, where countless Westerns were filmed on location. A prologue follows, chronicling the history of the Navajo nation from the cliff dwellers of two thousand years past to the time in which the film is set, the second decade of the twentieth century.

Dix appears as Nophaie, the son of a chief, a strong, sympathetic, tragic Indian on a modern reservation. For fifty years, the United States government has been in control of the reservation, which is barren and desolate except for a single valley which services the tribe with water and food. Booker (Noah Beery), the crooked assistant of Indian agent Amos Halliday (Charles Crockett), purchases the Navajos' best horses for twenty-five dollars and sells them for one hundred dollars. Nophaie complains to the agent, who testily refers him to Booker. The Indian finds Booker at the schoolyard, forcing his attentions on Marion Warner (Lois Wilson), a white schoolteacher; and Nophaie almost beats him for his actions. Gekin Yashi (Shannon Day), a young Indian who secretly loves Nophaie, sees the Indian and teacher together and becomes jealous, but keeps her feelings to herself because she admires Marion.

The following day, Booker again visits the schoolhouse. Marion does not respond to his attention, so he tries to take her into his arms and steal a kiss. Nophaie happens to enter—he is returning some books—and fights Booker, who is joined by two of his cohorts who pass by and see the battle through a window. Nophaie overcomes all three and then runs off into the hills.

Several weeks later, Earl Ramsdale (Malcolm McGregor), an army procurement officer, arrives to purchase horses for the government's use in World War I. The Indians, who know that they have in the past been cheated by Booker, are afraid to sell to Ramsdale. Marion tells the captain that Nophaie is the only man who will be able to convince the Indians to part with the animals, and if Ramsdale will assure his safety, she will get word to him. Soon, he arrives with a column of Navajos and horses. The Indians sell the horses and also enlist in the army because they are proud to serve their country as Americans.

Nophaie is sent overseas, where he is promoted to sergeant and is assigned to a company commanded by Ramsdale. Both men are in love with Marion, who cares for Nophaie, but is unable to admit her feelings. At the front, the company has been cut off from the rest of the infantry, and Ramsdale is severely wounded. A white soldier attempts to make a run through no man's land to report the company's position, but he is killed. Nophaie then tries and succeeds. He also returns to his platoon and carries Ramsdale to safety. The captain talks of Marion in a manner that makes Nophaie realize he has a rival for the schoolteacher.

After the war, Nophaie returns to the reservation where Booker is now in charge of the agency. White men now are working the fields, the Indians having been pushed into the hills where they live in squalor. Booker tells Nophaie that Marion has gone east to marry Ramsdale. The Indian also discovers Gekin Yashi dead, and Booker is to blame. Nophaie wanders into the hills and prays for guidance. Meanwhile, Marion arrives back at the reservation, and she is not married to Ramsdale. The Indians declare war and plan to attack the agency. Nophaie learns this and decides to warn the whites. When he sees Marion, he is even more determined to prevent the raid.

Booker machine-guns the attacking Indians, mowing them down without compassion. Nophaie runs into the street and is shot by the agent. The fighting halts. Then, Gekin Yashi's father kills Booker with an arrow. The dying Nophaie tells his people to return home and submit to the rule of the United States government. Submission, he explains, is inevitable. The Indians are taken by his words and promise to obey. Ramsdale arrives with word that Booker has been deposed as agent, but of course, it is too late. Nophaie dies in Marion's arms.

It is accepted without argument in *The Vanishing American* that, despite bad men like Booker, the white man is more fit to rule the land than the Indian. This is a natural progression, as the white civilization has advanced beyond the red man's. Nophaie realizes that his people will never again be the sole inhabitants of America: a more radical scenario might have stressed that the white man and his government have broken countless treaties made with Indian tribes and have practically jailed the red men on reservations.

Still, however, *The Vanishing American* remains an intelligent, lyrical, handsomely produced study of injustice and the plight of the Indian. Although sometimes sentimental, it perceptibly shows the problems of a red man adjusting to a white civilization. The focus is not the Indian on the warpath, but the Indian as a human being who is heroic, passionate, sad—and who happens to be a native American. The filmmakers also contrast the sorry state of the reservation to the Indians' patriotism and willingness to fight and die for their country. They do not, however, resort to a phony, unrealistic finale with white and red man united as brothers. Instead, Nophaie and Booker both die—the only practical denouement—with the Indian urging his people to give in to the inevitability of the white man's rule, for there will be no happy ending for the red man, the vanishing American.

Dix, the epitome of the "strong, silent" leading man, dominates *The Vanishing American* with his sensitive performance, and he is ably supported by Lois Wilson. They had previously appeared together in *The Call of the Canyon* (1923) and *To the Last Man* (1923), both Westerns, and *Icebound* (1924), a love story; later, they co-starred in *Let's Get Married* (1926), with Dix as a football hero, and *Lovin' the Ladies* (1930), in which Dix portrays an electrician who poses as a playboy to win the affections of the Wilson character. They were involved romantically offscreen as well; however, their most famous films were done separately. Wilson's best film is James Cruze's epic Western, *The Covered Wagon* (1923); Dix's is the Academy Award-winning *Cimarron* (1931), which earned him his only Oscar nomination for Best Actor. Noah Beery, brother of Wallace, father of Noah, Jr., and one of the top character actors of the era, is quite good as Booker. In fact, with Walter Long, Sam De Grasse, George Siegmann, Brandon Hurst, Montagu Love, and a few others, Beery was one of the silent screen's great villains.

The film is unquestionably the most outstanding in the career of its director, George B. Seitz. Before *The Vanishing American*, he was in charge of Pearl White serials, and later, he worked on Andy Hardy features. Among his better Westerns are *Wild Horse Mesa* (1925), also based on a Zane Grey story, and *The Thrill Hunter* (1933), with Buck Jones.

The Vanishing American received good reviews. Zane Grey was particularly pleased with the film, singling out for praise Seitz, production supervisor Lucien Hubbard, screenwriter Ethel Doherty, and Dix. The film, made with the assistance of the Navajo and Hopi Indian nations and the United States Army, was shot on location at various points throughout the Southwest including, in addition to Monument Valley, the Painted Desert, Navajo Mountain, the Rainbow Bridge, Sagi Canyon, and the Grand Canyon. It was remade in 1955 as a forgettable "B"-grade Western. The director was Joseph Kane, and the stars were Scott Brady, Audrey Totter, Forrest Tucker, Gene Lockhart, and Jim Davis.

Rob Edelman

VARIETY

Released: 1926
Production: Erich Pommer for Ufa; released by Paramount
Direction: E. A. Dupont
Screenplay: E. A. Dupont; based on the novel *The Oath of Stephen Huller*
by Friederich Hollaender
Cinematography: Karl Freund
Length: 8 reels/7,800 feet

> *Principal characters:*
> Boss Huller ....Emil Jannings
> Bertha ....Lya de Putti
> Artinelli ....Warwick Ward
> The Wife of Boss ....Maly Delschaft

When *Variety* was released in the United States in 1926, two of its stars—
Emil Jannings and Lya de Putti—had already been signed to come to America
to work at Paramount. *Variety* was, in fact, the next-to-last film in which
Jannings acted before leaving Germany, and by the time it premiered on
Broadway, Putti was already in America. Her screen career in the United
States was, at best, negligible, although she played the vamp in D. W.
Griffith"s *The Sorrows of Satan* (1927) in the manner of Theda Bara. She
died in New York, reputedly at only age thirty, from pneumonia contracted
when she was hospitalized either as a result of swallowing a chicken bone,
or, more likely, from a suicide attempt made because her career in America
had never caught on.

Jannings, however, did some of his best work in Hollywood, winning the
Motion Picture Academy's Best Actor Award in 1927-1928, the first year that
the awards were given, for his first two American features, *The Way of All
Flesh* (1927) and *The Last Command* (1928). American audiences were
already very familiar with what they had seen of him as imported from Germany, and his most recent work in *The Last Laugh* (1925), *Faust* (1926), and
Variety was highly praised. In fact, the weekly trade journal *Variety* had noted
in its review of the film that ". . .Emil Jannings can set himself down for an
American favorite in American-made pictures from the outset."

The film *Variety*, brilliantly written and directed by Ewald Andre Dupont,
who also came to Hollywood to Universal, should have been the first step in
a brilliant American career for Dupont; but Universal's next assignment for
him was a trite, over-sentimental film entitled *Love Me and the World Is Mine*
(1928), that was *ersatz* Erich Von Stroheim. It literally drove him back across
the Atlantic to direct in England and Germany. When he returned to Hollywood in 1933, he was not remembered for *Variety* and received nothing but
insignificant pictures to direct. His talent, which had flowered so brilliantly

with *Variety*, was tragically misused and utterly wasted. He died, almost unknown, of cancer in Hollywood in 1956.

When *Variety* first opened in the United States at the Rialto Theater in New York, its running time was noted as being ninety-two minutes, which is what it had been abroad. American censors, however, jumped on the picture because it dealt with adultery, and it was cut to seventy-five minutes. The entire role of the wife was omitted, and the story concerned itself with the Jannings character and his inamorata, the Putti character, who was now inferred to be his wife, on their way to sensational fame at the Wintergarten in Berlin. Fortunately, the missing seventeen minutes that had been clipped has been restored in recent screenings, and the picture plays as it should, with a quartet of characters that are fully three-dimensional.

The story begins in the warden's office of a prison, where a prisoner known as Boss Huller (Emil Jannings) is brought in to confront the warden. He is told that his wife and son (now ten years old) have petitioned for his pardon. Boss had refused to tell his story when he was sent to prison, and the warden urges him to do so now after all these years of silence, because it could lead to his release.

Thoughtfully, Boss considers the deal and then begins to talk. There is a lap dissolve to a sleazy carnival show in Hamburg, where Boss, who had been a great aerialist, is running a cheap dancing show, featuring his wife (Maly Delschaft), who had also retired from the act and now plays the piano for the show. She is, however, more attentive to the child that she had borne Boss than she is to her piano-playing.

A sailor brings a waif called Bertha (Lya de Putti) to Boss because the girl can dance. She is an orphan from Java, whose mother died aboard ship. Boss gives the girl a chance to break in on his dance act, but she is so young and attractive that when she does her seductive dance, a roughneck climbs upon the stage to hug her, and Boss has to drive him off. Bertha had been making a play for Boss, but he has put her off until the roughneck incident. He now decides that he will leave his wife and baby, return to Berlin with Bertha, and break her in as a trapeze artist, while he gets in shape to return to his work as a catcher in the act. They break in the act, and Bertha is a success, while Boss feels a return to power and vigor in the kind of work he likes doing. Also, Bertha is a real charmer, and for the first time, Boss knows that he is regaining his sexual drive.

They arrive at the Wintergarten in Berlin in time for the opening, and they are in luck. The great aerialist, Artinelli (Warwick Ward), is there too, but because his partner has suffered an accident and cannot work for a while, Artinelli will be forced to cancel his act if he cannot find a new partner. The Wintergarten management introduces Boss and Bertha to Artinelli, and the suggestion is made that he develop a trio act. Artinelli knows Boss' reputation as one of the best catchers in the business, and Artinelli is also not blind to

Bertha's charms. They rehearse, go on as a threesome, and become a sensation.

As photographed by Karl Freund and directed by Dupont under supervision by Erich Pommer, the trapeze act is breathtakingly performed with no nets, climaxed by a triple somersault. The atmosphere of the Wintergarten show is superbly and dramatically caught. It is as if one were there participating in the excitement.

On opening night, Artinelli gives Bertha a diamond ring for good luck and the next morning he entices her into his room, which is on the same floor and down the hall from the room occupied by Boss and Bertha. They become lovers, while Boss plays cards with his cronies. On another night, Artinelli takes Bertha to a fete, where they dance and do not return until four in the morning. Boss is furious, but his temperament is cooled by Bertha's wiles.

Everyone seems to know that Bertha is two-timing Boss, and a café artist sketches some cartoons of the three on a tabletop at the fete, indicating that Boss is being used. Boss sees the cartoons, and knowing the artist, he seeks him out. The artist admits that he himself had witnessed the boldness of the love-making at the fete.

It is again showtime, and as Boss looks out into the Wintergarten, he is plainly thinking of how he has been cheated and of how he might escape punishment were he to fail to catch Artinelli, allowing him to fall to his death. It happens, however, only in his imagination. When the act goes on, the suspense is maddening. Will Boss really yield to temptation and let his rival fall? The sequence is brilliantly photographed, with the full death-defying leaps terrorizing the film's audience as it drives the audience in the Wintergarten half mad with suspense.

The act, however, finishes without any accidental occurrence. The three artistes take their bows. Boss is ultimately too professional to fake a no-catch. After the performance, he asks Artinelli to tell Bertha that he will not be home until late. The two lovers feel free to spend another night together and go out to get drunk. In the small hours, the two return from their night on the town and say goodnight in the hall. When Artinelli goes to his room, he finds Boss there, waiting for him. Artinelli realizes that Boss knows he has been cuckolded and betrayed. Boss throws two knives point downward on the table, signifying that he will count to three. Artinelli seizes a knife on the count of three, and the two men struggle, falling to the floor as they hack at each other. Boss rises slowly, victorious, and walks down the hall to the room he shares with Bertha. As he enters, Bertha follows him with her eyes as he goes to the washbowl and washes the blood off his hands. She begins to whimper and then to scream, but Boss ignores her, and the camera follows him as he goes down the stairs and outside, where he stops a taxi and asks the driver to take him to the nearest police station.

There is a lap dissolve back to the warden's office as Boss finishes telling his story. The warden is attentive, and there is a hint that a pardon is possible now that the truth is known, and Boss may soon consequently rejoin his faithful wife and son, a free man.

DeWitt Bodeen

LE VOYAGE DANS LA LUNE
(A TRIP TO THE MOON)

Released: 1902
Production: Georges Méliès for Star Film
Direction: Georges Méliès
Screenplay: Georges Méliès; suggested by the novels of Jules Verne and H. G. Wells
Cinematography: Georges Méliès
Art direction: Georges Méliès
Costume design: Georges Méliès
Length: 1 reel/845 feet

> *Principal characters:*
> Not individually credited at this time, but in the 1930's, Georges Méliès wrote that Bleuette Bernon, Victor André, and he were three of the performers.

French director Georges Méliès is regarded today as one of the very first creative talents to work in cinema. In the words of film historian Lewis Jacobs, "Méliès started movies on a new course, broadened their scope, and focused attention upon their creative potentialities." Before he began making films, which was literally before motion pictures were invented, Méliès was a showman and professional magician who owned his own theater. His experiences with the theater and fantasy gave Méliès the background for his contributions to the development of motion pictures.

Because the early years of filmmaking were disorganized and experimental, with few accurate records or reports, it is usually impossible to determine with certainty who was the first to use the various techniques of cinema. What is more important is to identify the influential innovators of all countries discovering film, the ones who were noticed and imitated by their contemporaries so that their films demonstrated not only individual merits but also affected the manner in which films were made. In these first years of filmmaking, films were usually very short records of simple scenes. Indeed, the novelty of the process was so great at first that audiences watched films that simply showed workers walking out of a factory gate, or other equally uninspired subjects.

Méliès became the man who advanced the medium into filmic tricks, narrative, and theatricality. He began in France, in 1895 or 1896, making short films with little or no plot, but he discovered that the camera was a marvelous instrument for a magician. With it, he could make objects or people appear, disappear, change into other objects or people, or even appear several times in one frame. Legend has it that he learned of this technique when his camera accidentally jammed. He restarted it without moving it, and when he viewed the resulting film, he saw that objects that had been in front of the camera when it stopped but had moved before it started seemed to have instantly vanished. With his experience as a magician and his keen understanding of machinery, he was soon producing a whole spectrum of what are now called "special effects."

He pioneered in other areas also. Realizing that many scenes could be combined in sequence to form a narrative, he developed this form to the point that in 1899, he produced a film of *Cinderella* that lasted seven minutes and contained twenty separate scenes. This was an extremely long and involved film for that day. Also, Méliès drew upon his theatrical background to use professional actors and elaborate sets and costumes. Méliès was taking the art of film from the primitive stage, in which a moving image or a short amusing action was all a filmmaker tried to present, toward the day of sophisticated narrative and special effects.

There were, however, two areas of filmic technique that Méliès virtually ignored: editing and the placement and movement of the camera. His editing consisted of linking separate scenes together, just as they would be seen on the stage, and his camera placement was similarly stagebound. He put the camera in one position and had the scene acted out in front of it, without moving the camera to a different angle during a scene. Méliès had taken the art of cinema a long distance; others soon came along to discover that a scene could be divided into separate shots from several angles and that the scenes did not have to be presented in strictly chronological order.

For his films, Méliès was usually producer, director, cinematographer, set and costume designer, and a principal actor. He made hundreds of films, of which fewer than ninety still exist. The most frequently seen of his surviving films is *Le Voyage dans la Lune* (*A Trip to the Moon*) and a viewing of it proves (despite the poor quality of existing prints) that Méliès and his films are interesting in their own right, as well as being important milestones in the history of film. Into less than fifteen minutes, Méliès packs dramatic effects, humor, and invention that are still impressive today, especially when compared with a film from the same general time, *The Great Train Robbery* (1903), which was a highly successful American production.

The film begins with a meeting of astronomers that turns into a chaotic argument with the president of the society throwing books and papers at an opponent. Once the argument is over, and it is decided to make a trip to the moon, the film concentrates upon the preparations. The astronauts are to reach the moon inside a large projectile that will be fired from a huge cannon. Scenes show the casting of the enormous gun and the astronomers entering the projectile, which is then loaded into the gun. After the gun is fired, the projectile flies toward the moon and—in the most famous shot of the whole film—it lands in the eye of a very anthropomorphic man-in-the-moon face.

Once on the moon, the astronauts have several adventures and a dream.

In the dream, such visions as stars with women's faces in them are seen. After they awaken from the dream, they meet the Sélénites—as Méliès calls the inhabitants of the moon. These fantastic creatures with some resemblance to lobsters move about in an extraordinarily acrobatic manner (they were portrayed by acrobats from the Folies Bergère), and when they are struck by the astronauts they burst into countless pieces. The foreigners are captured by the Sélénites, but they finally escape and run back to their projectile, pursued by the moon creatures. Then, the projectile falls back to the earth (with one Sélénite still clinging to it) and into the sea. After it floats back to the surface, it is towed back to land, and the film ends with the astronauts receiving an enthusiastic reception.

Some of the films of Méliès can be criticized for relying too heavily upon photographic tricks, but in *Le Voyage dans le Lune*, these are subordinated to the playful and imaginative conception of the narrative. Also important and artistically rendered are the costumes and settings, all designed by Méliès.

It is impossible for a viewer today to appreciate how startling and revolutionary the films of Méliès were when they were first seen around the turn of the century. Rival film companies paid Méliès the undesired compliment of making copies of his films so that they could make money from his popularity without having to pay him any fees. For this reason and others, including Méliès' deficiencies as a businessman and the fact that the art of cinema was progressing so rapidly that within a few years it had assimilated most of his innovations and had progressed beyond him in other areas, Méliès made no films after 1911, and by 1923 he was bankrupt. The young art had no time or inclination to salute its pioneers, and it was not until the late 1920's that Méliès began to be recognized for his accomplishments. In 1931, he was given a Legion of Honor medal by the French government.

Timothy W. Johnson

WANDERER OF THE WASTELAND

Released: 1924
Production: Famous Players-Lasky; released by Paramount
Direction: Irvin Willat
Screenplay: George C. Hull and Victor Irvin; based on the novel of the same name by Zane Grey
Art titles: Oscar C. Buchheister
Cinematography: Arthur Ball
Length: 6 reels/5,775 feet

> *Principal characters:*
> Adam Larey .... Jack Holt
> Dismukes .... Noah Beery
> Mr. Roderick Virey .... George Irving
> Magdalene Virey .... Kathlyn Williams
> Ruth Virey .... Billie Dove
> Guerd Larey .... James Mason

It is to the credit of Carl Alfred "Doc" Willat that *Wanderer of the Wasteland* came to be the first full-length feature from a major studio to be filmed in Technicolor. "Doc" Willat was the older brother of director Irvin Willat, and he was one of the leaders of Technicolor. When he heard that Jesse L. Lasky had offered his brother the directorship of an adaptation of Zane Grey's *Wanderer of the Wasteland*, he came to Irvin and asked him if he thought he could get Lasky to agree to make the picture in Technicolor. Until then, Technicolor had not made a feature-length film for one of the major companies. Irvin Willat had been hesitant about doing the film, for most of his important work had been undersea dramas for Thomas Ince for release through Paramount, such as *Below the Surface* (1920) and *Behind the Door* (1920). Now, when he contemplated doing a Western, not only almost entirely out-of-doors on location but also in the desert, with all its softer, muted shades of color, as well as the brilliant hues of the morning and evening skies, he excitedly told his brother that he was confident that Lasky would agree to doing the film in Technicolor if he asked him personally.

Paramount was committed to filming *Wanderer of the Wasteland*, and Lasky, when convinced that the Technicolor cost would not be prohibitive, and that he would have the plus-value of a presold Zane Grey audience for it, gave his consent to Willat. Willat then got his company together and went out into the desert, even into Death Valley, for some of the scenes, and finished shooting the picture in six weeks.

Wanderer of the Wasteland had its Los Angeles premiere in June, 1924, and critics, delighted with its coloring, gave it an enthusiastic welcome. When it played New York in midsummer, viewers stood in line for tickets. The weekly

Variety critic, calling it "the biggest step in pictures since the close-up was first used," led all the critics in praising it. *Variety* went on to say,

> It is a work of art. That is the only expression to describe it. There have been color processes before, but none has given the screen anything of the perfect tones that are here. There are shots that one would swear were by Remington done in colors.

The story is set in the Great Southwest in the 1870's. As the film begins, two men pause at a gambling hall in a mining town. They are mining engineer Adam Larey (Jack Holt) and his brother, Guerd (James Mason). Adam has recently met Ruth Virey (Billie Dove), the girl he loves. Later, he returns to the gambling hall to fetch his brother, only to find complete chaos. Guerd has lost all of his inheritance at the gaming table, and Adam catches Guerd in the very act of stealing from him in order to pay his debts. There are protests and angry words. The two brothers battle for possession of a handgun, the revolver goes off accidentally, and Guerd falls to the floor, wounded.

To save himself, Adam stumbles out into the night and disappears. He seeks refuge in the desert, fearing that he is cursed with the mark of Cain for having killed his brother. He falls victim to a vicious rattlesnake, but is saved by an old desert rat named Dismukes (Noah Beery), who frees Adam's blood of the rattler's venom. The two men then become wanderers together.

The plot now switches to the story of Ruth Virey's father, Roderick (George Irving) who is almost insane with jealousy. He thinks that every man who speaks to his wife, Magdalene (Kathlyn Williams), or even smiles at her in admiration, is trying to steal her from him. In the desert, he finds a deserted cabin built beneath an overhung cliff, and he forces Magdalene to come with him and live there so that he can be sure she is faithful to him. She is convinced that she is fated to die, for it is obvious that sooner or later there will be an avalanche of rocks, which will certainly destroy the cabin and anybody in it. Magdalene regrets only her enforced separation from her daughter Ruth, and when Adam appears on the scene, she welcomes him and asks him to take word to Ruth that she is well and that some day they will be together.

From a distance, Virey sees his wife speaking intimately to Adam and completely misunderstands their relationship. When Adam leaves and Magdalene returns to the cabin, Virey triggers the overhanging rock with timed explosives and goes down to confront his wife, to accuse her, and to die with her in the downfall of rock. The avalanche goes off on schedule, with a mighty explosion, and the rocks spill down upon the little cabin, crushing it and its occupants. Adam hurries to the cabin and finds a dying Magdalene who begs him with her last words to tell Ruth of her death.

Adam does so, and Ruth is torn between grief over her mother's tragedy and delight at seeing Adam again. She urges him to find his brother Guerd, who may be alive. Adam does find him very much alive, and, his conscience clear, he seeks out Ruth again, the woman he loves.

Wanderer of the Wasteland was a handsome production and the color breath-takingly beautiful, a wonderful preface to the Douglas Fairbanks production of *The Black Pirate* (1926). Color is used with remarkable dramatic effect in both of these early color films. For example, in *Wanderer of the Wasteland* there is a fight in the millrace, and the man trapped in the revolving wheel is obviously being cut to pieces because the mill water turns a bright bloody red, spreading out to embrace the stream. Another advantage of Technicolor in this film is that the beautiful Billie Dove as Ruth was even more lovely in color than in black and white.

These two films—*Wanderer of the Wasteland* and *The Black Pirate*—are perfect examples of what Technicolor could do for a feature production. There were far more advantages to using it than disadvantages, but producers were sparing of its use because of the cost and because with time the colors faded and were washed out. Additionally, it was obvious by 1927 that the forthcoming immediate innovation was going to be the perfection of sound, and improvements in color would have to wait. The waiting proved advantageous because by 1935 three-strip Technicolor was in use, and on its first venture in a feature, RKO's *Becky Sharp*, the result proved sensational. Like sound, color had come of age and was extraordinarily beautiful when designers such as Robert Edmond Jones and Rouben Mamoulian showed how dramatic it could be and how much the content itself could be heightened.

Wanderer of the Wasteland is still a landmark, because it was an exciting drama with a remarkable visual sense of color displayed in the action.

DeWitt Bodeen

WAR BRIDES

Released: 1916
Production: Lewis J. Selznick
Direction: Herbert Brenon
Screenplay: Herbert Brenon; based on the play of the same name by Marion Craig Wentworth
Cinematography: J. Roy Hunt
Length: 8 reels

Principal characters:

Joan	Nazimova
George	Charles Hutchinson
Franz	Charles Bryant
Eric	William Bailey
Arno	Richard Barthelmess
Amelia	Nila Mac
The mother	Gertrude Berkeley
The King	Alex Shannon
Lieutenant Hoffman	Robert Whitworth
Captain Bragg	Ned Burton
Minna	Theodora Warfield
A Financier	Charles Chailles

War Brides provided filmgoers in 1916 with three unique attractions: a story line with a timely message and a tragic, inspirational resolution; a heroine who demonstrates enough inner strength to take charge of her own fate; and the debut of the luminous Broadway star, Alla Nazimova, on the screen. Released on November 12 during the reelection of Woodrow Wilson whose campaign slogan was "He kept us out of war," *War Brides* is a stirring, highly emotional depiction of the horrors of war from the woman's point of view. The story's popularity charts the course of public sentiment from noninvolvement to active support of World War I. Originally a magazine sketch by Marion Craig Wentworth, *War Brides* became a success on the vaudeville circuit in 1915, primarily because of the popularity of its pacifist theme and the blazing performance of its star, Nazimova. Essentially a piece of antiwar propaganda, when transferred to the screen, *War Brides* enjoyed initial success before facing intense censorship pressures once the United States entered World War I.

War Brides was, in some ways, an unusual choice of vehicles for Nazimova to select for her entry into films. For a decade the Russian-born actress had been widely acclaimed in the theater, known for her great natural beauty, deep "telling" eyes, and exotic image. In *War Brides*, Nazimova played the part of a grief-stricken widow, devoid of glamour, and, hence, quite different from the public image she had cultivated. By her portrayal of Joan, however, Nazimova helped to popularize a new multidimensional type of heroine, who is capable not only of passion but also of the creativity and intellectual depth which had previously been attributed only to men.

Much publicity surrounded the making of this film. Nazimova had been refusing lucrative film offers for five years, until she was impressed with Herbert Brenon's "pure creative imagination" in directing *A Daughter of the Gods* (1916). Once Brenon, who had just entered into an agreement with producer Lewis J. Selznick, acquired the rights to *War Brides*, Selznick was eager to capitalize on the box-office potential of Nazimova's name, and he lured her into the project with a salary of thirty-thousand dollars for thirty days work. To insure publicity, they often posed before cameras as he handed her daily installments of one thousand dollars in bills or gold coins.

During the course of *War Brides*, Joan (Nazimova) is converted from an assertive labor organizer into a dependent, idolizing wife before finally emerging as a leader in charge of her own destiny. Living in a mythical kingdom filled with oppressed factory workers, Joan first demonstrates her humanitarianism and leadership abilities by organizing a strike for decent working conditions. When the factory owner accedes to the demands, Joan becomes a highly influential, respected community spokesperson. At a picnic held to celebrate the victory, Joan is accosted in a secluded nook by a rowdy villager. Too proud to admit helplessness by screaming, Joan appears defeated until the appearance of a towering young giant named Franz (Charles Bryant) sends the bully scurrying away. Awed by the presence of this brave young man, Joan spends the rest of the day talking to him, and soon they become engaged.

Franz is a farmer living with his mother (Gertrude Berkeley); sister, Amelia (Nila Mac); and three brothers, George (Charles Hutchinson), Eric, (William Bailey), and Arno (Richard Barthelmess). Franz explains that he, like all men in the kingdom, has received military training. His idealistic view of nobly defending his king and country if necessary contrasts sharply with Joan's vision of the carnage and destruction of war.

Meanwhile, the King (Alexander K. Shannon), unable to contain the jealousy he feels toward a neighboring monarch, begins preparation for an attack. Although the reference is veiled, this mythical king is clearly modeled on Kaiser Wilhelm, and the story is viewed as a demonstration of the German people's unwillingness to participate in the war.

Hearing rumors of war, Franz and Joan cut their engagement short and are married immediately. The once independent Joan now subsumes her self-assertiveness in total adoration of her husband, whom she believes can shield her from all the trials and pains of life.

The King soon declares war and Franz is one of the first to be called for service, but by now he has shed his romanticized view of war. Clinging to

Joan before his departure, he tries to prepare her for some of the dangers she may face if the village is invaded. When Joan closes her eyes, his descriptions induce images in her mind of ruthless invaders with contorted, fiendish faces, pillaging the homes and violating the women of the town. Some critics originally raised objections to what was branded the "almost revolting realism" of this scene because Brenon included numerous details which, combined with J. Roy Hunt's excellent photography, result in a strong visual impact.

With Franz at war, Joan loses her sense of purpose and sinks into a state of listlessness and apathy which lifts only intermittently as one by one her brothers-in-law are drafted. Joan is plagued by morbid dreams depicting Franz lying crumpled on the battlefield, as so she is not surprised when word comes of his death. In her agony, she reaches for the gun Franz left for her protection, but his mother convinces her that she must be strong.

As casualties mount, the King issues orders forbidding mourning and encouraging young single women to marry the soldiers who are going off to war. Seeing this as both a vital service to their country and a purpose in life, thousands of women become "war brides." Brenon captures a striking contrast in a church scene where wounded and dying soldiers are interspersed with cheery recruits leading their war brides to the altar. Recognizing the King's plan as a means of producing a new generation of soldiers to use as cannon fodder, Joan shakes off her apathy and begins effectively spreading the gospel of defiance. When Lieutenant Hoffman (Robert Whitworth) asks for her sister-in-law's hand, Joan persuades Amelia to refuse him. In retaliation, Captain Bragg (Ned Burton) threatens to have Joan executed, but upon learning that she is pregnant, he decides to imprison her instead. With the shortage of able-bodied men, a huge, shrewish women is recruited as Joan's jailer. Despite her forbidding exterior, Minna (Theodora Warfield) becomes converted to Joan's cause and eventually allows her to escape in time to plan a demonstration during the King's proposed visit.

On the day of the King's arrival, the women of the village flood the streets, each draped from head-to-toe in black mourning clothes. At Joan's direction, they form a great black ribbon lining the sides of the road. As the King's motorcade approaches Joan at the head of the line, Captain Bragg desperately threatens to shoot her if the women do not disband. The tension mounts as Joan, ignoring Bragg's threats, steps forward to confront the King with the women's demands—either there will be no future wars, or they will not produce children. Stepping back, Joan pulls Franz's gun from her robe, aims for her heart, and shoots, killing herself and her unborn child. Vowing to follow their martyr rather than sacrifice more children to war, the women lift up Joan's lifeless body before the eyes of the horrified King. This visually moving, tragic conclusion was hailed in 1916 as being probably the most powerful ending ever filmed and left the industry audience clapping after its initial showing.

The major flaws in *War Brides* probably stem from the addition of extra material and comic moments in the beginning to pad Wentworth's one act play for the screen. As a consequence, the first four reels were regarded as slow paced and artificial. Additional criticism centered on the poor choice of locale for the battle scenes which resulted in unrealistic positioning of soldiers in the trenches. In the last half, the drama built and sustained intensity, however, and reviewers expressed universal commendations for the conclusion.

Nazimova received rave reviews for her ability to convey strength, intelligence, and a variety of emotions. Her pantomimic talents produced a well-contoured, tragic figure, whose thoughts and feelings were easily shared by the audience. The entire cast was well balanced and forceful. Gertrude Berkeley as the mother received special notice for the quiet force of her performance, and Nila Mac as Amelia was appealing and effective. Richard Barthelmess' performance as Arno was impressive enough to launch his successful career.

War Brides is regarded as one of Brenon's best films, perhaps the best of his early efforts. The action in the film was easy to follow, close-ups were used to advantage, and subtitles were used effectively; and Hunt provided some stunning cinematography.

Both before and after its release, *War Brides* stirred controversy. In October, 1916, a month prior to his film's opening, Brenon petitioned the courts and received an injunction restraining the distribution of a hastily produced William Fox Corporation film entitled *The War Bride's Secret* with Virginia Pearson. Fox, fresh from a bitter dispute with Brenon over *A Daughter of the Gods*, had recently released his film to steal the box office from the upcoming Brenon production.

Although pacifism was still in vogue when *War Brides* was released, the Preparedness Campaign of 1916 was beginning to exert influence within the motion-picture world and films which discouraged enlistment were being carefully scrutinized. By April, 1917, with the United States adopting a war footing, *War Brides* came under fire from military and Bureau of Investigation officials for its vehement stand against all wars; bowing to pressure, many local exhibitors were induced to edit "objectionable" parts and/or preface the film with a slide extolling the virtues of enlisting to fight Prussian militarism in "the greatest of all wars." Brenon later said that the events surrounding *War Brides* was one of the greatest tragedies of his life. Despite its censorship and withdrawal in many areas, the film was a financial success, earning more than $300,000 in profits for Selznick. Unfortunately, there are at present no known copies of *War Brides* in existence.

Anne Louise Lynch

THE WARRENS OF VIRGINIA

Released: 1915
Production: Cecil B. De Mille for Jesse L. Lasky Feature Play Company; released by Paramount
Direction: Cecil B. De Mille
Screenplay: William C. deMille; based on his play of the same name
Cinematography: Alvin Wyckoff
Editing: Cecil B. De Mille
Length: 5 reels

Principal characters:
Agatha Warren	Blanche Sweet
Ned Burton	House Peters
General Warren	James O'Neill
Arthur Warren	Page Peters
Mrs. Warren	Mabel Van Buren
Bette Warren	Marguerite House
General Griffin	Dick La Reno
Sapho	Mrs. Lewis McCord

Cecil B. De Mille personally directed at least seventy films during his prolific career which began with *The Squaw Man* in 1914 and ended with *The Ten Commandments* in 1956. De Mille was born the younger of two sons of Henry Churchill deMille and Mathilda Beatrice in Ashfield, Massachusetts, on August 12, 1881. His father taught English at Columbia University, was a preacher, and also wrote plays, four of which were successful collaborations with David Belasco. After his father died, his remarkable mother turned the family home into a school for girls in order to obtain the funds to send her elder son, William, to Columbia University and Cecil to Pennsylvania Military College. She then formed her own theatrical agency, The DeMille Play Co. and proceeded to write successful stories and plays. Cecil did not care much for the environment at the military college and decided that the Spanish-American War offered more opportunity for derring-do. After being rejected because of his youth while trying to enlist, his mother decided that The Academy of Dramatic Arts in New York might be more agreeable to Cecil's sensibilities. While William was establishing himself as a playwright, Cecil, in 1900, made his debut as an actor in *Hearts Are Trumps*, a Charles Frohman production. While on tour with this play, he met and married an actress, Constance Adams, the daughter of a Boston judge.

Having discovered that writing was not his forte, Cecil became general manager of his mother's company while his brother became one of the better American playwrights. Cecil was in a position to meet many prominent people, and he had a knack for making the most of every opportunity. He collaborated on several operettas with a vaudeville musician by the name of Jesse L. Lasky, and in 1913, they became obsessed with Edwin S. Porter's film *The Great Train Robbery* (1903). De Mille and Lasky were very much impressed, as well, with Adolph Zukor the Hungarian-born film pioneer who had emigrated to the United States. Zukor had been a fur salesman, nickelodeon owner, and an independent producer before he bought the American film rights to the French four-reeler *Queen Elizabeth* (1912), with Sarah Bernhardt, and hired a legitimate theater to show the film when the motion-picture trust closed their houses to him. He organized a company called "Famous Players" in order to take the top stars of the stage and feature them in the film versions of their best plays. He persuaded the famous New York stage star James O'Neill (father of Eugene O'Neill) to film *The Count of Monte Cristo* (1913) and Minnie Maddern Fiske to appear in *Tess of the D'Urbervilles* (1913).

This idea of "Famous Players in Famous Plays" soon acquired many imitators, and American audiences were able to view such legitimate luminaries as Nat C. Hoodwin, James Hackett, and Lily Langtry on the motion-picture screen. The most important of these imitators was Lasky's Feature Play Company. De Mille and Lasky convinced Samuel Goldfish (later Samuel Goldwyn), an East Side glove seller, and Arthur Friend, a young attorney, to join them in their project. With the name of Belasco, whose support they enlisted to add prestige, these men became some of the most important figures in the film industry.

Elated by the praise the critics had bestowed on Zukor's *Queen Elizabeth* and the Italian-made feature *Quo Vadis?* (1912), Lasky, De Mille, Goldfish, and Friend got things under way in a matter of a few weeks, and the "Feature Play Company" was organized with the cash capital of twenty thousand dollars, with Lasky as president, Goldfish as vice-president and business manager, Friend as secretary and legal adviser, and De Mille acquiring the title of Director-General. They headed west to Los Angeles and in the small community of Hollywood, they found a large barn at the corner of Vine and Selma, where they made their headquarters. Their policy was "feature pictures only" which meant four or five reels minimum and a running time of an hour or more. This policy was in opposition to the two reel maximum of the General Film Company which controlled most of the picture houses. Zukor and his Famous Players were the only other adversaries of General at that point.

It was in the old barn that filming began on the Feature Play Company's first feature *The Squaw Man* with De Mille directing. Six reels long, this adaptation by Edwin Milton Royle from his own play of the same name starred Dustin Farnum as James Wynnegate the English Earl who, falsely accused of embezzlement, escapes to Wyoming where he rescues (and subsequently marries) an Indian girl from a villainous cattle rustler. This film is the only film of De Mille's canon in which he officially shares credit with another director, Oscar C. Apful. In 1914, De Mille directed, for his company, *The Virginian*, *The Call of the North*, *What's His Name*, *The Man from Home*, *Rose of the Rancho*, and began shooting *The Girl of the Golden West* and *The Warrens of Virginia* which was released in 1915.

The Warrens of Virginia, which was based on a play by William C. deMille and David Belasco, dealt with the subject of the American Civil War which had already become a cliché on stage but which would explode dramatically into new dimensions on screen in such films as this and *The Birth of a Nation* (also 1915). In *The Warrens of Virginia*, Agatha Warren (Blanche Sweet), daughter of the aristocratic General Warren (James O'Neill), falls in love with Ned Burton (House Peters) of New York. When the Civil War begins, Ned leaves his Southern sweetheart to join the Union forces in opposition to her father, who has taken command of many of the Southern troops. Ned becomes a lieutenant and a special correspondent who must try to learn about the arrival of a supply train. He is sheltered by Agatha who is still in love with him, although she is torn by their different sympathies. Most of the action takes place during the closing days of the war when General Warren's soldiers are suffering from a lack of supplies. Burton is eventually forced by his superiors to use his intimacy with the Warren family to conduct a ruse which leads to the destruction of a supply train coming to relieve the Confederate army. When Burton is captured, Agatha, still in love, offers him a means of escape, but he is too proud to accept. Only the timely surrender of General Robert E. Lee saves him from being shot. In the end, Agatha and Ned are reunited and marry.

The spectacular effects that were possible on screen proved that film was a better medium for war drama than the stage. The lavish scale of the production coupled with an attention to detail made the film much more impressive to the audience. The ambushing of the Confederate supply train and the destruction of the powder wagons; the martial incidents; the starving, ragged, Confederate troops juxtaposed with the satisfactory condition of their enemies; the battle behind the trenches; the contrasting conditions of the South before, and then near the close of, the Civil War; all seemed more dramatic than the earlier Belasco production, which had had a highly successful run in the theater and became a drama classic. Mary Pickford was only fifteen when she played in the original production of the play which co-starred the young Cecil B. De Mille playing her older brother. Of the film version, the *Motion Picture News* of February 20, 1915, suggested that "The realistic battle scenes . . . are featured in the film version in such a true to life manner that the subject is worthy of being termed educational."

Cecil B. De Mille began to be known outside the industry with his spectacle *Carmen* (also 1915) which contained elements of what would become De Mille's trademarks and were already discernible in *The Warrens of Virginia*: genuine sets instead of flat, painted scenery; actors speaking lines even though sound was not yet invented; faithfulness to minor details, a concern for production values; and theatrical realism. His spectaculars such as *King of Kings* (1927), *Cleopatra* (1934), *The Crusades* (1935), *Samson and Delilah* (1949), *The Greatest Show on Earth* (1952), and *The Ten Commandments* (1956) set an unequaled precedent for this style and genre of film, and only D. W. Griffith can be said to have created as many screen stars as Cecil B. De Mille. In 1916, Zukor merged his Famous Players with Lasky's Feature Play Company and acquired Paramount to create a combine active in production, distribution, and exhibition. De Mille's films were all released under that company's aegis throughout its various name changes.

Tanita C. Kelly

WAY DOWN EAST

Released: 1920
Production: D. W. Griffith
Direction: D. W. Griffith
Screenplay: Anthony Paul Kelly, elaborated by D. W. Griffith; based on the
stage play of the same name by Lottie Blair Parker and Joseph R. Grismer
Cinematography: G. W. Bitzer and Hendrik Sartov
Editing: James Smith and Rose Smith
Length: 13 reels/10,500 feet

Principal characters:
Anna Moore .... Lillian Gish
Her mother .... Mrs. David Landau
Lennox Sanderson .... Lowell Sherman
David Bartlett ....·............... Richard Barthelmess
Squire Bartlett .... Burr McIntosh
Martha Perkins .... Vivia Ogden
Maria Poole .... Emily Fitzroy

D. W. Griffith is now recognized as one of the most important and influential figures in the history of the cinema. In the words of film historian
Arthur Knight: "He created the art of the film, its language, its syntax." He
accomplished this in literally hundreds of short (one- or two-reel) films and
in his first full-length masterpiece, *The Birth of a Nation* (1915). Ironically,
because of a variety of reasons, Griffith's career faltered after the rather
steady progression through the short films to the critical and financial success
of *The Birth of a Nation*. He was to make many films after 1915, but only
three or four are today regarded as classics or as full expressions of his genius.
One of these is *Way Down East* (1920), although even this film has its detrac-
tors, including those who attempt to dismiss it as merely Victorian melodrama.

To be sure, the plot is Victorian melodrama. The film was made from a
stage play of the same name written by Lottie Blair Parker and Joseph R.
Grismer. It was such a success after its introduction in 1897 that it toured the
country for years. By the time Griffith bought the rights to film it (for an
astounding $175,000), it was already regarded as old-fashioned. Indeed, many
of the people who had worked with Griffith for years thought he had made
a terrible mistake and that it would be impossible to make a successful film
from the play. Among the doubters was Lillian Gish, who was to play the
heroine. Griffith hired Anthony Paul Kelly to write the screenplay, but
apparently it was Griffith himself who wrote most of the final script. It is not
in the script, however, that the power and excellence of *Way Down East* is
found; it is in the directing, the editing, and the acting.

The plot centers on the story of Anna Moore (Lillian Gish), who lives with her mother (Mrs. David Landau) in a small New England village. Because of their lack of money, her mother asks her to seek aid from their wealthy relatives in Boston. She is, however, treated poorly by the relatives, but attracts the attention of an unprincipled playboy named Lennox Sanderson (Lowell Sherman). He tricks her into a fake marriage and then tells her that she must return to her home and keep the marriage a secret. She does so until she has to write him that there is a "tender new reason" that their secret can no longer be kept. Sanderson responds by telling her that they are not really married, leaving her to cope as best she can.

Some time later, Anna's mother dies, and, as the title card explains, Anna "hides away with her shame in the village of Belden." There she gives birth, but the baby is not well and soon dies in her arms as she huddles in her small rented room. After being told that the child would be damned if it died unbaptized, Anna performs a baptism herself. Later, suspecting that Anna has no husband, her landlady, Maria Poole (Emily Fitzroy), evicts her from the room and sends her pitifully carrying her few possessions down the road to look for work. She finds a position at the Bartlett farm, despite the reservations of Squire Bartlett (Burr McIntosh) about hiring someone whose past they do not know. As coincidence would have it, Sanderson lives directly across the road. He tries to persuade Anna to leave, but to no avail. Meanwhile, the squire's son, David (Richard Barthelmess), falls in love with Anna, but when he tells her of his feelings, she says—without explanation—that he must never speak of it again.

The plot begins building to its climax when Maria Poole visits the Bartlett village, sees Anna, and tells the local gossip, Martha Perkins (Vivia Ogden), her story. After Martha relays the news to the Squire, he goes to Belden to confirm it, and when he learns that it is true, he orders Anna out of his house during a blinding snowstorm. She leaves, but not before denouncing Sanderson, who is that very evening a guest at the Bartlett house. David Bartlett then attacks Sanderson and goes into the storm to find Anna. She has collapsed on the frozen river, but the ice is beginning to break up, and when David finds her, she is floating toward the falls on a large piece of ice. In an exciting sequence, he rescues her at the last moment. The Squire then asks her forgiveness, which she grants; Sanderson offers to marry her and is refused. The film ends with Anna and David being married along with two other Bartlett village couples in a triple wedding.

It is obviously not the plot that made *Way Down East* Griffith's most profitable film excluding *The Birth of a Nation*. Gish has written that when she first read the story, she did not see how she could make the character of Anna convincing. Under Griffith's direction, however, she did so. In fact, part of the success of the film can be attributed to the fact that everything is taken seriously and played seriously. There are two or three minor comic characters, but neither the director nor the principal actors show any condescension toward the material, even though there is an over-seriousness in the titles.

At the center of *Way Down East* is Gish as Anna. Under Griffith's direction, she shows the innocence and trusting naïveté of the young woman without making her seem either simpleminded or overly pathetic. There are, to be sure, scenes of pathos, most notably the one in which Anna, alone and friendless, holds her dying baby as its hands grow cold. It is the subtlety of Gish's acting that keeps the scene from bathos without diminishing its emotional impact. Throughout the film, Gish exhibits a wide range of emotions, although complete happiness is reserved for the end. Even when Anna is supposedly marrying Sanderson, she has a bit of doubt and must be reassured by him.

In his overall design of the film, Griffith has also contributed to its impact. He does this by linking or contrasting separate people or events through editing, and he also contributes to the suspense, excitement, or emotion of many scenes through editing. For example, during the mock marriage David Bartlett awakes from a troubled dream. At that point Anna has not met him and the audience does not know his significance to the story. This device simply informs viewers that he will have a part in the story to come. Also, the contrast between two people is sometimes dramatically underscored by a cut directly from one to the other. The most forceful of these occurs when the film cuts directly from Anna holding her dead baby to Sanderson enjoying the good life on his estate. There is also a skillfully edited sequence in which Martha Perkins is interrupted by a barn dance on her self-appointed mission to tell Anna's story to the Squire. Meanwhile, Sanderson is threatening Anna by saying that he will reveal her past. Then, when Perkins is finally able to recount Anna's "sin" to the Squire, his son David is at the same moment professing his love to Anna. Finally, the rescue of Anna from the ice that is about to float over the falls is edited extremely well in order to build up the excitement, although the situation was becoming something of a cliché, even in 1920.

The blizzard scenes were shot largely in a real blizzard in New York, and some of the ice scenes were shot in the winter in Vermont and then combined with others shot in the summer using painted blocks of wood for the ice. The falls toward which Anna is floating are represented by brief shots of Niagara Falls. She was apparently never in danger of going over the falls, but the exposure to the cold and snow was a serious problem since her hair and eyelashes frequently froze.

Way Down East had been used as a title to an earlier film in 1914, but it was not based on the play by Parker and Grismer. Griffith's film was re-released in 1931, slightly reedited by the director and with the addition of a musical sound track. In 1935, Twentieth Century-Fox (for reasons that are today difficult to understand) decided to remake the film, but the remake only proved that the plot was extremely difficult to present in a believable and artistic manner. Once again it was shown that the talent of Griffith was necessary to fashion the material into a work that film critic Stanley Kauffmann has called "a picture of persistent strength and of exceptional interest in American cultural history."

Timothy W. Johnson

THE WEDDING MARCH

Released: 1928
Production: Adolph Zukor and Jesse L. Lasky for Famous Players-Lasky; released by Paramount
Direction: Erich Von Stroheim
Screenplay: Erich Von Stroheim and Harry Carr
Cinematography: Ben Reynolds and Hal Mohr
Art direction: Richard Day
Music: J. S. Zamecnik
Length: 24 reels/10,721 feet

> *Principal characters:*
> Prince Nicki von
> Wildeliebe-Rauffenberg .... Erich Von Stroheim
> His father, Prince Ottokar .... George Fawcett
> His mother, Princess Maria .... Maude George
> Mitzi Schrammell .... Fay Wray
> Martin Schrammell .... Cesare Gravina
> His wife, Katherina .... Dale Fuller
> Wine-garden keeper .... Hughie Mack
> Schani Eberle .... Matthew Betz
> The Magnate, Schweisser .... George Nichols
> His daughter, Cecilia .... ZaSu Pitts
> Emperor Franz-Josef .... Anton Wawerka

The career of Erich Von Stroheim is regarded as one of the most tragic in Hollywood history. Few directors of his acknowledged genius have suffered careers as aborted as this controversial autocrat. His entire directorial output was nine motion pictures, most of which were either released in edited versions of which he did not approve or were not completed by him at all.

In addition, his greatest masterpiece, *Greed* (1923), remains the greatest of the "lost" films, and *The Wedding March*, his second greatest masterpiece, survives only in part. Originally intended to be two films, *The Wedding March* and *The Honeymoon*, the sole surviving print of *The Honeymoon* was destroyed by a fire in the Paris Cinémathèque. Fortunately, these two films do survive pictorially in book versions compiled by film historian Herman Weinberg: *The Complete Greed* (1972) and *The Complete Wedding March* (1975).

Historically, Von Stroheim ranks among the top dozen motion-picture directors and is perhaps the most individualistic *auteur* of all the early pioneers. At the same time, he was also one of the most egocentric, autocratic, and controversial men in his profession. He found it absolutely impossible to work within the studio system or in any atmosphere which dictated controls over his creativity—there simply was no room for two dictators. His mortal enemy was "the Front Office," and yet his excessive and expansive habits, his obsession with detail, and his addiction to over-shooting footage was repeated time after time with almost a masochistic compulsion to bring the Front-Office wrath down atop his bald head. Von Stroheim's greatest enemy was Von Stroheim himself. His only form of survival was to eke out a career as an actor—and he was at times a great actor—and it is that career for which he is remembered by most filmgoers, as opposed to film historians.

He was born Erich Oswald Stroheim in Vienna in 1885, and although he cultivated the myth that he had been a cavalry officer and a member of the Austrian aristocracy, he was in fact the son of a simple German-Jewish merchant, and he had added the "Von" to his name to further perpetuate the myth. He emigrated to the United States in 1909 and spent the next several years actually hustling a variety of mundane jobs, including being a traveling salesman for a lingerie company, a job which would seem to have appealed to his Freudian instincts.

Eventually, John Emerson hired him as military adviser and actor in *Old Heidelberg* (1915), after which he went to work for D. W. Griffith as an assistant and also acted in *The Birth of a Nation* (1915) and *Intolerance* (1916). In 1917, he played the part of a Prussian officer in Wesley Ruggles' *Old France* and thereafter was frequently typecast in that role.

Ever hustling, he finally talked Universal's Carl Laemmle into allowing him to direct, and his debut was *Blind Husbands* (1919), the first of a trilogy on adultery. His work was immediately recognized as intellectual, Freudian, and pictorially impressive, but from the start his unorthodox work habits made studio executives wary. He completed the trilogy with *The Devil's Passkey* (1919) and *Foolish Wives* (1922) and then was removed from his production of *Merry-Go-Round* (1923), a feature which was completed by Rupert Julian.

That situation precipitated his move from Universal to M-G-M, where he shot forty-two reels of *Greed* in nine months. M-G-M took the final editing out of his domain and assigned him to the commercial project, *The Merry Widow* (1925), starring Mae Murray and John Gilbert. Shot in fourteen reels and released in twelve, it was to be his *only* commercially successful film as a director.

M-G-M had planned a third project, *East of the Rising Sun* starring Constance Talmadge, but Nicholas Schenck vetoed it, and Von Stroheim, and paved the way for Von Stroheim to enter into independent production with producer P. A. Powers.

Powers approached Von Stroheim to write and direct a film which would make a star out of Powers' girl friend Peggy Hopkins Joyce. At their meeting, Von Stroheim expressed no interest in Joyce but managed to convince Powers to back a story he had in mind called *The Wedding March*.

Powers was so impressed by Von Stroheim's storytelling and acting abilities that he agreed and convinced Paramount's Jesse L. Lasky to release the picture. The plot of *The Wedding March* is relatively simple but what would finally end up on screen was an entirely different matter. It was full of Von Stroheim's personal sexual yearnings and a re-creation of the Vienna of which he pretended to have been a part.

In the film, Prince Nicki von Wildeliebe-Rauffenberg (Erich Von Stroheim) is the son of decadent and impoverished Prince Ottokar (George Fawcett) and Princess Maria (Maude George) in pre-World War I Austria during the last decaying days of the Hapsburg dynasty.

The family's financial destitution forces them to demand that their son marry a rich girl. On the festive day of the Corpus Christi parade, Prince Nicki's horse bolts and injures a beautiful young maiden named Mitzi Schrammell (Fay Wray). She is the daughter of a violinist, Martin (Cesare Gravina), who plays in the orchestra of the wine-garden managed by Mitzi's mother, Katherina (Dale Fuller). The Corpus Christi processional scene is stunningly impressive in all its pomp and ceremony and the first meeting of these two lovers—with no words spoken between them—is equally and contrastingly beautiful in its simplicity. It is immediately apparent that they are instantly in love with each other.

Prince Nicki visits Mitzi in the hospital in a scene noted for its imaginative lighting and gauze filtered camera, after which Prince Nicki begins to court Mitzi at the wine-garden where she plays the harp in the orchestra. Her parents frown on the courtship, aware of the Prince's superior social position, but the couple's love is all-consuming, and one evening Mitzi gives herself to the Prince.

In the meantime, Nicki's father has made the acquaintance of a rich, vulgar cornplaster magnate named Schweisser (George Nichols), who has an eligible daughter named Cecilia (ZaSu Pitts). In a drunken scene between Prince Ottokar and Schweisser, which takes place with the two of them groveling on the floor of a brothel in the middle of an orgy (as only Von Stroheim could film orgies), the two fathers seal the fate of their children by arranging their marriage. Tragically, the shy, homely Cecilia has a crippled foot.

Mitzi's present suitor is the lowly butcher, Schani Eberle (Matthew Betz), who, upon hearing of Prince Nicki's betrothal, plans to kill the Prince as he exits the Cathedral St. Stefan's on his wedding day. Mitzi dissuades Schani by promising to marry him and part one ends with the grand marriage ceremony of Prince Nicki and Cecilia.

To many who saw the second part, *The Honeymoon*, when it was released in Europe in 1931 as *Mariage de Prince*, it is regarded as the more interesting half of the film. It takes place in a Tyrolean castle where Nicki and Cecilia spend their honeymoon. The urbane Nicki is Freudianly shown removing the shoe and stocking from Cecilia's deformed foot which renewed comment about Von Stroheim's own foot fetish.

Mitzi marries the butcher, but he realizes that she still loves Nicki, and so he sets out to kill him. He arrives at the hunting lodge and fires a bullet through a window but kills Cecilia instead of the Prince, and then dies himself trying to escape down the mountain. With dramatic irony and cynicism, Von Stroheim's Prince is now free to marry Mitzi, but he discovers she has entered a convent and the Prince rides off to battle in a war which will see the ruin of the Austrian Empire.

Von Stroheim began *The Wedding March* in June, 1926, and by its completion, or what Paramount executives determined was the completion (for by this time Powers had sold his interests to that studio), he had shot thirty-three hours of film at a reported cost of $1,125,000. Paramount ordered the film cut, first by another autocrat, Josef von Sternberg, then Julian Johnson, then still further, until eventually a truncated version of 10,400 feet was released to very mixed reviews in 1928. It was released in Europe in 1929, but Von Stroheim forbade Paramount, through a clause in his contract, to release the second part in the United States, and it was only seen abroad.

Von Stroheim's excesses involved building thirty-six sets, many of which were opulent reconstructions in exact detail of sights in Vienna. These included the sunburst altar of Cathedral St. Stefan's topped by the huge crucifix against a background of stained glass and bronze grill, as well as wooden pews carved to the exact dimensions of the originals. In addition, he had a complete Tyrolean hunting lodge built atop Mount Alice, 12,000 feet up in the High Sierra. Then there is the famous story of his ordering one thousand pairs of silk undergarments for the extras playing the aristocrats so they might at least feel aristocratic even though the lingerie itself would never be seen on film. Apocryphal as this particular story may be, however, it is indicative of the manner in which Von Stroheim worked—as if he wanted to bankrupt the moneymen. To his own exasperation, however, all his behavior did was to thwart his own efforts to create. Soon that power would be denied him forever, and all he would have left was an acting career in which there would be many clichéd Prussian officer portrayals and only an occasional good assignment.

For the most part, critics did not know what to make of *The Wedding March*. All were aware that this was not the film Von Stroheim had made, and yet they knew there would be little chance of ever seeing what he had really created, so their assessment of the badly edited version that went into release was almost universal: taken in short sections, individual scenes (as some critics felt *all* of Von Stroheim's work should be assessed), the film, they admitted, had many scenes which were strikingly original and moving—the Corpus Christi processional, the hospital scene, and the wedding, for example. All agreed, however, that even in this incomplete version, Von Stroheim allowed too much extraneous material to overshadow his story, and he never seemed able to edit himself. The beautifully romantic scenes were criticized for going on too long, and most critics quickly tired of what seemed like an avalanche of apple blossoms, that, while pictorially beautiful, seemed ready to snowbound the entire picture. As Paul Rotha wrote in *The Film Till Now*, "In the copy presented to the public, *The Wedding March* was lacking in unity, uncertain in treatment and crudely interspaced with cheaply written titles, but, for the student of the cinema, it contains some beautiful passages."

Von Stroheim's directing career ended completely in 1933, but he did continue acting, and two of his most outstanding efforts were in Jean Renoir's *La Grande Illusion* (1937) and Billy Wilder's *Sunset Boulevard* (1950). Shortly before his death in 1957, he was honored by the British Film Institute after which he told the press: "Over the vast, syphilitic wound that has been my career, this has been a small but welcome plaster [bandage]." In 1965, the New York Film Festival screened a 132-minute version of *The Wedding March* for a whole new generation of filmgoers who had never seen it.

Ronald Bowers

WEST OF ZANZIBAR

Released: 1928
Production: Tod Browning for Metro-Goldwyn-Mayer
Direction: Tod Browning
Screenplay: Elliott Clawson and Waldemar Young; based on an original screen
   story by Chester Devonde and Milbourn Gordon
Titles: Joseph W. Farnham
Cinematography: Percy Hilburn
Editing: Harry Reynolds
Length: 7 reels/6,150 feet

> *Principal characters:*
> Flint .... Lon Chaney
> Crane .... Lionel Barrymore
> The Doctor .... Warner Baxter
> Maizie .... Mary Nolan
> Flint's wife .... Jane Daly

   Director Tod Browning, who collaborated with actor Lon Chaney on eight silent films between 1925 and 1929, with each one becoming more fanatically obsessive than the last, seemed to find a perfect companion for his cinematic vision. Their films together were among the most off-beat thrillers ever made, with themes of mutilation, castration, sexual humiliation, and maniacal revenge obvious in almost every reel. Of these eight, *West of Zanzibar* is possibly the weirdest and certainly one of the strangest films ever produced by M-G-M, the studio known particularly for family-oriented films.

   In *West of Zanzibar*, Chaney plays a clown-magician named Flint who plies his trade in a music hall in the infamous Limehouse section of London. The film opens with his specialty: transforming a skeleton in an upright coffin into a lovely woman (Jane Daly), who happens to be his wife. Yet, on this particular night, even as Flint is backstage removing his makeup and flirting with her, she is planning to leave him for an ivory trader named Crane (Lionel Barrymore). He subsequently catches Crane kissing her and gets into a fight with him which results in his being thrown over a balustrade, which breaks his legs. Flint vows revenge on Crane. The film then flashes forward twenty years to an African village.

   Shaven-headed and crippled, Flint is now a tyrant known as Dead Legs, "the thing that crawls," presiding over a remote outpost with morbid glee. His wife has long since died (three months after leaving him as it turns out). Flint, believing her baby girl to have been fathered by Crane, put her in a brothel on his arrival in Africa, where she was reared to womanhood by whores. Flint is waiting for the day when Crane will show up at this forsaken spot so that he can reunite him with the daughter, Maizie (Mary Nolan), to show him the kind of woman she has become.

Meanwhile, an alcoholic doctor (Warner Baxter) takes care of Flint and looks after Maizie when the former magician flies into his periodic rages. The doctor is in love with Maizie but is too lethargic and dissipated to flee the outpost with her.

When Crane finally does appear, he is treated to the spectacle of Maizie being tortured by Flint, who has stirred up the natives to make Crane's daughter a human sacrifice. Ironically, however, it is Flint who is tortured since it is discovered that Maizie is really his daughter. Yet, Flint has gone too far in fanning the natives' enthusiasm for a human sacrifice, so in order to save the intended victim, Maizie, he pulls his skeleton-in-the-coffin trick one last time, substituting himself for his daughter to atone for twenty years of mistreatment. One of the last shots in the film shows Flint burning on a stake.

Considered a pulp nightmare, *West of Zanzibar* makes perfect sense, because only in pulp melodrama does one find such perverted plans for revenge. No where else would a crippled magician wait twenty years in such a terrible place instead of actively seeking the man who mangled him. Viewers never do discover why Flint hides himself in an obscure African hideout, although the darkness of Africa may be intended as a symbol for the darkness of his soul.

Browning, however, wants more than simple entertainment with a neatly tied, utterly logical story. The world of *West of Zanzibar* is a symbolic dream state where a ruined artist whips the local cannibals into a bloodthirsty frenzy with his magic tricks, living for the day when these monsters, under his control, will torture and maim on command.

Flint is an ugly sight through all this, as he slithers about on his dead limbs and descends from his grass hut bedroom by means of a knotted rope, then climbs into his wheel chair on arm strength alone. He is an utterly possessed demon, determined to get even with the man who wronged him even if the revenge costs more than it is worth.

It may be obsessive and illogical, but *West of Zanzibar* is not a bad film. It is an extraordinary piece of work that engulfs the viewer in a steaming, fetid milieu unlike any other. Even more incredible is that this skin-crawling jungle was created entirely on the M-G-M lot, yet the set designs and vivid, hallucinogenic black-and-white photography are so convincing that the audience believes that the film is actually in the heart of a dark continent; not the real Africa, but a twisted, surreal one tainted by evil thoughts and worse deeds.

Warner Baxter's performance as the doctor is equally amazing. Baxter was usually a debonair, mustachioed actor in conventional dress in an urban setting, but here he plays totally against type, even to the point of joining the natives in a crazy tribal dance. This was the most uninhibited that he had ever been allowed to become onscreen, and it did wonders for his career. The following year, Baxter was cast as the Cisco Kid in *In Old Arizona* (replacing director Raoul Walsh who had lost an eye in a car accident), winning a Best Actor Oscar for playing a dashing, earthy Mexican hero.

The other major cast members also turn in memorable performances. Lionel Barrymore is chillingly callous as the ivory huckster, Crane, although he does overact somewhat when lording over Flint in the final reel. Mary Nolan is sympathetic and also good as the young woman who learns too late who her real father is.

Good as the supporting cast is, *West of Zanzibar* is overwhelmingly a Browning-Chaney film, wringing the maximum shock value out of the concept and its climax, even though the finale is not entirely credible. If Chaney has such complete command over these savages, surely he would be able to rescue both himself and his daughter so that he could do penance by being a real father to her; a stake-burning is too easy an out.

After *West of Zanzibar*, Chaney and Browning made one more film together, the almost equally perverse *Where East Is East* (1929), in which Chaney plays a big-game hunter who heads a very strange household.

Oddly enough, Browning did not direct Chaney in the talking remake of their first film together, *The Unholy Three* (1930), but was set to direct him in the title role of *Dracula*, when Chaney died of throat cancer. Action director Jack Conway was assigned to *The Unholy Three* and what could have been an interesting talkie for Chaney (his only one) is instead a poor imitation of the silent version. Conway had absolutely no feeling for such bizarre material, and the end result is a turgid, incoherent film with midget actor Harry Earles mumbling his lines. Chaney does well under the adverse circumstances, however, and revealed a pleasant although gravelly voice.

Browning and Chaney had a marvelous four years together, creating a number of crazy cinematic spectres that would seldom be equaled or surpassed. For all the apparent morbidity of the Browning-Chaney oeuvre, their films are more imaginative and have more blood-curdling impact on the subconscious than almost all of the so-called horror films of the late 1970's and early 1980's.

Sam Frank

WHAT PRICE GLORY?

Released: 1926
Production: Winfield R. Sheehan for Fox Film Corporation
Direction: Raoul Walsh
Screenplay: James T. O'Donohoe; based on the play by Maxwell Anderson
and Laurence Stallings
Titles: Malcolm Stuart Boylan and Laurence Stallings
Cinematography: J. Barney McGill, with John Marta and John Smith
Length: 12 reels/11,400 feet

> *Principal characters:*
> Captain Flagg .... Victor McLaglen
> First Sergeant Quirt .... Edmund Lowe
> Charmaine de la Cognac .... Dolores Del Rio
> Cognac Pete .... William V. Mong
> Shanghai Mabel .... Phyllis Haver
> Mother's Boy .... Leslie Fenton

What Price Glory? began as a play by Maxwell Anderson and Laurence
Stallings that became a hit on Broadway in 1924. It amazed audiences with
its rough language and its irreverent portrayal of wartime marines who were
more concerned with women, drink, and their feuds with one another than
they were with fighting the enemy or with the patriotic motivations for doing
so. Indeed, the language was thought so strong that many speeches were
rewritten in milder terms after the opening night. At any rate, despite, or
perhaps because of, the outrage in some quarters about the language and its
disrespectful treatment of soldiers, the play was a great success with the
public.

A year later, in 1925, King Vidor's war film *The Big Parade* also achieved
great popular success and inspired Fox Film Corporation to buy the film rights
(for an impressive $100,000) to *What Price Glory?* The adaptation for the
screen was done by James T. O'Donohoe although one of the authors of the
play, Laurence Stallings, did collaborate with Malcolm Stuart Boylan on the
titles. Raoul Walsh, who had begun his career in films a dozen years earlier
as both an actor and an assistant director to D. W. Griffith, was chosen to
direct. Walsh had, in fact, played John Wilkes Booth in Griffith's *The Birth
of a Nation* (1915) but abandoned acting to concentrate on directing.

A great deal of time, effort, and expertise were devoted to the production
of the film, which took seven months to complete. Veterans of World War
I were hired both as technical consultants and as extras. It is claimed that
every extra in the film was a veteran. The battle scenes were so realistically
staged that explosions could be heard and sometimes felt in many residential
neighborhoods in Los Angeles. Less than one-tenth of the finished film,

however, consists of war footage. Most of the film takes place away from the battlefield.

The film that emerged from this planning and production is mainly a service comedy, although it is also partly a war story and partly a protest against the waste and injustice of war. It gains its effect not only from the script and from the strong direction but also from the fine performances from its principal actors—Victor McLaglen, Edmund Lowe, and Dolores Del Rio.

The film begins in China with the introduction of Captain Flagg (Victor McLaglen) and First Sergeant Quirt (Edmund Lowe), two soldiers who love wine and women but hate each other. As viewers will see throughout the film, it is usually a competition for a woman that provokes the fights between Flagg and Quirt. In Peking, it is Shanghai Mabel (Phyllis Haver) who causes their first brawl. Throughout the film a characteristic of the director is noticed: the first view of a woman is usually not of her face but of her derriere.

After a brief visit to the Philippines, the film arrives at its primary location, France, and reveals the most attractive object of the attentions of Flagg and Quirt thus far—Charmaine de la Cognac (Dolores Del Rio). She is described in a title as being "fascinated by the men who stop at her smile on their way to die." Her father, "Cognac Pete" (William V. Mong) runs an eating and drinking establishment in which Flagg is quartered when he arrives with the American forces. Charmaine and Flagg immediately begin a lighthearted liaison that is more sensual than romantic. In fact, film historian Kevin Brownlow has written that it is impossible for a present-day audience to realize how daring was "the utterly unabashed sexual content of the love scenes" in the film. Another element of *What Price Glory?* that shocked some and delighted others was the profanity uttered by Flagg and Quirt. None of the profane words was in the titles, but most viewers could read lips well enough to understand at least some of what was said. Many reviewers at the time mentioned this, and it has continued to be one of the most remembered and most remarked-upon features of the film.

Flagg is soon called to the front and separated from Charmaine. There follows a sequence of the women of the village saying good-bye to the soldiers and then a well-crafted montage of superb battle footage. After the fighting, Flagg is rewarded with a ten-day leave, which he spends by enjoying the wine and women of the town of Bar-le-Duc. Before he leaves, however, he is dismayed to find that Quirt has been assigned to his outfit and will take over his command while he is on leave. Flagg and Quirt immediately resume their scrapping with such statements as "I'd as soon find a skunk in my sleeping bag" appearing in the titles and stronger ones on their lips.

As Flagg had suspected, Charmaine transfers her affections to Quirt once Flagg leaves. Indeed, when Flagg returns, he finds that the garters he had given Charmaine are now on the shirtsleeves of Quirt. There is also an episode in which Charmaine's father demands that the man who "wrecked" his daughter marry her and give him five hundred francs. (His speaking French to the Americans is cleverly conveyed by titles in French that are flashed on the screen very rapidly.) At first, Flagg thinks he is the object of the father's wrath (or greed), and Quirt finds the situation hilarious, but then they find that it is Quirt who is accused, and it is time for Flagg to find the humor in the circumstances. Charmaine, however, refuses to marry Quirt, and the men are called back to the front.

The second battle sequence is longer and more emotionally forceful than the first. There are visually splendid night battle scenes, but also scenes of the wounded in the underground dressing station. One young soldier who has always been called "the mother's boy" (Leslie Fenton) calls for his mother and then dies in Flagg's arms. In this battle Quirt is wounded.

Both Flagg and Quirt go back to Charmaine and continue to quarrel with each other. Quirt tells Flagg, "I can beat you fighting and thinking and talking and—loving." Before they are ordered back to the front again, Charmaine tells Flagg that he has her heart but Quirt has her love. Then as the soldiers leave, Quirt decides to forget his wound and joins them. He shakes hands with his old adversary and the two march off together, Quirt supported by Flagg. They leave a despairing Charmaine who says that they came back twice but will not return a third time.

What Price Glory? has gained some reputation as a pacifistic film, and this could be supported by quoting some of the titles, such as Flagg's entry in his diary after the first battle sequence—"The horror of it haunts me." The second battle sequence is ended with a title that states that "the blood and youth of nations had been sacrificed for the mastery of a village." On the other hand, however, there is a speech in which Flagg approvingly tells his young soldiers that they have been baptized in blood, and "I'm as proud of you as America should be." The director, Raoul Walsh, has also noted that the overall portrayal of the marines in the film is that they were "happy-go-lucky guys with gals and this and that." In fact, he claims that the film promoted enlistments in the Marine Corps.

All in all, *What Price Glory?* has perhaps suffered too much from comparisons with the original play (some reviewers said that it sentimentalized the characters and incidents) and with *The Big Parade*. Perhaps Robert E. Sherwood in *Life* magazine summarized the film best as a "fine, stirring, straightforward movie." It was remade by John Ford in 1952 and starred James Cagney and Dan Dailey.

Timothy W. Johnson

WHEN KNIGHTHOOD WAS IN FLOWER

Released: 1922
Production: Cosmopolitan; released by Paramount
Direction: Robert G. Vignola
Screenplay: Luther Reed; based on the novel of the same name by Charles Major
Cinematography: Ira Morgan and Harold Wenstrom
Art direction: Joseph Urban
Costume design: Gretl Urban Thrulow
Music: Victor Herbert and William Frederick Peters
Length: 12 reels/11,618 feet

Principal characters:
Mary Tudor	Marion Davies
Henry VIII	Lyn Harding
Louis XII	William Norris
Charles Brandon	Forrest Stanley
Duke of Buckingham	Pedro de Cordoba
Sir Edwin Caskoden	Ernest Glendinning
Francis I	William Powell
Cardinal Wolsey	Arthur Forrest
Grammont	Gustav von Seyffertitz
Will Sommers	Johnny Dooley
An Adventurer	George Nash

When the film *When Knighthood Was in Flower* was released on September 14, 1922, it had the distinction of being the most expensive film ever made and boasted that one of its sets was two blocks long. The cast-list included many stars, a large supporting cast, and the most lavish decor ever designed. Praised by critics as a masterpiece, this historical spectacular was based on Charles Major's best-selling novel of the same name, a pomp and ceremony swashbuckler depicting the conflict between King Henry VIII and his sister Mary Tudor.

In the film, the fiery temper of the Princess Mary (Marion Davies) erupts into rebellion when her brother, King Henry VIII (Lyn Harding), announces that she is to marry King Louis XII of France (William Norris) for political reasons. Henry VIII arranges this marriage rather than make her turbulent romance with Charles Brandon (Forrest Stanley) legal. The tyrannical and temperamental Henry had a great deal with which to contend in the form of his rebellious younger sister in this colorful interpretation of history. After many threats, fights, cajolery, and a thwarted elopement attempt, Mary finally acquiesces to the King's demands in order to save her "commoner" lover from decapitation. She marries Louis XII on the condition that she be able to choose her second husband. King Louis does not live long, and although

King Francis I (William Powell) connives to make Mary his wife, she marries Brandon, finally with the blessing of her brother Henry.

While the film's musical-comedy characterizations are somewhat questionable as historical fact, the story is highly entertaining, and Marion Davies, as the petulant Mary Tudor, rather surprisingly gives an excellent interpretation of the spirited Princess. As *The New York Times* review of the film stated, "She really outdoes herself . . . really seems to have caught the spirit of the role, even if, at times, she gives the impression that she is well-drilled in the part." Contemporary reviews often criticized Davies' performances for their lack of spontaneity, but modern critics are usually more complimentary of her talents.

The incredible detail of the spectacle and the extraordinary art decoration by Joseph Urban adds considerably to the enjoyment of the film. Cosmopolitan indulged director Robert G. Vignola with an incredible budget, which he lavished on settings and costumes faithful to the period of the film. Urban had decorated palaces and built bridges in Europe before coming to the United States to design scenery for the Metropolitan Opera. Later, he became production manager for Cosmopolitan where he re-created magnificently, the period of Henry VIII for *When Knighthood Was in Flower*.

To put the magnitude of the art direction into perspective, some 340 costumes were specially imported from London, and Giddings & Co. of Fifth Ave., New York, made the gowns. Every prop in the film had to be a real antique or a perfect reproduction. For example, it took George Henry, a French woodcutting artist, three months to carve the elaborate doors and ornamental work. Bashford Dean, the foremost authority on ancient armor in America, and former curator of the Metropolitan Museum of Art, was commissioned to find suits of armor which could actually be used in scenes of combat. To this end, Dean obtained many suits of genuine tilting armor from European royalty. Antique, Gothic tapestries, valued at $125,000 each, and other genuine art objects were rented from private collectors as well as from commercial dealers. Cartier furnished the jewelry and diamonds in antique settings, and P. W. French & Co. supplied the priceless silverware which decorated the banquet tables in the film.

There were more than three thousand extras and dozens of horses used in the scene which takes place in front of Notre-Dame; actors and animals that paraded through the bricked streets of Cosmopolitan's reconstructed Paris, on which there were thirty-two separate buildings designed in the old French style. The job of building the sets was so extensive, in fact, that two other studios had to do additional construction. One built a duplicate of the great hall in Hampton Court, in which the historic incidents of the film were supposed to have taken place, and the other constructed the interior of Notre-Dame Cathedral, where the wedding of Louis XII and Princess Mary occurred and where she was eventually crowned Queen. The barge in which Princess

Mary rode to her birthday party was reconstructed on a river in Connecticut, and the tournament at which she first saw Brandon was filmed in Stamford, Connecticut.

Among the more spectacular costumes in the film were those of King Henry VIII, a fifty pound suit, and of Mary, a twenty-five pound wedding dress of pearl-decorated ermine and silver cloth. Fifteen assistant directors under the general supervision of first assistant Philip Carle were employed only to manage the details and the extras, while the same number of cameramen were shooting miles of film on the lavish production.

The scene depicting Mary at the altar, appealing her lover's execution, is unforgettable, as is the elopement sequence in which the lovers ride through a storm, equaled only by Rhett Butler and Scarlett O'Hara's ride through the blazing sets in *Gone with the Wind* (1939). Other important scenes include the provocative juxtaposition of Mary in her elegant bedchamber with a brilliant dueling sequence.

In addition to Davies, the star-studded cast includes Lyn Harding as King Henry VIII, an English actor-manager, who expertly re-creates the role for which he became famous. Harding physically bore a resemblance to a painting of Henry VIII by court painter Hans Holbein. Forrest Stanley, often Davies' leading man, is very handsome and dashing as Charles Brandon. William Norris as Louis XII, Pedro de Cordoba as the Duke of Buckingham, Arthur Forrest as Cardinal Wolsey, the dancer-contortionist Johnny Dooley as Will Sommers the King's jester, and George Nash as An Adventurer are all excellent and offer varied and highly effective performances.

Tanita C. Kelly

WHERE ARE MY CHILDREN?

Released: 1916
Production: Universal
Direction: Lois Weber and Phillips Smalley
Screenplay: Lois Weber; based on an original story by Lucy Payton and Franklyn Hall
Cinematography: no listing
Length: 5 reels

Principal characters:

Richard Walton, District Attorney	Tyrone Power, Sr.
Mrs. Walton	Helen Riaume
Mrs. Brandt	Marie Walcamp
Walton's housekeeper	Cora Drew
Lillian, her daughter	Rene Rogers
Roger, Mrs. Walton's brother	A. D. Blake
Dr. Malfit	Juan De La Cruz
Dr. Homer	C. Norman Hammond
The maid	Mary MacLaren

Although Lois Weber was trained to be a concert pianist, she had an uncle who persuaded her to become a musical-comedy leading lady at his Chicago theater. It was there that she met and married Phillips Smalley, and they entered films shortly afterward in New York City as a team. They wrote, directed, co-produced, and acted in motion pictures and eventually went to Hollywood and Universal, where they both enjoyed great popularity. Weber especially did well because she concentrated on direction and is probably the screen's most important female director of the silent period. The leading ladies she discovered for Universal included Mary MacLaren, Mildred Harris, Claire Windsor, and Billie Dove, every one of whom became a star in her own right.

Weber had a penchant for a highly exploitable kind of production, and *Where Are My Children?*, which deals with abortion and birth control, is a film far ahead of its time. Without the prologue and brief epilogue, it would be acceptable in today's market. Maurice Maeterlinck would have loved the prologue, and, in effect, it was already written by him in his play *The Blue Bird*. Beyond the Portals of Eternity, there are three types of children waiting to be born: what were then called "chance children"; those who are born physically defective; and those with sound bodies and minds, who are really wanted by their parents. Society might be benefited by the elimination of "chance children" and those who are defective, and for this reason the circulation of information about birth control should be encouraged and practiced. Such is the opinion of district attorney Richard Walton (Tyrone Power,

Sr.), the leading character in *Where Are My Children?* He believes, like Margaret Sanger and Emma Goldman, that the means toward attaining this ideal of eugenics should be placed within the reach of those who are poor and uneducated. Mr. Walton does realize, however, that one day soon such a plan for life will boomerang, and he will be the one who suffers.

Richard Walton wants to have children of his own, but his social butterfly wife (Helen Riaume) does not want to relinquish her activities for nine months, and more if she is going to nurse and attend a child in its infancy. When a friend of hers, Mrs. Brandt (Marie Walcamp) confides that she is pregnant, Mrs. Walton obligingly turns her over to her personal physician, Dr. Malfit (Juan De La Cruz). For a price, Dr. Malfit will try almost anything. He has kept Mrs. Walton from conceiving and helped her when she did, in spite of everything, and now he assists Mrs. Brandt in ridding herself of an unwanted child with an abortion. Mrs. Brandt is eternally grateful, for she is soon back to the afternoon bridge parties and teas for which her gay social circle lives.

Mrs. Walton has a young and rakish brother, Roger (A. D. Blake), visiting her, and the housekeeper's daughter, Lillian (Rene Rogers), comes to live for a time with her mother (Cora Drew) in the Walton house. When Roger sees the pretty young girl under the same roof as he, he cannot wait to seduce her. Lillian is ignorant of the consequences of her seduction, but Mr. Walton is the first to realize that something is sadly wrong with Lillian. When the innocent Lillian suddenly realizes that she is pregnant, she tells Roger that she must have his help. Roger, furious at being trapped by Lillian, goes to his sister, and Mrs. Walton gives him the address and number of Dr. Malfit to pass on to Lillian.

Lillian consults Dr. Malfit, and he tries to abort her unwanted child, but something goes wrong; this time he blunders, but not before Lillian, dying, confesses the truth to her mother. The grief-stricken housekeeper goes directly to Richard Walton. It is useless to place the blame on Roger, because his sister has helped him leave the country. Walton discovers that the culprit is Dr. Malfit, and he is prosecuted fully. Malfit then writes Mrs. Walton, threatening exposure unless she comes to his aid and procures a lighter sentence from her husband. Mrs. Walton, however, is helpless, and Dr. Malfit receives a heavy sentence. In revenge, he sends his datebook to Walton, with all the pages marked on which Mrs. Walton herself paid him a visit.

Thus, Richard Walton becomes aware of his wife's deception. He comes to her with the datebook in hand and asks fiercely, "Where are my children?" Mrs. Walton, repentant, begs forgiveness, but his answer is to repeat the question with accusative force, "Where are my children?" She realizes that what he is doing is tantamount to naming her as a murderess, but at the same time he realizes that he also is guilty. Society has made them criminals, her by actually aborting a child conceived and him by lending his influence to the making of many other criminals.

Wherever *Where Are My Children?* played, audiences were visibly moved by the force of the drama. Universal released the picture on a state rights basis, and the audience was wide and entirely receptive. It was the first major success for the Smalleys. Mary MacLaren who had a small role as the maid in the Walton home was selected by Weber to star in *Shoes* (1916), the sad tale of a poor working girl who gives up her virtue for the price of a pair of good shoes. In the late 1920's, Weber had two big successes with Billie Dove vehicles, *The Marriage Clause* (1926) and *The Sensation Seekers* (1927), and Cecil B. De Mille used her to pronounced effect at Producers Distributing Corporation, especially with Leatrice Joy in *The Angel of Broadway* (1927).

Weber's husband, Phillips Smalley, continued to be employed regularly when talkies came in. After he died, she married a second time. Despite her decline in income she made no changes in her life-style, and she died broke in 1939. Screenwriter Frances Marion, to whom Weber gave employment when both were working for Oliver Morosco, came forward and paid the funeral expenses and debts that Weber had managed to incur.

DeWitt Bodeen

WHERE THE PAVEMENT ENDS

Released: 1923
Production: Rex Ingram for Metro Pictures Corporation
Direction: Rex Ingram
Screenplay: Rex Ingram; based on the short story "The Passion Vine," by
   John Russell
Cinematography: John F. Seitz
Editing: Grant Whytock
Length: 8 reels/7,706 feet

> *Principal characters:*
> Motauri .... Ramon Novarro
> Matilda Spener .... Alice Terry
> Pastor Spener .... Edward J. Connelly
> Captain Hull Gregson .... Harry T. Morey
> Napuka Joe, his servant .... John George

"Where the pavement ends, there Romance begins" is the anonymous quote that gave writer John Russell a title for his book of short stories of faraway places. The volume contains a haunting short story called "The Passion Vine," but when Rex Ingram filmed that story, he decided to call his picture *Where the Pavement Ends* because it is one of the most romantic of all Russell's stories, and could only happen far away from civilization. It was Ingram's ninth feature to be released by Metro, and he made it away from Hollywood pressures, shooting most of the film on the coast of Florida and a portion of it in Cuba.

He gathered around him the people with whom he liked to work: his wife Alice Terry; his favorite leading man, Ramon Novarro; cinematographer John F. Seitz; and film editor Grant Whytock. With his cast and crew and far from Hollywood interference, Ingram's picture took on a luscious native beauty.

Hollywood, however, did intrude on Ingram's isolated group. Before leaving for Florida, Ingram had gone to New York City, where he talked privately to Marcus Loew, who was the eastern head of Metro (or Metro-Goldwyn-Mayer, as the studio was then in the process of becoming). Ingram was assured that when the studio did the film *Ben-Hur* (1925), he would be named its director. *Ben-Hur* was the one story property that he wanted to make, and certainly no other director was as well equipped as he to make that film a testament to beauty. He went to Florida to make *Where the Pavement Ends* with the assurance from Loew that *Ben-Hur* might even be his next film.

Louis B. Mayer, the new head of the studio's production department, however, did not want so rare a plum as *Ben-Hur* to go to Ingram, who, he felt, was personally inimical to him. With Ingram more than three thousand miles away, Mayer operated quickly. He named Charles Brabin as director of *Ben-Hur* and approved a cast, most of whom later had to be changed during production. Ingram was about two-thirds through shooting *Where the Pavement Ends* when he received word of Mayer's betrayal. He lost his temper and a day's work berating Mayer; but then he pulled himself together and went on with *Where the Pavement Ends*, determined to give it the best that was in him. Consequently, a more beautiful picture was never made. Every frame is a thing of rare and wondrous beauty. It is sad that so much loveliness survives only in stills, for *Where the Pavement Ends* is a "lost" film.

It tells a simple story that is both lyrical and impassioned. The hero, Motauri (Ramon Novarro), a native boy of the islands, is a pagan, a hero uncorrupted by the excesses of Christianity, which have tainted the Wallis Islands in the South Pacific, where the story is set. In the island community there lives a lonely group of Protestant missionaries, with only one young female, Miss Matilda Spener (Alice Terry), the daughter of Pastor Spener (Edward J. Connelly). They were originally from New England, but Miss Matilda has grown to young womanhood on an island where there is no other white woman. She exists in a kind of dream world, surrounded by beauty and spends her time reading poetry and playing hymns in her father's church on the melodeon. Her father is so absorbed in his teachings that he does not realize how selfish he has, in fact, become.

Pastor Spener is also extremely corruptible. He is greedy for money, which makes him blind to the vulgarities of Captain Hull Gregson (Harry T. Morey), a rich trader whose store is the center of all trade in the island village. In order to get into the good graces of Pastor Spener, Gregson announces that he will no longer sell intoxicating liquors to the natives. This, of course, so pleases Spener that he is receptive to the idea of a future marriage between his daughter and Gregson.

Matilda, however, loathes Gregson, finding him utterly revolting, and the mere thought of being married to him is highly offensive to her. Yet, there is no one on the island to help her resist her father's corrupt desires, and so she is not in a position to spurn Gregson. There is only Motauri, the young island chieftan, whose own island is within boating distance from the one on which the Speners live. Motauri, in fact, has his own boat and often rows from his island to stand outside the mission church when Miss Matilda plays songs on the melodeon. He stands directly outside the window and mouths the words that she sings. They become friends, and by arrangement, she frequently meets him near the huge passion vine not far from her father's church. Neither she nor Motauri realizes that Captain Gregson is aware of their secret meetings. He has, in fact, spied upon them through a telescope and viewing their happiness in each other's company has only made him more determined to claim Matilda as his own.

When Matilda learns of her father's plan to marry her to Gregson, she realizes that Motauri is her only chance for salvation. He is elated when she consents to marry him. They plan to run away together and go immediately to Motauri's island, where she will take him as her husband in a native ceremony. Captain Gregson watches their meeting through his telescope, however, and quickly sets up a plan to trap them before they can get away.

Because they do not want to be seen together passing through the little village, Motauri carries her down a perilous waterfall, aided greatly by a clinging passion vine. They hope to find his boat where he had beached it, but it is not in the ravine where he had always hidden it, nor is there any sign of another boat in the immediate vicinity. Gregson has worked fast, and the boats are all hidden. The only course remaining is for Matilda to remain where she is while Motauri seeks a substitute vessel. As he searches for a boat, however, Motauri is apprehended by Gregson himself and forced to accompany him to the captain's shack.

Meanwhile, the sky is darkening and the wind is rising, signaling a hurricane. Matilda, alone now, begins to regret her rash decision to run off with Motauri and attempts to make her way back to her father's church before the storm increases in intensity. At the same time, Motauri turns on Gregson, and the two men fight fiercely. Gregson tries to kill Motauri, but he is himself the victim of the struggle and is slain by Motauri.

Miss Matilda manages to get to Gregson's shack and finds Motauri about to make his way back to her. Frantically, she tells him that she cannot marry him and begs for forgiveness. She collapses, and Motauri carries her back through the wind and the rain to her father's church, where he deposits her on the veranda. He touches her unconscious face tenderly and then takes a bag of pearls, the only wealth that he has in the world, and presses it into her hand. Now there is nothing to make him want to go on living. He returns to the top of the ravine, grasps the passion vine, and then swings out and drops into the turbulent waterfall. Days later, on a clear morning, Matilda and her father give up their now hopeless attempt to run a missionary colony and sail back to New England.

Novarro's growing popularity as a star made exhibitors demand that the picture not end unhappily, so Ingram shot a second ending where it is proved that Motauri's parentage is white under his lovely tan, and consequently, Pastor Spener consents to his daughter's marriage to her pagan lover. Ironically, though, all of England and Europe preferred the original, tragic ending, and that was the one most frequently shown, except in the American "Bible Belt." Equally ironic was the situation of *Ben-Hur*, because the original company was called back to Hollywood, where, save for Carmel Myers as Iras and Francis X. Bushman as Messala, a new company was selected and sent to Italy, headed by Novarro as Ben-Hur. The film was released in 1925, a great success, even without Ingram.

DeWitt Bodeen

THE WHISPERING CHORUS

Released: 1918
Production: Cecil B. De Mille for the Artcraft Pictures Corporation; released by Famous Players-Lasky/Paramount
Direction: Cecil B. De Mille
Screenplay: Jeanie Macpherson; based on the novel of the same name by Perley Poore Sheehan
Cinematography: Alvin Wyckoff
Editing: Cecil B. De Mille
Art direction: Wilfred Buckland
Length: 6 reels

Principal characters:
John Tremble .... Raymond Hatton
Jane Tremble .... Kathlyn Williams
John Tremble's mother .... Edythe Chapman
George Coggeswell .... Elliott Dexter
Longshoreman .... Noah Beery
Chief McFarland .... Guy Oliver
F. P. Clumley .... Tully Marshall
Channing .... James Neill
Evil Face/Temptation .... Gustav von Seyffertitz
Good Face/Self-Sacrifice .... Edna Mae Cooper

One of the first psychological studies of a man's inner conflict on film is Cecil B. De Mille's *The Whispering Chorus*, a psychovisual presentation of the temptations pro and con leading to a man's ultimate decisions. De Mille did it pictorially with an evil face (Gustav von Seyffertitz) and a good face (Edna Mae Cooper) as they advise the hero on how he should decide his course of action, and, in several instances, he shows a multiple collection of materialized faces of conscience assailing the man's mind.

Early in the picture it is established that *The Whispering Chorus* is made up of those voices that speak to every soul, the voices that guide one toward right or wrong. The hero, John Tremble (Raymond Hatton), heard the voice of Temptation and followed it to the depths of degradation, until the voice of Self-Sacrifice caused him to give up his life so that happiness might come to the woman he loved.

John Tremble is a bookkeeper who is tempted to change one figure on his books so that he can get money to obtain a few of the best things in life. Unfortunately for him, after he has yielded to temptation, word arrives at the office where he works that the authorities are coming on the following day to balance the books. Tremble is desperate. He is happily married, and his wife, Jane (Kathlyn Williams), has not minded all of the sacrifices she has had to make, nor has his mother (Edythe Chapman), who lives with the couple.

They have all been invited to go to the theater for a holiday performance, but John, pleading that some last-minute work at the office must be done, urges them to go ahead and he will join them during the intermission. With the stolen money he had planned to buy his wife a simple silk dress to which she was attracted, but outside the dress store, he is induced to join a crony in a game of cards. Hoping that luck may come his way, he yields to persuasion and thus loses all of his embezzled money.

He wanders the wintry streets down to the river, intending to drown himself in the icy waters, but he discovers a body drifting in the backwaters and pulls it ashore. The dead man is very like him in height and weight, and it is thus that the idea of changing identities is born. He changes clothes with the corpse and then disfigures the face so that it cannot be recognized. He makes certain that there is proper identification of himself on the man's body and then he leaves him, certain that the mutilated body will soon be discovered and identified as that of the missing John Tremble.

The body is discovered, declared a victim of violence, and identified by Jane Tremble as that of her husband. She is stunned with grief, and the only consolation that comes to her is from John Tremble's boss, George Coggeswell (Elliott Dexter), a distinguished businessman rising to importance in the world of banking. As time goes by, Coggeswell finds himself attracted more and more to Jane, but she remains faithful to John's memory although she is drawn to Coggeswell. Time passes, and John Tremble is eventually declared legally dead. Jane finally yields to Coggeswell, and they are married.

Meanwhile, John has slipped faster and lower on the social scale until he is no more than a derelict with no resemblance to the man he had been. The police, however, have never given up in their search for the missing murderer of John Tremble. Meanwhile, Coggeswell is rising in political importance and runs for governor of the state, an election he wins; he is doubly happy when Jane informs him that she is soon to become a mother.

Tremble is drawn to the cottage where his mother now lives happily, and a detective, who has followed him on the advice of a neighbor, sees his mother give food to a tramp. Something about the tramp, however, intrigues the detective, and he keeps a close watch upon the house. Tremble's mother recognizes him as her long lost son and has a heart attack. Before she dies, she makes John swear to keep his true identity a secret so that Jane will not be named as a bigamist and her unborn child, a bastard. The detective arrests John, and when evidence points to his relationship at one time in the past to Tremble, the suspect is accused of murder and put on trial. The supreme irony is that, in fact, he goes on trial for his own murder.

Tremble, aware that he may be executed as his own murderer, in a weak moment reveals that he is really Tremble, but it is too bizarre an admission to be believed. The only one who has doubts of his identity is Jane, who is able to see John in his cell. John tries to persuade her that he had lied, and she, wanting to believe that he is not really her husband, allows herself to be convinced that he is a stranger.

In the dawn, Coggeswell rises and joins Jane, not realizing that she is still torn by a shred of doubt. In his cell, John Tremble meets with those who will lead him to the death chamber. He falters once, but regains his composure, enters the chamber, and the door closes upon him.

The Whispering Chorus told a searing story that was unlike anything De Mille ever had done before, and he looked upon it as his finest achievement, as gripping as *The Cheat* (1915), but with many more psychological truths. Critics greatly praised it, admitting its effect as powerful, but doubting that the public would accept it. They were right. Audiences found it morbid and resisted its double-exposed drama.

De Mille's principals were three of Hollywood's finest actors, and they gave of their best. Kathlyn Williams had played many dramatic roles at Selig, where she had been the top female star of that studio in such dramas as *The Spoilers* (1914), *The Rosary* (1915), and *The Ne'er Do Well* (1916). De Mille used her three times—in this feature as well as in *We Can't Have Everything* (1918) and as the Fairy Godmother in *Forbidden Fruit* (1921). Elliott Dexter played more male leads for De Mille than any other player at Paramount, but the role of Coggeswell was one of his most sympathetic. Raymond Hatton had his most important and challenging role in *The Whispering Chorus* and drew excellent notices for his performance.

Paramount, aware of the dramatic value of the story, essentially remade it as *The Way of All Flesh*, Emil Janning's first film in America, and for that film and *The Last Command*, Jannings won an Oscar as Best Actor of the year 1927-1928, the first year of the Awards. *The Way of All Flesh* was remade a second time in 1940, with Akim Tamiroff in the lead, but the picture was virtually ignored.

De Mille did learn something important from making *The Whispering Chorus*: he never again was tempted by the power of a downbeat story. After the film's failure to find any popularity with audiences, he determined to give them what they wanted: sex, luxury, and satiric comedy. By the next year, he was producing such box-office hits as *Don't Change Your Husband*, *Why Change Your Wife?*, *Male and Female*, and a whole series of marital extravaganzas. Yet, until *The King of Kings* (1927), when anybody asked him, "What is your favorite picture, Mr. De Mille?" he answered with a rueful smile, "*The Whispering Chorus*."

DeWitt Bodeen

WHITE GOLD

Released: 1927
Production: C. Gardner Sullivan for De Mille Pictures; released by Producers Distributing Corporation
Direction: William K. Howard
Screenplay: Garrett Fort, Marian Orth, and Tay Garnett; based on the play of the same name by J. Palmer Parsons
Titles: John Krafft and John Farrow
Cinematography: Lucien Andriot
Editing: John Dennis
Art direction: Anton Grot
Length: 7 reels/6,108 feet

Principal characters:
Dolores Carson .... Jetta Goudal
Alec Carson .... Kenneth Thomson
Sam Randall .... George Bancroft
Carson, Alec's father .... George Nichols
Homer .... Clyde Cook

The story told in *White Gold* takes place in Arizona near the Mexican border on a large sheep ranch; thus, the sheep themselves provide the explanation of the title. Technically, it is a Western, but it has none of the accoutrements of the usual Western. Perhaps that is because Cecil B. De Mille had more than a small part in its production, working very closely with director William K. Howard. Another reason is that it sprang from a play that was originally set in Australia.

It is a tightly knit story. It opens with Alec Carson (Kenneth Thomson), a young sheep farmer, in a cantina which is on the Mexican side of the border. He has traveled to the town for supplies. At the cantina, he is much taken with Dolores (Jetta Goudal), the chief entertainer, who dances and accompanies herself on the guitar. Before he leaves the town and goes back to his ranch, he proposes to Dolores, and she accepts.

He drives his carriage through beautiful country on the way back to the ranch, with sheep grazing on every piece of land. The thick cumulus clouds hang dramatically over the scene, but Dolores is anxious and excited to see his ranch house, where she will be the only female for miles around. At last, he turns in at the gate, and his house is only a single-storied farmhouse with a bunkhouse behind it where the sheepherders live. Only Homer (Clyde Cook), the cook, and Alec's old, grizzled, complaining father (George Nichols) are on hand to receive Alec and his beautiful bride when they arrive. Homer is overjoyed that there will now be a lady of the house, but old Carson is not only surprised that his son has taken a wife, but also that he has picked such a beautiful one.

Dolores is delightful that first night. Alec and Homer are already captivated by her charms, but she senses that the old man not only dislikes her but also resents her presence in his son's house. He is even jealous when Alec and she retire for the evening to Alec's master bedroom.

The country is suffering from a drought, and when the dry, hot wind starts to blow again the following morning, it only fans old Carson's bitterness. Everybody is taut and nervous, and Alec even snaps at his father when the old man casts aspersions on Dolores' virtue. Why would she be singing and dancing in a bordertown cantina if she were not one of the devil's breed?, he asks. Alec reminds his father that he is now Dolores' husband and the old man had best watch himself when she is around.

At this point, an itinerant sheepherder named Sam Randall (George Bancroft) appears looking for work. He is hired at once by old man Carson who notices that Randall is interested in Dolores. Randall, at the instigation of Carson, tries to be friendly with Dolores, but she quickly puts him in his place. Tempers are short, however, and Dolores is on Randall's mind more frequently than not. She, however, goes about her business and never comes to life except in the presence of her husband.

Old Carson's constant insinuations about Dolores irritate Alec, but he refuses to refute them, thus causing a quarrel between himself and Dolores one evening because he is so passive. He, frustrated, slams out of the house to spend the night in the bunkhouse. Randall at first battles his conscience about Dolores' vulnerability but finally succumbs to his lesser nature. He decides to go after her and moves to the door. It is unlocked, and he softly turns the knob and enters the room.

The following morning Randall is found in the master bedroom, shot to death. Alec's father immediately says that in the middle of the night, he had awakened and seen Randall creeping into the bedroom, and when he went to the door, he saw Dolores surrendering to Randall's passion. Old man Carson is in his element, but Alec, troubled, looks questioningly at Dolores, who is staring straight ahead, saying nothing. The old man breaks in and admits to shooting Randall because he was raping Alec's wife, and she was not struggling against him.

Dolores still says nothing; she neither denies nor confirms the accusation, nor does she defend her actions. Alec looks at her fiercely and demands that she talk; she draws herself up proudly and says, staring into his eyes, "I am waiting for my husband to believe in me." This so shatters Alec that he can only sink into a chair, not knowing what to believe. Old Carson's eyes are gleaming because he knows that he has almost won his case. Dolores then turns and walks into the bedroom, closing the door.

A little later she leaves the house. The wind is blowing, and she lifts her shawl so that it covers her head. She is carrying all that she is taking with her in one small bundle. She starts walking down the road, then pauses for a moment at a mud hole and takes from her waist a hand gun. She looks at it, the proof of her innocence had she wanted to display it to her husband, the proof that it was she who slew Randall when he attacked her. She throws the gun into the mud hole and continues to walk to the border village.

White Gold is a very strong story, the best and most completely realized of all the films Goudal did for De Mille at Producers Distributing Corporation. It is a mood piece, but it is remarkably taut, and although it is a seven-reel feature, there is not an extraneous moment in it. Goudal is the only woman, and the audience's sympathy is with her. Dolores is the strongest role De Mille gave Goudal to perform, and she plays it with consummate artistry, overshadowing all her male support.

Goudal had a curious but brief career. She had come from Europe to the New York stage, where she made a hit in two plays, *The Hero* and *The Elton Case*. Everything she did on the screen glittered with a strange exoticism. She worked for De Mille in *The Road to Yesterday* (1925) and for D. W. Griffith in *Lady of the Pavements* (1929). She actually sued De Mille over a misinterpretation of her contract and won the case, so he never used her again, despite the fact that he had starred her brilliantly in *Three Faces East* (1926), a drama of espionage in World War I, as well as in *White Gold*. There is something heroic in her mien in *White Gold* when she triumphantly walks off alone, only pausing to dispose of the weapon that could have proved that she was a virtuous woman forced to kill in order to maintain her virtue. She was definitely one of the shining lights of the silent screen.

DeWitt Bodeen

THE WHITE ROSE

Released: 1923
Production: D. W. Griffith for United Artists
Direction: D. W. Griffith
Screenplay: Irene Sinclair (D. W. Griffith)
Cinematography: G. W. Bitzer, Hendrik Sartov, and Hal Sintzenich
Length: 10 reels/9,800 feet

Principal characters:
Bessie "Teazie" Williams .... Mae Marsh
Marie Carrington .... Carol Dempster
Joseph Beaugarde .... Ivor Novello
John White .... Neil Hamilton
"Auntie" Easter .... Lucille La Verne
"Apollo," a servant .... Porter Strong

In 1922, D. W. Griffith directed *Orphans of the Storm*, a spectacle set during the French Revolution focusing on the lives of two sisters, one of whom is blind, who lose track of each other in teeming Paris. The film had to earn a great deal of money for its director, who was in debt; unfortunately, it was not the kind of success Griffith needed so desperately at this point in his career. It was based on an old play, *The Two Orphans*, filmed as a short in 1911 and again with Theda Bara in 1915; an Italian-made *Two Orphans* was released in America prior to the opening of Griffith's version, which undoubtedly cut into the film's box office.

The director was struggling artistically as well as financially. He next made *One Exciting Night* (1922), a hackneyed murder mystery starring Henry Hull and Carol Dempster which has nevertheless been credited as the first of its genre. He fortunately redeemed himself stunningly with his next film, *The White Rose*, a tale of the rural South which was savaged by the critics but is still an intriguingly complex motion picture highlighted by a sparkling Mae Marsh performance.

The plot is, on the surface, a superficial Victorian soap opera replete with unlikely plot coincidences and racial stereotypes; lamentably, the black servants are even referred to as "darkies." Underneath, however, the characters—especially the three leads—are multidimensional human beings who transcend the cardboard scenario.

Bessie Williams (Mae Marsh), with the appropriate nickname of "Teazie," is a poor, orphaned waitress eking out a living in an inn outside New Orleans. Although as virginal as any Griffith heroine, she is nevertheless a coquette. She flirts with men and has earned a reputation as a "loose woman," but she is still "innocent." Bessie adores Joseph Beaugarde (Ivor Novello), a wealthy, priggish young man who was recently graduated from a seminary. After attending a ball given by the parents of his girl friend, Marie Carrington (Carol Dempster), a woman of high social standing, Beaugarde sets out on a trip to learn more about the world. He and Bessie meet at the inn, and while he is repulsed by her flirtatiousness, he is also attracted to her. He seduces her, believing her to be a mere jezebel, but the girl, who really was a virgin, gives birth to a baby without Beaugarde's knowledge.

Meanwhile, Beaugarde has gone home to his plantation in the Louisiana bayous. He feels guilt over his treatment of Bessie, however, because he really loves her. He channels his emotions into his work, and his vivid sermons win him popularity. Beaugarde is informally engaged to Marie, who in turn has repressed her feelings for John White (Neil Hamilton), a grocery clerk, because of his poor-white-trash background. White cares for Marie, but believing that his pursuit of her is hopeless, he, too, goes out into the world. Later, he becomes a successful author after writing a book entitled *Life Through a Grocer Shop's Window*. Marie is then able to admit her love for the boy she once ignored.

Because of her illegitimate child, Bessie loses her job, and she cannot find another. She is evicted from her lodging and is now an outcast. In one heartbreaking scene, she uses a discarded dog box for her baby, whose father she refuses to name. When she inadvertently but conveniently strays near the Beaugarde plantation, a black servant couple, "Auntie" Easter and "Apollo," a mammy and butler (Lucille La Verne and Porter Strong, white actors in blackface), find Bessie near death and give her shelter in a log cabin. Marie helps to nurse Bessie, and Beaugarde is summoned. He discovers that this is the woman he had mistreated and is finally able to acknowledge his true feelings for her. She, too, is still in love with him, as she always has been. Marie forgives Beaugarde for his affair with Bessie, and without animosity, she agrees to break their engagement. He relinquishes his ties with the Church, and Bessie and Beaugarde are married immediately.

There are a number of symbols of morality in the film. Bessie and Beaugarde have been redeemed by their love—and matrimony. In the first part of the film, Beaugarde treats a poor alcoholic testily, but later, he helps the old man find shelter. He is now truly a religious man, more so than when he was in the pulpit. Even the servants, who had been living together without benefit of a marriage license, are wed. Beaugarde nurses Bessie and their baby as if they are dying roses, and at the finale, Griffith focuses in on a close-up of a rose.

The White Rose is slow-paced, but the director chose to unravel the scenario in this manner. Griffith, who wrote the film under the name "Irene Sinclair," lets his camera linger on his actors and the natural settings, mostly in long shots, and allows the picture to tell the story. He is not concerned with montage or quick cutting. The film, shot on location in Franklin and St. Martinsville, Louisiana, with interiors filmed in rented space at the Hialeah

Studios outside Miami, is composed not of a mixture of long and medium shots and close-ups, but of simple, beautifully composed shots of gardens, lakes, trees, the ball at the Carrington plantation. Edited together, they imply peacefulness, permanence, warmth, and loving feelings. The sequences of Bessie in the city, however, particularly in a dance hall, are harshly lit. They reek of shoddiness and of the despair Bessie feels when she is homeless with her fatherless baby. Metaphorically, Griffith eloquently captures Bessie's emotional state. Although not in keeping with the visual and stylistic advances made by other directors during the 1920's, *The White Rose* is still a quiet, beautiful, complex, and dramatic motion picture.

The film is also graced with an exceptional performance by Mae Marsh. A Griffith heroine in *The Birth of a Nation* (1915) and *Intolerance* (1916), Marsh is perfectly cast as Bessie; she is a creature of nature, as at home in the countryside as the flowers and trees. Marsh's career had declined since she left Griffith with whom she had also worked in many of his Biograph shorts. *The White Rose* is a stunning comeback for her. She movingly conveys helplessness and confusion, yet she still tenaciously protects the name of the man she loves. Unfortunately, Bessie Williams was her last role for Griffith, and her final great characterization on the screen.

Marsh is ably supported by Ivor Novello, the Welsh-born matinee idol in his first American film. Best recalled, perhaps, for his title role in Alfred Hitchcock's first thriller *The Lodger* (1926), Novello played the innocent man accused by circumstances of being Jack-the-Ripper. Also lending their support to the film were Neil Hamilton, who was acclaimed as the "new Richard Barthelmess" and went on to star in Griffith's epic *America* (1924) and the underrated *Isn't Life Wonderful* (1924), and Carol Dempster, a young actress who started in films as an extra in *Intolerance* and who Griffith unsuccessfully tried to mold into another Marsh and Lillian Gish. Dempster, never a top star, was quickly forgotten by most film devotees. She is most appealing here, however, and later played opposite Hamilton in *Isn't Life Wonderful* and *America*.

The reviewers, however, treated *The White Rose* cooly. They criticized not the film but its director by complaining that the scenario chronicled yet another innocent girl whose purity is threatened. Griffith insisted on directing scenarios which stressed a conservative sentimentality that was outmoded during the 1920's. Yet, the debt that all filmmakers owed Griffith is immeasurable: he, more than anyone else, united the theatrical and documentary aspects of film. In so doing, he invented the grammar of the motion picture.

Despite its pictorial beauty, *The White Rose* was yet another in a series of box-office failures that ruined Griffith. The director consulted several clergymen during the shooting, as he was very concerned about reaction to the film from the clerical community. Still, religious groups objected to his depiction of a fallen minister, and, in some areas, *The White Rose* was banned. It closed after barely playing on Broadway, and its maker went further into debt. Griffith had signed Novello to a seven-picture contract, but the other films in the deal were never made.

Long before the advent of sound, Griffith was critical and commercial poison. He made two talkies—*Abraham Lincoln* (1930) and *The Struggle* (1931)—and, although credited to Hal Roach, *One Million B.C.* (1940) was also directed by him. The pioneer filmmaker died in 1948, an alcoholic has-been.

Rob Edelman

WHITE SHADOWS IN THE SOUTH SEAS

Released: 1928
Production: Cosmopolitan for Metro-Goldwyn-Mayer
Direction: W. S. Van Dyke and Robert J. Flaherty
Screenplay: Ray Doyle; based on the novel of the same name by Frederick O'Brien
Titles: John Colton
Cinematography: Clyde De Vinna (AA), George Nogle, and Bob Roberts
Editing: Ben Lewis
Length: 9 reels/7,968 feet

Principal characters:
Matthew Lloyd .... Monte Blue
Fayaway .... Raquel Torres
Sebastian .... Robert Anderson

White Shadows in the South Seas—often erroneously referred to as "White Shadows *of* the South Seas"—could easily have been entitled *Greed*. Along with Erich Von Stroheim's 1923 classic film of that name and John Huston's *The Treasure of the Sierra Madre* (1948), the film is an ironic, grim, refreshingly unsentimental saga of lust for wealth. It is the story of a man who finds—and who is, tragically, not satisfied with—paradise. It also convincingly proclaims that the white man's chief gift to simpler races is not the Bible but disease and degradation.

In the film, Matthew Lloyd (Monte Blue), an alcoholic, disenchanted doctor, lives on the island of Hikuero, a pearl lagoon in the South Pacific. He is educated and sophisticated, yet his life is a mystery. Only he himself knows what strange fortune has resulted in his addiction to drink and his move to the island, and he will not talk about the matter. Although a derelict beachcomber perfectly content to pass his days forgetting his past in an alcoholic haze, he is not unaware that Sebastian (Robert Anderson), an unscrupulous pearl trader, has been greedily cheating the natives. Lloyd's better instincts have not yet been obliterated by the drink, and he defends a native against the trader's aggression.

For this effort, Sebastian connives to shanghai the doctor aboard a plagued schooner. Lloyd is tied to the wheel of the death ship, which is then set adrift. He is alone and unable to sail the ship, whose crew has died of cholera. It floats for several weeks in the open Pacific. The food and water have all been consumed, and the doctor would surely starve, but the schooner is caught in a typhoon and washes ashore on a virgin island. The natives, who have never seen a white man before, come to his rescue and adopt Lloyd as one of their own.

Time passes, and Lloyd, who is revered as a god, is carefree and comfortable with his existence on the isle. He and Fayaway (Raquel Torres), the daughter of the chief, fall in love, but she is "tapou"—the islands' vestal virgin who, by custom, must wed only the chief of another island tribe. The doctor despairs of ever having Fayaway, until one day he saves the life of her younger brother. The lad, overtaken by cramps while swimming, has gone under; the physician successfully resuscitates him, and the grateful chief permits Lloyd to take his daughter for a wife.

Lloyd has now been completely regenerated by life on the island and the pure love of Fayaway. His "white man's instincts" return, however, and he becomes obsessed with greed. He can no longer enjoy his idle existence. The island is rich in pearls, and he dreams of returning to "civilization," selling them, and becoming wealthy. He thinks that the conversion of the pearls to gold will make him even more content.

Lloyd decides that he must leave the island, so he lights a fire on the top of a mountain in the hope of attracting a passing ship. Fayaway senses his discontent and follows him to try to persuade him not to carry out his plan. At first he does not listen, but finally he accedes to her wishes when he realizes he would be unable to take her with him. The fire has already been started, however, and is seen by the men aboard a ship captained by Sebastian. The trader orders an investigation, and the ship sets sail in the direction of the island.

Sebastian and his crew land and quickly assess the island's wealth when they notice the ornaments adorning the native women. The natives are unaware of the value of the pearls, so the men have no trouble inveigling them into parting with the gems; they trade for them with cheap calico, worthless brass knickknacks, and glass diamonds. Sebastian and his cronies are not satisfied to leave the island in peace, however, and they attack the tribe's women.

Lloyd has observed the trading, but he is willing to let it pass. He reasons that the pearls will be removed from the island eventually anyway, and if they are taken now, he will not be tempted by them later. He will not stand for any assault on his adopted people, though, and comes to their defense. Sebastian responds by singling out Fayaway for his attentions. The doctor saves his wife, but he is also mortally wounded by a bullet from the trader's pistol. Sebastian can now set up a trading post, cheat the natives, and introduce them to liquor. Their lives become dominated by the white men, and the result is misery and grief.

Like René Clair's *À Nous la Liberté* (1931) and Charles Chaplin's *Modern Times* (1936), *White Shadows in the South Seas* is critical of the so-called "advancements" of society. The first two films, however, are satires: *White Shadows in the South Seas* is a gripping drama of how money and lust can separate and alienate men from nature and one another. The island is a Garden of Eden—even though it is without any of the modern comforts.

Once it is tainted by the white man's "civilization," all of its beauty and appeal are irrevocably lost. Its inhabitants are no longer innocent and happy; their lives—like Lloyd's, at the beginning of the film—become darkened by alcohol and false contentment, as well as cruelty, lust, and disease.

The film is also, with its location shooting on the Marquesas Islands in the South Seas and the participation of various aboriginal tribes, a successful blend of documentary and fiction. *White Shadows in the South Seas* was co-directed by Robert Flaherty, the pioneer documentary filmmaker who had previously made *Nanook of the North* (1922) and *Moana* (1926) and went on to shoot *Tabu* (1931, with F. W. Murnau), *Man of Aran* (1934), and *Louisiana Story* (1948). Jesse L. Lasky had hired Flaherty to make *Moana*, also shot in the South Seas; the director had lived in Samoa for a year before he began shooting.

Flaherty filmed *Moana* using panchromatic stock, black-and-white film stock that is sensitive to the light of all colors and results in a reasonably accurate rendering of color as seen by the eye. Previously, films had been shot on orthochromatic stock, which is insensitive to red. In *White Shadows in the South Seas* the new stock enabled Flaherty to capture the subtle gradations in clouds and the skin tones of the natives, and as a result, the film's cinematography is no less than exquisite.

Flaherty painstakingly prepared each of his film projects. Metro-Goldwyn-Mayer pressured him to speed up production while working on location. He eventually quit and was replaced by W. S. Van Dyke, who was respected for his ability to speedily complete his assignments.

Van Dyke, who began his career as an actor and assistant to D. W. Griffith, had been directing since 1918. *White Shadows in the South Seas* is his outstanding silent feature—even though it does have a synchronized musical score and sound effects. His other credits include *Trader Horn* (1931), *Tarzan, the Ape Man* (1932), *Manhattan Melodrama* (1934), *The Thin Man* (1934), *Naughty Marietta* (1935), *San Francisco* (1936), and *Marie Antoinette* (1938). The director has no critical reputation among film scholars, but is known mainly as an efficient technician who could bring in a film under budget and on schedule, and he indeed made more than three films a year for a quarter of a century. A perusal of his filmography, however, reveals a director of more than adequate talent. After observing William Powell and Myrna Loy in *Manhattan Melodrama*, he persuaded M-G-M to cast them as Nick and Nora Charles in *The Thin Man*. For this alone, he should have earned an Academy Award instead of the sarcastic sobriquet "One take Woody."

Monte Blue was a silent-film star whose credits date back to Griffith's *Intolerance* (1916). He also appeared in that director's *Orphans of the Storm* (1922) and enjoyed a successful career as a leading actor in dozens of films throughout the 1920's. Unfortunately, he was yet another actor unable to remain a star after the demise of the silent cinema. He had supporting roles, bit parts, and walk-ons in scores of features into the 1950's, including *Lives of a Bengal Lancer* (1934), *G-Men* (1935), *Dodge City* (1939), *Life with Father* (1947), and *Key Largo* (1948).

Raquel Torres had a relatively brief screen career playing fiery sirens in early talkies. The Mexican-born actress made her screen debut in *White Shadows in the South Seas*, which, along, with the Marx Brothers' *Duck Soup* (1933), is easily her best film. Robert Anderson, who had last appeared with Blue in *Intolerance*, infrequently appeared in supporting roles throughout the silent era.

Clyde De Vinna won an Academy Award for his cinematography on the film, however, various sources also list George Nogle and Bob Roberts as cinematographers along with De Vinna. Possibly some of the best location shooting was the work of Roberts, who had worked with Flaherty on *Moana*. *The New York Times* deservedly named the film to its "Top Ten" list for 1928.

Rob Edelman

THE WHITE SISTER

Released: 1923
Production: Charles H. Duell for Inspiration/Metro
Direction: Henry King
Screenplay: George V. Hobart and Charles V. Whittaker; based on the novel
of the same name by Francis Marion Crawford
Titles: William Ritchey and Don Bartlett
Cinematography: Roy F. Overbaugh
Editing: Duncan Mansfield
Art direction: Robert M. Haas
Length: 9 reels/10,055 feet

Principal characters:

Angela Chiaromonte	Lillian Gish
Captain Giovanni Severi	Ronald Colman
Marchesa de Mola	Gail Kane
Monsignor Saracinesca	J. Barney Sherry
Prince Chiaromonte	Charles Lane
Madame Bernard	Juliette La Violette
Professor Ugo Severi	Sig Serena
Filmore Durand	Alfredo Bertone
Count del Ferice	Roman Ibañez
Mother Superior	Corloni Talli
General Mazzini	Giovanni Viccola
The Archbishop	Giuseppe Pavoni
Bedouin Chief	Sheik Mahomet
Commander Dorato	Duncan Mansfield

During her prime as a leading heroine of silent films, Lillian Gish specialized in portraying frail, vulnerable, victimized heroines who nevertheless had inner fortitude and great endurance. *The White Sister*, one of her most popular pictures, provided her with the quintessence of such a role. Based upon the once popular novel by Francis Marion Crawford (1854-1909), published the year of the author's death, *The White Sister* is the story of Angela Chiaromonte (Lillian Gish), a sheltered Italian aristocrat who is her father's favorite. When her father, Prince Chiaromonte (Charles Lane) is thrown from his horse during a hunt and dies of his injuries, an unscrupulous older half-sister, the Marchesa de Mola (Gail Kane), steals and burns his will, successfully claims the right of inheritance, dispossesses Angela, and expels her from the family palace. Angela's fiancé, Captain Giovanni Severi (Ronald Colman), does not care about her inheritance and wants to take care of her, but unfortunately, he is ordered off to war, and in a North African campaign, he is captured by Bedouins and held prisoner. Believing the report that her lover is dead, the grief-stricken Angela enters a convent and eventually becomes a nun.

After a prolonged imprisonment, Giovanni escapes and returns to Italy, eager to marry his sweetheart; but he is forbidden to communicate with anyone until he has made his report to the Ministry of War. The only person he is allowed to see is his brother Ugo (Sig Serena), a seismologist who has invented a volcanometer, a sort of barometer to measure the pressures leading to an eruption of Mt. Vesuvius. On Giovanni's return, the brother is in a hospital, where it turns out that Angela is serving as a nurse. She and Giovanni pass several times without recognizing each other; when the shock of recognition comes, she faints. Although her lover is now alive, she has made a vow of absolute and eternal service to the church and is told that her marriage to Christ is as binding as that to any earthly husband. Giovanni, however, refuses to accept the fact that she has taken a lifelong vow of chastity and can never marry him. Failing to take Angela from the convent, he tricks her into a meeting during which he tries to persuade her to sign a letter asking the Pope to absolve her from her vows, which she would never have taken had she not been the victim of a misunderstanding. Having made her vows, however, Angela will not go back on them, regardless of circumstances. It is a classic confrontation between love and duty. In his grief and frustration, Giovanni briefly threatens to violate her vow of chastity by forcing her to his will, but his better nature triumphs, and he remains the gallant gentleman, allowing her to return safely to her convent.

At this point, the volcanometer reacts violently, and Vesuvius erupts spectacularly. The overflowing lava causes a dam to break, and the city is hit by a disastrous flood. Angela's wicked half-sister, overcome by the fumes and flood, crawls to a church, where Angela finds her dying. Before her death, the Marchesa confesses her sins, and Angela forgives her. Giovanni has ridden off to warn the townspeople of the coming flood waters, but though he saves most of them, he is swept away himself and drowned.

In terms of plot, *The White Sister* is a melodramatic tearjerker, but the film transcends the material through sensitive performances and superior production and direction. Gish personally selected *The White Sister* as a vehicle for herself, and it was her first film after she left D. W. Griffith, for whom she had worked for a dozen years. To direct this independent production, she chose Henry King, whose *Tol'able David* (1921) had impressed her. A leading man had not been cast, and Gish and King were rather desperate to find the right person, before the company sailed for Italy to make the film on location. One night, King and his wife went to the theater in New York to see Ruth Chatterton in *La Tendresse* and found themselves greatly impressed with one of her supporting players, a young actor from England named Ronald Colman. Colman had made a few short, obscure British films but was basically a stage actor who had only recently made his debut on Broadway. King gave him a screen test, put a mustache on him, and decided to cast him as the male lead in *The White Sister*. By contrast to the often overdone histrionics of silent-screen acting, Colman was impressive for his restraint and controlled performance. The reviewers found that he acted "with precision, economy and quiet force," and Colman was launched on one of the most successful careers in motion pictures. King was perceptive in discovering leading men; he later introduced Gary Cooper and Tyrone Power to films. Gish also gave her usual stellar performance as the plaintive, long-suffering heroine.

The White Sister was the first major American film to be made in Italy. King (who was later to make *Romola*, 1924—also with Gish and Colman—and *Prince of Foxes*, 1949, in Italy) made the most of locations in Naples, Sorrento, Capri, Lago Montagna, Tivola, and the outskirts of Rome; and cinematographer Roy Overbaugh caught the Mediterranean look that makes *The White Sister* visually outstanding. Clearly, it was not made on a Hollywood lot, with California exteriors, and the film benefits greatly by its attention to authentic detail. Francis Marion Crawford was a Catholic and King (who later made *The Song of Bernadette*, 1943) became a Catholic convert; thus the film treats the religious scenes with sensitivity and respect, including the first filming ever of the ceremony in which a nun is married to the church.

The only real problem is the ending—a sort of disaster *ex machina*, which resolves the moral and emotional dilemma by killing Giovanni and thus removing any further temptation. Although the eruption and flood are spectacular and visually awesome, they tend to turn the film from a serious character study and an examination of a relogous controversy into a disaster epic.

Running to twelve reels, *The White Sister* opened in New York on September 5, 1923; for its general release the following April, it was cut to nine reels. Despite the fact that modern religious stories were supposed to be death at the box office, it was an immense hit, so much so that M-G-M remade it in 1933 with Helen Hayes and Clark Gable. The remake, filmed in California, was a much more standard Hollywood product, and the 1923 silent film remains the classic version.

Robert E. Morsberger

WHY WORRY?

Released: 1923
Production: Hal Roach for Hal Roach Studios; released by Pathé
Direction: Fred Newmeyer and Sam Taylor
Screenplay: Sam Taylor
Cinematography: Walter Lundin
Editing: Thomas J. Crizer
Length: 6 reels/5,500 feet

> *Principal characters:*
> Harold Van Pelham .... Harold Lloyd
> The Nurse .... Jobyna Ralston
> Colosso ....John Aasen
> The Valet .... Wallace Howe
> Jim Blake .... James Mason

Why Worry? has more gags and laughs than almost any other silent comedy. The gags may not be as memorable or as hilarious as Harold Lloyd's climb up the skyscraper in *Safety Last* (1923), or Charles Chaplin's Oceana roll in *The Gold Rush* (1925), or Buster Keaton's chase by boulders in *Seven Chances* (1925). Nevertheless, the gags in *Why Worry?* were all original, brilliant, and evoked genuine, almost nonstop laughter from the audience.

The character with whom Lloyd is generally identified, is the ambitious young man in *Safety Last* who doubles as a human fly in order to secure an advancement, or the go-getter in *The Freshman* (1925) who lets his body be used as a tackling dummy by the football team, hoping that the act will win him popularity—characters that fit well within the American frame of mind during the 1920's. In *Why Worry?*, however, Lloyd played a young man with no ambitions or get-up-and-go, a hypochondriac who is solely concerned with his imaginary ills. Surprisingly enough, this character gets the audience's sympathy and reflects a personality much more honest than the young man so desperate to succeed in *Safety Last* or the fellow who wants to be socially accepted in *The Freshman*.

The film opens with a close-up of a story on the society page of a newspaper, announcing that the town's most eligible bachelor has departed for the tropics in search of peace and rest. Harold Van Pelham (Harold Lloyd) makes his entrance by arriving shipside in an ambulance and is carried aboard on a stretcher. Accompanying him is a remarkably pretty nurse (Jobyna Ralston) who is a picture of sympathy and devotion. She is obviously in love with Harold, but he is so concerned about his imaginary illnesses and pills that he does not see it, and one also gets the impression that he would not want human contact anyway because of germs.

During the voyage, Harold begins talking to one of his fellow passengers in the next deck chair and describes his life as a series of one terrible disease after another. He concludes by saying that he has had everything but smallpox, whereupon the man replies, "Well, I've got that." Immediately, Harold destroys a number of deck chairs getting away, and then he watches his body continuously for spots.

The ship docks at an island called Paradiso; but the island is anything but a paradise because a band of guerrillas is taking over the capital. A spy reports to the guerrilla leader that a representative of the world bank is soon to arrive in Paradiso to make a report on conditions. Orders are given to watch out for the representative and to make his stay uncomfortable.

Harold makes a sudden entrance when his wheelchair zooms down the gang plank and darts through town and into the guerrillas' headquarters. He manages to offend them all by treating them as servants and then strolls out, leaving them amazed and certain that he is the bank representative. He then walks about the town with his nurse and valet (Wallace Howe) unaware of the revolution going on about him. Even when a man is shot and slumps forward over a horse rail, Harold only thinks the man is bowing. The nurse and valet are frightened and abandon him; then, when he asks a band of revolutionaries for directions to the hotel, he is given an escort to jail instead. At the station he signs his name to a list of those to be shot at dawn, thinking that it is the guest register. Harold is thrown into jail with a nine-foot wild man named Colosso (John Aasen). The giant is frightened by the single-mindedness of Harold and willingly does his bidding, which involves breaking out of prison. When Harold pulls out a decayed tooth for Colosso, the giant becomes Harold's devoted servant. They fight the entire guerrilla band, winning only by Colosso's strength and Harold's cunning.

John Aasen actually was a nonprofessional who took over the role of Colosso after a giant from the Ringling Brothers Circus suddenly died, and Lloyd took marvelous advantage of his size. Colosso is used by Harold to carry a huge cannon on his back and a box of cannon balls around his neck, thus becoming a two-man army. The devastation they inflict on the guerrillas was done with a vast array of well-conceived sight gags played at a breakneck pace. Audiences could always depend on Lloyd comedy to keep them thrilled from beginning to end.

Lloyd probably worked harder at his craft than either Keaton or Chaplin. Watching his films always makes one gasp at the intricacy and precision of his stunts. It is even more remarkable when one realizes that Lloyd was missing two fingers on one hand, the result of an accident in which a prop bomb exploded in his hand during a publicity photo session earlier in his career.

Lloyd was the first of the major comedians to hire and retain on a full-time basis several gag writers, which explains Lloyd's steady output of high-quality features during the 1920's. Chaplin, on the other hand, developed his own comedy material and was dependent on his own inspiration for his films; thus, he only created three feature-length films during the 1920's, compared to Lloyd's twelve. Future comedians such as Bob Hope noted this and insured the quality and quantity of their own films by employing gag men on a full-time basis.

Jobyna Ralston was to continue as Lloyd's leading lady for his next five features, always a perfect accomplice for his sensitive slapstick. Her best role came in his next feature, *Girl Shy* (1924), in which she turns an extremely shy boy into a devoted lover. *Why Worry?* was her first teaming with Lloyd; he needed a new leading lady because he had married his former one—the lovely Mildred Davis from *Safety Last, Doctor Jack* (1922), and *Grandma's Boy* (1922). Ralston left Lloyd to play Richard Arlen's sweetheart in *Wings* (1927), and she later married Arlen in real life.

Lloyd and Davis lived in the biggest mansion in Beverly Hills, and despite many personal problems, they remained together until her death in 1969. When Lloyd died in 1971, he was a very wealthy man still living in the monument he built in Beverly Hills. Luckily for film audiences, he kept excellent prints of all his films in vaults he had built into the house in the 1920's. It is sad that not more of the silent stars preserved their films. It was only through luck that some of Keaton's films thought to be lost were preserved; they were found hidden in a house in which he had not lived for thirty years.

Lloyd's output of 166 short comedies, eleven silent features, and seven talking features is unparalleled in quantity and quality. Not all the shorts are gems, especially the ones using the Lonesome Luke character, which he dropped in favor of the more popular one of a bespectacled young man, but they all show a great amount of work, with a tendency to improve in technique from release to release. Lloyd was always fond of saying that he would rather scrap a feature, no matter what the cost, than disappoint his fans, who expected thrills and laughs galore and always got them.

Larry Lee Holland

WILD ORANGES

Released: 1924
Production: Goldwyn/Cosmopolitan
Direction: King Vidor
Screenplay: King Vidor; based on the novel of the same name by Joseph Hergesheimer
Cinematography: John W. Boyle
Length: 7 reels/6,837 feet

> *Principal characters:*
> Nellie Stope .... Virginia Valli
> John Woolfolk .... Frank Mayo
> Paul Halvard .... Ford Sterling
> Lichfield Stope, the grandfather ..... Nigel De Brulier
> Iscah Nicholas .... Charles A. Post

Wild Oranges is a psychological study in fear which is indicative of the mastery King Vidor had gained as a film director. In the next year, 1925, his studio, M-G-M, would release the first of his big screen productions, *The Big Parade*, and he would then be well on his way to heading the list of important younger directors.

He was thoroughly adept at handling storytelling through cinemagraphic techniques. *Wild Oranges* opens with a close shot of a piece of paper lying at the side of the road. The camera pulls back, and in the distance a village church is seen, from the open doors of which, a small bridal party is emerging. The bride and groom get into the open carriage and start off with a show of last-minute exuberance. As the horse nears the scrap of paper, it flutters and then rises on the vagrant wind, sweeping up in to the eyes of the horse, frightening the animal. The horse begins to race wildly, and the bride hangs on desperately to the carriage standard, while the groom tries to bring the animal to a halt. With a sudden lurch, the carriage turns sideways, throwing the bride out. The groom gains control of the horse and stops it, then he leaps out and runs back to where his bride lies at the side of the road. He takes her in his arms and bows his head over her. There is no hope, though, for she is dead.

Thus begins the story of John Woolfolk (Frank Mayo), made a widower within minutes of his marriage, told visually, without any subtitles. The action itself is beautifully self-explanatory, and so needs only to be followed by an expository title, telling how John Woolfolk, seeking solitude because of his tragedy, goes to sea, cruising down the coast in his yacht, with only one helper, Paul Halvard (Ford Sterling), not putting into port, not wanting to see or even talk to other human beings.

Early one evening his yacht is anchored in a secluded overgrown harbor on the Georgia shore. The scent of wild oranges is in the air, excessively fragrant, but the fruit, when tasted, is suddenly sharp and inedible. There is no sign of human habitation, but then Woolfolk, raising binoculars to his eyes, focuses in on the nude figure of a young girl, who has slipped into the water to bathe. She now discovers the anchored boat in the little harbor, swims ashore, and disappears from sight. Woolfolk realizes now that there is the semblance of a dwelling beyond the beach, but there is no sound in the air except the native sounds of swamp life and the occasional howl of a dog.

In the morning, the air is fresh and cool and still laden with the scent of wild oranges. John Woolfolk rows ashore, seeking a well or spring where he may get a store of fresh water. While he finds a well and fills his containers, he senses eyes watching him. He moves toward the house near the beach, which is an old, decrepit Southern mansion, literally falling to pieces. It is here, as he mounts the steps of the porch, that he encounters the girl, Nellie Stope (Virginia Valli), a girl of the lost wilderness, frightened, but intelligent and pretty. She cautions him to go away, but he wants to know about her, and especially why she is here in the swampland.

Gradually, reluctantly, she tells him about herself. She came to the swamp as an orphaned child with her aged grandfather. As a young man, dreading any show of violence, her grandfather, Lichfield Stope (Nigel De Brulier), had taken his wealth, bought the secluded old mansion, and with his granddaughter had come here to live, hiding away from the Civil War that then was tearing the country apart. He has become very old and senile, afraid of his very shadow, and Nellie has grown up in a world that is a refuge of her own dreams.

She shows Woolfolk a fragment of a handbill advising that a giant homicidal maniac known as Iscah Nicholas has escaped from jail and is at large. He is dangerous, has already been known to kill, and may do so again. Nellie confides that everything was lonely but bearable about her existence with her grandfather until the day that Iscah came stumbling onto the scene from the swamp waters, like a beast from another world. Now he has taken over, terrorizing her weak-hearted grandfather and threatening her with every kind of violence. He has made both of them victims of his evil presence, and the very thought of him makes Nellie a terror-stricken child. He has disappeared as is his habit, but he will come back, and Nellie pleads with Woolfolk to sail away and forget her and her problems, for if Iscah returns and finds Woolfolk in the harbor, he will not be content until he has torn him apart.

Woolfolk rows back to his boat with the precious store of water, but he is resolved to rescue Nellie and her grandfather. Meanwhile, Iscah (Charles A. Post) returns. He is a giant of a man and extremely belligerent. He suspects the worst when he sees the yacht at anchor in the bay, and when Nellie pleads ignorance of who is aboard, he picks her up bodily and splashes through the swamp water, setting her on a tree stump, laughing sadistically when alligators swim about the trunk, trying to climb it. Nellie almost faints from hysteria, but Iscah relents, scares the alligators off, and brings her to safety.

When night falls, Woolfolk manages to get ashore unseen and warns Nellie that on that same night he will return to get her and her grandfather and take them to his boat, so that they will escape to safety. Nellie agrees to accompany him, and she promises to have her grandfather with her ready to escape.

A great silence falls over the house. A wind is rising, teasing the loose shutters, rattling the old weather-beaten shingles on the roof, and setting the lone rocking chair in motion on the porch. There is no sign of Iscah anywhere. Nellie waits until it is time, and then she and her terror-stricken grandfather steal down the stairway, with the light of a lone candle to guide them. As they reach the foot of the stairs, Nellie is suddenly confronted with the giant bulk of Iscah, who has been waiting for them. Her grandfather is so shocked that he has a heart attack and literally dies of fright on the stairs. Nellie tries to elude the strength of her captor, but Iscah gets her back to the upstairs bedroom and ties her onto the bed.

Meanwhile, Woolfolk steals ashore. The house is dark and quiet when he goes inside. A lamp has been left burning and Woolfolk goes to the stairs, where he finds the dead body of Lichfield Stope. Afraid of the worst, he climbs the stairs quickly and discovers Nellie tied to the bed. He frees her, and she accompanies him downstairs. Once again Iscah blocks their passage at the foot of the staircase, and he lunges for Woolfolk. A terrible fight ensues, man against the almost inhuman brute, while Nellie cringes against the wall, watching in terror.

The fight is the most dramatic on film since the first version of *The Spoilers* (1914). The two men accidentally knock over the lamp, which catches the room on fire, then Iscah and Woolfolk fight their way out of the house. Outside, the wind has risen to gale force, and Iscah's dog, which has been tied up, pulls at its leash, howling and spitting to be free.

Woolfolk manages to knock out Iscah briefly, stunning him temporarily into a stupor. Woolfolk then seizes Nellie's hand, and they run for the rowboat. Iscah recovers and stumbles out onto the pier, shooting at the dinghy as it reaches the yacht, and Nellie and Woolfolk manage to tumble aboard. Iscah fires wildly after them, while the burning old mansion sends a ghastly light over the scene.

The dog, pulling savagely at its leash, manages to tear free, and runs out onto the pier madly, attacking and ripping with its claws the huge maniac brute of a man, knocking him into the water. Paul Halvard is fatally wounded by one of Iscah's bullets, and Woolfolk is not of much use because all of his strength is gone. With their help, however, Nellie seizes the helm of the yacht and guides it through the shallows and out into the open sea across the bar. Woolfolk staggers to aid her at the helm. As the film ends she lifts her head to the storm, which is subsiding as quickly as it rose, and cries, "I'm free! I'm no longer afraid!"

Wild Oranges proved to be one of the most absorbing and fast-moving suspense melodramas ever filmed in the silent era. Its very silence, aided by a musical score, gave it a maniacal pace as the action rose steadily to a desperate peak, each climax surpassing the preceding one. It is a classic Gothic tale, with terror evident in virtually every scene.

The settings on the Georgia coast were beautiful, and the performances by the four actors and the lone actress were perfect. With its thrills, adventure, and maddening suspense, Vidor's *Wild Oranges* is a mood classic.

DeWitt Bodeen

WILD ORCHIDS

Released: 1929
Production: Metro-Goldwyn-Mayer
Direction: Sidney Franklin
Screenplay: Willis Goldbeck (adaptation), with Hans Kraly (continuity) and
   E. Richard Schayer (continuity); based on the story "Heat" by John Colton
Titles: Marion Ainslee
Cinematography: William Daniels
Editing: Conrad A. Nervig
Length: 11 reels/9,235 feet

> *Principal characters:*
> Lillie Sterling .... Greta Garbo
> John Sterling .... Lewis Stone
> Prince De Gace .... Nils Asther

Greta Garbo is now known as one of the greatest of screen actresses for her many famous sound films, such as *Camille* (1937) and *Ninotchka* (1939), but at the end of the 1920's, she was a celebrated silent star. Although it is now hard to believe, studio executives at M-G-M were afraid that Garbo could not be successful in sound films (largely because of her Swedish accent) and delayed her sound debut. Even though most studios, including M-G-M, began making sound films by the end of 1928, it was not until 1930 that Garbo made her first talking picture, *Anna Christie.*

Garbo had been brought to Hollywood in 1925 with her mentor, the Swedish director Mauritz Stiller. According to most accounts, M-G-M was interested only in Stiller and accepted Garbo reluctantly, however this is probably not the case. Her first film, *The Torrent* (1926), was a great success, and soon she was established as an American film star. Reluctant to tamper with success in the unsettled early days of sound films, the studio continued to feature her in silent films. This was probably a wise course, as it turned out, because Garbo's 1929 films represented the culmination of the technique of the silent film rather than the primitive beginnings of the sound film.

An ideal example of this period in Garbo's career, when she was still making silent films while most of the motion-picture industry had turned to sound, is *Wild Orchids*. It is the story of a woman who finds herself pursued by a tempestuous Javanese prince although she is married to a stolid American businessman. Until the excessive amount of melodrama in its last part, the film is a fine study of passion and repression, adventure and duty.

As the film opens, a wealthy businessman, John Sterling (Lewis Stone) and his young wife Lillie (Greta Garbo) embark from San Francisco on a voyage to inspect plantations in the Orient. Something of Sterling's character is soon seen when he brushes off Lillie's invitation to look back at the city as the ship pulls away. Instead, he begins working on papers from his briefcase. Soon, however, Lillie is confronted with a man who is the antithesis of her husband. As she walks down a long empty corridor in the ship, she is startled by a door opening and a Javanese prince who bursts into the corridor whipping his servant. A close-up shows Lillie's fear and revulsion. Prince De Gace (Nils Asther), however, exhibits neither shame nor embarrassment, only an obviously sensual interest in Lillie.

The film then establishes and maintains a constant tension as Lillie tries to fend off the Prince without telling her husband what is going on. She does try to tell him the first time the Prince attempts to kiss her, but he falls asleep. The Prince has even befriended Sterling so that he can spend time with Lillie. The Prince also invites the two of them to stay at his palace while they are in Java. Throughout this middle section, the film frequently underlines the contrast between the staid Sterling and the exotic, sensual Javanese prince.

For example, on the ship Sterling and Lillie sleep in separate beds, and when the Prince shows them their accommodations in the palace, Sterling's only reaction is "Good Lord—a double bed." He is relieved when he finds that the bed is for Lillie alone and that the Prince has a completely separate room for him. Later, they are entertained with an elaborate and exotic Javanese dance. Afterward, Sterling goes to bed, but Lillie tries on the dancer's costume. She goes to her husband's bedroom to show him how she looks, but he merely dismisses her with the remark that she looks silly.

Still resisting the continuing advances of the Prince, Lillie insists on going on a plantation inspection tour with Sterling. She hopes this will get her away from the Prince, but she discovers instead that he is also going. After they are caught in a rainstorm, Sterling leaves Lillie in a cottage and unwittingly leaves the Prince with her for protection. Here Lillie, for the first time, responds to the Prince's kisses, but they are interrupted by Sterling's return.

Sterling decides that Lillie must be in love with the Prince and devises a complicated scheme for revenge that provides a melodramatic last act for the film. Without accusing Lillie and the Prince of anything, Sterling insists that they all go on a tiger hunt. On the hunt, Sterling gives the Prince an unloaded gun, intending to shoot him or let him be killed by a tiger. When a tiger does attack the Prince, however, Sterling kills the tiger and saves the life of his rival. He then prepares to leave both Java and Lillie behind, but when he enters his expensive touring car, Lillie is waiting for him. She says that he is "the only man I ever loved," and they embrace as the car drives off. The last shot shows a Javanese servant feeding the swans in front of the Prince's castle.

Wild Orchids succeeds in establishing and developing the tepid life of Lillie and her husband and contrasting it with the passion represented by Java, where "the orchids grow wild and their perfume fills the air." Garbo is especially effective in conveying the latent adventurousness and sensuality of the young wife. She and the script also make vivid Lillie's ambivalence as she begins to see and experience the new world in which "The everlasting heat strips everyone of all pretense."

Neither Garbo nor the other actors nor the director, Sidney Franklin, can make the melodrama of the last act convincing. Yet, Franklin does make striking use of light and shadow and the moving camera, so that, on the whole, *Wild Orchids* is a fine Garbo vehicle.

Timothy W. Johnson

THE WIND

Released: 1928
Production: Metro-Goldwyn-Mayer
Direction: Victor Seastrom
Screenplay: Frances Marion; based on the novel of the same name by Dorothy
  Scarborough
Titles: John Coltons
Cinematography: John Arnold
Editing: Conrad A. Nervig
Art direction: Cedric Gibbons and Edward Withers
Length: 8 reels/6,721 feet

> *Principal characters:*
> Letty Mason .... Lillian Gish
> Lige .... Lars Hanson
> Wirt Roddy .... Montagu Love
> Cora .... Dorothy Cumming
> Beverly .... Edward Earle
> Sourdough .... William Orlamond

Lillian Gish is one of the greatest actresses and *faces* in all cinema. She has been making films for about as long as they have existed—from early two-reelers for D. W. Griffith at Biograph seventy years ago to Robert Altman's *A Wedding* (1978). Gish's softness and great imagination made her a star in many Griffith classics, such as *The Birth of a Nation* (1915), *Intolerance* (1916, as the young girl rocking the cradle of humanity), *Hearts of the World* (1918), *Broken Blossoms* (1919), *True Heart Susie* (1919), *Way Down East* (1920), and *Orphans of the Storm* (1922).

In *The Wind*, a depressing but hauntingly beautiful drama directed by Victor Seastrom, the protagonist is not really any one character but a wind which constantly blows sand and almost drives the heroine insane. Gish's performance as Letty is sincere and no less than brilliant; and the film, a startling study of mental disintegration caused by an individual's actions and reactions to unfamiliar surroundings, is a masterpiece.

The story concerns Letty Mason (Lillian Gish), a gentle, refined, delicately reared young woman from Virginia, who journeys by train to the ranch of her cousin Cora (Dorothy Cumming), which is on the Texas prairie. On the train, she meets Wirt Roddy (Montagu Love), of Fort Worth, who is attracted to her and implies that he is interested in marriage. At the ranch, Letty endears herself to Cora's husband, Beverly (Edward Earle), and their children. Cora is jealous, though, which only aggravates Letty's loneliness. Cora accuses Letty of husband-stealing and forces her to leave.

Alone, penniless, and with nowhere to go, Letty decides to accept Roddy's "invitation," but she learns that he already has a wife. Hastily, she marries Lige (Lars Hanson), a curly-haired cowboy who, with the older Sourdough (William Orlamond), had met her at the train station and driven her by buckboard across the prairie to her cousin's ranch. Letty does not love Lige, an awkward, kind-hearted man, but she decides to make the best of the situation. Lige knows her feelings and generously offers to send her back to Virginia once he earns the money.

During a violent sandstorm, when Letty finds herself alone in her cabin while Lige is away on a round-up of wild horses, Roddy suddenly appears. He attacks her, and she is helpless against his brute strength. He rapes Letty and, after spending the night with her, implores her to leave with him. She refuses, and in a desperate instant, she shoots him with one of her husband's guns, drags his body outside, and buries it behind a bulwark Lige had constructed to keep the sand away from the cabin. The wind, however, lifts the sand from Roddy's corpse, as the helpless, half-mad Letty looks on through the window, and she believes that the dead Roddy has returned to haunt her. She turns around only to see Lige, who has come home from the round-up. She realizes that she has survived and is now no longer alone as they embrace in the last frames of the film.

Gish's performance in *The Wind*, along with her work as Hester Prynne in *The Scarlet Letter* (1926)—which, like *The Wind*, was directed by Victor Seastrom, written by Frances Marion, and co-starred Lars Hanson—is arguably the most memorable of her career; both are definitely among the best ever on film. She is at her peak during the climactic windstorm. As the wind rages, she is at first unusually still. She is not calm, though, she is practically in a daze, overwhelmed by the wind. She becomes frightened and attempts to follow Lige, but the force of the storm pushes her violently back inside the cabin. She is alone. Her terror mounts as she gazes stupidly at a swinging door. Her shoulder hides her mouth, and her eyes dominate the screen.

When Roddy arrives, he joins the wind in serving as her jailer. He rapes her, yet she still somehow manages to survive: she has been subjected to unbearable physical and psychological pressure, yet she still has the courage to shoot the evil Roddy, who has been menacing her throughout the film. Perhaps by this time, she is even mad as she glances down at the gun in a quick, strange manner. Yet, she will still not be left alone. Her hysteria becomes even more evident as she drags Roddy's bulky body outside for burial. She becomes conscious of a horrible silence and is then stunned by the sound of the wind changing direction. She stares out the window and watches in amazement as the wind uncovers the sand from the corpse. Her fingers seem to scratch at the window. Her eyes almost pop out of her face; they are accentuated because, again, her mouth is covered. Her hysteria is complete.

In Dorothy Scarborough's novel and Marion's scenario, Letty, tortured beyond endurance, wanders off alone into the desert at the finale and disappears into the storm. The film was written and shot in the spirit of the novel, with Irving Thalberg supervising the production and agreeing to leave the conclusion intact. After a successful preview, Gish left the studio, but the Metro-Goldwyn-Mayer Eastern office decided that *The Wind* must end happily. Seastrom and the cast were therefore reassembled, and the ending reshot. A discouraged Seastrom and Hanson then returned to their native Sweden.

Except for its resolution, *The Wind* is a harshly detailed chronicle of the relationship between the mind and nature. A storm rages both in Letty's head and on the prairie. Her fight to survive the seemingly ever-present wind is a battle to keep her sanity. She is a quiet, sweet woman thrust into a hostile environment, where nature is brutal and man has become brutalized.

Seastrom's precise direction assists immeasurably in conveying the passion and emotion in the scenario. (Originally, Clarence Brown was scheduled to make the film, but was instead sent to Alaska to direct *The Trail of '98*, released the same year as *The Wind*.) With Mauritz Stiller, discoverer and mentor of Greta Garbo, Seastrom dominated the Swedish film industry during the second decade of the century—the Golden Age of Swedish films. He came to Hollywood in 1923 to work for Samuel Goldwyn, and directed, among other projects, *He Who Gets Slapped* (1924), with Lon Chaney, Norma Shearer, and John Gilbert; and *The Divine Woman* (1928), with Garbo and Hanson. He was an actor as well: he played in a number of Stiller's and his own films and gave his greatest performance decades later as Professor Borg, a man about to die, in Ingmar Bergman's *Wild Strawberries* (1957). Hanson, a Swedish matinee idol, came to America at the insistence of Seastrom. He never became a name performer here, but still acted for Seastrom in *The Divine Woman*, *The Scarlet Letter*, and *The Wind*.

Exteriors for *The Wind* were filmed in the Mojave Desert around Bakersfield, California. Eight airplane propellors, aided by smoke pots and sand, created the windstorm. The temperature during the shooting was 120 degrees, and the sulphur smoke burned and nearly destroyed Gish's hair. The film coating was melting from its celluloid base; it had to be packed in ice, rushed to laboratories in Culver City, thawed, and, finally, developed.

The result, however, even with the change in ending, was too "artistic." M-G-M executives, unsure of how to market the film, kept it on the shelf and finally released it as the novelty of talkies was beginning to forever doom silent-film production. In 1925, Gish had signed a six-picture, $800,000 deal with the studio. After *The Wind*, the fourth of five films she made for M-G-M—the others were *La Bohème* (1926), *The Scarlet Letter*, *Annie Laurie* (1927), and *The Enemy* (1928)—the agreement was mutually terminated.

Rob Edelman

WINGS

Released: 1927
Production: Lucien Hubbard for Famous Players-Lasky; released by Paramount (AA)
Direction: William A. Wellman
Screenplay: Hope Loring and Louis D. Lighton; based on a story by John Monk Saunders
Cinematography: Harry Perry
Editing: Lucien Hubbard
Length: 13 reels/12,682 feet

Principal characters:
Mary Preston	Clara Bow
John "Jack" Powell	Charles "Buddy" Rogers
David Armstrong	Richard Arlen
Cadet White	Gary Cooper
Sylvia Lewis	Jobyna Ralston
Patrick O'Brien	El Brendel
Air Commander	Richard Tucker
Sergeant	Gunboat Smith
David's mother	Julie Swayne Gordon
David's father	Henry B. Walthall

It is arguable that *Wings* was actually the best film of 1927 and 1928, and that it deserved to win the first Academy Award for Best Picture. Among the competitors, certainly *Sunrise* is a far greater film and has weathered the years more successfully, while Frank Borzage's *7th Heaven* would be a more popular choice on a purely emotional level. Yet, *Wings* does offer some of the finest aerial fight sequences filmed up to that time, and its antiwar propaganda is stronger than that expressed in *The Big Parade* (1925) and *What Price Glory?* (1926). Further, it did, deservedly, make a star of Charles "Buddy" Rogers, a young man from Kansas who had recently graduated from the Paramount School of Acting, and it did present Clara Bow with one of her best screen roles. She never looked more beautiful than in *Wings*.

The idea of *Wings* originated with writer John Monk Saunders, who had been a member of the flying corps during World War I, but who had not seen active service in Europe. Getting his first major directorial opportunity with *Wings* was William A. Wellman, who had also served in the flying corps and was later to direct four other features dealing with air adventures, *The Legion of the Condemned* (1928), *Young Eagles* (1930), *Men with Wings* (1938), and *Lafayette Escadrille* (1958). Richard Arlen, the film's co-star, had served in the Royal Flying Corps and was an accomplished aviator, but Buddy Rogers had to learn to fly for *Wings*, during the shooting of which he claims to have spent 150 to two hundred hours in the air.

Wings opens with a title announcing "To those young warriors of the sky whose wings are folded about them forever this motion picture is reverently dedicated." The audience is then introduced to a small Middle Western town, as far as possible removed from scenes or thoughts of war, in which John "Jack" Powell (Buddy Rogers) and David Armstrong (Richard Arlen) have little fondness for each other, since both are in love with the same girl, Sylvia Lewis (Jobyna Ralston, an actress of considerable talent best remembered today for her performances opposite Harold Lloyd in many of his comedies made during the 1920's). Jack is oblivious to "the girl next door," Mary Preston (Clara Bow), who is secretly in love with him, and when he leaves to enlist in the flying corps, he takes with him a locket from Sylvia which she had intended for David.

With documentary thoroughness, *Wings* depicts the two men's training for the flying corps, during which their enmity is forgotten in the thrill of comradeship. One of the moving scenes which sets *Wings* apart from other dramas takes place at this point, when a veteran flyer, Cadet White (played by a young and virtually unknown Gary Cooper), welcomes the two youths to his tent. He displays a fatalistic attitude toward flying and leaves as quietly as he was introduced into the film to do "a few figures of eight before dinner." He dies offscreen, and his two new buddies are left to gather together his belongings.

Soon the men are in war-torn France as members of the 39th Aero Squadron, where they are joined by Mary who has volunteered as an ambulance driver at the front. At this point, *Wings* re-creates the battle of St.-Mihiel—actually filmed on location, as was much of the film, near San Antonio, Texas—where the director takes the camera and thus the audience onto the planes themselves, giving a unique feeling of immediacy and personal involvement to the air fights. Jack Powell is forced down in no-man's-land, but he makes his way to safety, only to return to battle to bring down two enemy observation balloons. Jack and David are decorated, and, as a reward for their valor, given leave in Paris.

As a much needed relief from the scenes of war, brilliantly conceived as they may be, director and writer provide a lighthearted picture of Parisien nightlife, with Jack getting drunk. (Rogers recalls that in the interest of realism, Wellman insisted that he drink champagne until he was inebriated.) In a marvelous scene, Rogers as Jack Powell sees bubbles floating into the air from the champagne, providing a giddy effect for both the actor and audience. This sequence also boasts an often-praised, lengthy boom shot across the length of the nightclub. While in Paris, all leave is rescinded, but Jack is too drunk to know or to care. Mary goes in search of him and finds him in a drunken state in the arms of a French prostitute.

To lure Jack away, Mary discards her uniform and dons an evening dress—

giving a hint of the Clara Bow flapper image which was such a 1920's phenomenon. She takes Jack to his hotel room, but while putting him to bed
discovers the locket with Sylvia's photograph. Changing back into her uniform, Mary is interrupted by the military police, who, surmising the worst,
arrange for her to be sent back to the United States in disgrace. Meanwhile,
Jack returns to his unit, totally unaware of Mary's sacrifice.

The major offensive is about to begin, but Jack and David quarrel over
Sylvia, with David trying to explain that Jack received the locket by mistake.
In the confusion of anger and animosity, David forgets his good-luck talisman.
He is shot down over enemy territory, but managing to evade the Germans,
he steals a German plane and heads toward the Allied lines. In the meantime,
Jack has learned of his friend's supposed death, and sets out alone on a
journey of revenge, shooting anything German that he sights. He spots a lone
German plane heading for the American lines, not comprehending that his
friend is in the cockpit. David recognizes Jack and begs him not to shoot, but
to no avial, and he crashes.

Jack lands close by, and, full of delight at his success, heads for the wrecked
plane meaning to take the cross on its fuselage as a trophy. As he approaches,
the body of his friend is lifted from the cockpit. In one of the greatest moments
of male comradeship captured on film, the two friends embrace in a final
scene of forgiveness and declaration of lasting platonic love. As David slips
away into death, Jack gently kisses him on the lips: buddies at the end.

Jack Powell returns home a hero, but also a disillusioned man. He visits
the parents of his buddy, played by Henry B. Walthall and Julia Swayne
Gordon (two actors whose careers go back to the cinema's beginnings and
who wring every last drop of emotion from their scene as the grieving parents).
Also, in the end, Jack realizes who his real love was and marries Mary.

Wings is a long film, more than two hours in length, and it is not totally
gripping throughout. Battle scenes, however well filmed, do get a little wear-
isome, and the relationship between the two men is not adequately developed.
The film has much to recommend it, however, and, with one or two reservations, one can echo critic Penelope Gilliat's sentiment that "*Wings* is truly
beautiful, and it deserved its Oscar."

Anthony Slide

THE WINNING OF BARBARA WORTH

Released: 1926
Production: Samuel Goldwyn for United Artists
Direction: Henry King
Screenplay: Frances Marion; based on the novel of the same name by Harold Bell Wright
Titles: Rupert Hughes
Cinematography: George Barnes and Gregg Toland
Editing: Viola Lawrence
Art direction: Carl Oscar Borg
Music: Ted Henkel
Length: 9 reels/8,757 feet

> *Principal characters:*
> Willard Holmes .... Ronald Colman
> Barbara Worth/Emigrant woman .... Vilma Banky
> Jefferson Worth .... Charles Lane
> Abe Lee .... Gary Cooper
> The Seer .... Paul McAllister
> James Greenfield .... E. J. Ratcliffe
> Tex .... Clyde Cook
> Pat .... Erwin Connelly
> Blanton .... Sam Blum

Along with John Gilbert and Greta Garbo, and Janet Gaynor and Charles Farrell, Ronald Colman and Vilma Banky were the leading love team in silent films. Their first film together, *The Dark Angel* (1925), was an immense success; and its producer, Samuel Goldwyn, seeing Colman and Banky's potential, looked for another suitable vehicle for them. The work he settled upon was *The Winning of Barbara Worth*; yet it seemed quite unsuitable to both stars, who made it reluctantly. Goldwyn, however, was perceptive, for the film not only established Colman and Banky as a team, but it is also the best remembered of their five films together.

The scenario by Frances Marion is based upon a 1911 novel by Harold Bell Wright, one of the most popular American writers in the first quarter of the twentieth century. In the 1970's and 1980's, popular "romantic" novels tend to feature steamy sex adventures of innocent damsels abducted and ravished by bandits or other sordid types, or to deal with kinky sex and violence among the super rich; but during the opening years of the century, this type of fiction was full of moral uplift. During that time, no novelist was more popular or morally uplifting than Harold Bell Wright; a Harold Bell Wright bookmark lists some of his titles as *That Printer of Udells* ("A story of practical Christianity, A Vigorous Story"), *The Shepherd of the Hills* ("An inspiration to the simple life, A Sweet Story"), *The Calling of Dan Matthews* ("The ministry of daily life, A Vital Story"), and *The Winning of Barbara Worth* ("The ministry of capital, A Clean Story"). The reverse side of the bookmark describes *The Winning of Barbara Worth* as "As clean a story as man ever wrote—a story with big incidents, strong people, high ideals and the Spirit of the West."

Goldwyn and Marion were less interested in the story's cleanliness and "sane, wholesome message" (the blurb makes the story sound like an episode of *Little Orphan Annie*) than they were with the dramatic potential of "big incidents, strong people," and "the Spirit of the West." Here, they thought, was a story that might rival the epic scope and popular success of such recent films as *The Covered Wagon* (1923) and *The Iron Horse* (1924). It has a twentieth century setting, however, and deals with the then recent project of irrigating and reclaiming from the desert the Imperial Valley of California.

In Wright's fictionalized account of this project and in the film version, the valley is owned by Jefferson Worth (Charles Lane), a pioneer settler who, a generation earlier, had discovered an emigrant woman (Vilma Banky) lost and dying in the desert. Worth had rescued her infant daughter Barbara and adopted her. As the story proper begins, Barbara (also played by Vilma Banky) is the princess of the ranch, a wholesome outdoor girl admired by all the men and beloved by Abe Lee (Gary Cooper), an employee of her father. Making an alliance with a group of Eastern financiers, Worth plans a massive project to dam the Colorado River and thus reclaim his desert land for irrigation farming. As chief engineer of the project, he brings west a New Yorker named Willard Holmes (Ronald Colman). Although the novel describes him as "a thoroughbred and a good individual of the best type that the race has produced," Holmes is at first a misfit in the West, a greenhorn who seems too refined for the territory. He is a foil to Abe Lee, the simple, unsophisticated, but sturdy ranch hand who is Holmes' chief rival for Barbara's love. Holmes, however, quickly adapts and proves himself a man's man with the best of them. Dashing and debonair, he woos Barbara while Lee stands around in inarticulate and shy frustration.

An unscrupulous Eastern financier, James Greenfield (E. J. Ratcliffe) tries to make the dam with inferior materials and specifications. When Holmes discovers this, Greenfield tries to discredit him. Holmes, however, persuades Jefferson Worth to authorize him to start a rival dam. When Abe Lee discovers that Greenfield's dam is about to burst, he races to warn the settlers who will be flooded, but Greenfield's hired gunmen pin him down in a canyon. Holmes, however, gets through to him, shoots one of the gunmen, and he and Lee manage to ride out to give the alarm. Lee is killed, but Holmes succeeds in saving the settlers. Greenfield, however, is caught in his own flood and washed away. Without further obstruction, Holmes completes his dam, irrigates the valley, and wins the hand of Barbara Worth.

Until the spectacular flood at the end, this narrative lacks the epic scope for which Goldwyn had hoped. It is more concerned with the triangle among Holmes, Barbara, and Lee and with the corrupt plotting of Greenfield than with the conquest of the Colorado River. As the title indicates, it deals more with the winning of Barbara Worth than the winning of the West. Unlike the novel, the film makes no attempt to preach "The Ministry of Capital"; indeed, its effect is quite the reverse, as the villain is an unscrupulous financier. Without Wright's didacticism, the story is lively enough, with considerable human interest, and the film was one of the most popular of 1926.

Much of the picture was shot in the austere Black Rock Desert of northern Nevada, where an entire town was built. The film benefited from the rugged location and from the impressive photography of George Barnes and Gregg Toland (Toland would later be the cinematographer for *The Grapes of Wrath*, 1939, and *Citizen Kane*, 1941), who captured the harsh beauty of the desert and the drama of howling sandstorms and the climactic flood.

In casting, *The Winning of Barbara Worth* is most notable for introducing Gary Cooper as a film actor. Previously, Cooper had been no more than an extra, and he applied to director Henry King for a job as a rider in the film. King, however, gave him a small part on the strength of a screen test that Cooper had brought along. Another actor, Herold Goodwin, had already been cast as Abe Lee, and numerous scenes between Colman and Banky had already been shot. Since Goodwin was involved in making another film at Warners, King (who had discovered Colman for *The White Sister* in 1923 and would later discover Tyrone Power for *Lloyds of London* in 1936) decided to take a chance on Cooper and promoted him to the key role of Abe Lee, at a salary of sixty-five dollars a week. Cooper was nervous before the camera, but this quality resulted in the sort of shy, sensitive underplaying that was appropriate for the role, and audiences responded positively to his natural performance. In *Tol'able David* (1921), King had done a skilled job of bringing out an appealing rustic innocence in Richard Barthelmess, and he had a similar success with Cooper.

Colman and Banky had objected to Goldwyn's casting them in a Western. Both stars (Colman, the debonair Englishman, and Banky, the delicate Hungarian) thought they would be out of their element and some reviewers agreed. They nevertheless gave stellar performances (their accents being no obstacle in a silent film), playing together so well that audiences clamored for more. Goldwyn subsequently cast them together in three more films—*The Night of Love* (1927), *The Magic Flame* (1927), and *Two Lovers* (1928), all costume swashbucklers. When sound films became the rule in 1929, Banky's thick Hungarian accent sent her into retirement; but Colman, with one of the most distinctive voices in film history, went on to greater triumphs. Their five films together had made them one of the legendary love teams of silent films, and *The Winning of Barbara Worth* is the one for which they are best remembered.

Robert. E. Morsberger

WITCHCRAFT THROUGH THE AGES
(HÄXAN)

Released: 1920
Production: Svenska Biografteatern
Direction: Benjamin Christensen
Screenplay: Benjamin Christensen
Cinematography: Johan Ankerstjerne
Art direction: Richard Louw
Length: 12 reels

Principal characters:
Satan .... Benjamin Christensen
The Witch ....Maria Pedersen
The Nun .... Clara Pontoppdian
The Monk ....Elith Pio
The Fat Monk .... Oscar Stivolt
The Kleptomaniac .... Tora Teje
Chief Inquisitor ....Johs Andersen

The Swedish film *Witchcraft Through the Ages* is an early masterpiece which deals with the occult and the bizarre. Scandinavian filmmakers and artists often have been noted for their preoccupation with horror and the supernatural; from the great playwright August Strindberg through the classic filmmaking of Mauritz Stiller, Victor Seastrom, Carl Dreyer, Detlev Sierck (Douglas Sirk), and Ingmar Bergman, horror and/or the metaphysical have been as central to the cinematic vision as death and solitude. Like the Germans, Scandinavian filmmakers in general have not been concerned with the famous American action sequences which D. W. Griffith initiated. They are interested instead in a certain ambience which depicts subconscious states. It is the evil and obsessive nature of the subconscious, moreover, that predominates in the Danish, Swedish, and German cinema.

Written and directed by Benjamin Christensen, *Witchcraft Through the Ages* was first released in Sweden under the title *Häxan* in 1920, and then released in the United States in 1922 under the new title. Three years in the making, the film actually preceded Robert Wiene's groundbreaking expressionist horror classic, *The Cabinet of Dr. Caligari* (1920). Beautifully shot and sharply cut, *Witchcraft Through the Ages* is a remarkable example of the cinema of the fantastic. The passage of more than sixty years has not dulled its initial impact. The nauseating detail of its Black Masses and torture scenes, and its frequent nudity and debauchery shocked everyone who saw it in the 1920's and angered American audiences whose tastes were not as sophisticated as those of European audiences. Considered exploitative of nudity and perversion in 1922, the film, today, can be appreciated for its unusual and imaginative imagery on a par with Ken Russell's *The Devils* (1971). Fantastically conceived and directed, the film holds its audience spellbound while, at the same time, the audience is taught, in a somewhat didactic and documentary fashion, the history of witchcraft and the ignorance often associated with it.

The film opens with a gallery of terrifying artwork by medieval painters such as Hieronymus Bosch, Lucas Cranach, Pieter Breughel, and Albrecht Dürer and is followed by a series of episodes of bizarre images depicting the power of witches in the Middle Ages. The characters appear to have stepped from these primitive paintings, engravings, and woodcuts. A pointer is used to direct the audience's attention to the significant elements of the artwork, and then the film proceeds into a fictional documentary depicting the efforts of foolish, frightened human beings trying to comprehend evil and the unknown.

Employing a fictional work within a nonfictional framework was quite radical for a 1920 feature film. The psychoanalytic-documentary framing device not only serves to demonstrate the film's thesis that primeval fears (given names such as anxiety and hysteria) can darken knowledge, but it also enhances the effect of the narration which was added to the 1969 American re-release sound version of *Witchcraft Through the Ages*. Novelist William Burroughs' weary-voiced irony combines with the dissonant, incongruent, modern-jazz score to provide precisely the right continuity for the wildly imaginative costumes and *mise-en-scène*. Through the power of montage, the film suggests that while Sigmund Freud and Carl Jung have changed the terminology associated with the occult, fear and its causes remain the same. Burroughs' ironic humor is most effective when he makes contemporary comparisons with images such as the poor old hag who is being alternately pampered by the "kind" official and tortured by the "cruel" one in order to confess to witchcraft. This routine, Burroughs dryly suggests, is "still being used in police stations of the world."

The film, which vacillates between the hilarious and the horrifying, depicts not only the persecution of witches but also the related perversions in monasteries and convents. The images are often strikingly bare. For one powerful sequence which depicts nuns running amok—obscene and barbaric experiments and demons ravishing their victims—Christensen recruited deformed old women from a hospital in Copenhagen, and the director gleefully plays the Devil himself. Freely intercutting past, present, and future, Christensen examines hysteria in the modern woman as well. He uses stop-motion photography, animation, and reverse printing while allowing much of the artistic burden to rest on brilliant lighting techniques and tinted film stock. The mechanics of sorcery, the devious machinations of the Devil in a dry-ice Hell, the orgies of Satan's disciples, the witch trials, and the God who is revealed as a criminal divinity whose agents on earth (the church) repress and oppress mankind are greatly enhanced by ingenious costuming and makeup.

While the sleeping heroine's adventures seem somewhat like a horrific satire on *The Perils of Pauline* (1916), the Devil worship as an outlet for suppressed sexuality and frustration is as timely as *The Exorcist* (1973).

With the exception of Dreyer, Danish filmmakers are relatively unknown in America, and yet before World War I, Denmark was the leading country in *avant-garde* films. Danish filmmakers were highly influential in Europe, particularly in the development of German film. Up to 1920, the Danish films were primarily thrillers, romances, comedies, and melodramas. Only two or three directors aspired to perfect film, as did such directors as Stiller and Seastrom in Sweden. Holger Madsen, judging from his works *Opium Dreams* and *The Spirits* (both 1914), was one of the first Danish film stylists as was August Blom, who did a screen version of *Atlantis* as early as 1913. Neither of these two directors, however, were as important as Christensen, one of the greatest and yet least known of the early filmmakers.

Christensen was a medical student, opera singer, actor, and wine merchant before becoming a film director. In 1912, he began writing films. In 1913, he became successful as a film actor and also directed his first film, *The Mysterious X* (*Det hemmelighedsfulde X*), whose images were just as impressive as those of Erich Von Stroheim's *Foolish Wives* (1922), which was made years later. *Witchcraft Through the Ages* was an astonishing technical achievement that shows early that Christensen was obsessed with light and composition. His cameraman, Emil Dinesen, and he were far ahead of their contemporaries in the employment of *chiaroscuro* lighting. Christensen, like Griffith, was able to grasp intuitively the emotional and psychological effect of montage, and his editing was remarkably advanced. He, too, understood the language of film. In 1915, Christensen made *Night of Vengeance*, which tells the story of a convict who returns home after a long prison sentence to find his child. The images, lighting, camerawork, and editing surpassed his earlier achievement.

In 1920, Christensen went to Sweden to direct *Witchcraft Through the Ages*, the film that inspired Dreyer to praise Christensen's work. Christensen's subsequent career was somewhat enigmatic. *Witchcraft Through the Ages* led to a contract with Ufa in Germany, where he acted in Dreyer's *Mikaël* (1924) and directed three films of his own, including *Seine Frau* and *Die Unbekannte* (both 1924). Then in 1926, on the strength of his success with *Witchcraft Through the Ages*, Christensen was brought to America where he made a number of horror films. He wrote and directed *The Devil's Circus* (1926), with Norma Shearer, and *Mockery* (1927), a Lon Chaney film, for M-G-M. He directed another film in the horror genre for Associated First National, *Hawk's Nest* (1927), and then did three tongue-in-cheek horror mysteries for the same producer, Richard Rowland, at Associated First National: *The Haunted House* (1928), with Chester Conklin; *The House of Horror* (1929); and *Seven Footprints to Satan* (1929), with Thelma Todd. *Seven Footprints to Satan*, adapted from Abraham Merritt's novel, was the last horror film made before silents disappeared. After making this highly imaginative thriller, Christensen returned to Denmark where he remained until his death in 1959.

Christensen was inactive in cinema for ten years after leaving the United States, but then, at sixty, he resumed his career with some success directing *Children of Divorce* (1939), *The Girl* (1940), *Come Home with Me* (1941), and *The Lady with the Light Gloves* (1943).

Tanita C. Kelly

THE WOMAN ALL MEN DESIRE
(DIE FRAU, NACH DER MAN SICH SEHNT)

Released: 1929
Production: Terra-Film
Direction: Curtis Bernhardt
Screenplay: Ladislaus Vajda; based on the novel *Die Frau, Nach der Man Sich Sehnt* by Max Brod
Cinematography: Kurt Courant
Length: 6 reels/7,743 feet

> *Principal characters:*
> Stascha .... Marlene Dietrich
> Henry Leblanc .... Uno Henning
> Doctor Karoff ....Fritz Kortner
> Mrs. Leblanc .... Frida Richard

Marlene Dietrich, with her sultry German accent, is generally thought of as an actress of only talking pictures, but *The Woman All Men Desire* proves beyond a doubt that she was a very talented and beautiful performer for silent films as well. Her silent-film performances might be better known, however, had she made them in Hollywood instead of Germany. *The Woman All Men Desire* dispels another Dietrich myth: that Josef von Sternberg was the person who made her the epitome of glamour, a Pygmalion shaping a Galatea from a lump of shapeless clay. In this film, she is wildly beautiful, with the mysterious eyes and high cheekbones that are her trademarks.

Dietrich had the benefit of another excellent director in his silent film, Curtis Bernhardt. He would later be brought to Hollywood by Warner Bros. and be responsible for directing one of Bette Davis' best pictures, *A Stolen Life* (1946), and one of Joan Crawford's best, *Possessed* (1947). Bernhardt had a flair for helping actresses rise above their material and used that talent when he directed Dietrich in *The Woman All Men Desire.*

The Woman All Men Desire (also known as *The Woman One Longs For* and *Three Loves*) has Dietrich playing a beauty named Stascha. Stascha is traveling in a train through the snowy German countryside with a middle-aged, portly man called Doctor Karoff (Fritz Kortner). He has murdered her husband for her, and they are running from the police. She would like to get rid of Karoff, but he doggedly watches her, for he has paid a high price for her: murder. She is more than a little frightened of him; his eyes seem terribly intense when they watch her, and he is viciously jealous of every man she meets.

They sit together in their private compartment. The world outside is white with snow, but inside the mood is dark and heavy. When Karoff lights a cigar, she disdainfully tells him that she is going out into the aisle for some air. He watches her leave through his monacle. As she stands in the aisle, facing the window, but lost in her thoughts, a good-looking young man steps out from another private compartment and instantly is stunned by her beauty. He is Henry Leblanc (Uno Henning), who has recently married a pretty girl in order to combine his family's ailing factory with her family's prosperous company. His new bride, in fact, is in the compartment changing into her negligee and has modestly sent him out for a moment.

Stascha, suddenly aware that she is not alone, turns and catches him staring at her. She quickly turns and looks out the window, yet is pleased with the young man's interest. She watches out of the corner of her eyes as he takes out a cigarette and lights it, so she also takes one from her purse. Hypnotized, he watches her put the cigarette to her lips and then with a start realizes that she is waiting for him to light it for her. After he lights her cigarette, white smoke streams from her chiseled nostrils, and the young man is completely bewitched by her. He looks back for a second to the door of his compartment, where his bride (Frida Richard) is in bed fluffing the pillows and waiting for her husband to return. Stascha moves closer to him and with a frightened expression, whispers in his ear, "You must help me. A man is forcing me to leave with him."

Just then Karoff opens the door, and she steps back from Henry. Karoff is not happy when he sees them, and with a forced smile, he takes her arm and escorts her back into the compartment. Before the door closes, she looks back at the young man and beseeches him with her eyes.

He stands alone for a dazed minute and then remembers that he must go back to his compartment. His bride wonders why he seems so distant when he sits on the edge of the bed. She puts her arms around him, but he simply pats her hand and tells her that he is going out for a cigarette.

Meanwhile, Stascha is being scrutinized by Karoff. Their stop is coming up, so he must go attend to their luggage. When he leaves, he sees Henry standing in the aisle and gives the young man a menacing look. The moment that Karoff passes to the next car, however, Stascha rushes out into Henry's arms. She lies there in a half faint, and he kisses her. The title cards show Stascha saying: "We are getting off at the next stop. We will be at the Grand Hotel. Please come. I need your help. You can see how he is. I must go back inside now."

As she pulls away from Henry, he holds her hand, and Karoff enters the car in time to see them. Her face blanches, but as he walks menacingly toward them, the fear on her face is quickly replaced with gaiety, and she turns to Karoff, saying, "This is my cousin, Henry. Henry, this is Dr. Karoff. Such a small world."

Karoff suspiciously greets Henry and then hurries Stascha off. They gather their wraps, the train stops, and they get out. She looks back at Henry as Karoff pulls her onward. Henry watches them step down onto the platform, snow blowing about them, the steam from the locomotive blocking them from his view in gusts. Stascha looks back at the window in which Henry stands with eyes that seem to beg for him, but Karoff pulls her into a taxicab. The train lurches forward and begins to leave the station. Henry suddenly realizes that he now must make a decision: follow Stascha or go back to his wife. The wheels click faster and faster as the train builds up speed. He looks at the door of his compartment, then looks at the taxi traveling to the big hotel on the hill. He is torn between passion and duty. His hand reaches for the emergency stop line, and he pulls it, causing the train to stop. He then jumps out into a cold world that will end with Stascha's and Karoff's deaths, and his own dishonor.

The film was not a major one in Dietrich's career, but is an exemplar of the type of film which she made even before *The Blue Angel* (1930) brought her international recognition.

Larry Lee Holland

A WOMAN OF PARIS

Released: 1923
Production: Charles Chaplin for United Artists
Direction: Charles Chaplin
Screenplay: Charles Chaplin
Cinematography: Rollie Totheroh and Jack Wilson
Editing: Monta Bell
Length: 8 reels/5,800 feet

Principal characters:
Marie St. Clair	Edna Purviance
Pierre Revel	Adolphe Menjou
Jean Millet	Carl Miller
Jean's mother	Lydia Knott
Jean's father	Charles K. French
Paulette	Malvina Polo
Orchestra Conductor	Karl Gutman
Masseuse	Nellie Bly Baker
Maitre d'hotel	Henry Bergman
Valet	Harry Northrup
Station porter	Charles Chaplin

In 1923, Charles Chaplin, the world's most popular comedian, did something quite extraordinary. He directed a film which was not a comedy, nor a great popular success, and in which he made only a cameo appearance. The film was *A Woman of Paris*, and despite its enthusiastic reception by critics at the time, it proved to be too far afield of what audiences had come to expect from their beloved Little Tramp. Consequently, the film remained somewhat of a "lost classic" until recent years, when it began to appear more and more frequently in revival houses around the country.

To audiences accustomed to the innocence and irrepressible high spirits of Chaplin's comedies, the film comes as something of a surprise. Chaplin's story of a country girl's fall from grace in the big city is a theme which has found its way into hundreds of films over the years. What sets *A Woman of Paris* apart is the attitude it takes toward its story and the ways in which its characters are allowed to develop. Here, viewers find no trusting young innocent tricked out of her virtue by the villain's promises of marriage. *A Woman of Paris* is a cool, hard-edged look at the elegant, decadent life-style of the sophisticated upper classes of Parisian society.

The film's story traces the experiences of Marie St. Clair (Edna Purviance), a girl from a small village in France. Marie's domineering father has made her life at home unbearable, and she and the man she loves, Jean Millet (Carl Miller), are planning to run away and get married. Arriving at the train station, Jean buys their tickets and is then forced to return home for more money. When he reaches his parents' house, he learns that his father (Charles K. French) is gravely ill, and, feeling that he cannot leave his family at such a time, he telephones Marie at the train station. Upset and confused, Marie believes that Jean has changed his mind and is making excuses to avoid leaving. Knowing she cannot return home, she boards the train for Paris alone.

Time passes, and Marie becomes the mistress of Pierre Revel (Adolphe Menjou), a cynical yet charming playboy who knows the power his money gives him, particularly over Marie. As Pierre's mistress, Marie's life-style is one of luxury and sophistication, with maids to look after her needs and jewels and furs at her fingertips. Although her life with Pierre is one she enjoys, she chafes under his insistence that he will never marry her. One day, she suddenly encounters Jean and his mother (Lydia Knott), who are now living in Paris while Jean works as an artist. Learning of Marie's situation with Pierre, Jean declares that he still loves her and wants to marry her. Marie decides to accept his proposal, although it will mean giving up her wealthy life-style for that of a poor artist's wife. When she overhears Jean quarreling bitterly about her with his mother, however, she returns to Pierre.

In desperation, Jean follows Pierre to a nightclub. Out of his element in Pierre's world, Jean's violent confrontation with his rival ends with his own humiliation, and he shoots himself in the club's lobby. When Jean's mother learns of his death, she vows to kill Marie for her part in Jean's unhappiness. Finding the girl mourning over her son's body, however, she relents and the two women share their grief over Jean's death.

Shocked and remorseful because of the tragedy for which she is responsible, Marie moves to the country with Jean's mother, where they open a home for orphans. Finding happiness at last through her love for the children in her care, Marie has cut all ties with her former way of life. One day, as she sits on the back of a cart with two of the children, an expensive car passes them, heading toward Paris. The car carries Pierre, who has remained as carefree and callous as he was when Marie knew him in Paris. Neither one sees the other, and as Marie's cart carries her down the road, Pierre's companion wonders whatever happened to Marie St. Clair. Pierre has no answer and no interest in the question.

The key to the tone of *A Woman of Paris*, and to its artistic success, is the character of Marie. As played by Edna Purviance, Marie is believable both as the troubled young woman in love at the film's beginning, and as the sophisticated "kept woman" she becomes later in the film. Marie's life as Pierre's mistress is shown to be quite a pleasant one, although she speaks frequently of her desire to marry. Their manner together is relaxed and playful, and there is no suggestion that she is anything other than a willing participant in the arrangement—an unusual attitude for an American film to take in 1923. The film carries this aspect of Marie's character even further in a scene in which she and Pierre quarrel. She denounces him and their way of life, swearing she will reform, and as a symbol of her defiance, she throws the pearls Pierre has given her out the window. When she sees that a passing bum has picked them up, however, she races down to the street to retrieve them, her "new leaf" vanishing at the thought of actually losing the pearls.

Chaplin's original intention of writing *A Woman of Paris* was to provide a vehicle for Purviance, his longtime co-star. She had first appeared with Chaplin in the 1915 short *A Night Out* and had continued as his leading lady during the next eight years. During that period, she was never able to achieve recognition as a star in her own right, and *A Woman of Paris* was Chaplin's attempt to provide her with a role which would best display her talents, as well as giving her a chance to appear onscreen without his overshadowing presence. Her performance in the film is excellent, and she moves Marie from innocence to jaded experience with ease. Indeed, the film contains performances from all of its cast members that are remarkable for their natural and unmannered quality. It is to Chaplin's credit that the film remains free of overdramatizing and theatricality on the part of its actors.

A Woman of Paris did bring stardom to one of its leading players, but it was not Purviance. Adolphe Menjou, perfectly cast in the role of the dapper, high-living playboy, enjoyed a long career dating from his success in Chaplin's film. Throughout his career, Menjou would play a number of roles which were essentially variations on the character of Pierre Revel. As for Purviance, despite her favorable reception in the film, she remained "Chaplin's leading lady" in the public's mind, and the film failed to spark the interest in her for which both she and Chaplin had hoped.

A Woman of Paris remains surprising even today for its frank portrayal of social mores among the Parisian elite. This casual depiction of its subject matter, together with the fact that Pierre Revel suffers no punishment or guilt at the film's close, sets *A Woman of Paris* apart from the majority of films of its day. Its rediscovery and reappraisal has added a new dimension to audiences' traditional conception of Chaplin's work. Although it differs greatly from such Chaplin classics as *The Gold Rush* (1925) and *City Lights* (1931), *A Woman of Paris* can now take its place among the ranks of Chaplin's better films. It has waited nearly sixty years for that honor.

Janet E. Lorenz

A WOMAN OF THE WORLD

Released: 1925
Production: Famous Players-Lasky; released by Paramount
Direction: Malcolm St. Clair
Screenplay: Pierre Collings; based on the novel *The Tattooed Countess* by
Carl Van Vechten
Cinematography: Bert Glennon
Length: 7 reels/6,353 feet

Principal characters:
Countess Elnora Natatorini .... Pola Negri
Gareth Johns .... Charles Emmett Mack
Richard Granger ....Holmes Herbert
Lennie Porter .... Blanche Mehaffey
Sam Poore ....Chester Conklin
Lou Poore .... Lucille Ward
Judge Porter .... Guy Oliver
Mrs. Bierbauer .... Dot Farley

There are two worthwhile aspects of *A Woman of the World*: first and foremost, Pola Negri as its star; and second, a very playable, funny scenario adapted from Carl Van Vechten's novel *The Tattooed Countess*. Van Vechten probably never thought that he had written an amusing story of American mores, but it becomes precisely that when directed by a master of the comic touch, both subtle and broad, such as Malcolm St. Clair.

Negri was never more charming than when she starred in a light comedy. Most of the time when she was the top female star of Paramount's western studio, she acted in dark tragedies such as *Bella Donna* (1923) or *The Cheat* (1915) or that evocatively entitled drama, *Men* (1924). Once in a while, however, a light farce was given to her, and *A Woman of the World* was one of those rare occasions. The screen's leading tragedienne had a chance to be blithe and gay-hearted, and she must have relished it, for *A Woman of the World* is a mixture of sophistication, broad humor, and, at least once, tongue-in-cheek melodrama.

As the film fades in, the Countess Elnora Natatorini (Pola Negri) is discovered enjoying the sunshine on the French Riviera, when she quite accidentally learns that the man she loves is having an affair with another woman, a wealthy beauty. The Countess Elnora had thought that her own relationship with the man would last forever, and she wears the crest of her lover tattooed delicately on her forearm. She decides that she has had enough of the man's fickle promises, however, and she promptly writes a cousin, Sam Poore (Chester Conklin) living in Maple Valley, which is somewhere in the American Middle West, that she is coming to visit him and his portly wife, Lou (Lucille

Ward). The Poores are very impressed when the Countess cables them that she is on her way. Sam is so delighted that he goes out in his suspenders and mows the lawn, but he catches his suspenders on a fence, and his pants drop to his ankles, causing him to run quickly back indoors.

Maple Valley has never seen so exotic a beauty as the Countess Elnora, and she causes a local sensation. Her train is not on time, so she arrives at the little wayside railway station a half-hour late. She engages a car and is driven to Sam Poore's home, where the elite of Maple Valley have gathered to receive her. She is smoking a cigarette in a long holder when her car is driven down Main Street, and although the town's efficient district attorney, Richard Granger (Holmes Herbert), has just raided the local dance hall, and the girls are being loaded into the jail-wagon, everybody pauses to watch the Countess as her car is driven past them on Main Street. The girls are open mouthed and applaud enviously, while Granger is indignant to see a woman boldly smoking a cigarette in public. He halts the Countess' car, but he is speechless with rage as he faces this exotic phenomenon, who only smiles calmly and signals the driver to move onward. The district attorney lets the car by, but this incident is only the beginning of their conflicts.

Everybody wants to give a party for the visiting celebrity, and the Countess obliges by wearing her wardrobe of fashionable French clothes. When the townspeople note the tattoo she wears, Sam Poore explains to everyone, "For love of a man she did it." At a county fair, the reception committee has had the nerve to tack up a card informing the crowds that anybody can talk to a "real countess for 25 cents."

Gareth Johns (Charles Emmett Mack) is a clerk in the district attorney's offices, and when he is chosen to bring big bouquets of flowers from Granger to the Countess, he immediately falls in love with her, as does every other man, young and old, in town, and the Countess loves being treated like a celebrity.

The women, however, gossip and are convinced that the countess is a "bad" woman. Since Granger is heading an antivice campaign, the women persuade him to run the wicked woman out of town. At a church bazaar, he gives her orders to leave Maple Valley, and there follows a sequence which is based on a real incident in the life of Lola Montez, the real life courtesan of Gold Rush days; she marched to a newspaper editor's office and horsewhipped him publicly when he maligned her in his paper. There is an unforgettable moment when Negri, as the Countess, marches down Main Street, the camera tracking her, and she looks like a black panther out to avenge a deadly wrong. Granger does not flinch when she horsewhips him, but she falls exhausted into his arms, and they finally come together in a passionate embrace. Thus, the film ends as the "bad" woman and the righteous district attorney realize that they are in love.

Negri was magnificent, although her vehicle became a wild farce comedy, and all the characters of Maple Valley, including the self-righteous Richard Granger, are completely one-dimensional, almost comicstrip characters.

Negri's career almost ended when talkies came in at the end of the 1920's. She had a charming continental accent, but no star with an accent lasted long in Hollywood during the early days of the talkies, except Greta Garbo, who became an even greater star when she spoke, somewhat late, in 1930.

Negri returned to Europe in the early 1930's where she charmed European audiences again in foreign language versions of *Mazurka* (1935), singing in a voice huskier and sexier than Marlene Dietrich's, and *Madame Bovary* (1937). She returned to RKO to star in *A Woman Commands* (1932), but she had been gone too long from the scene. The script was mediocre, and the only thing worth comment was Negri singing "Paradise," which is a standard now and a lovely, lilting song.

Some years later, she came back again for another farce for Hal Roach, *Hi Diddle Diddle* (1943). Years later, she left Europe for good and eventually came back once more to play in an important cameo in a Walt Disney romantic comedy with Hayley Mills, *The Moonspinners* (1964). That film was a distinct hit, but Negri, like her onetime supposed rival at Paramount, Gloria Swanson, had better things to do. She wrote her autobiography, *Memoirs of a Star*, and retired to live in San Antonio, Texas. The millionairess, in whose home she resided, died and left Negri a wealthy woman.

"I would relinquish neither internal scars nor external glories," she has said when asked if she would change any part of her life. "I have wept and laughed, been foolish and wise. There is even a center edge of triumph in the peacefulness of my present life."

DeWitt Bodeen

THE WOMAN THAT GOD FORGOT

Released: 1917
Production: Cecil B. De Mille for Artcraft Pictures Corporation; released by Paramount
Direction: Cecil B. De Mille
Screenplay: Jeanie Macpherson
Cinematography: Alvin Wyckoff
Editing: Cecil B. De Mille
Art direction: Wilfred Buckland
Length: 6 reels

Principal characters:

Tecza, daughter of Montezuma	Geraldine Farrar
Alvarado	Wallace Reid
Montezuma	Raymond Hatton
Guatemoco	Theodore Kosloff
Cortez	Hobart Bosworth
Taloc, the high priest	Walter Long
Tecza's handmaiden	Julia Faye
Aztec woman	Olga Grey

Cecil B. De Mille is best remembered as the director of spectacular Biblical and historical costume epics; in fact, two-thirds of his sound films fall into this category. In his silent films, however, De Mille approached the past cautiously. In *Joan the Woman* (1917), the story of Joan of Arc is a flashback from a modern story set in World War I; a vision of Joan inspires an English officer to carry out a seemingly suicidal mission. In *Male and Female* (1919), a version of James M. Barrie's *The Admirable Crichton*, De Mille introduced a fantasy flashback to ancient Rome; *Manslaughter* (1922) also has a flashback to a Roman orgy, and *Adam's Rib* (1923) has a caveman sequence. In *The Road to Yesterday* (1925) a train wreck sends the modern characters back into the seventeenth century to become once more the forebears from whom they are reincarnated. Even De Mille's silent version of *The Ten Commandments* (1923) devotes only a short opening sequence to the story of Moses and the Exodus; most of the film consists of a modern story in which one brother breaks the commandments and comes to a bad end, while the other keeps them. It was not until *The King of Kings* (1927) that De Mille cut loose and devoted a full eighteen reels to a picture set entirely in the past. From then on, he stopped moving back and forth in time; his subsequent costume epics, all of them sound films, stay completely in their Biblical or historical setting.

The Woman That God Forgot (1917) is notable as De Mille's first attempt ᵗo make a historical epic entirely on its own terms, with no modern parallels. ᵣwo years before, he had lured Geraldine Farrar from the opera stage to star opposite Wallace Reid in a silent version of *Carmen*; the next year, he starred her in *Temptation* and then paired her again with Reid in *Maria Rosa* (1916) and *Joan the Woman*. *Joan the Woman*, his most ambitious film to date, was so well received that De Mille looked for another historical romance in which to co-star the popular team of Farrar and Reid. Jeanie Macpherson, who wrote most of the scenarios for his silent films, presented De Mille with a love story set during the conquest of Mexico.

In *The Woman That God Forgot*, Guatemoco (Theodore Kosloff), the leading Aztec warrior, is in love with Tecza (Geraldine Farrar), the daughter of Montezuma (Raymond Hatton); yet she does not return his love. She finds Guatemoco too fierce and arrogant and rejects his suit. Meanwhile, word has reached the Aztec capital that a band of white-skinned warriors have landed in Mexico and are marching against Montezuma. Taloc (Walter Long), the high priest, persuades Montezuma that human sacrifices are necessary to appease the wrath of the gods: "Each day in the temple thou shalt sacrifice one living maiden—until the fair-skinned strangers shall have gone." The first victim that Taloc selects is Tecza's favorite handmaiden (Julia Faye). Horrified, Tecza refuses to submit to the sacrifice and hides her favorite in a basket. Later, however, the handmaiden is captured and slaughtered on the sacrificial altar.

To drive away the invading army, Montezuma sends emissaries to the white men with gifts of gold, which he hopes will satiate their greed, but it only inflames it further. Cortez (Hobart Bosworth), in turn, sends his best captain, Alvarado (Wallace Reid), to Montezuma with a demand for the Aztec's surrender. Enraged, Montezuma orders Alvarado taken prisoner and offered as a sacrifice. Alvarado draws his sword, slashes his way out of the audience chamber, and escapes to the battlements of the city, where he fights off most of the guard but is wounded by an archer. By a fortunate accident, he stumbles into the chambers of Tecza who has admired the stalwart stranger. She shelters him from the search party headed by Guatemoco, and as she nurses him back to health, they become lovers. Eventually, however, Guatemoco discovers the Spaniard and takes him prisoner, and Montezuma decrees Alvarado's death as a sacrifice to the gods. To save her lover, Tecza goes at night to the Spanish camp and guides Cortez and his army into the city. Just as Taloc is about to plunge his knife into Alvarado, Spanish archers kill the high priest. Alvarado rejoins the invading army, and in a spectacular battle, the Aztecs are defeated. To mourn the defeat of her people, Tecza secludes herself in an isolated valley, but Alvarado finds her there, persuades her that he loves her faithfully, and they are united in a Christian marriage. "I should like to be a Christian—if I may be your Christian," she tells him.

Clearly, the plot greatly oversimplifies history and turns the complexities of the conquest of Mexico into a lurid melodrama. The story of a love affair between the daughter of Montezuma and Alvarado, however, had twice been the theme of a historical novel, *The Fair God* (1873) by Lew Wallace and *Montezuma's Daughter* (1893) by H. Rider Haggard. For some years before De Mille filmed *The Woman That God Forgot*, there had been negotiations for a film of *The Fair God*, which along with Wallace's *Ben-Hur* (1925), was one of the most popular historical romances of the late nineteenth century. The Selig Polyscope Company had wished to film *The Fair God* on location in Mexico but were prevented by the revolution in progress there. In 1915, D. W. Griffith proposed to film it but abandoned the project in favor of *Intolerance*. The Lasky Feature Company bid for the film rights, but Wallace's son Henry declined the offer. Thus, when *The Woman That God Forgot* appeared, with the same historical background as *The Fair God* and some of the same characters, including a daughter of Montezuma who is in love with Alvarado, Henry Wallace sent a reporter to a screening to take down the titles, in preparation to filing suit for violation of copyright. An earlier suit by Wallace in response to an unauthorized 1907 Kalem production of *Ben-Hur* had been a landmark case in establishing the rights of authors to payment and permission for film versions of their works.

In the present instance, however, Wallace did not have a case, for De Mille's film and *The Fair God* have only superficial resemblances. In Wallace's novel, Guatemozin is the noblest of the Aztec princes and becomes the emperor after the death of Montezuma. He loves and is beloved by Tula, Montezuma's older daughter. It is a younger daughter, Nenetzin, who loves Alvarado. Alvarado's unsuccessful rival for her hand is a young warrior named Hualpa. In the battle of La Noche Triste, both Hualpa and Nenetzin are killed. *The Fair God* has a genuinely epic scope and would have provided a picture in far more depth and complexity of the Aztec empire and the Spanish conquerors than anything De Mille attempted. Had Griffith filmed it, he might have made an early film classic, for it has many of the elements of the Babylonian sequences of *Intolerance*, the picture that he made instead.

Compared to *Intolerance*, *The Woman That God Forgot* is crudely handled. The acting is in the florid style that then prevailed in opera, from which De Mille had lured Farrar, and indeed the film is rather like an Aztec *Aida*. To play Guatemoco, De Mille selected Theodore Kosloff, a Russian dancer from the Imperial School of Ballet in Moscow, who was then on tour in the United States. Kosloff, De Mille thought, "could add a desirably barbaric note to the part of Guatemoco." Kosloff's strong accent and erratic English kept him from acting in sound films, but he became a lifelong friend of De Mille and directed the choreography of many of his later films. Another lifelong friend who appeared in most of De Mille's subsequent pictures was Julia Faye, who made her debut in the small part of Tecza's handmaiden. The rest of the cast had all been in *Joan the Woman* and constitute almost a stock company for De Mille's silent films. Farrar and Reid co-starred in one more De Mille picture, *The Devil Stone* (1917). Farrar made a few more films for other directors and then abandoned motion pictures to return to the opera stage. Reid starred in one subsequent De Mille film, *The Affairs of Anatol* (1921), but he became addicted to morphine, and his death of drug addiction in 1923 was one of the major scandals of Hollywood in the 1920's.

De Mille's direction is energetic, if crude, and the climactic battle up the sides of an Aztec teocalli is genuinely impressive in its spectacle. To avoid reconstructing an entire pyramidal temple, De Mille found a hill of the proper size and dimensions and covered it with the exterior walls and stairways of the temple, on which the battle is fought. *The New York Times* found the fighting "unusually realistic," and De Mille credited the success of his spectacular scenes to "treating extra players as players, not just extras . . . if the director regards each individual as an individual and lets each one know and feel that a real performance is expected of him, that director will get a real performance."

It is this attention to detail that gives De Mille's epics their vitality, from *The Woman That God Forgot* to *The Ten Commandments* (1956). The two films have something of a similar plot, in that each is a clash of cultures, and the relationship among Montezuma, Tecza, Guatemoco, and Alvarado is rather like that of the Pharaoh Sethi, Nefretiri, Rameses, and Moses in the latter film. In its own right, *The Woman That God Forgot* is more of a curiosity than a classic of the silent screen, but it is a significant work in the career of De Mille and contains the ingredients that he was to develop more fully in his celebrated Biblical and historical epics.

Robert E. Morsberger
Katharine M. Morsberger

WOMAN'S PLACE

Released: 1921
Production: Joseph M. Schenck Productions; released by Associated First National
Direction: Victor Fleming
Screenplay: John Emerson and Anita Loos; based on their original story
Cinematography: no listing
Length: 6 reels/5,645 feet

> *Principal characters:*
> Kay Gerson .... Constance Talmadge
> Jim Bradley .... Kenneth Harlan
> Freddy Bleeker .... Hassard Short
> Amy Bleeker .... Florence Short
> Mrs. Margaret Belknap .... Ina Rorke

Anita Loos and John Emerson were very forward thinking when they devised the plot for *Woman's Place.* In fact, the plot is so up-to-date that it is surprising that it has not been remade today. Women had had the vote for only a few years when *Woman's Place* was released, but the salient truths about the sexes in politics have not changed over time.

In the film, Kay Gerson (Constance Talmadge), is an up-to-date, vivacious young woman, and when she decides to enter the mayoral contest, she does so because politics interest her scatterbrained mind and because her fiancé, Freddy Bleeker (Hassard Short), is positive that he is going to win the race. Kay finds it unbearable that anybody could be so egotistical as to be totally sure that he will win; thus, she decides to announce her candidacy, knowing that if all else fails, she can vamp a few voters into supporting her.

Freddy is amused by her actions at first, but then becomes indignant, and finally worried because Kay's platform is so irresistible that he is certain anybody would vote for her instead of him. Amused by both of them is Jim Bradley (Kenneth Harlan), because he has long been attracted to Kay's fresh outlook on life. Bradley is the political boss of the city, and it amuses him that a pretty, gayhearted flapper could intrigue an entire town.

Kay asks a few favors of Bradley, and he quickly and graciously grants them. Kay's and Freddy's campaigns are blockbusters. Everybody, male and female, turns out to see Kay, if for no other reason then to have a look at her attractive wardrobe. A few of the women show up, however, because they are curious as to what she will say.

Freddy's campaign is spirited, but he can arouse little enthusiasm from the potential voters, most of whom are in the hall that Kay has hired. Even Jim Bradley is there, cheering her on, and watching what is happening with a very amused twinkle in his eye.

Election Day arrives, and the turnout is extremely heavy. Practically everybody in town who can vote is out to make their choice. When the votes are counted, however, a very curious thing is noticed. All of the women, except Kay, vote for Freddy, while all the men vote for Kay. Her vote for herself is the only female vote she gets, and since there are more women in town who have registered to vote than men, Kay is the loser, defeated by her own sex.

She is not, however, really the loser. She and Freddy had long ago lost interest in each other, and now Jim pushes his personal campaign to win Kay's love. She says that she will marry him gladly, because he is the boss of the town, and she knows exactly how to get what she wants out of him. He admits that she is right, and he is ready to give it, and the audience knows that she will be the real boss.

The film was charmingly directed by Victor Fleming at a rapid pace, and it boasted some of the best subtitles that the Loos-Emerson collaboration ever produced. The story is built on only one situation—the mayoral contest—but the subtitles are classics of wit. Loos and Emerson wrote twelve screenplays for Constance Talmadge, most of them original and only a few from plays or popular novels. Loos also wrote the screenplay for *The Matrimaniac*, which Talmadge did with Douglas Fairbanks in 1916, when both Fairbanks and Talmadge were at Triangle.

Talmadge, until her mid-1920's achievements, almost always worked with the same people. Harrison Ford, for example, was her leading man in thirteen features, and Kenneth Harlan in six. She liked people around her whom she knew and with whom she felt comfortable. She was sure of both Ford and Harlan and developed an easy style with both actors. The first romantic farces that she did were adaptations of popular comedies first done with great success in the theater by actresses such as Margaret Illington, Grace George, or Marie Tempest. She was on safe ground with them, and it was not until 1919 when she did her first original story by Loos and Emerson, *A Temperamental Wife*, that she hit her amusing casual stride. Her later comedies were more elaborate, but they still possessed an unaffected charm. Like Norma Talmadge, her sister, she was uniquely a product of the silent screen. She had her greatest success as The Mountain Girl in D. W. Griffith's superb classic *Intolerance* (1916), but no film she did after that bore any relationship to her lone performance for Griffith. *Intolerance* shaped her as an actress, and she went on from there.

Constance never made a talking feature. She realized, in 1927, without trying to make a romantic talkie, that the new era of the sound film was not for her. She was persuaded to make a screen test for one, doing a scene from the Zoë Akins comedy *The Greeks Had a Word For Them* (1932), but she was not even interested enough to see the results and referred to it sometimes as the most embarrassing experience of her life. When her sister Norma made two "clinkers" in sound, she cabled from the Riviera, where she was enjoying herself: "Leave them while you're looking good and thank God for the trust funds Momma set up." Norma took her advice and quit at once.

Constance had married and divorced three husbands, when she met stockbroker Walter Michael Giblin in 1939 and married him. It was a very happy marriage that lasted until his death in May, 1964. Then when her other sister, Natalie (who for a time had been married to Buster Keaton), died, she moved to California and lived at the Beverly Wilshire Hotel, seeing few people and making no new friends. By that time all of her old friends had died or had moved to Santa Barbara and Europe. She died in 1973 at the age of seventy-three. *The Times* of London noted that she was the wisest of the Talmadge girls and concluded:

> Her retirement was due to the advent of sound, and not to any failure to keep abreast of the times, for she had taken to playing the sophisticated "vamp" type of woman of the world which the young Joan Crawford was soon to establish as a part of the American scene.

DeWitt Bodeen

ZAZA

Released: 1923
Production: Allan Dwan for Famous Players-Lasky; released by Paramount
Direction: Allan Dwan
Screenplay: Albert Shelby LeVino; based on the play of the same name by
  Pierre Berton and Charles Simon
Cinematography: Harold Rosson
Costume design: Norman Norell
Length: 7 reels/7,076 feet

Principal characters:
Zaza	Gloria Swanson
Bernard Dufresne	H. B. Warner
Duke de Brissac	Ferdinand Gottschalk
Aunt Rosa	Lucille La Verne
Florianne	Mary Thurman
Nathalie, the maid	Yvonne Hughes
Rigault	Riley Hatch
Stage Manager	L. Rogers Lytton
Apache	Ivan Linow

Between 1919 and 1922, Gloria Swanson made six films directed by Cecil B. De Mille, and under his careful tutelage, she developed into one of the most important stars of the day. Her screen image was that of the young sophisticate, a glamorous heroine of great beauty and natural hauteur. Both on screen and off, she was exactly what the public believed a film star should be.

After making her sixth film with De Mille, he advised her to move on to better things, paving the way for her to enter into a productive and profitable association with another director, Allan Dwan. Beginning in 1923, with *Zaza*, Swanson made eight films with Dwan: *A Society Scandal* (1924), *Manhandled* (1924), *Her Love Story* (1924), *Wages of Virtue* (1924), *The Coast of Folly* (1925), *Stage Struck* (1925), and *What a Widow* (1930).

In her films with Dwan, she maintained her sophisticated clotheshorse image; but she also developed her natural abilities as a comedienne and mimic which were evident early in her career when she had worked for Mack Sennett in Keystone Kops comedies. Her films with Dwan were for the most part charming "Cinderella" comedies, primarily stories about shopgirls or waitresses who have flings with society.

Zaza, the story of a saucy French soubrette, who renounces her wealthy suitor when she discovers he is married but, through fate, wins him in the end, was a variation on the Cinderella theme.

Zaza is based on a story by Albert Shelby LeVino and was filmed in 1915 by Famous Players (Paramount) with the beautiful Pauline Frederick as the star and co-directed by Edwin S. Porter and Hugh Ford. Earlier, *Zaza* had been a popular stage vehicle for the French actress Réjane and for Mrs. Leslie Carter. Ruggiero Leoncavallo also fashioned it into an opera for Geraldine Farrar, who enjoyed a great personal success with it at the Metropolitan Opera during the 1920's.

Following her departure as one of De Mille's regular stars, Swanson found herself at odds with the management of Paramount and had become disenchanted with the roles the studio assigned her and of working in Hollywood. In like manner, Dwan at this period in his career was also unhappy with Paramount management. B. P. Schulberg had been put in charge of production at Paramount, and Dwan recalled that he then hired several relatives to supervise activities and all they did was hang around the set and bother him all day. Dwan finally asked to be allowed to make several pictures in New York, where Paramount owned the Astoria Studios on Long Island. Management agreed, and the first project he chose was *Zaza*.

It was the handsome, harddrinking Marshall (Mickey) Nielan who first brought Dwan and Swanson together. One evening over dinner, Dwan described the project to Swanson, who immediately agreed. Dwan assured her that she would have beautiful gowns, designed by Norman Norell, but he pointed out that this was not going to be merely another costume film.

Swanson recalls that "With difficulty Allan Dwan convinced Mr. Lasky and Mr. Zukor to let me try one realistic picture with a role I could get my teeth into." The two studio chieftains acquiesced, and Dwan set up production in New York and located a mansion on Long Island which would double as a French chateau in the film.

Swanson says that there was "a wonderful sense of revolution and innovation" at the Astoria Studios, and the cast and crew were like a happy band of gypsies throughout the filming. "Zaza," she adds, "turned out to be the fastest, easiest, most enjoyable picture I ever made."

Zaza (Gloria Swanson) is a combination of lovable gamine and childish, devil-may-care petulance. She was the gaudily bedecked singing star of the Théâtre de l'Odéon, a French provincial open-air theater somewhat like vaudeville, in St. Etienne.

Zaza lives with her Aunt Rosa (Lucille La Verne) and spends her carefree existence performing at l'Odéon and flirting with the many rich male patrons. Her "specialty" is a singing act she performs on a swing high above the heads of the audience. In her gaudy, bizarre, and sexy costumes which make her look like an overdecorated Christmas tree, she sings, swings, and displays her shapely legs to the men's delight.

Her rival at the club is another soubrette, Florianne (Mary Thurman), who is jealous of Zaza's popularity. One evening, Zaza and Florianne get into a wild, scratching fight which is witnessed by the aristocratic Bernard Dufresne (H. B. Warner), who falls in love with Zaza. Dufresne explains that he must soon return to Paris where he will take up a post in the French government. One evening, in a jealous rage, Florianne cuts the rope on Zaza's swing only enough so that it will snap in the middle of her act. Zaza swings out over the audience, the rope breaks, and she is seriously injured. During her long convalescence, Dufresne is torn between staying near her and returning to Paris, and eventually he has to leave.

The recuperated Zaza then follows Defresne to Paris where she discovers that he is married and a father. She renounces him, resolves to reform her vulgar ways and make something of herself, and goes on, in true Cinderella fashion, to become a glamorous and celebrated opera star courted by the Duke de Brissac (Ferdinand Gottschalk). Eventually, Zaza and Dufresne meet again, and Zaza learns that his wife has died, leaving him free to marry and live happily ever after with her.

Zaza was a true Cinderella story with touches of adultery and the wages of sin, that was enlivened by both Swanson's animated performance and by Dwan's spirited direction. Dwan's technique of direction included using the script as a blueprint and allowing the actors room enough to improvise. Critics praised Swanson and Dwan but most commented that H. B. Warner was miscast as the aristocratic suitor.

Swanson showed considerable range as an actress in this role. Her early scenes as the singing, dancing strumpet are delightfully animated and at times almost slapstick in their physicality, and her cheap costumes and frizzily curled hair create a realistic portrait of the gauche prostitute.

When the film changes locale to Paris in 1900, Swanson is predictably glamorous and sophisticated as the opera star who is courted by a titled beau. Audiences expected these trappings of glamour in every Swanson film, and she was unique in her delineation of sophisticated sex appeal.

Dwan's remarkable career is one of the least appreciated in motion-picture history for the simple reason that so few of the more than eight hundred films with which he was associated have survived. He was, like D. W. Griffith and De Mille, a pioneer whose career spanned the birth and growth of American film. He was born in Canada in 1885 (he died in 1981 at the age of ninety-six) and started out in show business as a lighting man at Essanay in 1909. He directed hundreds of one- to four-reelers, and with *David Harum* (1915), he invented the dolly shot (in which the camera is able to move, mounted on a dolly). He was technically inventive, was greatly influenced by Griffith— who frequently sought out Dwan for technical advice—and a major contributor to the success of Douglas Fairbanks, with whom he made eleven films including *Manhattan Madness* (1916) and *A Modern Musketeer* (1917). The two also made the spectacular *Robin Hood* (1922), which was, at a cost of one million dollars, the most expensive film made up to that time.

He directed Norma Talmadge and Erich Von Stroheim in *Panthea* (1917), to great critical success, and earned praise for the very human *Big Brother*

(1923). His eight productions with Swanson were popular moneymaking films, but his career faltered during the early days of sound, and by 1934, he was serving duty at Fox in their B-unit. It is this latter part of his career, however, for which he is remembered because so many of the earlier films are lost. Among his successes during this time were Shirley Temple's *Heidi* (1937) and *Rebecca of Sunnybrook Farm* (1938), and *Suez* (1938) with its famous typhoon sequence.

In 1945, he signed an eight-year contract with Republic where he was stuck with mostly second-rate material but continued unabated and undefeated. In the last segment of his career, which ended in 1961, he was relegated to direct mostly Westerns, but there was an occasional good assignment along the way such as *Sands of Iwo Jima* (1949), *Montana Belle* (1952), and *Escape to Burma* (1955).

Dwan's career is one which should not be forgotten, and it is unfortunate and regrettable that neither the Motion Picture Academy nor any of the other "prestigious" and often self-serving preservation organizations failed to honor this giant at some point during his remarkable ninety-six lucid years.

Ronald Bowers

TITLE INDEX

Numbers shown in **boldfaced type** refer to films discussed in the essays in Volume I.

II

TITLE INDEX

III

DIRECTOR INDEX

Titles in quotation marks refer to the essays in Volume I.

V

DIRECTOR INDEX

DIRECTOR INDEX

SCREENWRITER INDEX

Titles in quotation marks refer to the essays in Volume I.

SCREENWRITER INDEX

XIII

CINEMATOGRAPHER INDEX

Titles in quotation marks refer to the essays in Volume I.

MAGILL'S SURVEY OF CINEMA

CINEMATOGRAPHER INDEX

XIX

CINEMATOGRAPHER INDEX

EDITOR INDEX

Titles in quotation marks refer to the essays in Volume I.

PERFORMER INDEX

Titles in quotation marks refer to the essays in Volume I.

AASEN, JOHN
   Why Worry? III-1238
ABBOTT, MARION
   Tol'able David III-1140
ABEL, ALFRED
   Metropolis II-733
ABEL-GANCE, MARGUERITE
   Fall of the House of Usher, The I-418
ACKER, JEAN
   Lombardi, Ltd. II-665
ACORD, ART
   Cleopatra I-322
ADAIR, ALICE
   Private Life of Helen of Troy, The III-883
ADAMS, CLAIRE
   Big Parade, The I-212
   Penalty, The II-858
ADAMS, KATHRYN
   Baby Mine I-165
ADAMS, LIONEL
   Janice Meredith II-597
   Thaïs III-1105
ADORÉE, RENÉE
   Big Parade, The I-212
   Bohème, La I-253
AINSWORTH, SYDNEY
   Doubling for Romeo I-377
AITKEN, SPOTTISWOODE
   Avenging Conscience, The I-162
   Birth of a Nation, The I-216
   Goose Woman, The II-494
AKIN, MARY
   Charley's Aunt I-292
ALBA, MARIA
   Mr. Robinson Crusoe II-761
ALDEN, MARY
   Birth of a Nation, The I-216
ALDERSON, ERVILLE
   America I-137
   Sally of the Sawdust III-943
ALEXANDER, BEN
   Hearts of the World II-537
ALEXANDER, RICHARD
   City Girl I-310
   Mysterious Lady, The II-778
ALI, GEORGE
   Peter Pan II-862
ALLEN, ALFRED
   Kaiser, Beast of Berlin, The II-616
ALLEN, C. J.
   Foolish Wives II-440
ALLEN, RICA
   Daughter of the Gods, A I-361
ALLISON, MAY
   Fool There Was, A II-437
   Masked Rider, The II-720
ANDERS, GLENN
   Sally of the Sawdust III-943

ANDERSEN, JOHS
   Witchcraft Through the Ages III-1257
ANDERSON, ERVILLE
   Isn't Life Wonderful II-584
ANDERSON, FLORENCE
   Blue Bird, The I-244
ANDERSON, JAMES
   Freshman, The II-457
ANDERSON, PHILIP
   Man, Woman, and Sin II-696
   Redskin III-911
ANDERSON, ROBERT
   Heart of Humanity, The II-534
   White Shadows in the South Seas III-1231
ANGELO, JEAN
   Nana II-781
ANKEWICH, CAMILLE (see MANON, MARCIA)
ANTONOV, ALEXANDER
   Potemkin II-880
APOLLON, UNI
   Mare Nostrum II-709
APPLEGATE, ROY
   Sally of the Sawdust III-943
ARBUCKLE, MACLYN
   Janice Meredith II-597
ARBUCKLE, MRS. MACLYN
   Janice Meredith II-597
ARBUCKLE, ROSCOE "FATTY"
   Hollywood II-554
   "Roscoe "Fatty" Arbuckle" I-92-94
ARGUS, EDWIN
   Janice Meredith II-597
ARLEN, RICHARD
   Beggars of Life I-195
   She's a Sheik III-972
   Wings III-1251
ARNOLD, JESSIE
   Shoes III-975
ARTAUD, ANTONIN
   Napoleon II-787
   Passion of Joan of Arc, The II-854
ARTEGA, SOPHIA
   Sadie Thompson III-931
ARTHUR, GEORGE K.
   Hollywood II-554
   Her Sister from Paris II-546
ASCOT, CHARLES
   Blue Bird, The I-244
ASHTON, SYLVIA
   Greed II-514
ASTHER, NILS
   Our Dancing Daughters II-835
   Single Standard, The III-991
   Wild Orchids III-1245
ASTOR, GERTRUDE
   Cat and the Canary, The I-289
   Strong Man, The III-1066

PERFORMER INDEX

BENEDICT, BROOKS
  Freshman, The II-457
BENNETT, ALMA
  Lost World, The II-671
BENNETT, BELLE
  Stella Dallas III-1049
BENNETT, CHARLES
  America I-137
  Tillie's Punctured Romance III-1136
BENNETT, CONSTANCE
  Cytherea I-350
  Goose Woman, The II-494
BENNETT, ENID
  Robin Hood III-921
BENOIT, VICTOR
  Fool There Was, A II-437
BENSON, ANNETTE
  Squibs Wins the Calcutta Sweep III-1035
BENTLEY, BEATRICE
  Toll of the Sea, The III-1143
BERANGER, ANDRÉ
  Are Parents People? I-149
  Beau Brummell I-183
  Birth of a Nation, The I-216
  Bright Shawl, The I-256
  Broken Blossoms I-259
  Grand Duchess and the Waiter, The II-497
  So This Is Paris III-1008
BEREGI, OSCAR
  Camille I-280
BERGMAN, HENRY
  Gold Rush, The II-485
  Kid, The II-622
  Modern Times II-764
  Woman of Paris, A III-1264
BERKELEY, GERTRUDE
  War Brides III-1189
BERKHART, HARRY
  Masked Rider, The II-720
BERLE, MILTON
  Tillie's Punctured Romance III-1136
BERLEY, ANDRÉ
  Passion of Joan of Arc, The II-854
BERNA, ELSA
  Passion II-850
BERNARD, ARMAND
  Miracle of the Wolves, The II-754
BERNARD, SYLVIA
  Sparrows III-1021
BERNHARDT, SARAH
  Queen Elizabeth III-889
BERRELL, GEORGE
  Straight Shooting III-1063
BERTONE, ALFREDO
  White Sister, The III-1235
BERWIN, ISABEL
  Prunella III-886
BESSERER, EUGENIE
  Anna Christie I-142
  Coast of Folly, The I-326
  Flesh and the Devil II-431
  Lilac Time II-657
BETZ, MATTHEW
  Wedding March, The III-1201
BIANCHI, KATHERINE
  Blue Bird, The I-244

BILLINGS, GEORGE
  Hands Up! II-527
BILLINGTON, FRANCILLA
  Blind Husbands I-232
BIRD, CHARLOT
  Mantrap II-706
BISWANGER, ERWIN
  Metropolis II-733
BLACKTON, J. STUART
  Humorous Phases of Funny Faces II-562
BLAKE, A. D.
  Where Are My Children? III-1215
BLAND, R. HENDERSON
  From the Manger to the Cross II-461
BLINN, HOLBROOK
  Janice Meredith II-597
  Rosita III-928
BLUE, EDGAR WASHINGTON
  Beggars of Life I-195
BLUE, MONTE
  Affairs of Anatol, The I-133
  Marriage Circle, The II-716
  Orphans of the Storm II-831
  Pettigrew's Girl II-865
  So This Is Paris III-1008
  White Shadows in the South Seas III-1231
BLUM, SAM
  Blue Bird, The I-244
  Winning of Barbara Worth, The III-1254
BLYTHE, BETTY
  Queen of Sheba, The III-892
BLYTHE, GILBERT
  Anne of Green Gables I-146
BOARDMAN, ELEANOR
  Crowd, The I-347
  Memory Lane II-723
  Tell It to the Marines III-1095
BOARDMAN, TRUE
  Tarzan of the Apes III-1091
BOLAND, EDDIE
  Kid Brother, The II-625
BOLES, JOHN
  Fazil I-425
BONNER, PRISCILLA
  Charley's Aunt I-292
  Red Kimono, The III-905
  Strong Man, The III-1066
  Three Bad Men III-1116
BORDEN, EDDIE
  Battling Butler I-179
BORDEN, OLIVE
  Three Bad Men III-1116
BORIO, JOSEPHINE
  Fazil I-425
BOSWORTH, HOBART
  Big Parade, The I-212
  Joan the Woman II-601
  My Best Girl II-775
  Oliver Twist II-821
  Woman That God Forgot, The III-1270
BOW, CLARA
  "Acting Style in Silent Films" I-7
  Black Oxen I-223
  Dancing Mothers I-354
  Down to the Sea in Ships I-380
  Mantrap II-706
  Wings III-1251

PERFORMER INDEX

XXIX

PERFORMER INDEX

PERFORMER INDEX

PERFORMER INDEX

L

CHRONOLOGICAL LIST OF TITLES

1902

Voyage dans la Lune, Le

1903

Great Train Robbery, The

1906

Humorous Phases of Funny Faces

1908

Assassination of the Duke de Guise, The

1909-1910

Life of Moses, The

1912

From the Manger to the Cross
Kerry Gow, The
Queen Elizabeth
Quo Vadis?

1913

Count of Monte Cristo, The
Student of Prague, The
Traffic in Souls

1914

Avenging Conscience, The
Bargain, The
Cabiria
Christian, The
Judith of Bethulia
Mabel at the Wheel
Spoilers, The
Squaw Man, The
Tess of the Storm Country
Tillie's Punctured Romance

1915

Battle Cry of Peace, The
Birth of a Nation, The
Carmen
Cheat, The
Coward, The
Fool There Was, A
Italian, The
Regeneration
Warrens of Virginia, The

1916

Civilization
Daughter of the Gods, A
Dumb Girl of Portici, The
Hell's Hinges
Intolerance
Masked Rider, The
Oliver Twist
Romeo and Juliet
Shoes
Snow White
War Brides
Where Are My Children?

1917

Baby Mine
Barbary Sheep
Blue Jeans
Cleopatra
Flame of the Yukon, The
Joan the Woman
Narrow Trail, The
Panthea
Polly of the Circus
Poor Little Rich Girl
Rebecca of Sunnybrook Farm
Straight Shooting
Tale of Two Cities, A
Thaïs
Woman That God Forgot, The

1918

Blue Bird, The
Hearts of the World
Kaiser, Beast of Berlin, The
Mickey
Prunella
Sinking of the Lusitania, The
Stella Maris
Tarzan of the Apes
Whispering Chorus, The

1919

Anne of Green Gables
Blind Husbands
Broken Blossoms
Eyes of Youth
Follies Girl, The
Heart of Humanity, The
His Majesty, the American
J'Accuse!
Lombardi, Ltd.
Male and Female
Miracle Man, The
Passion
Pettigrew's Girl
Red Lantern, The
True Heart Susie

1920

Cabinet of Dr. Caligari, The
Dr. Jekyll and Mr. Hyde
Golem, The
Last of the Mohicans, The
Madame X
Mark of Zorro, The
One Week
Penalty, The
Remolding Her Husband
Sex
Suds
Way Down East
Witchcraft Through the Ages

Affairs of Anatol, The
Blot, The
Dream Street
Forever

Four Horsemen of the Apocalypse,
 The
Glorious Adventure, The
Great Moment, The
Kid, The
Miss Lulu Bett
Old Swimmin' Hole, The
Queen of Sheba, The
Sentimental Tommy
Sheik, The
Sin Flood, The
Three Musketeers, The
Tol'able David
Woman's Place

1922

Blood and Sand
Cops
Doubling for Romeo
Down to the Sea in Ships
Foolish Wives
Manslaughter
Nanook of the North
Nosferatu
Oliver Twist
Orphans of the Storm
Robin Hood
Squibs Wins the Calcutta Sweep
Three Must-Get-Theres, The
Toll of the Sea, The
Under Two Flags
When Knighthood Was in Flower

1923

Anna Christie
Atonement of Gosta Berling, The
Bella Donna
Bright Shawl, The
Covered Wagon, The
Driven
Extra Girl, The
Girl I Loved, The
Hollywood
Hunchback of Notre Dame, The
Merry-Go-Round
Our Hospitality
Rosita
Safety Last
Ten Commandments, The

Tramp, Tramp, Tramp
Variety
What Price Glory?
Winning of Barbara Worth, The

1927

Camille
Cat and the Canary, The
College
End of St. Petersburg, The
Flesh and the Devil
Gaucho, The
Gentleman of Paris, A
Hotel Imperial
Italian Straw Hat, An
Kid Brother, The
King of Kings, The
Man, Woman, and Sin
Metropolis
My Best Girl
Napoleon
October
Private Life of Helen of Troy, The
7th Heaven
She's a Sheik
Sorrows of Satan, The
Stark Love
Student Prince in Old Heidelberg, The
Sunrise
Surrender
Tell It to the Marines
Tracked by the Police
Underworld
White Gold
Wings

1928

Beggars of Life
Cameraman, The
Chien Andalou, Un
Circus, The
Crowd, The
Docks of New York, The
Fall of the House of Usher, The

Fazil
Four Sons
Last Command, The
Lilac Time
Lonesome
Mysterious Lady, The
Our Dancing Daughters
Passion of Joan of Arc, The
Sadie Thompson
Show People
Spies
Steamboat Bill, Jr.
Storm over Asia
Wedding March, The
West of Zanzibar
White Shadows in the South Seas
Wind, The

1929

Arsenal
Big Business
Lady of the Pavements
Man with a Movie Camera
Pandora's Box
Redskin
Single Standard, The
Wild Orchids
Woman All Men Desire, The

1930

City Girl
Earth

1931

City Lights

1932

Mr. Robinson Crusoe

1936

Modern Times